Lecture Notes in Computer Science 7783

Commenced Publication in 1973
Founding and Former Series Editors:
Gerhard Goos, Juris Hartmanis, and Jan van Leeuwen

Audun Jøsang   Pierangela Samarati
Marinella Petrocchi (Eds.)

Security
and Trust Management

8th International Workshop, STM 2012
Pisa, Italy, September 13-14, 2012
Revised Selected Papers

 Springer

Volume Editors

Audun Jøsang
University of Oslo
Department of Informatics
P.O. Box 1080 Blindern
0316 Oslo, Norway
E-mail: josang@mn.uio.no

Pierangela Samarati
Università degli Studi di Milano
Dipartimento di Informatica
Via Bramante, 65
26013 Crema, Italy
E-mail: pierangela.samarati@unimi.it

Marinella Petrocchi
National Research Council (CNR)
Institute of Informatics and Telematics (IIT)
Via G. Moruzzi, 1
56124 Pisa, Italy
E-mail: marinella.petrocchi@iit.cnr.it

ISSN 0302-9743   e-ISSN 1611-3349
ISBN 978-3-642-38003-7   e-ISBN 978-3-642-38004-4
DOI 10.1007/978-3-642-38004-4
Springer Heidelberg Dordrecht London New York

Library of Congress Control Number: 2013936249

CR Subject Classification (1998): K.6.5, K.4.4, E.3, D.4.6, C.2, J.1

LNCS Sublibrary: SL 4 – Security and Cryptology

Typesetting: Camera-ready by author, data conversion by Scientific Publishing Services, Chennai, India

Printed on acid-free paper

Springer is part of Springer Science+Business Media (www.springer.com)

Preface

These proceedings contain the papers selected for presentation at the 8th International Workshop on Security and Trust Management (STM 2012) held September 13–14, 2012, in conjunction with the 17th European Symposium on Research in Computer Security (ESORICS 2012), in Pisa, Italy.

In response to the call for papers, 57 papers were submitted to the workshop. These papers were evaluated on the basis of their significance, novelty, and technical quality. As in previous years, reviewing was "double-blind": The identities of reviewers were not revealed to the authors of the papers and identities of authors were not revealed to the reviewers. The Program Committee meeting was held electronically, yielding intensive discussion over a period of two weeks. Of the papers submitted, 20 were selected for presentation at the conference, giving an acceptance rate of 35%. The workshop also includes an invited talk by Carmela Troncoso, whose PhD thesis "Design and Analysis Methods for Privacy Technologies" was awarded the 2012 ERCIM WG STM Best PhD Thesis Award.

An event like this does not just happen; it depends on the volunteer efforts of a host of individuals. There is a long list of people who volunteered their time and energy to put together the workshop and who deserve special recognition. Thanks to all the members of the Program Committee, and the external reviewers, for all their hard work in the paper evaluation. We are also very grateful to all those people whose work ensured a smooth organization process: Javier Lopez, Chair of the Security and Trust Management Working Group, for his support and advice; Fabio Martinelli, for his support as General Chair of ESORICS 2012; Giovanni Livraga, for taking care of publicity and of the workshop website; the members of the IIT Security Group and IIT Scientific Secretariat, for fulfilling local duties at the workshop; and Sara Foresti for collating this volume.

Last but certainly not least, our thanks go to all the authors who submitted papers, and to all the attendees who contributed to the workshop discussions. We hope you find the proceedings stimulating and a source of inspiration for your future research and practical development work.

Audun Jøsang
Pierangela Samarati
Marinella Petrocchi

Organization

General Chair

Marinella Petrocchi   National Research Council - CNR, Italy

Program Chairs

Audun Jøsang   University of Oslo, Norway
Pierangela Samarati   Università degli Studi di Milano, Italy

Publicity Chair

Giovanni Livraga   Università degli Studi di Milano, Italy

STM Steering Committee

Theo Dimitrakos   British Telecom, UK
Javier Lopez (Chair)   University of Malaga, Spain
Sjouke Mauw   University of Luxembourg, Luxembourg
Stig F. Mjølsnes   Norwegian University of Science and
     Technology, Norway
Babak Sadighi   SICS, Sweden
Pierangela Samarati   Università degli Studi di Milano, Italy
Ulrich Ultes-Nitsche   University of Fribourg, Switzerland

Program Committee

Rafael Accorsi   University of Freiburg, Germany
Rose-Mharie Åhlfeldt   University of Skövde, Sweden
Alessandro Armando   Università degli Studi di Genova, Italy
Gilles Barthe   IMDEA Software, Spain
Jason Crampton   Royal Holloway University of London, UK
Naranker Dulay   Imperial College London, UK
Mathias Ekstedt   KTH Royal Institute of Technology, Sweden
Carmen Fernández-Gago   University of Málaga, Spain
Sara Foresti   Università degli Studi di Milano, Italy
Jochen Haller   SAP Research, Germany
Michael Huth   Imperial College London, UK

Sushil Jajodia   George Mason University, USA
Christian Jensen   Technical University of Denmark, Denmark
Henrik Johnsson   Blekinge Institute of Technology, Sweden
Lalana Kagal   MIT, USA
Günter Karjoth   IBM Research, Switzerland
Stewart Kowalski   Stokholm University, Sweden
Giovanni Livraga   Università degli Studi di Milano, Italy
Javier Lopez   University of Málaga, Spain
Fabio Martinelli   National Research Council - CNR, Italy
Sjouke Mauw   University of Luxembourg, Luxembourg
Catherine Meadows   US Naval Research Laboratory, USA
Stig Mjølsnes   Norwegian University of Science and
                           Technology, Norway
Masakatsu Nishigaki   Shizuoka University, Japan
Marina Papatriantafilou   Chalmers University of Technology, Sweden
Günter Pernul   University of Regensburg, Germany
Silvio Ranise   Fondazione Bruno Kessler, Italy
Ketil Stolen   University of Oslo, Norway
Vipin Swarup   The MITRE Corporation, USA
Sotirios Terzis   University of Strathclyde, UK
Mahesh Tripunitara   University of Waterloo, Canada

External Reviewers

Bielova, Nataliia   Moyano, Francisco
Broser, Christian   Muller, Tim
Carbone, Roberto   Omerovic, Aida
Enderlein, Robert   Reisser, Andreas
Erlandsson, Fredrik   Rocha Flores, Waldo
Fu, Zhang   Sala, Massimiliano
Fuchs, Ludwig   Saracino, Andrea
Gjøsteen, Kristian   Seehusen, Fredrik
Gulisano, Vincenzo   Tudor, Valentin
Holm, Hannes   Weber, Michael
Jhawar, Ravi   Wickel, Jochen
Jonker, Hugo   Zanetti, Luca
Meier, Stefan   Zhao, Haifeng

Table of Contents

Distributed Systems and Physical Security

Authentication

Security Policies

Cost-Aware Runtime Enforcement
of Security Policies⋆

Peter Drábik, Fabio Martinelli, and Charles Morisset

IIT-CNR, Security Group
Via Giuseppe Moruzzi 1, 56124 Pisa, Italy
`firstname.lastname@iit.cnr.it`

Abstract. In runtime enforcement of security policies, the classic requirements on monitors in order to enforce a security policy are soundness and transparency. However, there are many monitors that successfully pass this specification but they differ in complexity of both their implementation and the output they produce. In order to distinguish and compare these monitors we propose to associate cost with enforcement.

We present a framework where the cost of enforcement of a trace is determined by the cost of operations the monitor uses to edit the trace. We explore cost-based order relations on sound monitors. We investigate cost-optimality of monitors which allows considering the most cost-efficient monitors that soundly enforce a property.

Keywords: runtime enforcement, cost, constructible monitors.

1 Introduction

An enforcement mechanism is a program in charge of controlling the actions of a target over a system, such that the sequences of actions submitted to the system satisfy a security policy. For instance, a security policy can state that the user of a database cannot execute a request to remove a table she does not own, or that an application downloaded onto a mobile operating system cannot modify the core functionality of the system. An enforcement mechanism can therefore be seen as a monitor between a target, seen as a black-box, and a system, such that only correct sequences of actions are executed by the system.

In the context of runtime enforcement, the classic requirements on monitors in order to enforce a security policy are soundness, i.e. producing only correct output, and transparency, i.e. acting invisibly on correct input [1]. However, there are many monitors that successfully pass this specification but differ in complexity of both their implementation and the output they produce for incorrect input [2]. In order to distinguish and compare these monitors we propose to associate cost with enforcement.

For a motivating example consider a museum which has a policy that no child should be inside without the presence of a guard. A monitor processing

⋆ This research was supported by the EU FP7-ICT project NESSoS under the grant agreement n. 256980.

the queue of visitors is requested a decision upon seeing a child in the case that no guard is inside the museum. Such an input trace is considered incorrect and the responsibility of the monitor is to turn it to a correct one. There are many ways to do it, for example to refuse the entrance to any further visitor, or a less drastic one to refuse the entrance to that child. The current theory of runtime enforcement does not offer any way to compare these two solutions and say which one is better. In this paper we argue that cost can be a convenient tool for doing so. For example, cost could be associated with the lost gain from the tickets not sold, which would favour the second solution.

In this work we present a framework for considering the editing cost of enforcement. First we adopt a high level view on enforcement, where we see runtime monitors as functions. In real life, we can construct only monitors that upon processing an action have to decide only based on the current action and the past trace. Following this intuition, we introduce a class of constructible monitors, which are monitors that at each step choose performing one of the specified operations on the input action: either to accept it, suppress it or to substitute or insert a sequence of actions. Moreover, such a monitor in each step outputs a non-empty sequence of symbols. We argue that this concept of monitor is close to the nature of runtime enforcement.

For a constructible monitor, the cost of enforcement of a trace is determined by the cost of operations the monitor uses to edit the trace. The cost enables to compare monitors and we introduce two cost-based order relations on sound constructible monitors, one based on pointwise comparison for each trace and another one on the expected cost for a set of traces. The minimality in this order relations allows us to reason about cost-optimal monitors. Moreover, we prove that (under some reasonable assumptions) each cost-optimal monitor is transparent, which justifies the classic concept of transparency [1].

We believe that our approach can be useful to a security designer in three ways. Firstly, it allows her to calculate the actual cost of enforcing a given policy with a given monitor. Secondly, it provides a way of comparing two correct monitors to choose the more cost-efficient one. Finally, the "optimal" monitor(s) can be defined, together with the minimal expected cost for enforcing a policy.

The article is structured as follows. In Section 2 we recast the topic of runtime enforcement in the framework of functions, after which in Section 3 we introduce the class of constructible monitors. For these we develop the notion of cost of enforcement in Section 4 and investigate cost-optimal monitors in Section 5. Finally we relate our work with the literature and discuss possible extensions of our work in Section 6.

2   Runtime Enforcement

As we said in the introduction, a monitor is responsible for enforcing a policy over a system. We consider the three following entities: the *target* is an active entity sending actions to the system; the *system* is a passive entity waiting for actions from the target, and executing them; the *monitor* is an entity between the target and the system, receiving actions from the target and sending actions to the system. We now introduce the notion of traces, together with some usual notations, and then we express the notion of policy and monitor.

Actions, traces. The monitor observes the *actions* of the target, we denote $\mathcal{A}$ the set of security-relevant ones. Let $\mathcal{A}^*$ denote the set of all finite sequences over $\mathcal{A}$. A *trace* is a finite sequence of actions, that is the set of traces $\mathcal{T} \subseteq \mathcal{A}^*$. For the purposes of runtime monitoring, which acts on all prefixes of the traces we assume that $\mathcal{T}$ is prefix-closed. In this work we consider only security policies over finite traces. This is a choice made by many approaches in the field of enforcement, e.g. [1,3,4,2]. The treatment of infinite traces is left for future work. By σ we refer to a trace and by ϵ we refer to the empty trace. We write $\sigma; \tau$ to denote the concatenation of two traces. By $\sigma^{<k}$ we denote the prefix of σ constituted of the first $k - 1$ actions, while σ^k means the k-th action of the trace, where the initial action is σ^0. Lastly, by $\leq$ we denote the relation of being a prefix of a trace.

Properties. Following most existing approaches in the context of run-time enforcement, we consider security policies defined in terms of individual executions of the program. A *security property* is a computable predicate $P \subseteq \mathcal{T}$ and a trace σ that satisfies the property P is called *correct* (denoted as $P(\sigma)$), and a trace that does not satisfy the property is called *incorrect* (denoted as $\neg P(\sigma)$). In this paper we focus on reasonable properties, those which always hold for the empty trace: $P(\epsilon)$. Note that this is a classic restriction made in the field of runtime enforcement [1]. Among reasonable properties, the category of *safety properties* has been particularly studied. Intuitively, with a safety property, an incorrect trace cannot be extended into a correct one. Formally a reasonable property $P \subseteq \mathcal{T}$ is a safety property iff $\forall \sigma_1, \sigma_2 \in \mathcal{T} \ \neg P(\sigma_1) \wedge \sigma_1 \leq \sigma_2 \Rightarrow \neg P(\sigma_2)$ [5,6].

Monitors. We choose in this work to model the runtime *monitor* as a function on sequences of actions. While this is a view directly adopted by later works on runtime monitoring, such as by Bielova and Massacci [2], it is present indirectly in the original approach by Ligatti et al. [1], since the operational semantics of the security automaton takes the full trace as an input and, after possibly many multi-steps transitions, outputs another trace. So, a monitor processes the input trace action by action and produces the output trace: $M : \mathcal{T} \to \mathcal{T}$.

Enforcement – soundness and transparency. We recall the classic notions of soundness and transparency of enforcement. Soundness implies that all outputs of the monitor must obey the security property. Transparency requires that monitors operate invisibly on executions that satisfy the property already.

Definition 1. *A monitor* $M : \mathcal{T} \to \mathcal{T}$ *soundly enforces property* P *iff* $\forall \sigma \in \mathcal{T} :$ $P(M(\sigma))$. M *transparently enforces* P *iff* $\forall \sigma \in \mathcal{T} : (P(\sigma) \Rightarrow M(\sigma) = \sigma)$.

If the property P is understood from the context, we might omit it and say that monitor M is sound and transparent, respectively.

Table 1. Monitors

mon.	description	sound	transp.
M_0	insert no guard, suppress all	✓	✗
M_1	insert no guard, suppress all children	✓	✗
M_2	insert no guard, suppress children when no guard is in	✓	✓
M_3	insert a guard before the whole trace	✓	✗
M_4	insert a guard upon seeing the first child when no guard is in	✓	✓
M_5	insert a guard upon seeing the first child	✓	✗
M_6	insert a guard before each child	✓	✗
M_7	insert no guard, let everybody in	✗	✓

Running Example. *The security policy in a museum distinguishes between two types of visitors: adults and children. While adults can enter on their own, children can be inside only in a presence of a guard. In this setting, the (abstract) target "produces" sequences of visitors and guards as a trace of actions from $\mathcal{A}$, where the possible action can be the entering of an adult* a, *a child* c *or a guard* g.

In particular, we consider the set of traces $\mathcal{T} \subseteq \mathcal{A}^*$ which consists of all traces of finite length over $\mathcal{A}$. For instance the trace acc *means that the first to enter is an adult and then two children and* agcc *says that the children are preceded by a guard.*

The security policy is expressed as a property P_M on traces, where $P_M(\sigma) \Leftrightarrow (\sigma^k = c \Rightarrow \exists i < k \text{ s.t. } \sigma^i = g)$. We can see that $\neg P_M(\text{acc})$ but $P_M(\text{agcc})$. Note that P_M is a safety property, as an incorrect trace cannot be extended to a correct one.

In Table 1, we list some approaches to enforcement and monitors that implement them. For example consider the monitor M_2, that implements the enforcement mechanism which lets enter all adults, but lets in children only when there are guards inside. We have that $M_2(\text{acc}) = a$ but agcc *is left unaltered by M_2. It is easy to see that M_2 soundly and transparently enforces P_M. Another approach could be not to let in anyone, i.e. a monitor M_0 such that $M_0(\sigma) = \epsilon$ for all $\sigma \in \mathcal{T}$, which is sound for P_M but clearly not transparent.*

3   Constructible Monitors

Traditionally, a monitor can be any function from traces to traces. However, as we can see in the example, in real life we can construct only monitors that upon processing an action have to decide only based on the current action and the past trace. Following this intuition, in this section we define a class of monitors that we consider constructible. We believe that such a view accurately reflects the nature of runtime monitoring.

3.1   General Definition

Intuitively, a constructible monitor is a monitor which for each input action, based on the seen past trace, takes a decision and outputs a non-empty sequence of actions.

That is, since a monitor is a function from traces to traces, the output of the monitor needs to be defined for each prefix of a trace. Moreover, with each subsequent action, the output of the monitor is strictly incremental.

Definition 2. *A monitor* $M : \mathcal{T} \to \mathcal{T}$ *is considered to be* constructible, *if for each* $\sigma \in \mathcal{T}$ *and for all* $0 \leqslant i < |\sigma|$ *we have* $M(\sigma^{<i}) < M(\sigma^{<i+1})$.

We can see that the definition corresponds to the intuitive specification above. Indeed, for each seen action the output of the monitor is only based on that action and the preceding ones. At the time of the decision the monitor is in possession of no information about the future of the trace. Moreover, the requirement of a non-empty output at all times excludes postponing the decision by outputting an empty trace.

Class of constructible monitors. We define the class of constructible monitors $\mathsf{CM} = \{M : \mathcal{T} \to \mathcal{T} \mid M \text{ is constructible}\}$.

We observe, that not all monitors are constructible. We illustrate this fact on our running example. Consider a monitor M defined so that if there is at most one child in the whole trace it must be suppressed, and in all other cases a guard is inserted at the beginning of the trace. Therefore, we have for example $M(\mathtt{ca}) = \_\mathtt{a}$ and $M(\mathtt{cc}) = \mathtt{gcc}$ where the action $\_$ signalises an action suppression. We can see that monitor M does not satisfy the definition of constructibility, because $M(\mathtt{c})$ cannot be a non-empty prefix of both $\_\mathtt{a}$ and $\mathtt{gcc}$ since there is none. Intuitively, the reason for M not being constructible because at seeing the first child, the monitor needs to decide whether to suppress it or send a guard before, but at the point of the decision there is no way of knowing if more children will come.

Dealing with suppression. As we can see, the output at each step of the enforcement can be arbitrary, but not empty. Therefore, suppressing an action in the sense of removing it completely from the trace is not possible by a constructible monitor. The reason is that it is necessary to signalise the suppression to the system. We assume that a system understands such a signal and even requires it. This function can be for example performed by a special wait action $(\_)$, which in the set of actions. Otherwise $\_$ is considered a normal action, which means that there is no restriction on its use or its presence in the output of the target.

In the example above, the interaction of the target (the queue of visitors) and the monitor is synchronous. Therefore the suppression of a child occupies a visitor's turn, and that is why we must signalise such an event in the output trace by a $\_$ action. It corresponds to the fact that in that particular turn no one will enter the museum. The system (the museum) must be able to handle the wait action. Similarly the target could produce such an action to model a situation where at some turn there is no one at the entrance. Such a scenario is a valid one and the monitor should be able to deal with it. Such a case is represented by the $\_$ in the input trace.

Power of constructible monitors. Under the assumptions of soundness and transparency, the power of constructible monitors is equal to the one of Schneider's security automata [7] and to precise enforcement of edit automata of Ligatti et al. [1].

Lemma 1. *Given any property P, there exists a monitor M in CM such that M enforces soundly and transparently P iff P is a safety property.*

The proof of this lemma is analogous to the case of precise enforcement in edit automata in Ligatti et al. [1].

3.2   Specifying Constructible Monitors

In each step of runtime monitoring, a constructible monitor produces an increment of the output trace.

A convenient way to build constructible monitors is by specifying how to obtain this piece of output based on the past trace and the current action.

We abstract the decision process into a *selector* function $f : \mathcal{T} \times \mathcal{A} \to Ops$, where Ops is a set of atomic operations. Given a trace σ and an action a, $f(\sigma, a)$ stands for the decision taken for a considering that the previous trace is σ^1.

In a second step, we define the semantics of each atomic operation over traces. This decomposition allows us to make explicit the power of editing of the monitor.

For instance, if we were to consider the set $Ops = \{acc\}$, where acc stands for the acceptance of an action, then any monitor would be bound to accept every trace, since no other operation is available. In the following, we consider the $Ops = \{acc, sub(\tau), sup, ins(\tau)\}$, where $sub(\tau)$ stands for the substitution of an action by a non-empty sequence $\tau \in \mathcal{A}^+$, sup for the suppression of an action and $ins(\tau)$ for the insertion of a non-empty sequence $\tau \in \mathcal{A}^+$.

The semantics of the atomic operations is given with the function $opsem : Ops \times \mathcal{A} \to \mathcal{A}^+$. In the following, we consider the semantics given by:

$$
opsem(op, a) = \begin{cases} a & \text{if } op = acc \\ \tau & \text{if } op = sub(\tau) \\ \_ & \text{if } op = sup \\ \tau; a & \text{if } op = ins(\tau) \end{cases}
$$

Note that the semantics function $opsem$ respects the requirement from the definition of constructible monitors and always returns a non-empty trace increment.

Finally, given a selector f, we define the monitor $M_f : \mathcal{T} \to \mathcal{T}$ as the concatenation of $opsem(f(\sigma^{<i}, \sigma^i), \sigma^i)$, for any $0 \leqslant i < |\sigma|$.

The class of monitors that are constructible according to Definition 2 and the class of monitors definable through selectors coincide. It can be easily checked

---

[1] To some extent, a selector can be seen as an analogue to the functions δ, γ and ω used for edit-automata [1] with the exception that the action cannot be suppressed "silently".

that each monitor with a selector is constructible. For the other direction, note that for any constructible monitor $M : \mathcal{T} \to \mathcal{T}$, there exists at least one selector f such that $M_f(\sigma) = M(\sigma)$ for all $\sigma \in \mathcal{T}$. We denote the following selector for M as f_M.

Let us denote for a $\tau \in \mathcal{A}^*$ and $a \in \mathcal{A}$ as $tracedif(\tau, a)$ the difference between what M outputs for traces τ and $\tau; a$, i.e. $M(\tau); tracedif(\tau, a) = M(\tau; a)$. Then

$$
f_M(\tau, a) = \begin{cases} acc & \text{if } tracedif(\tau, a) = a \text{ and } a \neq \_ \\ sup & \text{if } tracedif(\tau, a) = \_ \\ ins(\tau') & \text{if } tracedif(\tau, a) = \tau'; a \text{ for some } \tau' \in \mathcal{A}^+ \\ sub(tracedif(\tau, a)) & \text{otherwise} \end{cases}
$$

Note that f_M is only one of the selectors f for M such that $M_f(\sigma) = M(\sigma)$ for all $\sigma \in \mathcal{T}$ and there exist others, for example $f'_M = sub(tracedif(\tau, a))$. Even if the semantics of these two monitors is the same, we will show in the next section that their cost of enforcement might differ. More importantly, the fact that any constructible monitor can be defined through a selector function enables us to concentrate in the rest of the paper only on constructible monitors with a given selector.

Running Example. *Actually, all the monitors M_0 through M_7 described in the previous section are constructible, provided that in the case of suppression they produce the $\_$ action included in $\mathcal{A}$. This also illustrates that when one wants to specify a runtime-monitor, intuitively always reasons in terms of constructible monitors.*

For example monitor M_2 can be specified by using the selector f_2 as follows:

$$
f_2(\tau, a) = \begin{cases} sup & \text{if } a = \mathrm{c} \text{ and } \mathrm{g} \notin \tau \\ acc & \text{otherwise} \end{cases}
$$

4   Cost of Enforcement

In the previous section, we have introduced a simple and intuitive way to build a monitor, using a selector. A monitor can therefore be seen as a function that to a trace output by the target associates a sequence of atomic operations. In this section we introduce the idea that enforcing a property, and in particular modifying the trace input by the target, should come with a cost. In other words, we want to make explicit the cost for the monitor to transform the input trace into the output trace.

Hence, we first introduce a basic cost-model, based on cost of atomic operations, which we extend to the cost of enforcing a single trace, and a set of traces. The cost enables to compare monitors and we introduce a cost-based order relation on sound monitors for a property.

4.1   Cost

Cost domain. The cost of transformation is expressed by a value – the smaller the value, the better. We consider values from the cost domain $(\mathbb{C}, \leqslant, \bot, \top, +)$ such that $\leqslant$ is a well-founded total order, $\bot$ is the minimal element of $\leqslant$, $\top$ the maximal element and $+$ is a cost aggregation function, such that that $c \leqslant c + c'$ and $c' \leqslant c + c'$. Moreover, $\bot$ and $\top$ are the neutral and absorbing elements for $+$, respectively. In general, we use $\bot$ to denote the absence of cost, and $\top$ to denote an unreachable cost. For instance, a possible cost domain is $(\mathbb{R}^+, \leqslant, 0, \infty, +)$.

Operation costs. In the same way that we define the semantics of each atomic operation in *Ops* for each action in $\mathcal{A}$ with the function *opsem* in Section 3, we associate cost with each operation and each action with the function *opcost* : $Ops \times \mathcal{A} \to \mathbb{C}$.

Running Example. *We want to express the fact that denying the entrance to the museum to an adult or to a guard costs 4, to a child costs 3 and inserting a guard costs 5. Given an atomic operation op and an action a, we therefore define the function opcost as:*

$$opcost(op, a) = \begin{cases} 0 & \text{if } op = acc \text{ or } (op = sup \text{ and } a = \_) \\ 4 & \text{if } op = sup \text{ and } a \in \{\mathbf{a}, \mathbf{g}\} \\ 3 & \text{if } op = sup \text{ and } a = \mathbf{c} \\ 5 & \text{if } op = ins(\mathbf{g}) \\ \infty & \text{otherwise} \end{cases}$$

To some extent, associating an atomic operation with an infinite cost could be used to denote that some operations are not possible. For instance, the idea of observable actions introduced in [8], on which a monitor cannot stop, can be modelled as associating an infinite cost with their suppression. We leave the characterisation of enforceable policies based on the cost of their enforcement for future work.

Cost of editing a trace. Given a monitor built using a selector, the total cost of enforcement of this monitor for a given trace can be calculated as the sum of the cost of each atomic operation.

Definition 3. *Given a selector f, a monitor M_f built using this selector and a trace σ in $\mathcal{T}$, we define the cost function $\mathsf{cost}_{M_f} : \mathcal{T} \to \mathbb{C}$ as:*

$$\mathsf{cost}_{M_f}(\sigma) = \sum_{0 \leqslant i < |\sigma|} opcost(f(\sigma^{<i}, \sigma^i), \sigma^i)$$

We remark that different sequences of operations might cost differently even if they produce the same output. For example for general actions a and b and c, the transformation from ac to abc can be done either by accepting a and inserting b upon seeing c, or by substituting a by ab and accepting c. In general these two

Table 2. Enforcement

σ	M_0		M_1		M_2		M_3		M_4		M_5		M_6		M_7	
ϵ	ϵ	0	ϵ	0	ϵ	0	ϵ	0	ϵ	0	ϵ	0	ϵ	0	ϵ	0
_a	__	4	_a	0	_a	0	g_a	5	_a	0	_a	0	_a	0	_a	0
aa	__	8	aa	0	aa	0	gaa	5	aa	0	aa	0	aa	0	aa	0
cc	__	6	__	6	__	6	gcc	5	gcc	5	gcc	5	gcgc	10	cc	0
ca	__	7	_a	3	_a	3	gca	5	gca	5	gca	5	gca	5	ca	0
ga	__	8	ga	0	ga	0	gga	5	ga	0	ga	0	ga	0	ga	0
gc	__	7	g_	3	gc	0	ggc	5	gc	0	ggc	5	ggc	5	gc	0
aaaa	____	16	aaaa	0	aaaa	0	gaaaa	5	aaaa	0	aaaa	0	aaaa	0	aaaa	0
cccc	____	12	____	12	____	12	gcccc	5	gcccc	5	gcccc	5	gcgcgcgc	20	cccc	0
caaa	____	15	_aaa	3	_aaa	3	gcaaa	5	gcaaa	5	gcaaa	5	gcaaa	5	caaa	0
gaaa	____	16	gaaa	0	gaaa	0	ggaaa	5	gaaa	0	gaaa	0	gaaa	0	gaaa	0
gccc	____	13	g___	9	gccc	0	ggccc	5	gccc	0	ggccc	5	ggcgcgc	15	gccc	0

sequences can have different cost. Therefore, what is important for assigning the cost is the intent of the modeller when creating the selector function for the monitor.

Running Example. *In Table 2 we can see the result of enforcement of monitors M_0 through M_7 on several traces, together with the cost.*

Expected cost of editing a set of traces. Sometimes a particular subset of the set of all traces produced by the target is of interest. For such a set, the expected cost of enforcement can be defined. We define a function $expcost_M : \mathcal{P}(\mathcal{T}) \to \mathbb{C}$, that for a set of traces T computes the *expected cost* of editing of traces in T.

Definition 4. *Let T be a set of traces, f be a selector function and opcost : Ops $\to \mathbb{C}$ a function assigning cost to operations. The function $expcost_{M_f} : \mathcal{P}(\mathcal{T}) \to \mathbb{C}$ is defined as follows*

$$expcost_{M_f}(T) = \frac{\sum_{\sigma \in T} \text{cost}_{M_f}(\sigma)}{|T|}.$$

Running Example. *Suppose that the maximum number of visitors that can come in one day is 30, that is $T = \mathcal{T}^{30}$. Then $expcost_{M_2}(T) = 2.99$.*

Intuitively, if T were associated with a probability distribution, we could extend $expcost_M$ be weighting the cost of each trace by its probability. We leave this extension for future work and we consider that all traces are equiprobable.

4.2 Cost-Based Comparison of Monitors

The interest of comparing monitors is to provide the security designer with a way of choosing a more efficient monitor which guarantees the correct functionality. That is why in this section we concentrate only on monitors that produce correct output at all times, i.e. on sound monitors. Note that transparency is intrinsically related to cost, so we drop it at this point of the paper to establish its relation to cost in the following section.

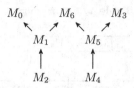

Fig. 1. Pointwise order between monitors

Pointwise comparison. We start with a natural way of comparing monitors – the pointwise comparison. Clearly, if for each trace a monitor spends less for enforcement than another one, it can be considered more cost-efficient.

Definition 5. *Let M and M' be monitors from* **CM**. *We define the relation* more cost-efficient *for monitors as follows:*

$$M \sqsubseteq M' \text{ iff } \forall \sigma \in \mathcal{T} : \text{cost}_M(\sigma) \leqslant \text{cost}_{M'}(\sigma).$$

Running Example. *The monitor M_2, which lets enter all adults but lets in children only when there are guards inside is assigned cost as follows:* $\text{cost}_{M_2}(\sigma) = opcost(sup, \text{c}) \cdot n_k$, *where n_k is the number of* c*s not preceded by any* g *in σ.*

As for monitor M_0, which prevents anyone from entering the museum, the cost is $\text{cost}_{M_0}(\sigma) = opcost(sup, \text{c}) \cdot \#_\text{c}(\sigma) + opcost(sup, \text{a}) \cdot \#_\text{a}(\sigma) + opcost(sup, \text{g}) \cdot \#_\text{g}(\sigma)$.

Intuitively, monitor M_2 should be more cost-efficient than the monitor M_0. In fact, none of these two monitors introduces any guards, and each child that is prevented from entering by M_2 is prevented also by M_0. Since this is true for each trace in $\mathcal{T}$, we have that $M_2 \sqsubseteq M_0$. The order between all sound monitors M_0 through M_6 according to $\sqsubseteq$ can be seen on Figure 1. For instance, we can see that in order to soundly enforce P_M there is no point in choosing M_0 since it is less cost-efficient than M_2 on each trace. Note that both M_2 and M_4 are more cost-efficient than the others, but they are incomparable.

Comparison by expected cost. In practice, it is quite difficult to obtain a monitor that is pointwise more cost-efficient than another monitor. The reason is, that frequently one monitor can be more cost-efficient on a set of traces, but less cost-efficient on another. In such a case the two monitors are incomparable according to $\sqsubseteq$. That is why we introduce another order relation, a comparison based on the expected cost which can serve as a distinguishing criterion.

Definition 6. *We define the relation* globally more cost-efficient *for monitors M and M' on the set of traces T as follows: $M \trianglelefteq^T M'$ iff $expcost_M(T) \leqslant expcost_{M'}(T)$.*

If we take as T the set $\mathcal{T}^n$ of all fixed-length traces of length n from $\mathcal{T}$, we write $\trianglelefteq^{\mathcal{T}^n}$ as $\trianglelefteq^n$.

It is easy to see that the order relation $\trianglelefteq^T$ is total, that is each two constructible monitors are comparable.

Running Example. *We are interested in comparing monitors M_2 and M_4, which are incomparable according to $\sqsubseteq$.*

It is easy to see[2] , that for short traces, i.e. small n monitor M_2, is more efficient. For long traces instead, M_4 becomes more convenient. This is due to the fact that when the trace to come is long enough, then inserting a guard is more efficient, because on average enough children will arrive to justify the cost for the guard. If the trace is not long enough, it is convenient to suppress all children.

It is possible to derive the n^* where this shift occurs. Note, that it is possible to combine these two strategies and obtain a monitor that subsumes both these monitors. More details on this matter, along with a table containing actual expected costs (Table 3), are included in the following section.

Relationship between pointwise and global order relations. It is clear that the pointwise order between two monitors implies the global order between them. That is if $M \sqsubseteq M'$ then $M \trianglelefteq^T M'$ for any T. The reason is that if the cost is smaller for each trace in a set, then for sure also the expected cost, which is the average of the cost on that set, is better. In general, the converse implication does not hold, in particular there can be two monitors, and one monitor is better on one trace in T, the other monitor is better on another trace in T, but the first maintains a better expected (average) cost on T.

5 Cost-Optimal Constructible Monitors

There are many sound and transparent constructible monitors for any safety property. The security designer might want to choose the one that minimises the cost of enforcement, that is in a way the best out of the monitors that perform their task well. In this section we consider sound cost-optimal monitors. Transparency is not required, in fact it is derived as cost-optimality in one of the special cases.

We associate the notion of cost-optimality with the minimality in the cost-based order relation. We call cost-optimal monitors the elements for which no element is smaller.

Definition 7. *We say that monitor M is $\sqsubseteq$-optimal ($\trianglelefteq^T$-optimal) iff there is no $M' \in$ CM such that $M' \sqsubset M$ ($M' \lhd^T M$).*

5.1 Cost-Optimality for $\sqsubseteq$

Consider, for a property P, the set of monitors that soundly enforce P. Now since $\sqsubseteq$ is a preorder on CM, on this set there exist minimal elements. That

---

[2] Formulas for computing the expected cost of monitors M_2 and M_4 can be found in the technical report [9].

means that for each property P there always exists at least one cost-optimal sound constructible monitor.

We call a monitor *absolutely* $\sqsubseteq$-optimal, if it the smallest element in CM w.r.t. $\sqsubseteq$, i.e. it is more cost-efficient than any other constructible monitor. It is worth noting, that in general there is no absolutely $\sqsubseteq$-optimal monitor, since there can be more than one incomparable minimal elements.

Running Example. *As can be seen on Figure 1, both monitors M_2 and M_4 are more cost-efficient that the rest of monitors in our example. It can be shown that for a general set of traces $\mathcal{T}$, there is no monitor that is strictly better than M_2 or M_4. Therefore both of them are $\sqsubseteq$-optimal. However, M_2 and M_4 are incomparable as we showed in the previous section. It follows that there is no absolutely cost-optimal monitor to enforce the museum security policy.*

Transparency as cost-optimality. In the beginning of this section we decided to relax the classic requirements of enforcement by dropping transparency. Now we will motivate this choice by showing, that under assumptions very reasonable in practice, transparency is implied by $\sqsubseteq$-optimality. In other words, it is enough to concentrate on cost-optimal monitors in order to obtain transparent ones. In particular, let us assume that acc is the single cheapest operation. Then for safety properties by assuming soundness, cost-optimality implies transparency. Note that we only consider safety properties P, as constructible monitors only can soundly and transparently enforce these properties.

Lemma 2. *Let P be a safety property. Let opcost be such that $opcost(acc, x)$ is strictly less than $opcost(op, x)$ for all other operations op. If M_f is sound for P, then if it is $\sqsubseteq$-optimal then it is transparent for P.*[3]

We remark, that the converse implication does not hold, i.e. transparency does not imply cost-optimality. The reason is that transparency does not talk about incorrect traces. It can be the case that even a sound and transparent monitor can be subsumed by another sound and transparent monitor with lower cost on incorrect traces.

Running Example. *We can see, that monitors M_2 and M_4 are transparent. On the other hand, all other monitors modify the trace gc, which is correct, and therefore are not transparent.*

It is worth noting, that if suppression was the cheapest operation, a trivial monitor that suppresses everything is the absolutely $\sqsubseteq$-optimal one for any property P (even beyond safety). This suggests that having suppression as the cheapest operation is a degenerate case since it favours security by blocking in the sense "what is shut off is secure".

5.2   Cost-Optimality for $\lhd^T$

As we have seen, the pointwise order does not allow for determining the cost-optimal monitor that is more cost-efficient than all others. However, the criterion

---

[3] The proof can be found in the technical report [9].

of expected cost can be of help in establishing cost-based relationship between pointwise incomparable monitors. Now we show how it can be useful for finding the best monitor.

Since $\trianglelefteq^T$ is a total order on CM, there is always a minimal element, which corresponds to the smallest element, i.e., the $\trianglelefteq^T$-optimality coincides with the absolute $\trianglelefteq^T$-optimality. Note that each $\trianglelefteq^T$-optimal monitor must be also $\sqsubseteq$-optimal which can be readily seen by reasoning by contradiction.

A natural question is how to find or construct a cost-optimal monitor for a set of traces $\mathcal{T}^n$. In the general case of an arbitrary cost setting, the cost-optimal monitor exists, since the cost-induced order is a preorder on CM, but it might not be trivial to find it. A very non-efficient way of finding $\trianglelefteq^n$-optimal monitor would be to enumerate all the monitors (there is a finite number of them for a $\mathcal{T}^n$) and choose the one with the lowest expected cost. We leave the investigation of more efficient ways to find such monitors for future work. Nevertheless, in some cases the $\trianglelefteq^n$-optimal monitors can be specified directly, as is in the case of our running example.

Running Example. *Note that out of M_0 through M_7 the only candidates for $\trianglelefteq^n$-optimality are M_2 and M_4. Following the reasoning from the previous section, there are lengths n for which M_2 is more cost-efficient than M_4 on $\mathcal{T}^n$ and others on which it is the other way round. Actually, none of these two monitors is $\trianglelefteq^n$-optimal. A cost-optimal monitor combines the strategies of these two monitors.*

Let us define a monitor M^* such that knowing that traces have a fixed length n, upon seeing the first child it inserts a g unless it is no longer convenient for the expected cost because on average not enough children can enter any more. Recall that n^* is the borderline length between "short" and "long" traces from the previous section. We can compute n^* as the smallest n that satisfies $expcost_{M_2}(\mathcal{T}^n) > expcost_{M_4}(\mathcal{T}^n)$. Thus if there remains a trace of $m \geqslant n^*$ to be seen (including the current action), it is still better to insert a guard, but if $m < n^*$, then instead it is better to suppress all children. In our case $n^* = 6$.

So the monitor M^* is defined through the selector function f^* as follows

$$f^*(\tau, x) = \begin{cases} ins(g) & \text{if } x = c \text{ and } g \notin \tau \text{ and } n - |\tau| \geqslant 6 \\ sup & \text{if } x = c \text{ and } g \notin \tau \text{ and } n - |\tau| < 6 \\ acc & \text{otherwise} \end{cases}$$

We show that M^* has the optimal expected cost on traces of length n, i.e. $\forall M \in \mathsf{CM} : expcost_{M^*}(\mathcal{T}^n) \leqslant expcost_M(\mathcal{T}^n)$. Proof: consider a trace σ of length n. On each prefix of σ that does not contain c, it can be easily seen that an optimal monitor M' should accept all actions. When a prefix of σ ends with a c, an optimal monitor should accept if a g is already in the prefix. Any other action would lead to a bigger expected cost. If there is no g in the prefix, then the optimal monitor should, based on the average number of cs in all the possible extensions of length n of the current prefix, insert g iff it costs less than the expected cost of suppression of all the cs. This is exactly the way in which M^* works, and thus it is cost-optimal with respect to $\trianglelefteq^n$.

Table 3. Expected costs of M_2, M_4 and M^*

T	$\mathcal{T}^1$	$\mathcal{T}^2$	$\mathcal{T}^3$	$\mathcal{T}^4$	$\mathcal{T}^5$	$\mathcal{T}^6$	$\mathcal{T}^7$	$\mathcal{T}^8$
$expcost_{M_2}(T)$	0.75	1.31	1.73	2.05	2.29	2.47	2.60	2.70
$expcost_{M_4}(T)$	1.25	1.88	2.19	2.34	2.42	2.46	2.48	2.49
$expcost_{M^*}(T)$	0.75	1.31	1.73	2.05	2.29	2.39	2.45	2.47

The expected cost of monitor M^* can be seen in Table 3. On traces shorter that 6, it has expected cost exactly as M_2, and it is less than that of M_4. Starting from traces of length 6, M^* outperforms both M_2 and M_4. The difference between the three monitors is illustrated on several traces from $\mathcal{T}^8$ as follows: if a child comes at the first turn, i.e. $\sigma =$ caaaaaaa, then $M_2(\sigma) = $ _aaaaaaa, $M_4(\sigma) = $ gcaaaaaaa and M^* acts as M_4 because it is convenient to put a guard since on average enough children will come to pay off for the cost of the guard. If the first child comes at the last turn instead, , i.e. $\sigma = $ aaaaaaac, it is no longer convenient to send in a guard and M^* acts as M_2 on σ thus $M^*(\sigma) = $ aaaaaaa_.

It is also worth noting that since the trace length n is a part of the definition of M^*, a monitor for $n = n'$ and $n = n' + 1$ behave differently. In particular, if a monitor M^* is $\trianglelefteq^{n'}$-optimal, it will not necessarily be $\trianglelefteq^{n'+1}$-optimal. We also remark, that since the constructibility of M^* depends vitally on the prior knowledge of the trace length by the monitor, if the security expert defining the monitor is not in possession of the information about the length of traces on which the monitor will be applied, such a monitor cannot be constructed. This issue is worth further investigation and is left as future work.

6   Conclusions

Discussion and related work. Since Schneider's seminal work [7], runtime enforcement of policy using security automata has been a well-studied subject in the literature, such as [1,10,3,11]. We do not detail here all these approaches, and we refer to [12] for an extensive survey. However, to the best of our knowledge, our approach is the first one to deal with the problem of cost of enforcement.

Recent research has argued that the original definition of effective enforcement [1] is inadequate because it does not sufficiently constrain the behaviour of the monitor when it is faced with a possible violation of the security policy [12]. Researchers have revisited the notion of enforcement by a monitor have proposed alternative ones.

Bielova and Massacci [2] propose to apply a distance metrics known from string analysis in order to capture the similarity between traces. With help of this distance metrics they propose a new requirement on the enforcement mechanism, called predictability, which is based on the following principle "for each illegal trace – if it is close enough to a legal one, it should be projected close enough to that trace". They leave the problem of characterising the class of properties that can be enforced by a predictable enforcement mechanism as open. Our proposal, using cost-optimal monitors, restated using similar vocabulary would be "for each illegal trace – (at all times) it should be projected onto the closest legal trace" where the distance is given by the cost of operations used for editing the trace. We prove, that for each safety property there is a cost-optimal monitor that soundly enforces this property.

Another attempt at a more restrictive concept of enforcement is the corrective enforcement of Khoury et al. [13]. Their approach is to group together related sequences into equivalence classes, and then limit the monitor so that it can only return an output sequence equivalent to the input. Moreover they use a partial order on sequences to obtain better results than with equivalence. The drawback of their approach is that restrictions on the treatment of incorrect sequences must be defined explicitly by the user for each property.

Edit automata [1] have also been identified as being too powerful, because they can use buffering and make the enforcement decisions with information about entire trace at its disposal. Bielova and Massacci [4] investigate subclasses of automata as delayed automata, all-or-nothing automata and Ligatti automata. We believe that our paradigm of constructive monitors is close to the practical nature of runtime enforcement, as we oblige the monitor to decide at each step only based on the information it can obtain from the current action and the past trace. To certain point this is similar to the concept of precise enforcement of Ligatti et al. [1] and therefore it comes as no surprise that this class of monitors enforces soundly and transparently only safety properties.

Our model of constructible monitor bears similarities to the MRA model of Ligatti and Reddy [3], which obliges the monitor to returns a result to the target application before seeing the next action it wishes to execute. Our model, instead, requires that the monitor outputs a non-empty trace before seeing the next action, but does not provide any feedback to the target.

Future work. It would clearly be interesting to leverage the fact that our cost model is parameterized to consider more practical operations inspired by real scenarios, for instance a complex treatment of buffering in our cost framework, with positive/negative costs. In addition, a general approach for constructing the optimal monitor for a cost model would be worth investigating, for instance by using recent work linking decision theory and access control [14].

Furthermore, our framework paves the way for investigations about quantitative aspects of runtime enforcement [15]. The present is only a first attempt to consider cost in the context of monitoring, where all traces are seen as equiprobable. A straightforward extension could be done when in possession of probabilistic information about traces, which would represent a more accurate notion of expected cost. Other dimensions to be treated in a quantitative manner include considering impact/benefit of traces and penalty for not respecting the policy.

Conclusion. In this paper we have presented a framework where the cost of enforcement is determined by the cost of operations used by monitor. The classic requirements on enforcement of security policies, soundness and transparency, leave a margin for specifying the behaviour of the monitor on incorrect inputs.

We argue that the cost of enforcement can serve as a distinguishing criterion for sound monitors for safety policies. We investigate cost-optimality of monitors and show that under reasonable assumptions it justifies the concept of transparency. We demonstrate the approach on a case study of a museum security policy and show how to find the cost-optimal monitor to enforce the policy.

References

1. Ligatti, J., Bauer, L., Walker, D.: Edit automata: Enforcement mechanisms for run-time security policies. International Journal of Information Security 4(1-2), 2–16 (2005)
2. Bielova, N., Massacci, F.: Predictability of enforcement. In: Erlingsson, Ú., Wieringa, R., Zannone, N. (eds.) ESSoS 2011. LNCS, vol. 6542, pp. 73–86. Springer, Heidelberg (2011)
3. Ligatti, J., Reddy, S.: A theory of runtime enforcement, with results. In: Gritzalis, D., Preneel, B., Theoharidou, M. (eds.) ESORICS 2010. LNCS, vol. 6345, pp. 87–100. Springer, Heidelberg (2010)
4. Bielova, N., Massacci, F.: Do you really mean what you actually enforced? IJIS, 1–16 (2011)
5. Alpern, B., Schneider, F.B.: Recognizing safety and liveness. Distributed Computing 2(3), 117–126 (1987)
6. Lamport, L.: Proving the correctness of multiprocess programs. IEEE Trans. Software Eng. 3(2), 125–143 (1977)
7. Schneider, F.B.: Enforceable security policies. ACM Trans. Inf. Syst. Secur. 3, 30–50 (2000)
8. Basin, D., Jugé, V., Klaedtke, F., Zălinescu, E.: Enforceable security policies revisited. In: Degano, P., Guttman, J.D. (eds.) Principles of Security and Trust. LNCS, vol. 7215, pp. 309–328. Springer, Heidelberg (2012)
9. Drábik, P., Martinelli, F., Morisset, C.: Cost-aware runtime enforcement of security policies. Technical Report TR-11-2012, IIT-CNR (2012)
10. Ligatti, J., Bauer, L., Walker, D.: Run-time enforcement of nonsafety policies. ACM Transactions on Information and System Security 12(3), 1–41 (2009)
11. Fong, P.W.L.: Access control by tracking shallow execution history. In: IEEE Symposium on Security and Privacy, pp. 43–55. IEEE Computer Society (2004)
12. Khoury, R., Tawbi, N.: Which security policies are enforceable by runtime monitors? a survey. Computer Science Review 6(1), 27–45 (2012)
13. Khoury, R., Tawbi, N.: Using equivalence relations for corrective enforcement of security policies. In: Kotenko, I., Skormin, V. (eds.) MMM-ACNS 2010. LNCS, vol. 6258, pp. 139–154. Springer, Heidelberg (2010)
14. Martinelli, F., Morisset, C.: Quantitative access control with partially-observable Markov decision processes. In: Proceedings of CODASPY 2012, pp. 169–180. ACM (2012)
15. Martinelli, F., Matteucci, I., Morisset, C.: From qualitative to quantitative enforcement of security policy. In: Kotenko, I., Skormin, V. (eds.) MMM-ACNS 2012. LNCS, vol. 7531, pp. 22–35. Springer, Heidelberg (2012)

Enforcing More with Less:
Formalizing Target-Aware Run-Time Monitors

Yannis Mallios[1], Lujo Bauer[1], Dilsun Kaynar[1], and Jay Ligatti[2]

[1] Carnegie Mellon University, Pittsburgh, USA
{mallios,lbauer,dilsunk}@cmu.edu
[2] University of South Florida, Tampa, USA
ligatti@cse.usf.edu

Abstract. Run-time monitors ensure that untrusted software and system behavior adheres to a security policy. This paper defines an expressive formal framework, based on I/O automata, for modeling systems, policies, and run-time monitors in more detail than is typical. We explicitly model, for example, the environment, applications, and the interaction between them and monitors. The fidelity afforded by this framework allows us to explicitly formulate and study practical constraints on policy enforcement that were often only implicit in previous models, providing a more accurate view of what can be enforced by monitoring in practice. We introduce two definitions of enforcement, target-specific and generalized, that allow us to·reason about practical monitoring scenarios. Finally, we provide some meta-theoretical comparison of these definitions and we apply them to investigate policy enforcement in scenarios where the monitor designer has knowledge of the target application and show how this can be exploited to make more efficient design choices.

1   Introduction

Today's computing climate is characterized by increasingly complex software systems and networks, and inventive and determined attackers. Hence, one of the major thrusts in the software industry and in computer security research has become to devise ways to *provably guarantee* that software does not behave in dangerous ways or, barring that, that such misbehavior is contained. Example guarantees could be that programs: only access memory that is allocated to them (memory safety); only jump to and execute valid code (control-flow integrity); and never send secret data over the network (a type of information flow).

A common mechanism for enforcing security policies on untrusted software is run-time monitoring. Run-time monitors observe the execution of untrusted applications or systems and ensure that their behavior adheres to a security policy. This type of enforcement mechanism is pervasive, and can be seen in operating systems, web browsers, firewalls, intrusion detection systems, etc. A common example of monitoring is system-call interposition (e.g., [12]): given an untrusted application and a set of security-relevant system calls, a monitor intercepts calls made by the application to the kernel, and enforces a security policy

A. Jøsang, P. Samarati, and M. Petrocchi (Eds.): STM 2012, LNCS 7783, pp. 17–32, 2013.

by taking remedial action when a call violates the policy (Fig. 1). In practice, several instantiations of monitors could be used in this scenario. Understanding and formally reasoning about each is as important as understanding the general concept, since it allows important details to be captured that might be lost at a higher level of abstraction. Two dimensions along which instantiations can differ are: (1) *the monitored interface*: monitors can mediate different parts of the communication between the application and the kernel, e.g., an input-sanitization monitor will mediate only inputs to the kernel (dashed lines in Fig. 1); and (2) *trace-modification capabilities*: monitors may have a variety of enforcement capabilities, from just terminating the application (e.g., when it tries to write to the password file), to being able to perform additional remedial actions (e.g., suppress a write system call and log the attempt).[1]

Despite the ubiquity of run-time monitors, their use has far outpaced theoretical work that makes it possible to formally and rigorously reason about monitors and the policies they enforce. Such theoretical work is necessary, however, if we are to have confidence that enforcement mechanisms are successfully carrying out their intended functions.

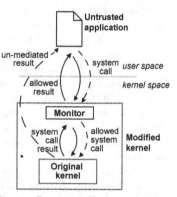

Several proposed formal models (e.g., [23,17]) make progress towards this goal. They use formal frameworks to model monitors and their enforcement capabilities, e.g., whether the monitors can insert arbitrary actions into the stream of actions that the target wants to execute. These frameworks have been used to analyze and characterize the policies that are enforceable by the various types of monitors.

Fig. 1. System-call interposition: dashed line shows an input-mediating monitor; solid line an input/output-mediating monitor.

However, such models typically do not capture many details of the monitoring process, including the monitored interface, leaving us with practical scenarios that we cannot reason about in detail. In our system-call interposition scenario, for example, without the ability to model the communication between the untrusted application, the monitor, and the kernel, it may not be possible to distinguish between and compare monitors that can mediate all security-relevant communication between the application and the kernel (solid lines in Fig. 1) and monitors that can mediate only some of it (dashed lines in Fig. 1).

Some recent models (e.g., [18,13]) allow reasoning about bi-directional communication between the monitor and its environment (e.g., application and kernel), but do not explicitly reason about the application or system being monitored. In practice, however, monitors can enforce policies beyond their operational enforcement capabilities by exploiting knowledge about the component that they are monitoring. For example, a policy that requires that every file that is opened

---

[1] In this paper we do not consider mechanisms that arbitrarily modify the target application, such as by rewriting.

must be eventually closed cannot, in general, be enforced by any monitor, because the monitor cannot know what the untrusted application will do in the future. However, if the monitored application always closes files that it opens, then this policy is no longer unenforceable for that particular application. Such distinctions are often relevant in practice—e.g., when implementing a patch for a specific type or version of an application—and, thus, there is a need for formal frameworks that will aid in making informed and provably correct design and implementation decisions.

In this paper, we propose a general framework, based on I/O automata, for more detailed reasoning about policies, monitoring, and enforcement. The I/O automaton model [19] is a labeled transition model for asynchronous concurrent systems. We chose I/O automata because we wanted an automata-based formalism, similarly to many previous models of run-time enforcement mechanisms, but with enough expressive power and established meta-theory to model asynchronous systems (e.g., communication between the application, the monitor, and the kernel).Our framework provides abstractions for reasoning about many practical details important for run-time enforcement, and, in general, yields a richer view of monitors and applications than is typical in previous analyses of run-time monitoring. For example, our framework supports modeling practical systems with security-relevant actions that the monitor cannot mediate.

We make the following specific contributions:

- We show how I/O automata can be used to faithfully model target applications, monitors, and the environments in which monitored targets operate, as well as various monitoring architectures (§3).
- We extend previous definitions of security policies and enforcement to support more fine-grained formal reasoning of policy enforcement (§4).
- We show that this more detailed model of monitoring forces explicit reasoning about concerns that are important for designing run-time monitors in practice, but about which previous models often reasoned only informally (§5.2). We formalize these results as a set of lower bounds on the policies enforceable by any monitor in our framework.
- We demonstrate how to use our framework to exploit knowledge about the target application to make design and implementation choices that may lead to more efficient enforcement (§5.3). For example, we exhibit constraints under which monitors with different monitoring interfaces (i.e., one can mediate more actions than the other) can enforce the same class of policies.

Limitations. The goal of this paper is to introduce an expressive framework for reasoning about run-time monitors, and illustrate how to use it for meta-theoretical analysis of run-time enforcement. Due to space constraints, we omit or abbreviate several important aspects of the discussion, including: (1) Real-world examples: We provide simple examples to illustrate the use and advantages of our framework (§3), but do not encode any complex real-world scenarios. I/O automata-based modeling of complex applications requires mostly stand-alone work (e.g., [15,2]), and we defer to future work such examples for run-time monitoring. (2) Translation of previous models: We omit translations of previous models of monitors (e.g., edit automata [17]) or auxiliary notions for defining enforcement (e.g., transparency [17]). Examples of modeling previously studied monitors can be found in our technical report [20]; a discussion of why *transparency* is non-essential in expressive frameworks, such as ours, can be found in [18]. (3) Formal presentation: When the notational complexity needed to formally define I/O automata and our framework obscures underlying insights, our presentation is not fully formal; a more formal treatment can be found in our technical report [20].

Roadmap. We first briefly review I/O automata (§2). We then informally show how to model monitors and targets in our framework and discuss some benefits of this approach (§3). Then, we formally define policies and enforcement (§4), and show examples of meta-theoretical analysis enabled by our framework: (a) lower bounds for enforceable policies (§5.2), and (b) constraints under which seemingly different monitoring architectures enforce the same classes of policies (§5.3).

2   I/O Automata

I/O automata are a labeled transition model for asynchronous concurrent systems [24,19]. Here we informally review aspects of I/O automata that we build on in the rest of the paper; please see our technical report [20] for a more formal treatment. We encourage readers familiar with I/O automata to skip to §3.

I/O automata are typically used to describe the behavior of a system interacting with its environment. The interface between an automaton A and its environment is described by the ***action signature*** $sig(A)$, a triple of disjoint sets—$input(A)$, $output(A)$, and $internal(A)$. We write $acts(A)$ for $input(A) \cup output(A) \cup internal(A)$, and call output and internal actions *locally controlled*.

Formally, an I/O automaton A consists of: (1) an action signature, $sig(A)$; (2) a (possibly infinite) set of *states*, $states(A)$; (3) a nonempty set of *start states*, $start(A) \subseteq states(A)$; (4) a transition relation, $trans(A) \subseteq states(A) \times acts(A) \times states(A)$, such that for every state q and input action a there is a transition $(q, a, q') \in trans(A)$; and (5) an equivalence relation $Tasks(A)$ partitioning the set $output(A) \cup internal(A)$ into at most countably many equivalence classes.

If A has a transition (q, a, q') then we say that action a is *enabled* in state q. Since every input action is enabled in every state, I/O automata are said to be *input-enabled*. When only input actions are enabled in q, then q is called a *quiescent* state. The set of all quiescent states of an automaton A is denoted by $quiescent(A)$. The equivalence relation $Tasks(A)$ is used to define *fairness*, which essentially says that the automaton will give fair turns to each of its tasks while executing.

An ***execution*** e of A is a finite sequence, $q_0, a_1, q_1, \ldots, a_r, q_r$, or an infinite sequence $q_0, a_1, q_1, \ldots, a_r, q_r, \ldots$, of alternating states and actions such that $(q_k, a_{k+1}, q_{k+1}) \in trans(A)$ for $k \geq 0$, and $q_0 \in start(A)$. A ***schedule*** is an execution without states in the sequence, and a ***trace*** is a schedule that consists only of input and output actions. An *execution, trace,* or *schedule **module*** describes the behavior exhibited by an automaton. An execution module E consists of a set $states(E)$, an action signature $sig(E)$, and a set $execs(E)$ of executions. Schedule and trace modules are similar, but do not include states. The sets of executions, schedules, and traces of an I/O automaton (or module) X are denoted by $execs(X)$, $scheds(X)$, and $traces(X)$. Given a sequence s and a set X, $s|X$ denotes the sequence resulting from removing from s all elements that do not belong in X. Similarly, for a set of sequences S, $S|X = \{(s|X) \mid s \in S\}$.

The symbol ϵ denotes the empty sequence. We write $\sigma_1; \sigma_2$ for the concatenation of two schedules or traces, the first of which has finite length. When σ_1 is a finite prefix of σ_2, we write $\sigma_1 \preceq \sigma_2$, and, if a strict finite prefix, $\sigma_1 \prec \sigma_2$. $\Sigma^\star$ denotes the set of finite sequences of actions and Σ^ω the set of infinite sequences of actions. The set of all finite and infinite sequences of actions is $\Sigma^\infty = \Sigma^\star \cup \Sigma^\omega$.

An automaton that models a complex system can be constructed by *composing* automata that model the system's components. A set of I/O automata is *compatible* if their output actions are disjoint and the internal actions of each automaton are disjoint with all actions of the other automata. The composition $A = A_1 \times \ldots \times A_n$ of a set of compatible automata $\{A_i : i \in I\}$ is the automaton that has as states the Cartesian product of the states of the component automata and as behaviors the interleavings of the behaviors of the component automata. Composition of modules is defined similarly [24].

Unlike in models such as CCS [22], composing two automata that share actions (i.e., outputs of one are inputs to the other) causes those actions to become output actions of the composition. Actions that are required to be internal need to be explicitly classified as such using the *hiding* operation, which takes as input a signature and a set of output actions to be hidden, and produces a signature with those actions reclassfied as internal. *Renaming*, on the other hand, changes the names of actions, but not their types, i.e., renaming is a total injective mapping between sets of actions.

3   Specifying Targets and Monitors

We model targets (the entities to be monitored) and monitors as I/O automata, and denote them by metavariables $\mathcal{T}$ and $\mathcal{M}$. Targets composed with monitors are *monitored targets*; such an example is the modified kernel in Fig. 1. Monitored targets may themselves be targets for other monitors.

Building on the system-call-interposition example (Fig. 1), we now show how to model monitors and targets using I/O automata. Suppose the application's only actions are *OpenFile*, *WriteFile*, and *CloseFile* system calls; the kernel's actions are *FD* (to return a file descriptor) and the *Kill* system call. The application can request to open a file *fn*, and the kernel keeps track of the requests as part of its state. When a file descriptor *fd* is returned in response to a request for *fn*, *fn* is removed from the set of requests. The application can then write *bytes* number of bytes to, or close, *fd*. Finally, a *Kill* action terminates the application and clears all requests. Such a formalization, where the target's actions depend on results returned by the environment, was outside the scope of original run-time-monitor models, as identified also by recent work (e.g., [18,13]).

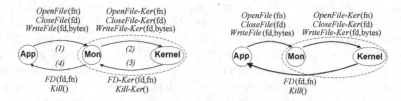

(a) Input/output-mediating monitor   (b) Input-mediating monitor

Fig. 2. I/O automata interface diagrams of kernel, application, and monitor

Fig. 2a shows I/O automata interface diagrams of the monitored system consisting of the application and the monitored kernel.[2] The application's and the kernel's interfaces differ only in that the input actions of the kernel are output actions of the application, and vice versa. This models the communication between the application and the kernel when they are considered as a single system. The kernel's readiness to always accept file-open requests is modeled naturally by the input-enabledness of the I/O automaton. Paths (2) and (3) represent communication between the monitor and the kernel through the *renamed* actions of the kernel (using the renaming operation of I/O automata), e.g., $OpenFile(x)$ becomes $OpenFile\text{-}Ker(x)$, and thus irrelevant to a policy that reasons about $OpenFile$ actions. Renaming models changing the target's interface to allow the monitor to intercept the target's actions. In practice, this is often done by rewriting the target to inline a monitor. Finally, we also *hide* the communication between the monitor and the kernel to keep it internal to the monitored target (denoted by the dotted line around the monitored kernel automaton). This models a monitoring process that is transparent to the application (i.e., the application remains unaware that the kernel is monitored).

In our system-call interposition example we described some choices that a monitor designer can make, such as choosing (1) the interface to be monitored, e.g., mediate only input actions, and (2) the trace-modification capabilities of the monitor. Choice (1) can be expressed in our model by appropriately restricting the renaming function applied to the target. For example, in Fig. 2b, we renamed only the input actions of the kernel (i.e., $OpenFile$, $CloseFile$, and $WriteFile$). This models monitors that mediate inputs sent to the target and can prevent, for example, SQL injections attacks. Similarly, renaming only the outputs of the target models monitors that mediate only output actions (and can prevent, for example, cross-site scripting attacks). Choice (2) is closely related to representing previous models of monitors in our framework; please see our technical report for more detail on this and on modeling different trace-modification capabilities [20].

4 Policy Enforcement

In this section we define security policies and two notions of enforcement: target-specific and generalized enforcement.

---

[2] The kernel's I/O automaton definition is shown in our technical report [20].

4.1   Security Policies

A *policy* is a set of (execution, schedule, or trace[3]) modules. We let the metavariables $\mathcal{P}$ and $\hat{P}$ range over policies and their elements, i.e., modules, respectively. The novelty of this definition of policy compared to previous ones (e.g., [23,17]) is that each element of the policy is not a set of automaton runs, but, rather, a pair of a set of runs (i.e., schedules or traces) and a signature, which is a triple consisting of a set of inputs, a set of outputs, and a set of internal actions. The signature describes explicitly which actions that do not appear in the set of runs are relevant to a policy. This is useful in a number of ways. When enforcing a policy on a system composed of several previously defined components, for example, the signatures can clarify whether a policy that is being enforced on one component also reasons about (e.g., prohibits or simply does not care about) the actions of another component. For our running example, if the signature contains only *Open*, *FD*, and *Kill*, then all other system calls are security irrelevant and thus permitted; if the signature contains other system calls (*SocketRead*), then any behaviors exhibiting those calls are prohibited.

Our definition of a policy as a set of modules resembles that of a hyperproperty [8] and previous definition of policies (modulo the signature of each schedule or trace module) and captures common types of policies such as access control, noninterference, information flow, and availability.

I/O automata can have infinite states and produce possibly infinite computations. We would like to avoid discussions of computability and complexity issues, and so we make the assumption that all policies $\mathcal{P}$ that we discuss are *implementable* [24], meaning that for each module $\hat{P}$ in $\mathcal{P}$, there exists an I/O automaton A such that $sig(A) = sig(\hat{P})$ and $scheds(\hat{P}) \subseteq scheds(A)$.

4.2   Enforcement

In §3 we showed how monitoring can be modeled by renaming a target $\mathcal{T}$ so that its security-relevant actions can be observed by a monitor $\mathcal{M}$ and by hiding actions that represent communication unobservable outside of the monitored target. We now define enforcement formally as a relation between the behaviors allowed by the policy and the behaviors exhibited by the monitored target.

Definition 1 *(Target-specific enforcement) Given a policy $\mathcal{P}$, a target $\mathcal{T}$, and a monitor $\mathcal{M}$ we say that $\mathcal{P}$ is **specifically soundly enforceable** on $\mathcal{T}$ by $\mathcal{M}$ if and only if there exists a module $\hat{P} \in \mathcal{P}$, a renaming function* rename, *and a hiding function* hide *for some set of actions Φ such that* $(scheds(\mathsf{hide}_\Phi(\mathcal{M} \times \mathsf{rename}(\mathcal{T})))|acts(\hat{P})) \subseteq scheds(\hat{P})$.

Here, $\mathsf{hide}_\Phi(\mathcal{M} \times \mathsf{rename}(\mathcal{T}))$ is the monitored target: the target $\mathcal{T}$ is renamed so that its security-relevant actions can be observed by the monitor $\mathcal{M}$; *hide* is applied to their composition to prevent communication between the monitor

---

[3] Our analyses equally apply to execution modules, but, for brevity, we discuss only schedule and trace modules.

and the target from leaking outside the composition.[4] If a target does not need renaming, rename can be the identity function; if we do not care about hiding all communication, *hide* can apply to only some actions. For example, suppose the monitored target from our running example (node with dotted lines in Fig. 2b) is composed with an additional monitor that logs system-call requests and responses. We would then keep the actions for system-call requests and responses visible to the logging monitor by not hiding them in the initial monitored target.

Def. 1 binds the enforcement of a policy by a monitor to a specific target. We refer this type of enforcement as *target-specific enforcement* and to the corresponding monitor as a target-specific monitor. However, some monitors may be able to enforce a property on any target. One such example is a system-call-interposition mechanism that operates independently of the target kernel's version or type (e.g., a single monitor binary that can be installed in both Windows and Linux). We call this type of enforcement *generalized enforcement*, and the corresponding monitor a generalized monitor.[5] More formally:

Definition 2 *(Generalized enforcement) Given a policy $\mathcal{P}$ and a monitor $\mathcal{M}$ we say that $\mathcal{P}$ is **generally soundly enforceable** by $\mathcal{M}$ if and only if for all targets $\mathcal{T}$ there exists a module $\hat{P} \in \mathcal{P}$, a renaming function rename, such that $(scheds(\mathcal{M} \times \mathsf{rename}(\mathcal{T}))|acts(\hat{P})) \subseteq scheds(\hat{P})$.*

Different versions of Def. 1 and 2 can be obtained by replacing schedules with traces (trace enforcement), fair schedules, or fair traces (fair enforcement); or by replacing the subset relation with other set relations (e.g., equality) for comparing the behaviors of the monitored target to those of the policy [18,5]. In this paper we focus on the subset and equality relations, and refer to the corresponding enforcement notions as *sound* (e.g., Def. 1) and *precise enforcement*.

No constraints are placed on the renaming and hiding functions in Def. 1 and 2, as this permits more enforcement scenarios to be encoded in our framework. For example, by α-renaming a target, which in practice means that we are ignoring it, and incorporating some of its functionality (if needed) in a monitor, we can encode a technique similar to the one used to automate monitor synthesis (e.g., [21]). Another reason for this choice, stemming from a meta-theoretical analysis of the two distinct notions of enforcement, is discussed next, in §4.3.

4.3   Comparing Enforcement Definitions

As an example of meta-theoretic analysis in our framework, we compare Def. 1 and 2. More specifically, one might expect target-specific monitors to have an advantage in enforcement, i.e., the class of target-specific monitors *should* enforce

---

[4] Since Def. 1 reasons about schedules (i.e., internal actions as well as input and output), hide$_\Phi$ is redundant: hiding reclassifies some output actions as internal, but does not remove them from schedules. We include it here to illustrate our framework's ability to expose that, in practice, the environment can be oblivious to the monitoring of the target application. In the rest of the paper we will omit the hiding operator.

[5] Monitors of previous models, such as [23] and [17], are generalized monitors.

a larger set of policies than the class of generalized monitors. Intuitively, this is because if a policy describes a behavior that is correctable for specific targets, but not for all targets, then there is no generalized monitor that can enforce that policy, even if target-specific monitors exist.[6]

Proposition 1. *Given a monitor* $\mathcal{M}$:

1. $\forall \mathscr{P} : \mathscr{P}$ *is **generally soundly enforceable** by* $\mathcal{M} \Rightarrow$
   $\forall \mathcal{T} : \mathscr{P}$ *is **specifically soundly enforceable** on* $\mathcal{T}$ *by* $\mathcal{M}$, *and*
2. $\exists \mathscr{P} \exists \mathcal{T} : (\mathscr{P}$ *is **specifically soundly enforceable** on* $\mathcal{T}$ *by* $\mathcal{M}) \wedge$
   $\neg(\mathscr{P}$ *is **generally soundly enforceable** by* $\mathcal{M})$.

Prop. 1 compares the definitions of enforcement (Def. 1 and 2) with respect to the same monitor, and shows that they capture the intuition that a monitor that enforces a policy without being tailored for a specific target can enforce the policy on any target, while the inverse does not hold in general.

However, we can get a deeper insight when trying to characterize the two definitions of enforcement in general, i.e., independently of a specific monitor. Surprisingly, in such a comparison the two definitions turn out to be equivalent.

Theorem 1. $\forall \mathscr{P} \forall \mathcal{T}$:
   $\exists \mathcal{M} : \mathscr{P}$ *is **specifically soundly enforceable** on* $\mathcal{T}$ *by* $\mathcal{M} \Leftrightarrow$
   $\exists \mathcal{M}' : \mathscr{P}$ *is **generally soundly enforceable** by* $\mathcal{M}'$.

The right-to-left direction of the theorem is straightforward: any generalized monitor can be used as a target-specific monitor. The other direction is more interesting since it suggests, perhaps surprisingly, that a generalized monitor can be constructed from a target-specific one. More specifically, given a monitor that enforces a policy on a specific target, we can use this *monitored target* as the basis for a monitor for any other target. In that case, security-relevant behaviors of the system would be exhibited only by the monitor (formally, all target actions would be renamed to become security irrelevant). For example, suppose that different versions of an application are installed on each of our machines. If we find a patch (i.e., monitor) for one version, then Thm. 1 implies that instead of finding patches for all other versions, we can distribute the patched version (i.e., monitored target) to all machines and modify the existing applications on those machines so that their behavior is ignored. This approach may apply if installing the patched version of the application on top of other versions is more cost-efficient than finding patches for all other versions.

Thm. 1 holds because Def. 1 and 2 place no restrictions on renaming functions (i.e., on how a monitor is integrated with a target). In practice, this interaction may be constrained. Thus, one might argue that it would be more natural for the only-if direction of the theorem to fail, since it erases the distinction between target-specific and generalized enforcement. The following theorem shows the effect of introducing such a constraint.

---

[6] Due to space constraints, proofs are given in our companion technical report [20].

Theorem 2. $\exists \mathscr{P} \exists \mathcal{T}$:

$\Big(\exists \mathcal{M}:\ \mathscr{P}$ *is* **specifically soundly enforceable** *on* $\mathcal{T}$ *by* $\mathcal{M}\Big)$ ***and***

$\neg\Big(\exists \mathcal{M}':\ \mathscr{P}$ *is conditionally* **generally soundly enforceable** *by* $\mathcal{M}'$, *i.e.,*

  for all targets $\mathcal{T}'$ *there exists a module* $\hat{P} \in \mathscr{P}$, *and a renaming function* rename, *such that if :*

   (C1) $\ acts(\hat{P}) \cap acts(\mathcal{T}') \neq \emptyset$, *and*

   (C2) $\ range(\mathsf{rename}) \subseteq acts(\mathcal{M}')$

  then $\big(scheds(\mathcal{M}' \times \mathsf{rename}(\mathcal{T}'))|acts(\hat{P})) \subseteq scheds(\hat{P}))\Big)$.

The first condition (C1) prohibits using an element of the policy that is irrelevant to the target that we are trying to monitor. For example, if a policy consists of one module that contains networking events (i.e., the signature of the module contains only network-related actions) and another that contains file-related events (e.g., a signature similar to the one of our system-call interposition example), then if we want to enforce that policy on a network card (i.e., a target that exhibits network actions but no file actions), we must use the former module.

The second condition (C2) ensures that the only way that we rename the target is to match the monitors interface. In other words, we may not arbitrarily rename the target so that nobody can "listen" to its actions.

Thm. 2 lists some conditions under which generalized and target-specific enforcement are not equivalent. More satisfying would be to identify a single constraint under which the equivalence would not hold for any policy or target; however, given the wide variety of enforcement scenarios in practice, we conjecture that no single constraint allows Thm. 2 to be universally quantified over all policies and targets, as Thm. 1 is. Since our goal is to introduce a framework general enough to accommodate as many practical scenarios as possible, we rely on the monitor designer to impose appropriate restrictions on renaming or monitors that accurately reflect the specific practical scenarios under scrutiny.

5   Bounds on Enforceable Policies

This section describes several meta-theoretic results, facilitated by the abstractions described thus far, that further our understanding of the general limitations of practical monitors that fit this model.

5.1   Auxiliary Definitions

I/O automata are input enabled—all input actions are enabled at all states. Several arguments can be made in favor of or against input-enabledness. For example, one can argue that input-enabledness leads to better design of systems because one has to consider all possible inputs [19]. On the other hand, this constraint may be too restrictive for practical systems [1].

In our context, we believe input-enabledness is a useful characteristic, since run-time monitors are by nature input-enabled systems: a monitor may receive input at any time both from the target and from the environment (e.g., keyboard or network). However, a monitor modeled as an input-enabled automaton can enforce only those policies that allow the arrival of inputs at any point during execution. This is reasonable: a policy that prohibits certain inputs cannot be enforced by a monitor that cannot control those inputs. We later combine this and other constraints to describe the lower bound of enforceability in our setting.

We say that a module (or policy) is *input forgiving* (respectively, *internal* and *output* forgiving) if and only if it allows the empty sequence and allows each valid sequence to be extended to another valid sequence by appending any (possibly infinite) sequence of inputs.

Definition 3 *A schedule module $\hat{P}$ is **input forgiving** if and only if:*
(1) $\epsilon \in scheds(\hat{P})$; and
(2) $\forall s_1 \in scheds(\hat{P}) : \forall s_2 \preceq s_1 : \forall s_3 \in (input(\hat{P}))^{\infty} : (s_2; s_3) \in scheds(\hat{P})$.

I/O automata's definition of executions allows computation to stop at any point. Thus, the behavior of an I/O automaton is *prefix-closed*: any prefix of an execution exhibited by an automaton is also an execution of that automaton.

Definition 4 *A schedule module $\hat{P}$ is **prefix closed** if and only if:*
$\forall s_1 \in \Sigma^{\infty} : \left(s_1 \in scheds(\hat{P}) \Rightarrow \forall s_2 \in \Sigma^{\star} : s_2 \preceq s_1 : s_2 \in scheds(\hat{P}) \right).$

These two characteristics are unsurprising from the standpoint of models for distributed computation, but describe practically relevant details typically absent from models of run-time enforcement. Our model, instead of making assumptions that may not hold in practice, e.g., that all actions can be mediated, takes a more nuanced view, which admits that some aspects of enforcement are outside the monitor's control, such as scheduling strategies for security-relevant actions that cannot be mediated. The above definitions help explicate these assumptions when reasoning about enforceable policies, as we see next.

5.2   Lower Bounds of Enforceable Policies

Another constraint that affects enforceability and is specific to monitoring is that, in practice, a monitor cannot always ignore *all* behavior of the target application. Some real monitors decide what input actions the application sees, but otherwise do not interfere with the application's behavior—firewalls belong to this class of monitors. In such cases, a monitor can soundly enforce a policy only if the policy allows all behaviors that the target can exhibit when it receives no input. We call such policies, and their modules, *quiescent forgiving* (recall the definition of a quiescent state from §2). This captures a limitation that was understood to be present in run-time monitoring, but that typically was not formally expressed. More formally:

Definition 5 *A schedule module* $\hat{P}$ *is* **quiescent forgiving** *for some* $\mathcal{T}$ *if and only if:*
$\forall e \in execs(\mathcal{T})$ *such that* $e = q_0, a_1, \ldots, q_n$:
$$\left(q_n \in quiescent(\mathcal{T}) \wedge \left(\forall i \in \mathbb{N} : 0 \leq i < n : q_i \notin quiescent(\mathcal{T}) \right) \right) \Rightarrow$$
$\left(sched(e) | acts(\hat{P}) \right) \in scheds(\hat{P}) \wedge (\forall i \in \mathbb{N} : 0 \leq i < n : (sched(q_0, \ldots, q_i) \mid acts(\hat{P})) \in scheds(\hat{P}))$.

The following theorem formalizes a lower bound: a policy that is not quiescent forgiving, input forgiving, and prefix closed cannot be (precisely) enforced.

Theorem 3. $\forall \mathscr{P} : \forall \hat{P} \in \mathscr{P} : \forall \mathcal{T} : \forall \mathsf{rename} :$
$\exists \mathcal{M} : \left(scheds(\mathcal{M} \times \mathsf{rename}(\mathcal{T})) | acts(\hat{P}) \right) = scheds(\hat{P}) \Rightarrow$
$\qquad \hat{P}$ *is input forgiving, prefix closed, and quiescent forgiving for* $\mathsf{rename}(\mathcal{T})$.

Thm. 3 reveals that monitors, regardless of their editing power, can enforce only prefix-closed properties (e.g., safety). In our context, even the equivalent of an edit monitor cannot enforce renewal properties (unlike in [17]), since, when constrained by prefix closure, renewal properties collapse to safety. This is because our model of executions allows computation to stop at any point, highlighting that the system may stop executing for reasons beyond our control, e.g., a power outage. In contrast, previous models assumed that a monitor's enabled actions would always be performed (e.g., [17]). In our framework, such guarantees are not built in, but can be explicitly added through fairness and other similar constraints on I/O automata [16]. This is another instance of our framework making explicit practical assumptions and constraints that affect enforcement. Earlier results about the enforcement powers of different types of monitors (e.g., that truncation monitors enforce safety and edit monitors enforce renewal policies) are also provable in our framework when we restrict reasoning to fair schedules and traces.

In practice, monitors typically reproduce at most a subset of a target's functionality. If a monitor composed with an application is to exhibit the same range of behaviors as the unmonitored application, it typically consults the target to generate these behaviors. In the system-call interposition example, for instance, the monitor cannot return correct file descriptors without consulting the kernel. Such monitors, which regularly consult an application, cannot precisely enforce (with respect to schedules) arbitrary policies even if they are quiescent forgiving, input forgiving, and prefix-closed. This is because input the monitor forwards to an application may cause the application to execute internal or output actions (e.g., a buffer overflow) forbidden by the policy, but which the monitor cannot prevent, since these are outside the interface between the monitor and the target.

On the other hand, in practice it is also common for the monitor (or system designer) to have some knowledge about the target. This knowledge can be exploited to use simpler-than-expected monitors to enforce (seemingly) complex policies. Although similar observations have been made before (e.g., program re-writing [14], non-uniformity [17], use of static analysis [7]), our approach formalizes them within a single framework, which allows new results that were beyond the scope of previous work, as we demonstrate in the following section.

5.3   Policies Enforceable by Target-Specific Monitors

As discussed in §3, our framework allows defining monitors that mediate different parts of the communication of a target with its environment, e.g., mediating a target's inputs and outputs or just its outputs. For brevity, rather than analyzing the policies enforceable by specific monitors, as done previously [23,17,18,14], we show an instance in which our framework enables formal results useful to designers of run-time monitors who have knowledge about the target application. This is a novel analysis of how some knowledge of the target can compensate (in terms of enforceability) for a narrower monitoring interface.[7]

In §3 we described two monitoring architectures: one where the monitor mediates the inputs and the outputs of the target, and another where it mediates just the inputs. Intuitively, an input/output-mediating monitor should be able to enforce a larger class of policies than an input-mediating one, since the former is able to control (potentially) more security-relevant actions than the latter (i.e., the outputs of the target). In other words, some policies should be enforceable by input/output mediating monitors, but not by input mediating ones:[8]

Theorem 4. $\exists \mathscr{P}$:
($\mathscr{P}$ *is generally precisely enforceable by some input/output-mediating* $\mathcal{M}_1$)$\wedge$
$\neg(\mathscr{P}$ *is generally precisely enforceable by some input-mediating* $\mathcal{M}_2$).

For the proof we pick a policy whose elements (i.e., modules) disallow all output actions (excluding the ones used for target-monitor communication) and a target that performs only output actions. An input-mediating monitor cannot enforce that policy on that target since it does not mediate its output, and thus it cannot generally enforce the policy. However, an input/output-mediating monitor will be able to enforce the policy, since whenever it receives any (renamed) actions from the target, it will just suppress them.

Thm. 4 establishes that some policies are generally enforceable by input/output-mediating monitors but not by input-mediating monitors. However, for some targets the two architectures are equivalent in enforcement power:

Theorem 5. $\forall \mathscr{P} : \forall \mathcal{T}$:
$\mathscr{P}$ *is specifically precisely enforceable on* $\mathcal{T}$ *by some input/output-mediating* $\mathcal{M}_1$
iff $\mathscr{P}$ *is specifically precisely enforceable on* $\mathcal{T}$ *by some input-mediating* $\mathcal{M}_2$
given that:
  (C1) $\mathscr{P}$ *does not reason about the communication between the monitor and the target,*
  (C2) $\forall \hat{P} \in \mathscr{P} : scheds(\hat{P})$ *is quiescent forgiving for* $\mathcal{T}$,
  (C3) $\forall \hat{P} \in \mathscr{P} : scheds(\hat{P}) \subseteq scheds(\mathcal{T})$, *i.e., the policy does not allow schedules that cannot be exhibited by the target, and*

---

[7] Another instance that focuses on the trace-modification capabilities of monitors and shows how arguments that were difficult to formalize in less expressive frameworks (e.g., [17]) can be naturally discussed in our model, can be found in [20].

[8] For brevity, we state theorems informally, omitting details necessary for the proofs. See our technical report [20] for detailed versions of the theorems and the proofs.

(C4) $\forall \hat{P} \in \mathscr{P} : \forall s \in scheds(\mathcal{T}) : \Big(s \notin scheds(\hat{P}) \Rightarrow \exists s' \preceq s : \big((s' \in scheds(\hat{P}))$
$\qquad \land \ (s' = s''; a) \land (a \in input(\mathcal{T}))$
$\qquad \land \ (\forall t \succeq s' : t \in scheds(\mathcal{T}) \Rightarrow t \notin scheds(\hat{P}))\big)\Big).$

Constraint C2 ensures that a target's outputs at the beginning of its execution, until it blocks for input, obey the policy. C3 ensures that an input/output-mediating monitor does not have an "unfair" advantage over an input-mediating one due to policies that require actions that a target cannot exhibit. C4 ensures that if a target receives input (from the monitor), then no behavior that it exhibits (until it blocks to wait for more input) will violate the policy; or, if it does, then that behavior can be suppressed without affecting the target's future behavior.

Thm. 5 shows how our framework can help to make sound decisions for designing monitors in practice. For example, consider a Unix kernel and the policy that a secret file cannot be (a) deleted or (b) displayed to guest users. To *precisely* enforce that policy, a monitor designer cannot in general use an input-mediating monitor: although it can enforce (a) by not forwarding commands like "rm secret-file", it cannot enforce (b), since it does not know whether the kernel can, for example, correctly identify guest users. However, if the designer knows that the specific kernel meets the constraints of Thm. 5, e.g., the kernel does not display secret files while booting (i.e., **C2**) and implements correct access-control for guest users (i.e., **C4**), then an input-mediating monitor suffices. The correctness of such design choices is not always obvious, and the above example shows how our framework can aid in making more informed decisions. Moreover, such decisions can benefit both efficiency (by not monitoring the kernel's output at run time) and security (since the monitor's TCB is smaller).

6   Related Work

The first model of run-time monitors, *security automata*, was based on Büchi Automata [23]. Since then, several similar models have extended or refined the class of enforceable policies based on the enforcement and computational powers of monitors (e.g., [17,11,10,4]). Unlike these works, we focus on modeling not just monitors, but also the target and the environment that monitors communicate with; this allows us to extend previous analyses of enforceable policies in ways that were out of the scope for previous frameworks [18].

Hamlen et al. described a model based on Turing Machines [14], and compared the policies enforceable by several types of enforcement mechanisms, including static analysis and inlined monitors. The main differences between this model and ours is that we explicitly model communication between the monitor, the target, and the environment, and we do not consider rewriting the target.

Recent work has revised these models or adopted alternate ones, such as the Calculus of Communicating Systems (CCS) [22] and Communicating Sequential Processes (CSP) [6], to more conveniently reason about applications, the interaction between applications and monitors, and enforcement in distributed systems. An example of a revised model are Mandatory Results Automata (MRA), which model the (synchronous) communication between the monitor and the target [18]. MRA's, however, do not model the target explicitly, making it difficult to derive results about enforceable policies in target-specific environments.

Among the works building on CCS or CSP is Martinelli and Matteucci's model of run-time monitors based on CCS [21]. Like ours, their model captures the communication between the monitor and the target, but their main focus is on synthesizing run-time monitors from policies. In contrast, we focus on a meta-theoretical analysis of enforcement in a more expressive framework.

Basin et al. proposed a practical language, based on CSP and Object-Z (OZ), for specifying security automata [3]. They focus on the synchronization between a single monitor and target application, although the language can capture many other enforcement scenarios. Our work is similar, but focuses on showing how to use such an expressive framework to derive meta-theoretical results on enforceable policies in different scenarios, instead of on the (complementary aspect) of showing how to faithfully translate and model practical scenarios.

Gay et al. introduced *service automata*, a framework based on CSP for enforcing security requirements in distributed systems [13]. Although CSP provides the abstractions for reasoning about specific targets and communication with the monitor, such investigation and analysis is not the focus of that work.

7   Conclusion

Formal models of run-time monitors have improved our understanding of the powers and limitations of enforcement mechanisms [23,17], and aided in their design and implementation [9]. However, these models often fail to capture details relevant to real-world monitors, such as how monitors integrate with targets, and the extent to which monitors can control targets and their environment.

In this paper, we propose a general framework, based on I/O automata, for reasoning about policies, monitoring, and enforcement. This framework provides abstractions for reasoning about many practically relevant details important for run-time enforcement, and, in general, yields a richer view of monitors and applications than is typical in previous analyses. We also show how this framework can be used for meta-theoretic analysis of enforceable security policies. For example, we derive lower bounds on enforceable policies that are independent of the choice of monitor (Thm. 3). We also identify constraints under which monitors with different monitoring capabilities (e.g., monitors that see only a subset of the target's actions) can enforce the same classes of policies (Thm. 5).

Acknowledgements. This work was supported in part by NSF grants CNS-0716343, CNS-0742736, and CCF-0917047; and by Carnegie Mellon CyLab under Army Research Office grant DAAD19-02-1-0389.

References

1. de Alfaro, L., Henzinger, T.A.: Interface automata. In: Proc. European Software Engineering Conference (2001)

2. Araragi, T., Attie, P.C., Keidar, I., Kogure, K., Luchangco, V., Lynch, N.A., Mano, K.: On Formal Modeling of Agent Computations. In: Rash, J.L., et al. (eds.) FAABS 2000. LNCS (LNAI), vol. 1871, pp. 48–62. Springer, Heidelberg (2001)
3. Basin, D., Olderog, E.R., Sevinc, P.E.: Specifying and analyzing security automata using CSP-OZ. In: Proc. ACM Symposium on Information, Computer and Communications Security, ASIACCS (2007)
4. Basin, D., Jugé, V., Klaedtke, F., Zălinescu, E.: Enforceable Security Policies Revisited. In: Degano, P., Guttman, J.D. (eds.) Principles of Security and Trust. LNCS, vol. 7215, pp. 309–328. Springer, Heidelberg (2012)
5. Bishop, M.: Computer Security: Art and Science. Addison-Wesley Professional (2002)
6. Brookes, S.D., Hoare, C.A.R., Roscoe, A.W.: A theory of communicating sequential processes. Journal of the ACM 31, 560–599 (1984)
7. Chabot, H., Khoury, R., Tawbi, N.: Extending the enforcement power of truncation monitors using static analysis. Computers and Security 30(4), 194–207 (2011)
8. Clarkson, M.R., Schneider, F.B.: Hyperproperties. In: Proc. IEEE Computer Security Foundations Symposium (2008)
9. Erlingsson, U., Schneider, F.B.: SASI enforcement of security policies: a retrospective. In: Proc. Workshop on New Security Paradigms (2000)
10. Falcone, Y., Fernandez, J.C., Mounier, L.: What can you verify and enforce at runtime? Intl. Jrnl. Software Tools for Tech. Transfer (STTT) 14(3), 349–382 (2011)
11. Fong, P.W.L.: Access control by tracking shallow execution history. In: Proc. IEEE Symposium on Security and Privacy (2004)
12. Garfinkel, T.: Traps and pitfalls: Practical problems in system call interposition based security tools. In: Proc. Network and Distributed Systems Security Symposium (2003)
13. Gay, R., Mantel, H., Sprick, B.: Service Automata. In: Barthe, G., Datta, A., Etalle, S. (eds.) FAST 2011. LNCS, vol. 7140, pp. 148–163. Springer, Heidelberg (2012)
14. Hamlen, K.W., Morrisett, G., Schneider, F.B.: Computability classes for enforcement mechanisms. ACM Trans. Program. Lang. Syst. 28(1), 175–205 (2006)
15. Hickey, J., Lynch, N.A., van Renesse, R.: Specifications and Proofs for Ensemble Layers. In: Cleaveland, W.R. (ed.) TACAS 1999. LNCS, vol. 1579, pp. 119–134. Springer, Heidelberg (1999)
16. Kwiatkowska, M.Z.: Survey of fairness notions. Information and Software Technology 31(7), 371–386 (1989)
17. Ligatti, J., Bauer, L., Walker, D.: Run-time enforcement of nonsafety policies. ACM Transactions on Information and System Security 12(3) (2009)
18. Ligatti, J., Reddy, S.: A Theory of Runtime Enforcement, with Results. In: Gritzalis, D., Preneel, B., Theoharidou, M. (eds.) ESORICS 2010. LNCS, vol. 6345, pp. 87–100. Springer, Heidelberg (2010)
19. Lynch, N.A.: Distributed Algorithms. Morgan Kaufmann Publishers Inc. (1996)
20. Mallios, Y., Bauer, L., Kaynar, D., Ligatti, J.: Enforcing more with less: Formalizing target-aware run-time monitors. Tech. Rep. CMU-CyLab-12-009, CyLab, Carnegie Mellon University (2012)
21. Martinelli, F., Matteucci, I.: Through modeling to synthesis of security automata. Electron. Notes Theor. Comput. Sci. 179, 31–46 (2007)
22. Milner, R.: A Calculus of Communicating Systems. Springer (1982)
23. Schneider, F.B.: Enforceable security policies. ACM Trans. Inf. Syst. Secur. 3(1), 30–50 (2000)
24. Tuttle, M.R.: Hierarchical correctness proofs for distributed algorithms. Master's thesis, Dept. of Electrical Engineering and Computer Science. MIT (1987)

Lazy Security Controllers[*],[**]

Giulio Caravagna[1], Gabriele Costa[2], and Giovanni Pardini[3]

[1] DISCO, Università degli Studi di Milano-Bicocca, Italy
giulio.caravagna@disco.unimib.it
[2] DIST, Università di Genova, Italy
gabriele.costa@unige.it
[3] Dipartimento di Informatica, Università degli Studi di Verona, Italy
giovanni.pardini@univr.it

Abstract. Security controllers follow the execution of the target systems to prevent security violations. In fact, by proactively observing the target, they are able to catch security violations before they occur and act consequently, such as by interrupting the execution. In this paper we define a novel category of security controllers called *lazy controllers*, a conservative extension of standard controllers which routinely suspend the observation of the target for different time spans, in order to reduce the cost of monitoring and increase performance, at the expense of the possibility of missing a violation.

We show how a proactive truncation controller can be extended to the lazy setting, and we formally characterize the relation between the length of suspended time spans and the actual violation risk, which constitutes the formal ground of our approach. This allows the actual time of suspension to be determined according to a given maximum bearable risk. Precisely, we formally investigate three classes of systems, namely non-deterministic, probabilistic, and stochastic systems.

1 Introduction

controllers are a common practice for guaranteeing that an application meets a security specification. In words, the problem statement is: *"Given a system S and a security policy φ, define an effective procedure to control that the execution of S does not violate φ"*.

In the last decades, the research on software security has seen a parallel evolution of static verification methods and security controllers. Since the main drawbacks of static analysis (such as false positives), can be easily overcome by controllers, several recent proposals [1–4] advocate the use of integrated frameworks for verification and monitoring.

An influential approach to the definition of security policies and controllers was introduced in [5], where a category of Finite State Automata (FSA), called *security automata*, is proposed for specifying security policies.

---

[*] This work has been partially supported by EU-funded projects FP7-257876 SPaCIoS.
[**] This work started when the three authors were employed at IIT-CNR, Pisa, Italy.

A. Jøsang, P. Samarati, and M. Petrocchi (Eds.): STM 2012, LNCS 7783, pp. 33–48, 2013.

A further contribution to security controllers was given in [6], in which they characterized a larger class of policies, i.e., *edit policies*, by means of the *edit automata* enforcing them. An edit automaton can decide whether to (*i*) allow, (*ii*) suppress or (*iii*) anticipate with a prefix the next action of its target. In [7,8] an automatic synthesis is defined using the target's specification. Although widely studied, open issues exist about their applicability in realistic contexts [9].

In this paper we define a new class of controllers, namely *lazy controllers*, which are able to suspend the observations for a certain time span. Unlike the standard controllers, a lazy controller may miss a security violation while suspended. Such violations are called *passive*, against the detected, *active* ones.

A discontinuous controller has various advantages which partially cope with the limitations described in [9]. In terms of performance and costs, monitors can be optimised by reducing the number of checks on the target. Another important advantage concerns the applicability. Indeed, a continuous and synchronous access to the target actions is quite restrictive for certain applications of security controllers. For instance, log auditing [10,11] is often used to check the last actions performed by a system without pausing its execution. Although a formalisation is still missing, log-based security analysis are used by real systems and some research was carried out for studying them, e.g., see [12].

A crucial aspect of the applicability of lazy controllers is the calculation of the *risk* deriving from suspending them. Indeed, scheduling the observations the proper way ensures that no passive violations occur, with a given probability of error bounded by a maximum risk value. Hence, increasing the risk threshold causes observations to be scheduled less frequently, so exploiting the advantages of lazy monitoring. Finding an optimal scheduling, i.e. one bounding the probability of passive violations to the risk, is a main issue when using lazy controllers.

Here we focus on *safety* properties, i.e., those writeable with the automata of [5], and define controller synthesis strategies for three kinds of target: (*i*) non-deterministic with non-instantaneous actions, (*ii*) probabilistic modelled as Discrete Time Markov Chains and (*iii*) stochastic modelled as Continuous Time Markov Chains. For each one, we provide an analytical measure of the risk of passive violations, so to allow the synthesis of optimal controllers, for any, arbitrarily small risk factor. Such results show that lazy controllers can indefinitely approximate the behaviour of traditional controllers by reducing the risk factor. Finally, they apply to scenarios in which the monitoring has a precise cost, so allowing a security trade-off between risk and budget.

The paper is structured as follows. In Sec. 2 we recall some background and in Sec. 3 we define lazy controllers. In Sec. 4 and 5 we discuss the synthesis of lazy controllers for specific targets. Finally, Sec. 6 concludes the paper.

2   Background

A *Labelled Transition System* (LTS) is a triple $(\mathcal{S}, \Lambda, \rightarrow)$ where Λ is a set of labels, $\mathcal{S}$ is a set of states and $\rightarrow \subseteq \mathcal{S} \times \Lambda \times \mathcal{S}$ is a set of labelled transitions. LTSs are often used to describe the behaviour of systems which allow for external

$$\text{(monitor)} \quad \frac{C \xrightarrow{a}_{\text{ctr}} C' \quad S \xrightarrow{a}_{\text{sys}} S'}{C \triangleright S \overset{a}{\Longrightarrow} C' \triangleright S'} \qquad \text{(T-monitor)} \quad \frac{C \xrightarrow{a}_{\text{ctr}} C' \quad \langle t, S \rangle \xrightarrow{a}_{\text{sys}} \langle t', S' \rangle}{\langle t, C \triangleright S \rangle \overset{a}{\Longrightarrow} \langle t', C' \triangleright S' \rangle}$$

Fig. 1. Semantics of truncation controllers for both the *untimed* and *timed* setting

observations. Observable actions are fired when the system performs a visible state change. Sometimes it can be useful to model state changes that produce no observable actions. In those cases, the set of labels is extended with the special symbol $\cdot \notin \Lambda$, which is used to label the corresponding transitions. As usual, we write $s \xrightarrow{\alpha} s'$ in place of $(s, \alpha, s') \in \rightarrow$.

As regards timed systems, we consider *Timed LTSs*, namely LTSs with states of the form $\mathbb{T} \times \mathcal{S}$, where $\mathbb{T}$ denotes the underlying time-domain of the system. Time domain $\mathbb{T}$ can be either discrete or continuous, and we assume a total order relation $\leq$ among its elements. A transition $\langle t, s \rangle \xrightarrow{\alpha} \langle t', s' \rangle$ describes a state change from s to s', occurring at time t', and exhibiting label $\alpha \in \Lambda$. Time cannot decrease, that is $t \leq t'$ for each transition. Transitions occur instantaneously, thus for all time instants x such that $t \leq x < t'$ the system is in state s. Besides the action labels in Λ, we assume an external observer to know the actual transition times $t, t' \in \mathbb{T}$.

We define *security controllers* both in the case of untimed systems and of timed systems, where the latter case is a trivial extension of the former.

Definition 1. *Let $\mathcal{S}$ be the set of states of a target, $\mathcal{C}$ the set of states of a controller, Σ a set of labels, and $\mathbb{T}$ a time-domain. An* **Untimed Security Controller** *is an LTS $(\mathcal{C} \times \mathcal{S}, \Sigma, \Longrightarrow)$ where $\Longrightarrow \subseteq (\mathcal{C} \times \mathcal{S}) \times \Sigma \times (\mathcal{C} \times \mathcal{S})$. A* **Timed Security Controller** *is a Timed LTS $(\mathbb{T} \times \mathcal{C} \times \mathcal{S}, \Sigma, \Longrightarrow)$ where $\Longrightarrow \subseteq (\mathbb{T} \times \mathcal{C} \times \mathcal{S}) \times \Sigma \times (\mathbb{T} \times \mathcal{C} \times \mathcal{S})$.*

We introduce *truncation controllers*, a particular kind of controllers that we use in the following sections for the synthesis of lazy controllers, both in the untimed and timed settings. Following the approach of [7], we define the truncation controllers by using a binary operator $\triangleright$ driving the execution of a target S under the scope of a controller C, denoted $C \triangleright S$. The truncation controller, and its extension to the timed setting by using the timed transition system of the target, are defined in the following.

Definition 2. *Let $(\mathcal{S}, \Sigma, \rightarrow_{\text{sys}})$ be the LTS describing the target system, and $(\mathcal{C}, \Sigma, \rightarrow_{\text{ctr}})$ be the LTS describing the behaviour allowed by the controller. A* truncation controller *is the security controller $(\mathcal{C} \times \mathcal{S}, \Sigma, \Longrightarrow)$ where $\Longrightarrow$ is the least transition relation defined by rule (**monitor**) from Figure 1.*

Definition 3. *Let $(\mathbb{T} \times \mathcal{S}, \Sigma, \rightarrow_{\text{sys}})$ be a Timed LTS describing the target system, and $(\mathcal{C}, \Sigma, \rightarrow_{\text{ctr}})$ be the LTS describing the behaviour allowed by the controller. A* timed truncation controller *is the timed security controller $(\mathbb{T} \times \mathcal{C} \times \mathcal{S}, \Sigma, \Longrightarrow)$ where $\Longrightarrow$ is the least transition relation defined by rule (**T-monitor**) from Fig.1.*

3   A Theory of Lazy Controllers

In this section we present a theory of *lazy controllers*, along with their *Structural Operational Semantics* (SOS) [13,14] which retains the standard theory of proactive controllers. In the next sections we prove theorems stating this relation and we explain how to build a lazy controller for a specific target in the style of [8]. Intuitively, we provide a framework into which standard controllers can be embedded, yielding lazy controllers.

We assume a set of *visible* actions $\Sigma = \{a, b, c, \ldots\}$ and we build from it the set of *unseen* actions $\widetilde{\Sigma} = \{\widetilde{a} \mid a \in \Sigma\}$. These two sets account for the fact that, depending on the observations scheduled by the controller, any action performed by the target can be either observed or not. We denote the set of the states of a proactive controller by $\mathcal{C}$, the set of the states of a target by $\mathcal{S}$ and the time-domain (e.g., discrete or continuous) underlying the target by $\mathbb{T}$. We define a lazy controller as follows.

Definition 4. *A lazy controller is a tuple* $(\mathcal{C}, \mathcal{S}, \Sigma, (\mathbb{T}, \leq), \Longrightarrow, \rightarrow_{\mathrm{lctr}}, \zeta)$ *where:*

- $\Longrightarrow \subseteq (\mathbb{T} \times \mathcal{C} \times \mathcal{S}) \times (\Sigma \cup \{\cdot\}) \times (\mathbb{T} \times \mathcal{C} \times \mathcal{S})$ *is the* active monitoring relation;
- $\rightarrow_{\mathrm{lctr}} \subseteq \mathcal{C} \times \widetilde{\Sigma} \times \mathcal{C}$ *is the* update relation *for unseen actions;*
- $\zeta : \mathcal{C} \times \mathbb{T} \to \mathbb{T}$ *is the* scheduling function;

As we discussed in Section 2, the relation $\Longrightarrow$ characterizes the input timed security controller. Such a relation is generally built by using a relation for the controller describing all the possible allowed behaviors, such as relation $\rightarrow_{\mathrm{ctr}}$ used for truncation controllers in Definitions 2 and 3. In lazy controllers, we also have an update relation $\rightarrow_{\mathrm{lctr}}$, which differs from $\rightarrow_{\mathrm{ctr}}$ by being defined over unseen actions in $\widetilde{\Sigma}$. Relation $\rightarrow_{\mathrm{lctr}}$ captures the operational notion of *activity logging*: as far as the controller is not observing the system, i.e., it is *idle*, every action is freely performed by the target and is logged. When the controller *wakes up* at any scheduled observation point, it examines the log in order to detect any passive violation, and acts according to its strategy, e.g., by truncating or editing the observed behaviour. Finally, it performs the scheduled observation, before looping this process. Therefore, the relation $\rightarrow_{\mathrm{lctr}}$ is actually a step-by-step operational definition of both the procedure of log checking and the recovery strategies.

Finally, function ζ provides the scheduling of the observations over the execution of the target. Notice that $\zeta(c, t) = t'$ is a function from a state c of the controller and the time t of the last action performed by the target to an observation time t'. In the next sections, when dealing with the synthesis of lazy controller, we show how to automatically create a function ζ starting from a security policy and a suitable description of the target system.

We now define the SOS of a lazy controller. In the following, we denote with $\alpha \in \Sigma \cup \{\cdot\}$ all the visible actions plus the special symbol $\cdot$, used for transitions not accounting for any action. A configuration is a tuple (t, C, k, S, h), written as $\langle t, \llbracket C \rrbracket_k \rhd \{\!\{ S \}\!\}_h \rangle$, with $t, k, h \in \mathbb{T}$, $C \in \mathcal{C}$, $S \in \mathcal{S}$. Let us denote by $\mathbb{D}$ the set of all configurations, and by $\mathbb{A} = \Sigma \cup \widetilde{\Sigma} \cup \{\cdot\}$ the set of labels. The semantics of a controller is the LTS $(\mathbb{D}, \mathbb{A}, \rightarrow_{lzy})$ where $\rightarrow_{lzy} \subseteq \mathbb{D} \times \mathbb{A} \times \mathbb{D}$ is the least transition relation defined by the following inference rules:

$$\text{(Sleep)} \quad \frac{\zeta(C,h) = k \qquad k > 0}{\langle t, \|C\|_0 \rhd \{|S|\}_h \rangle \xrightarrow{\cdot}_{lzy} \langle t, \|C\|_k \rhd \{|S|\}_h \rangle}$$

$$\text{(Monitor)} \quad \frac{\zeta(C,h) \leq 0 \qquad \langle t-h, C \rhd S \rangle \stackrel{\alpha}{\Longrightarrow} \langle t-h+x, C' \rhd S' \rangle \qquad h \leq x}{\langle t, \|C\|_0 \rhd \{|S|\}_h \rangle \xrightarrow{\alpha}_{lzy} \langle t-h+x, \|C'\|_0 \rhd \{|S'|\}_0 \rangle}$$

$$\text{(Log)} \quad \frac{\langle t-h, S \rangle \xrightarrow{a}_{sys} \langle t-h+x, S' \rangle \qquad C \xrightarrow{\tilde{a}}_{lctr} C' \qquad h \leq x < h+k}{\langle t, \|C\|_k \rhd \{|S|\}_h \rangle \xrightarrow{a}_{lzy} \langle t-h+x, \|C'\|_{k-(x-h)} \rhd \{|S'|\}_0 \rangle}$$

$$\text{(WakeUp)} \quad \frac{k > 0}{\langle t, \|C\|_k \rhd \{|S|\}_h \rangle \xrightarrow{\cdot}_{lzy} \langle t+k, \|C\|_0 \rhd \{|S|\}_{h+k} \rangle}$$

In those rules we make use of two *boxing operators* $\|\_\|\_$ and $\{|\_|\}\_$. If the time is t we write $\|C\|_n$, where $C \in \mathcal{C}$ and $n \in \mathbb{T}$, to denote that the controller has scheduled the next observation at time $t + n$. Differently, we write $\{|S|\}_h$, where $S \in \mathcal{S}$ and $h \in \mathbb{T}$, to denote that the target performed its last transition at time $t - h$ in the past. In both cases n and t denote relative times, hence from a configuration $\langle t, \|C\|_n \rhd \{|S|\}_h \rangle$ we derive all the possible behaviors of the target and the lazy controller in the time window $[t-h, t+n]$. By assuming the starting time to be t_0, all the possible behaviors of a lazy controller can be derived from the initial configuration $\langle t_0, \|C\|_0 \rhd \{|S|\}_0 \rangle$.

Rule (Sleep) states that, if at time t the controller is acting in the proactive mode $\|C\|_0$ and the next observation is scheduled at $t + k$, then the controller can idle till that time, hence becoming $\|C\|_k$. The label $\cdot$ of the transition means that this derivation does not involve any action of the target.

Rule (Monitor) states that if at time t a proactive controller must not wait further to observe the target, namely $\zeta(C, h) \leq 0$, then any action of the target started at previous time $t - h$ and completing at time $t - h + x$ should be proactively monitored. When so, we make use of the relation characterizing such a proactive controller, $\Longrightarrow$. Moreover, notice that by using the boxing operator for the target we are able to derive timed-transitions from the past time $t - h$, meaning that the passage of time is synchronous for S. We remark that, to have a good scheduling function, the next action should really be a passive violation, correctly prevented by the controller.

Rule (Log) states that if the time is t and the controller has scheduled the next observation at time $t + k$, then any action which S performs before $t + k$ is not controlled, but simply logged by means of the derivations of $\rightarrow_{lctr}$. In this time-window a passive violation may happen, not being detected up to time $t+k$. Finally, rule (Wakeup) makes the controller able to spend time autonomously and synchronously with the target S.

The following theorem[1] shows that lazy controllers are a conservative extension of standard proactive controllers. In fact, if a lazy controller never suspends the observations, then we obtain the same process as the proactive controller.

Theorem 1. *Let* $(\mathbb{T} \times \mathcal{C} \times \mathcal{S}, \Sigma, \Longrightarrow)$ *be a timed security controller. Let* $(\mathcal{C}, \mathcal{S}, \Sigma,$ $\mathbb{T}, \Longrightarrow, \rightarrow_{\text{lctr}}, \zeta)$ *be a lazy security controller with* $\rightarrow_{\text{lctr}}$ *arbitrarily defined and* ζ *such that* $\forall C \in \mathcal{C}, t \in \mathbb{T}. \ \zeta(C, t) = 0.$ *Then* $\forall t, t' \in \mathbb{T}, \ C, C' \in \mathcal{C}, \ S, S' \in \mathcal{S}, \ x \in$ Σ^*: $\langle t, C \triangleright S \rangle \overset{x}{\Longrightarrow}{}^* \langle t', C' \triangleright S' \rangle$ *iff* $\langle t, \|C\|_0 \triangleright \{|S|\}_0 \rangle \overset{x}{\longrightarrow}{}^*_{\text{lzy}} \langle t', \|C'\|_0 \triangleright \{|S'|\}_0 \rangle$.

4 Synthesis of Lazy Controllers

In this section we discuss the synthesis of lazy security controllers for non-probabilistic, probabilistic and stochastic targets (for a practical case study see [15]). In particular, we consider (i) non-deterministic Finite State Machines (FSMs) with non-instantaneous transitions, (ii) Discrete Time Markov Chains (DTMCs) and (iii) Continuous Time Markov Chains (CTMCs). We consider FSMs because they have been often used for system modelling and Markov chains because they are receiving major attention as formal descriptions of timed systems. We represent the targets as FSMs enriched with labelled (labels range over a countable domain) state transitions. The targets differ only for such labels, i.e. in (i) labels represent durations, in (ii) probabilities and in (iii) the parameters of exponentially-distributed random variables.

Here, we consider only *lazy truncation controllers* being the lazy version of the automata of [5]. They extend truncation controllers in a natural way, i.e., by interrupting an illegal execution either proactively or as soon as they wake up, after a violation. We argue that edit automata can be similarly adapted in the framework of lazy controllers from their standard specification. An investigation of these aspects is left as future work.

Below we discuss the synthesis steps of the controller. This is analogous for all the three types of FSMs since the states and transitions of a lazy controller can be synthesized independently from the interpretation of the labels, but rather by considering only its structure. Then, we conclude the synthesis strategy by defining the scheduling functions, which instead depend on the type of FSM.

Preliminaries. A *Finite State Machine* (FSM) is a tuple $M = (\Sigma, Q, \iota, \delta, F)$ where: Σ is a finite alphabet, Q is a finite set of states, $\iota \in Q$ is the initial state, $\delta \subseteq Q \times \Sigma \times Q$ is the set of (labelled) transitions, $F \subseteq Q$ is the set of final states. Given a FSM M, we denote its components as $(\Sigma_M, Q_M, \iota_M, \delta_M, F_M)$. Let us denote by Σ^n, with $n \in \mathbb{N}$ all words over the alphabet Σ of length n, and let $\Sigma^* = \bigcup_{n \in \mathbb{N}} \Sigma^n$ denote all the finite words over Σ. Also, we denote by Σ^ω all the *infinite* words (ω-words) over Σ, and let $\Sigma^\infty = \Sigma^* \cup \Sigma^\omega$.

A (finite) *path* π is a sequence of states $q_0, q_1, \ldots, q_k$ s.t. $\forall 1 \leq i \leq k. \ (q_{i-1}, \sigma_i, q_i)$ $\in \delta$. The finite word $\mathcal{W}(\pi) = \sigma_1 \sigma_2 \cdots \sigma_k \in \Sigma^k$ can be associated with such a sequence π. The set of all finite paths from q to q' is denoted $Paths(q, q')$. An infinite path π' is a sequence $q_0, q_1, \ldots, q_k, \ldots$ s.t. $\forall i \geq 1. \ (q_{i-1}, \sigma_i, q_i) \in \delta$. Again,

---

[1] Proofs are available at http://www.ai-lab.it/costa/publications/probsec.pdf

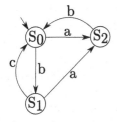

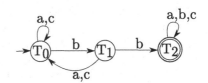

Fig. 2. The FSM of a target

Fig. 3. The FSM recognizing bad prefixes for the LTL property $\varphi = G\neg(b \wedge Xb)$

we can associate an infinite word $\mathcal{W}(\pi') \in \Sigma^\omega$ to such a path. The set of all infinite paths from q is denoted $Paths^\omega(q)$.

When a FSM is interpreted as an automaton on finite words its semantics is a *language* $L \subseteq \Sigma^*$. Given a FSM A, we denote its language on finite words as $\mathcal{L}(A)$, where $x \in \mathcal{L}(A)$ iff there is path from the initial state ι to any final state. Formally, $\mathcal{L}(A) = \{\mathcal{W}(\pi) \mid q \in F, \ \pi \in Paths(\iota, q)\}$.

A FSM A is said *deterministic* iff, for each state, there is exactly one transition for each symbol. Formally, $\forall q \in Q, \sigma \in \Sigma. \ \exists!q' \in Q. \ (q, \sigma, q') \in \delta$. We denote by $det(A)$ a deterministic FSM equivalent to A, i.e., s.t. $\mathcal{L}(det(A)) = \mathcal{L}(A)$. Given two FSMs A and $D = det(A)$, there always exists a mapping $\mu : Q_A \to \mathscr{P}(Q_D)$ which relates each state of A with a set of states of D. Note that $det(A)$ denotes *one* of the possible deterministic FSMs equivalent to A. We assume that, if A is deterministic, then $det(A) = A$.

We also recall the definition of the parallel composition of FSMs. Let $A = (\Sigma, Q_A, \iota_A, \delta_A, F_A)$ and $B = (\Sigma, Q_B, \iota_B, \delta_B, F_B)$ be two FSMs, using the same alphabet Σ. The *parallel composition* of A and B is defined as $A \parallel B = (\Sigma, Q_A \times Q_B, (\iota_A, \iota_B), \delta_{A\parallel B}, F_{A\parallel B})$, where $\delta_{A\parallel B} = \{((q_1, q_2), \sigma, (q_1', q_2')) \mid (q_1, \sigma, q_1') \in \delta_A, (q_2, \sigma, q_2') \in \delta_B\}$, and $F_{A\parallel B} = \{(q_1, q_2) \mid q_1 \in F_A \wedge q_2 \in F_B\}$.

We assume a computation of a non-terminating system to be represented as an infinite ω-*word* over Σ. A FSM can be seen as an automaton over ω-words, by using a proper acceptance condition. For automata over ω-words, here we only consider FSMs for which any possible transition is accepted. Thus, the set of final states F is not involved in the definition of the acceptance condition. We also define an ω-*automaton* as a FSM A whose semantics is the ω-language $\mathcal{L}^\omega(A) = \{\mathcal{W}(\pi) \mid \pi \in Paths^\omega(\iota)\}$.

To formally define safety properties, we recall some preliminaries. We first consider *bad prefixes* for a given language of infinite words $L \subseteq \Sigma^\omega$, which identify any finite word being not a prefix of an infinite word of the language. A language of infinite words $L \subseteq \Sigma^\omega$ s.t. each word not in L has a bad prefix is called *safety language*. Formally, a finite word $x \in \Sigma^*$ is a *bad prefix* for a language $L \subseteq \Sigma^\omega$ iff $\forall y \in \Sigma^\omega. \ xy \notin L$. Let BadPrefixes($L$) denote the set of all bad prefixes for a given language L. A language $L \subseteq \Sigma^\omega$ is a *safety language* iff $\forall w \in \Sigma^\omega \setminus L. \ \exists x \in \Sigma^*, y \in \Sigma^\omega. \ w = xy \ \wedge \ x \in \text{BadPrefixes}(L)$.

Let us denote by $\mathcal{A}_{bad(L)}$ a (non-deterministic) FSM recognizing the bad prefixes of a safety language L, i.e., $\mathcal{L}(\mathcal{A}_{bad(L)}) = \text{BadPrefixes}(L)$. Note that the language BadPrefixes(L) is closed under concatenation with arbitrary symbols, i.e. $\forall x \in \Sigma^*, \sigma \in \Sigma.\ x \in \text{BadPrefixes}(L) \implies x\sigma \in \text{BadPrefixes}(L)$. Hence, we can assume that $\mathcal{A}_{bad(L)}$ has exactly one final state ψ such that for each symbol σ there is a transition $\psi \xrightarrow{\sigma} \psi$, and no other transitions from ψ exist.

Let us consider a *safety property* φ, i.e., a property whose set $\mathcal{L}(\varphi)$ of infinite words satisfying it form a safety language. Then, a violation of a safety property always occurs after a finite execution of the system. We denote by $\mathcal{A}_{bad(\varphi)} = \mathcal{A}_{bad(\mathcal{L}(\varphi))}$ a (non-deterministic) FSM which recognizes the bad prefixes of the (language described by the) safety property φ, i.e., all words which do not satisfy the property.

Various formalisms, e.g., LTL formulae [16] or Büchi automata [17], include safety properties. We do not discuss the translation of a safety property φ into a FSM $\mathcal{A}_{bad(\varphi)}$ for its bad prefixes. Instead, we assume such a FSM to be given. We refer the reader to [18] for details on the construction of FSMs from LTL formulae and Büchi automata.

Synthesis of the Controller Structure. We consider a non-deterministic FSM $A = (\Sigma, Q_A, \iota^A, \delta_A, F_A)$ capturing all the possible behaviour for the target. In synthesizing the controller structure we abstract away from the type of labels which appear on the transitions of the enriched version of A. The FSM A is to be interpreted as an automaton over ω-words, moreover we assume $F_A = Q_A$ since the set of final states is not involved in the semantics of such a FSM.

Let φ be a safety property. In the proactive setting, a truncation controller can be defined from the deterministic FSM $C = det(\mathcal{A}_{bad(\varphi)})$, in which a transition is allowed only if it does not end up in the final state, i.e. if it does not cause a violation of the safety property. By exploiting Definitions 2 and 3, we can obtain a proactive controller with transition relation $\Longrightarrow$ with such a behaviour by using a transition relation $\rightarrow_{\text{ctr}}$ defined by the following inference rule.

$$(\text{good}) \quad \frac{\delta_C(c, \sigma) = c' \quad c' \notin F_C}{c \xrightarrow{\sigma}_{\text{ctr}} c'}. \tag{1}$$

According to the semantics of $\cdot \rhd \cdot$ from Definitions 2 and 3, such a definition of $\rightarrow_{\text{ctr}}$ is applicable to both untimed and timed systems. Slightly abusing notation, we denote the ensemble of the controller and the target as $\mathcal{A}_{bad(\varphi)} \rhd A$.

Recall from Section 3 that a lazy controller is completely specified by *(i)* an active monitoring relation $\Longrightarrow$, *(ii)* an update relation for unseen actions $\rightarrow_{\text{lctr}}$, and *(iii)* a scheduling function ζ. As regards the kinds of target that we consider, the corresponding lazy truncation controllers all share the same structure, and just the definition of the scheduling function ζ is different from one to another.

Example 1. Throughout this section we consider, as a running example, a target whose behaviour is described by the FSM shown in Figure 2, with alphabet $\Sigma = \{a, b, c\}$. We construct a controller for preventing the target to perform two consecutive b actions. Such a safety property can be formally expressed as the LTL formula $\varphi = G\neg(b \wedge Xb)$. Figure 3 shows the deterministic FSM recognizing the bad prefixes of φ, namely $det(\mathcal{A}_{bad(\varphi)})$.

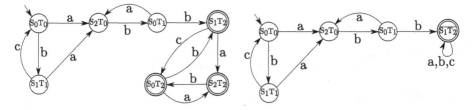

Fig. 4. The FSM C_0, obtained as the parallel of the target's FSM and the FSM recognizing bad prefixes

Fig. 5. The FSM C of the controller, constructed from C_0 (Figure 4)

We detail our construction only in the case of the untimed truncation controller, i.e., Definition 2. The construction in the timed case is analogous, and all the theorems can be easily restated by assuming a timed truncation controller as in Definition 3.

The lazy controller is constructed from the parallel composition of $det(\mathcal{A}_{bad(\varphi)})$ with a deterministic FSM equivalent to A, i.e., it is the FSM $C_0 = det(\mathcal{A}_{bad(\varphi)}) \parallel det(A)$. This allows the controller for tracking the actions performed by the target, which is necessary to determine an appropriate scheduling function ζ. In this case, the ensemble of the controller and the target becomes $(det(\mathcal{A}_{bad(\varphi)}) \parallel det(A)) \triangleright A$, which is equivalent to $det(\mathcal{A}_{bad(\varphi)}) \triangleright A$ according to the semantics of truncation controllers. This is formally proved by the following theorem.

Theorem 2. *Let $B \triangleright A$ be a truncation controller, with A being a non-deterministic FSM describing the behaviour of a target, and B a deterministic FSM describing the truncation controller. Let $D = det(A)$, and $C = B \parallel D$. Then, $\forall x \in \Sigma^*, \forall b' \in Q_B, d' \in Q_D, a' \in Q_A$: $(\iota_B, \iota_D) \triangleright \iota_A \overset{x}{\Longrightarrow}{}^* (b', d') \triangleright a'$ iff $\iota_B \triangleright \iota_A \overset{x}{\Longrightarrow}{}^* b' \triangleright a'$ where $(\iota_B, \iota_D), (b', d') \in Q_C$.*

The actual FSM describing the controller is obtained from C_0 by joining together all the final states in a unique final state ψ_{C_0} with a self loop for each symbol in Σ. We call a FSM of this kind *absorbing*, and we denote it as $C = absorbing(C_0)$ where the function *absorbing* is defined as follows.

Definition 5. *Let $C = (Q_C, \Sigma, \delta_C, \iota_C, F_C)$ be a deterministic FSM, with $absorbing(C)$ we denote a FSM $E = (Q_E, \Sigma, \delta_E, \iota_E, F_E)$ such that: (i) $Q_E = Q_C \setminus F_C \cup \{\psi_E\}$, with $\psi_E \notin Q_C$; (ii) $\delta_E = \{(\mu(c), \sigma, \mu(c')) \mid (c, \sigma, c') \in \delta_C\} \cup \{(\psi_E, \sigma, \psi_E) \mid \sigma \in \Sigma\}$; (iii) $\iota_E = \mu(\iota_C)$; (iv) $F_E = \{\psi_E\}$; where $\mu : Q_C \to Q_E$ is a mapping between the states of C and E such that $\forall c \in Q_C \setminus F_C. \mu(c) = c$ and $\forall c \in F_C. \mu(c) = \psi_E$.*

For the purposes of runtime monitoring, such a FSM C must be equivalent to C_0, in spite of the fact that the languages they recognize can be different. Such an equivalence is formally proved by the following theorem.

Theorem 3. *Let $C \triangleright A$ be a truncation controller, with A being the non-deterministic FSM of a target, and C a deterministic FSM such that $\forall c \in F_C. \delta_C(c, \sigma) \in F_C$.*

Let $E = absorbing(C)$. Then, $\forall x \in \Sigma^*, \forall c' \in Q_C, e' \in Q_E, a' \in Q_A : \iota_C \triangleright \iota_A \overset{x}{\Longrightarrow} {}^*c' \triangleright a'$ iff $\iota_E \triangleright \iota_A \overset{x}{\Longrightarrow}{}^*e' \triangleright a'$.

Example 2. Figure 4 shows the FSM $C_0 = det(\mathcal{A}_{bad(\varphi)}) \parallel det(A)$ obtained from the parallel composition of the FSM of the target, in Figure 2, and the FSM recognizing bad prefixes for φ, in Figure 3.

The FSM $C = absorbing(C_0)$, obtained from C_0 by collapsing all the final states in one, and for which there is a self loop for each possible symbol in the alphabet, is shown in Figure 5. Notice that C_0 has three final states $F_{C_0} = \{S_0T_2, S_1T_2, S_2T_2\}$, which are replaced in C by the only final state $\overline{S_1T_2}$.

The active monitoring relation $\Longrightarrow$ and the update relation for unseen actions $\to_{lctr}$ are both constructed from the target FSM A and the LTL safety property φ, since their definition does not depend on the type of FSM we consider. In particular, the active monitoring relation $\Longrightarrow$ corresponds to the timed truncation controller from Definition 3. The update relation for unseen actions $\to_{lctr}$, i.e., how the state of the controller is updated when an unseen action occurs, is defined as follows.

Definition 6. *The update relation for unseen actions $\to_{lctr}$ for a lazy truncation controller is the least relation defined by the following rules:*

$$\textbf{(asleep)} \quad \frac{\delta_C(c,a) = c' \quad c \notin F_C}{c \overset{\tilde{a}}{\to}_{lctr} c'} \qquad \textbf{(nil)} \quad \frac{a \in \Sigma \quad c \in F_C}{c \overset{\tilde{a}}{\to}_{lctr} c}.$$

Rule $\textbf{(asleep)}$ mirrors δ_C as far as non-final state are involved. As soon as the controller reaches a final state in F_C, rule $\textbf{(nil)}$ ensures that it remains in such a state while accepting any unseen actions, since a sleeping controller does not block unseen actions.

5   Synthesis of the Scheduling Functions

Here we define the scheduling functions for lazy controllers.

Scheduling Functions for Non-probabilistic Systems. We recall that we are considering a non-deterministic target $A = (\Sigma, Q_A, \iota_A, \delta_A, F_A)$, where $F_A = Q_A$, hereby enriched with a function $\theta : Q_A \times \Sigma \times Q_A \to \mathbb{R}^+$ denoting the durations associated with transitions. We assume $\theta(t) = 0$ for all $t \notin \delta_A$. The semantics of a target (A, θ) is the Timed LTS $(\mathbb{R}^+ \times Q_A, \Sigma, \to_{sys})$ where $\to_{sys}$ is the least transition relation defined by the following rule:

$$\frac{(q, a, q') \in \delta \quad \theta(q, a, q') = x}{\langle t, q \rangle \overset{a}{\to}_{sys} \langle t + x, q' \rangle}.$$

This relation is also valid for targets with discrete underlying time domain.

Recall that the controller is defined by the FSM $C = absorbing(B \parallel D)$, where $B = det(\mathcal{A}_{bad(\varphi)})$ and $D = det(A)$. Given a state $c \in Q_C$ of the controller, we define a function giving the shortest duration of any path from the current state c to the final state of C, denoted ψ_C. Let $\mu_C : Q_{B\|D} \to Q_C$ denote the mapping defining the *absorbing* function, and let $\mu_D : Q_A \to \mathscr{P}(Q_D)$ denote the mapping from the states of the FSM A to the states of the FSM $det(A)$. Let $\nu(c)$ denote the set of states of A which are mapped to a state $c \in Q_C$, i.e. $\nu(c) = \{a \mid \exists b, d.\ c = \mu_C(b, d) \wedge d \in \mu_D(a)\}$. Function $\nu(c)$ is also extended to paths as $\nu(c_1, \ldots, c_k) = \{a_1, \ldots, a_k \mid \forall 1 \le i \le k.\ a_i \in \nu(c_i)\}$. A function *duration* can be formally defined as follows: $duration(\pi) = \min\left\{\sum_{i=1}^{k} \theta(a_{i-1}, \sigma_i, a_i) \,\Big|\, a_0, \ldots, a_k \in \nu(\pi),\ \sigma_1 \cdots \sigma_k \in \Sigma^k\right\}$. Finally:

$$\zeta(c, h) = \min\{duration(\pi) \mid \pi \in Paths(c, \psi_C)\} - h. \tag{2}$$

Note that $\zeta(c, h)$ takes into account the fact that the last action from the target has been seen at time $t - h$. For this type of targets we can prove that no passive violation can happen if the scheduling function satisfies Equation 2.

Theorem 4. *Let A be a non-deterministic FSM describing the behaviour of the target, and $B = det(A_{bad(\varphi)})$ a deterministic FSM recognizing bad prefixes for a property φ. Let $D = det(A)$, and $C = absorbing(B \parallel D)$ be the FSM of the controller. Consider the lazy truncation controller $(\Longrightarrow, \to_{\mathrm{lctr}}, \zeta)$, with $\Longrightarrow$ as in Definition 3, $\to_{\mathrm{lctr}}$ as in Definition 6, and ζ as in Equation 2. Then, if $\iota_C \ne \psi_C$, the final state is never reached, i.e. $\forall t', k', h' \in \mathbb{R}^+,\ c' \in Q_C,\ a' \in Q_A$: $\langle 0, \|\iota_C\|_0 \triangleright \{\!|\iota_A|\!\}_0\rangle \to_{\mathrm{lzy}}^* \langle t', \|c'\|_{k'} \triangleright \{\!|a'|\!\}_{h'}\rangle$ implies $c' \ne \psi_C$.*

Scheduling Functions for Discrete Time Markov Chains. As a first probabilistic system we consider a target described by a homogenous *Discrete Time Markov Chain* (DTMC), i.e., a process jumping over a finite set of states, where at any time the probability of jumping to a state is completely determined in the state itself.

Definition 7. *A Discrete Time Markov Chain is a tuple $(S, \overline{s}, \mathbf{P})$ where (i) S is a finite set of states; (ii) $\overline{s}$ is the initial state; (iii) $\mathbf{P} : S \times S \to [0, 1]$ is a transition probability matrix, such that $\sum_{s' \in S} \mathbf{P}(s, s') = 1$ for all states $s \in S$.*

Each element $\mathbf{P}(s, s')$ gives the probability of a transition from s to s', i.e., $\mathbf{P}(s, s') = \mathbb{P}(X(k+1) = s' \mid X(k) = s)$ for any $k \ge 0$. A DTMC is a family of random variables $\{X(k) \mid k = 0, 1, 2, \ldots\}$ where $X(k)$, ranging over states, are observations made at discrete time-steps. Among others, these probabilistic processes satisfy the *Markov property*: the state at time k depends only on the state at time $k - 1$, and not on the states at previous times, i.e., the history.

We enrich this definition of DTMC with labels denoting actions on the transitions. We consider a target as the pair (A, θ), where $A = (\Sigma, Q_A, \iota_A, \delta_A, F_A)$, with $F_A = Q_A$, is a *deterministic FSM* enriched with $\theta : Q_A \times \Sigma \times Q_A \to [0, 1]$ giving the probability associated with each transition. Recall that the probabilities of all the transitions exiting from a state must sum up to 1. We also assume $\theta(t) = 0$ for all $t \notin \delta_A$. According to Definition 7 a labeled DTMC representing (A, θ) is a tuple $(Q_A, \mathbf{e}^{(\iota_A)}, \mathbf{P})$, where $\mathbf{e}^{(\iota_A)}$ is a unit vector (only in the position corresponding to ι_A there is a 1), and the transition probabilities $\mathbf{P} = [p_{ij}]$ are defined as $p_{ij} = \sum_{\sigma \in \Sigma} \theta(q_i, \sigma, q_j)$ when $Q_A = \{q_1, \ldots, q_n\}$.

$$\frac{(q, a, q') \in \delta}{\langle t, q \rangle \xrightarrow{\ a\ }_{\text{sys}} \langle t+1, q' \rangle} \qquad\qquad \frac{(q, a, q') \in \delta \quad x \in \mathbb{R}^{>0}}{\langle t, q \rangle \xrightarrow{\ a\ }_{\text{sys}} \langle t+x, q' \rangle}.$$

Fig. 6. Transition relation for DTMCs   **Fig. 7.** Transition relation for CTMCs

Our strategy for synthesizing the controller structure yields a FSM structurally analogous to some DTMCs having reachability properties, which we now discuss. Some terminology has to be introduced first: a DTMC state is *transient* (conversely *recurrent*) if any execution visits it only finitely many times. Differently, a state s is *absorbing* if it cannot be left, i.e., $\mathbf{P}(s, s) = 1$. A *terminating* DTMC is a Markov chain where all states are transient, except one which is absorbing. Intuitively, the controller we synthesize is structurally equivalent to a terminating DTMC. For these types of DTMCs the time to *absorption* T_s, i.e., the time it takes to enter the absorbing state, assuming the DTMC starts in state s, follows a well-known *Discrete Phase-type distribution* [19].

Definition 8. *Let* $(S, \bar{s}, \mathbf{P})$ *be a terminating DTMC, through a proper reordering of its states, we can always write* $\mathbf{P}$ *as* $\mathbf{P} = \begin{bmatrix} \hat{\mathbf{P}} & \rho \\ \mathbf{0} & 1 \end{bmatrix}$ *where (i)* $\hat{\mathbf{P}} \in [0, 1]^{(|S|-1) \times (|S|-1)}$ *restricts* $\mathbf{P}$ *to the transient states, (ii)* ρ *is a column vector which contains probabilities from each transient state to the absorbing one, and (iii)* $\mathbf{0}$ *is a zero row vector.*

A Discrete Phase-type (DPH) distribution, denoted $DPH(\boldsymbol{\tau}, \hat{\mathbf{P}})$, *is a row vector* $\boldsymbol{\tau} \in \{0, 1\}^{|S|-1}$ *specifying the initial probability distribution over transient states, and the matrix* $\hat{\mathbf{P}}$. *Its cumulative distribution function, i.e., the probability that the time* Δt *to the absorbing state is smaller or equal to* x, *is* $F(x) = 1 - \boldsymbol{\tau}\hat{\mathbf{P}}^x \mathbf{1}$ *for* $x \in \mathbb{N}$.

Given the system in a non-absorbing state s at time t, this distribution characterizes the probability of jumping to the absorbing state, in any number of steps, within time $t' > t$.

We now show why this distribution allows for analytically determining the probability that the lazy controller misses the detection of a violation. Given a DTMC (A, θ), its set of possible timed transitions is described by the transition relation $\rightarrow_{\text{sys}}$, defined in Figure 6, i.e., a special case of the non-probabilistic system where steps last 1 time-unit. The controller is the FSM $C = absorbing(det (\mathcal{A}_{bad(\varphi)}) \parallel A)$, since A is deterministic, and is equipped with a labelling function $\bar{\theta} : Q_C \times \Sigma \times Q_C \to [0, 1]$, built from θ, to obtain a labelled DTMC $(C, \bar{\theta})$. Let μ_C denote the mapping defining the *absorbing* function. Then, the labelling function $\bar{\theta}$, giving the transition probabilities, is such that $\forall c_1 \neq \psi_C, c_2 \in Q_C. \bar{\theta}(c_1, \sigma, c_2) = \theta(a_1, \sigma, a_2)$ where, for $i = 1, 2$, a_i is such that $\mu_C(c_i) = (b_i, a_i)$ for some b_i. Moreover, $\forall \sigma \in \Sigma. \bar{\theta}(\psi_C, \sigma, \psi_C) = 1/|\Sigma|$. The probabilities of looping in the final state are not important, as long as they sum up to 1, for correctness.

Recall that C has a unique absorbing state ψ_C in which the bad prefix of the target trace is recognized, i.e. the violation is detected. This proposition holds.

$$\mathbf{P} = \begin{bmatrix} 0 & 1/5 & 4/5 \\ 1/3 & 0 & 2/3 \\ 1 & 0 & 0 \end{bmatrix} \quad \mathbf{P'} = \begin{bmatrix} 0 & 1/5 & 4/5 & 0 & 0 \\ 1/3 & 0 & 2/3 & 0 & 0 \\ 0 & 0 & 0 & 1 & 0 \\ 0 & 0 & 4/5 & 0 & 1/5 \\ 0 & 0 & 0 & 0 & 1 \end{bmatrix} \quad \mathbf{R} = \begin{bmatrix} 0 & \frac{1}{1000} & \frac{1}{10} \\ 10 & 0 & \frac{1}{100} \\ 2 & 0 & 0 \end{bmatrix} \quad \mathbf{R'} = \begin{bmatrix} 0 & \frac{1}{1000} & \frac{1}{10} & 0 & 0 \\ 10 & 0 & \frac{1}{100} & 0 & 0 \\ 0 & 0 & 0 & 2 & 0 \\ 0 & 0 & \frac{1}{10} & 0 & \frac{1}{1000} \\ 0 & 0 & 0 & 0 & 0 \end{bmatrix}$$

Fig. 8. Probability and rate matrices

Proposition 1. *The DPH distribution of a DTMC $(C, \overline{\theta})$ is the distribution of the time until the next violation of the DTMC.*

Hence the probability of passive violations can be bounded by using such a distribution: given a state $c \in Q_C$, the function $\zeta(c, h)$ gives the maximum allowed time $\Delta t \in \mathbb{N}$ for which the probability of reaching the final state ψ_C from the current state c, within Δt time units, is less than a probability β. Formally, if the current state of the DTMC is c then the cumulative distribution function F of $DPH(\mathbf{e}^{(c)}, \hat{\mathbf{P}})$ gives the time for scheduling the next observation by solving

$$\Delta t = \max\{0, \max\{t \mid F(t) \leq \beta\} - h\} \tag{3}$$

where $\beta \in [0, 1]$ is a given probability of error. Notice that this corresponds to using the random variable $Y = (X - h)$ where $X \sim DPH(\tau, \hat{\mathbf{P}})$ and Y is the linear transformation of X and h. We remark that even though the exponential jumps of a DTMC are memoryless (i.e., the time past h could be disregarded if we considered exponential waiting times individually), the DPH and hence Y are not, requiring us to use h in equation (3). Moreover, the outmost max operation is required since X has infinite support, i.e., the probability that $x \in [0, h] \neq 0$. The following proposition states an important property for lazy controllers synthesized in this manner.

Proposition 2. *If $\zeta(c, h) = \Delta t$ with Δt a solution of equation (3) for some $\beta \in [0, 1]$, then the probability of a passive violation is bounded by β.*

Example 3. Consider the FSM of Figure 2 denoting a DTMC $(\{S_0, S_1, S_2\}, S_0, \mathbf{P})$, and let us build the terminating DTMC $(\{S_0 T_0, S_1 T_1, S_2 T_0, S_0 T_1, \overline{S_1 T_2}\}, S_0 T_0, \mathbf{P'})$ of Figure 5 where $\mathbf{P}$ and $\mathbf{P'}$ are shown in Figure 3.

The latter of these matrices is obtained from the former through the definition of parallel composition of FSMs. From $\mathbf{P'}$, by considering the top-left 4×4 sub-matrix, we extract $\hat{\mathbf{P}}'$. If we numerically solve equation (3) by varying the state-distribution τ to account for each possible state of the chain we obtain the following values for the scheduling function $\zeta(S_0 T_0, 0) = 4$, $\zeta(S_1 T_1, 0) = 4$, $\zeta(S_2 T_0, 0) = 1$, $\zeta(S_0 T_1, 0) = 0$, for the threshold $\beta = 0.2$. Thus, for instance, from $S_0 T_0$ with probability higher than 80% no passive violations will happen in the next 4 steps. If one lowers the threshold to $\beta = 0.05$ the observations need to be scheduled more frequently, e.g., in that case $\zeta(S_0 T_0, 0) = 2$.

Scheduling Functions for Continuous Time Markov Chains. A homogeneous *Continuous Time Markov Chain* (CTMC) is a probabilistic model of a target with an underlying continuous time domain, i.e., an analogous of a DTMC where a real valued clock underlies the system.

Definition 9. *A* Continuous Time Markov Chain *(CTMC) is a tuple* $(S, \bar{s}, \mathbf{R})$ *where (i) S is a finite set of states, (ii) $\bar{s} \in S$ is the initial state and (iii) $\mathbf{R} : S \times S \to \mathbb{R}^{\geq 0}$ is the transition rate matrix.*

The transition rate between each pair of states is described in the transition rate matrix $\mathbf{R}$, and represents the negative parameter of an exponential distribution. The time spent in a state $s \in S$ is exponentially distributed with rate $E(s)$, defined as $E(s) \stackrel{\text{def}}{=} \sum_{s' \in S} \mathbf{R}(s, s')$. The value $E(s)$, for a state s, is called the *exit rate* of s. From a CTMC an *embedded DTMC* can be retrieved by defining its transition probability matrix $\mathbf{P}(s, s') = \mathbf{R}(s, s')/E(s)$.

Targets whose behaviour is described as a CTMC generate executions where the sojourn time in a state is distributed according to an exponential distribution with parameter corresponding to the exit rate of the state, and in which the probabilistic jumps are resolved according to the embedded DTMC. The notions we introduced for DTMCs apply also to CTMCs where an *absorbing state* s is such that $E(s) = 0$. Also, labelled extensions of CTMCs can be obtained along the line of the labelled extensions of DTMCs.

Scheduling functions for CTMCs are defined similarly to the corresponding discrete case. In particular, the time until absorption is described by *Continuous Phase-type* (PH) distribution, as opposed to the DPH distribution of the previous case. Technically, given a set of states $Q_A = \{q_1, \ldots, q_n\}$, a labelled CTMC is described as a pair (A, θ), where $A = (\Sigma, Q_A, \iota_A, \delta_A, F_A)$, with $F_A = Q_A$, is a *deterministic* FSM, and $\theta : Q_A \times \Sigma \times Q_A \to \mathbb{R}^+$ gives the *rate* associated with each transition. As in the previous cases, we assume $\theta(t) = 0$ for all $t \notin \delta_A$. According to Definition 9, a labelled CTMC can be represented as a tuple $(Q_A, \mathbf{e}^{(\iota_A)}, \mathbf{R})$, where $\mathbf{e}^{(\iota_A)}$ is a unit vector with only a 1 in the position corresponding to the initial state ι_A, and $\mathbf{R} = [r_{ij}]$, namely the transition rates matrix, is such that $r_{ij} = \sum_{\sigma \in \Sigma} \theta(q_i, \sigma, q_j)$.

Definition 10. *Let $(S, \bar{s}, \mathbf{R})$ be a terminating CTMC, define its infinitesimal generator matrix $\mathbf{R}_{\text{in}}$ with entries $r_{i,j}^{in}$ where $r_{i,j}^{in} = r_{i,j}$ if $i \neq j$ and $r_{i,j} \in \mathbf{R}$, and $r_{i,i}^{in} = 1 - \sum_{j \neq i} r_{i,j}$. Then, (by possibly renumbering the states of the CTMC) define $\mathbf{R}_{\text{in}} = \begin{bmatrix} \hat{\mathbf{R}}_{\text{in}} & \boldsymbol{\rho} \\ \mathbf{0} & 0 \end{bmatrix}$ where (i) $\hat{\mathbf{R}}_{\text{in}} \in [0, 1]^{(|S|-1) \times (|S|-1)}$ restricts $\mathbf{R}_{\text{in}}$ to the transient states, (ii) $\boldsymbol{\rho}$ and $\mathbf{0}$ are as in Definition 8.*

A Continuous Phase-type *(PH) distribution $PH(\boldsymbol{\tau}, \hat{\mathbf{R}}_{\text{in}})$ is a row vector $\boldsymbol{\tau} \in \{0, 1\}^{|S|-1}$, i.e., the initial distribution over transient states and the matrix $\hat{\mathbf{R}}_{\text{in}}$. Its cumulative distribution function is $F(x) = 1 - \boldsymbol{\tau} e^{\hat{\mathbf{R}}_{\text{in}} x} \mathbf{1}$ for $x \in \mathbb{R}^+$ where $e^{(\cdot)}$ denotes matrix exponentiation.*

The set of possible timed transitions of a given CTMC (A, θ) is described by the transition relation $\to_{\text{sys}}$, defined in Figure 7. Note that, since the exponential distribution takes values in $[0, +\infty)$ such a relation defines infinite transitions.

As in the discrete case the controller is $C = absorbing(det(\mathcal{A}_{bad(\varphi)}) \parallel A)$ enriched with a labelling function $\overline{\theta} : Q_C \times \Sigma \times Q_C \to \mathbb{R}^+$. The definition of $\overline{\theta}$ is analogous to that of the DTMC, provided that the loop transition on the final state is $\forall \sigma \in \Sigma. \ \overline{\theta}(\psi_C, \sigma, \psi_C) = 0$. A continuous-time analogous of Proposition 1 can now be stated.

Proposition 3. *The PH distribution of $(C, \overline{\theta})$ is the distribution of the time until the next violation for such a CTMC.*

As in the discrete case such a chain is terminating and the absorbing state is ψ_C. Given a state $c \in Q_C$, function $\zeta(c, h)$ gives the maximum allowed time $\Delta t \in \mathbb{R}$ for which the probability of reaching the final state ψ_C from the current state c, within Δt time units, is less than a arbitrary probability β, as it was for DTMCs. The first time to reach the absorbing state follows a Continuous Phase-type distribution $PH(\mathbf{e}^{(c)}, \hat{\mathbf{R}}_{\text{in}})$ obtained from the CTMC $(C, \overline{\theta})$ according to Definition 10. Given its cumulative distribution function F the maximum time to sleep is again given by $\Delta t = \max\{0, \max\{t | F(t) \leq \beta\} - h\}$, which corresponds, when $\Delta t > h$, to solving

$$1 - \tau e^{\hat{\mathbf{R}}_{\text{in}}(\Delta t + h)} \mathbf{1} = \beta \tag{4}$$

since F is monotonic. As for DTMCs, h appears since the PH is not memoryless.

Proposition 4. *If $\zeta(c, h) = \Delta t$ with Δt a solution of equation (4) for some $\beta \in [0, 1]$, then the probability of a passive violation is bounded by β.*

Example 4. Consider the FSM of Figure 2 denoting CTMC $(\{S_0, S_1, S_2\}, S_0, \mathbf{R})$, and the CTMC $(\{S_0 T_0, S_1 T_1, S_2 T_0, S_0 T_1, \overline{S_1 T_2}\}, S_0 T_0, \mathbf{R}')$ (Fig. 5) where $\mathbf{R}$ and $\mathbf{R}'$ are as in Figure 3. As for DTMCs, the latter of these matrices is obtained from the former through the definition of parallel composition of FSMs. From $\mathbf{R}'$, considering the top-left 4×4 sub-matrix of the corresponding infinitesimal generator matrix $\mathbf{R}'_{\text{in}}$, we extract $\hat{\mathbf{R}}'_{\text{in}}$. If we numerically solve equation (4), by varying the state-distribution τ to account for each possible state of the chain, we obtain a scheduling function ζ such that $\zeta(S_0 T_0, 0) = 243.519992$, $\zeta(S_1 T_1, 0) = 243.609399$, $\zeta(S_2 T_0, 0) = 233.470649$, $\zeta(S_0 T_1, 0) = 232.969970$, for the threshold $\beta = 0.2$. Again, if one lowers the threshold to $\beta = 0.05$ the observations are scheduled more frequently, so for instance $\zeta(S_0 T_0, 0) = 63.259155$.

6   Conclusions

In this work we have proposed a novel class of security controllers, namely *lazy controllers*, and we have formally investigated the applicability of the framework to proactive truncation controllers. The novelty of our technique stands in the possibility of scheduling the security checks along the execution trace of the target, thus avoiding a costly continuous check of each action performed. Although this generates a risk factor of missing violating actions, it also extends the applicability of security monitors to many real-world scenarios, such as remotely logged systems. Moreover, we have formally analysed the risk of a security violation for the cases of non-deterministic, probabilistic and stochastic systems.

This constitutes the formal ground of our approach, which allows us to guarantee that a lazy controller never exceeds the maximum violation risk.

In this paper we have presented only the theoretical aspects of lazy controllers definition and synthesis. A prototype for remotely watching the execution of the OSGi implementation of a practical case study, showing the feasibility of our approach, has been presented in [15]. We leave as future work the extension to the lazy setting of other kinds of controllers, such as those based on edit automata.

References

1. Skalka, C., Smith, S.: Static enforcement of security with types. SIGPLAN Notices 35, 34–45 (2000)
2. Bartoletti, M., Degano, P., Ferrari, G.L., Zunino, R.: Types and effects for resource usage analysis. In: Seidl, H. (ed.) FOSSACS 2007. LNCS, vol. 4423, pp. 32–47. Springer, Heidelberg (2007)
3. Dragoni, N., Massacci, F., Naliuka, K., Siahaan, I.: Security-by-contract: Toward a semantics for digital signatures on mobile code. In: López, J., Samarati, P., Ferrer, J.L. (eds.) EuroPKI 2007. LNCS, vol. 4582, pp. 297–312. Springer, Heidelberg (2007)
4. Falcone, Y., Fernandez, J.C., Mounier, L.: What can you verify and enforce at runtime? Int. J. on Software Tools for Technology Transfer (STTT), 1–34 (2011)
5. Schneider, F.B.: Enforceable security policies. ACM Transactions on Information and System Security 3, 30–50 (2000)
6. Ligatti, J., Bauer, L., Walker, D.: Edit automata: enforcement mechanisms for run-time security policies. Int. J. of Information Security 4, 2–16 (2005)
7. Martinelli, F., Matteucci, I.: Through modeling to synthesis of security automata. Electronic Notes in Theoretical Computer Science 179, 31–46 (2007)
8. Martinelli, F., Matteucci, I.: Synthesis of local controller programs for enforcing global security properties. In: Proceedings of ARES 2008, pp. 1120–1127 (2008)
9. Falcone, Y.: You should better enforce than verify. In: Barringer, H., Falcone, Y., Finkbeiner, B., Havelund, K., Lee, I., Pace, G., Roşu, G., Sokolsky, O., Tillmann, N. (eds.) RV 2010. LNCS, vol. 6418, pp. 89–105. Springer, Heidelberg (2010)
10. Garfinkel, S., Spafford, G.: Practical Unix and Internet security, 2nd edn. O'Reilly & Associates, Inc., Sebastopol (1996)
11. Axelsson, S., Lindqvist, U., Gustafson, U., Jonsson, E.: An Approach to UNIX Security Logging. In: Proceedings of the 21st NIST-NCSC, pp. 62–75 (1998)
12. Abad, C., Taylor, J., Zhou, Y., Sengul, C., Rowe, K., Yurcik, W.: Log Correlation for Intrusion Detection: A Proof of Concept. In: Proceedings ACSAC 2003 (2003)
13. Plotkin, G.: A Structural Approach to Operational Semantics. In: Technical Report DAIMI FN-19, Denmark, Aarhus University (1981)
14. Plotkin, G.: The Origins of Structural Operational Semantics. In: Journal of Logic and Algebraic Programming. 60-61, 3–15 (2004)
15. Costa, G., Caravagna, G., Pardini, G., Wiegand, L.: Lazy Monitoring for Distributed Computing Environments. In: Proceedings of IMIS (2012)
16. Pnueli, A.: The temporal logic of programs. In: 18th FOCS, pp. 46–57. IEEE (1977)
17. Büchi, J.R.: On a Decision Method in Restricted Second-Order Arithmetic. In: Int. Cong. on Logic, Methodology, and Philosophy of Science, pp. 1–11 (1962)
18. Kupferman, O., Vardi, M.Y.: Model checking of safety properties. Formal Methods in System Design 19, 291–314 (2001)
19. Ross, S.M.: Introduction to Probability Models, 9th edn. Academic Press (2006)

Automated Analysis of Scenario-Based Specifications of Distributed Access Control Policies with Non-mechanizable Activities[*]

Michele Barletta[1], Silvio Ranise[2], and Luca Viganò[1]

[1] Dipartimento di Informatica, Università di Verona, Italy
{michele.barletta,luca.vigano}@univr.it
[2] FBK-Irst, Trento, Italy
ranise@fbk.eu

Abstract. The advance of web services technologies promises to have far-reaching effects on the Internet and enterprise networks allowing for greater accessibility of data. The security challenges presented by the web services approach are formidable. In particular, access control solutions should be revised to address new challenges, such as the need of using certificates for the identification of users and their attributes, human intervention in the creation or selection of the certificates, and (chains of) certificates for trust management. With all these features, it is not surprising that analyzing policies to guarantee that a sensitive resource can be accessed only by authorized users becomes very difficult. In this paper, we present an automated technique to analyze scenario-based specifications of access control policies in open and distributed systems. We illustrate our ideas on a case study arising in the e-government area.

1 Introduction

Access control aims at protecting data and resources against unauthorized disclosure and modifications while ensuring access to authorized users. An access control request consists of a *subject* asking to perform a certain *action* on an *object* of a system. A set of *policies* allows the system to decide whether access is granted or denied by evaluating some conditions on the attributes of the subject, the object, and the environment of the system (such as the identity, role, location, or time). For centralized systems, identifying subjects, objects, and the values of the attributes is easy since both subjects and objects can be adequately classified by identifiers that are assigned by the system itself. For open and distributed systems such as those based on web technology, the situation is more complex as web servers receive and process requests from remote parties that are

---

[*] The work presented in this paper was supported by the FP7-ICT-2009-5 Project no. 257876, "SPaCIoS: Secure Provision and Consumption in the Internet of Services", and by the "Automated Security Analysis of Identity and Access Management Systems (SIAM)" project funded by Provincia Autonoma di Trento in the context of the "Team 2009 - Incoming" COFUND action of the European Commission (FP7).

A. Jøsang, P. Samarati, and M. Petrocchi (Eds.): STM 2012, LNCS 7783, pp. 49–64, 2013.

difficult to identify and to bind with their attribute values. Hence, *certificates* or credentials, attesting not only the identity but also the attributes of parties, must be exchanged to correctly evaluate access control queries. In many situations, the creation and exchange of certificates require human intervention, e.g., to issue and sign a certificate or to pick one in a portfolio of available credentials. Furthermore—as observed in [19] among others—in distributed systems, a certificate can be accepted or rejected depending on the *trust relation* between the receiver and its issuer. Additional flexibility can be gained by chains of credentials and trust. In this context, guaranteeing that only trusted users can access sensitive resources becomes a daunting task.

Contributions. In this paper, we propose a technique for the automated analysis of access control systems (ACS) in presence of human activities for the creation and exchange of certificates together with trust management. Our approach combines a logic-based language with model checking based on *Satisfiability Modulo Theories (SMT)* solving. More precisely, we follow [17] and use *Constraint Logic Programming (CLP)* for the specification of policies and trust management with ideas adapted from [13]. The exchange of certificates and their interplay with the set of policies is modeled as a transition system of the type proposed in [18]. We show that interesting analysis problems of ACSs can be reduced to reachability problems. Our main contribution is a decidability result for the (bounded) reachability problem of a sub-class of transition systems that can encode the analysis of scenario-based specifications of ACSs, i.e., situations in which the exchange of certificates is constrained by a given causality relation. Another contribution is a technique to reduce the number of possible interleavings while visiting reachable states.

A Motivating Example. We consider a simplified version of the *Car Registration Office* (CRO) scenario in [4]. It consists of a citizen wishing to register his new car via an on-line service provided by the CRO (see Fig. 1). An employee of the CRO, Ed, checks if the request can be accepted according to some criteria. If so, Ed must store the request in a central repository CRep, which, in turn, checks if Ed is entitled to do so. To be successful, the storage request must be supported by three certificates: ise saying that Ed is an employee of the CRO, ish saying that Helen is the head of the CRO and cans saying that Helen granted Ed the permission to store documents in CRep. Role certificates must be signed by a trusted Certification Authority (CA) while Ed's permission certificate is signed by Helen; if these were not the case, the certificates should be

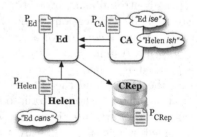

Fig. 1. The CRO scenario

rejected because the principal that signed the properties is *untrusted*. The generation of certificates (comics' balloons in Fig. 1) is a *non-mechanizable* activity whose execution depends on decisions that are not modeled in the system but only on the human behavior. Another issue is how the certificates are sent to

CRep in order to support Ed's storage request. It can be Ed to send the certificates along with the request (user-pull) or it can be CRep to collect the necessary certificates upon reception of Ed's request (server-pull). Each principal is equipped with trust and authorization policies ($P_{Ed}, P_{Helen}, P_{CA}, P_{CRep}$ in Fig. 1) that regulate the handling of security sensitive operations, such as the storing of a document in CRep (e.g., P_{CRep}) or the creation of a role certificate (e.g., P_{Helen}). These policies can be enforced locally or globally depending on the designer choice.

Organization. In Section 2, we give an overview of the main features of our approach, which we then detail in Section 3, where we formalize a class of access control schemas. In Sections 4 and 5, we present our main contributions: an automated analysis technique of scenario-based specifications and a heuristics for its scalability. In Section 6, we conclude and discuss related work. Due to lack of space, we point to the extended version [5] for proofs and more details.

2 Overview of the Main Features of Our Approach

Our goal is to automatically analyze situations in which (a) certificates are created or exchanged because of human intervention, (b) there is a need to reason about chains of credentials to establish the validity of a certificate, and (c) message exchanges comply with a causality relation.

Certificates and Non-mechanizable Activities. Inspired by [17,13], we use a variant of Constraint Logic Programming (CLP) to abstractly represent certificates and to specify and reason about the trust relationships among principals and the restrictions on delegating the ability to issue certificates. For the CRO scenario, the three certificates shown in Fig. 1 can be expressed as the following CLP facts: (F1) uknows(CA, a2i(Ed, ise)), (F2) uknows(CA, a2i(Helen, ish)), and (F3) uknows(Helen, a2i(Ed, cans)), where uknows represents the knowledge of a principal resulting from non-mechanizable activities only, called *internal* knowledge, and a2i is a constructor for the piece of knowledge about the binding of a property (e.g., being an employee, ise) with a principal (e.g., Ed).

Exchange of Certificates Among Principals. Distributed access control is based on exchanging certificates among principals so that access decisions can be taken by one principal with all the necessary information. In this paper, we do not deal with the problem of credential chain discovery (see, e.g., [19]), but we focus on credential distribution when solving a certain reachability problem. So, we need to specify the actions that change the state of the system, that is the content of the network and the internal knowledge of the principals involved. To this end, we use the notion of transition system introduced in [18] for access control systems as follows. The network of messages is modeled by a predicate msg with three arguments: the sender, the payload, and the receiver of the message. The action of p sending a message with payload x to q is written as

$$\mathsf{knows}(p, x) \Rightarrow \oplus \mathsf{msg}(p, \mathsf{said}(x), q) \tag{1}$$

where knows represents the knowledge of a principal, both internal and acquired from the reception of messages from other principals, and said transforms a piece of knowledge into an assertion that can be communicated to other principals. The fact that internal knowledge is knowledge can be expressed by the CLP rule

$$\mathsf{knows}(p, x) \leftarrow \mathsf{uknows}(p, x) \tag{2}$$

and the action of q receiving a message from p with s as payload is written as

$$\mathsf{knows}(q, \mathsf{s2i}(p, s)) \leftarrow \mathsf{msg}(p, s, q) \tag{3}$$

where s2i is a constructor for the piece of knowledge about the binding of the utterance s with a principal p. For example, the action of CA sending the certificate that Ed is an employee to Ed himself can be formalized as an instance of (1), the reception of such a certificate by Ed as an instance of (3), and the derivation that Ed knows that CA has uttered (and signed) the property about Ed being an employee—formally, $\mathsf{knows}(\mathsf{Ed}, \mathsf{s2i}(\mathsf{CA}, \mathsf{said}(\mathsf{a2i}(\mathsf{Ed}, \mathsf{ise}))))$—as an application of fact (F1) and rule (2). Note that Ed cannot claim to know that he is an employee since he does not know whether CA is trusted on emitting this type of utterances. For this, suitable trust relationships should be specified.

Trust Relationships Among Principals. We use again CLP rules. One rule is generic while the others are application dependent. The generic rule is

$$\mathsf{knows}(p, x) \leftarrow \mathsf{knows}(p, \mathsf{s2i}(q, \mathsf{said}(x))) \wedge \mathsf{knows}(p, \mathsf{a2i}(q, \mathsf{tdOn}(x))) \tag{4}$$

saying that a principal p may expand its knowledge to include the piece of information x as soon as another principal q has uttered $\mathsf{said}(x)$ and q is trusted on the same piece of knowledge x (the last part is encoded by the term $\mathsf{a2i}(q, \mathsf{tdOn}(x))$).

In the case of the CRO, we need also to consider four specific CLP rules, shown in Fig. 2, that encode the trust relationships among the various principals.

($P1$) says that a principal p can store documents in the CRep if p is an employee and p's head permits it, ($P2$) says that the content of any utterance of the CA is trusted, ($P3$) says that an utterance of a principal repeating an utterance of the CA is trusted, and ($P4$)

($P1$) $\mathsf{knows}(\mathsf{CRep}, \mathsf{a2i}(p, \mathsf{cans})) \leftarrow$
    $\mathsf{knows}(\mathsf{CRep}, \mathsf{a2i}(q, \mathsf{ish})) \wedge$
    $\mathsf{knows}(\mathsf{CRep}, \mathsf{a2i}(p, \mathsf{ise})) \wedge$
    $\mathsf{knows}(\mathsf{CRep}, \mathsf{s2i}(q, \mathsf{said}(\mathsf{a2i}(p, \mathsf{cans}))))$

($P2$) $\mathsf{knows}(p, \mathsf{a2i}(\mathsf{CA}, \mathsf{tdOn}(x)))$

($P3$) $\mathsf{knows}(p, \mathsf{a2i}(q, \mathsf{tdOn}(\mathsf{s2i}(\mathsf{CA}, \mathsf{said}(x)))))$

($P4$) $\mathsf{knows}(p, \mathsf{a2i}(q, \mathsf{tdOn}(\mathsf{s2i}(r, \mathsf{said}(\mathsf{a2i}(q, \mathsf{cans})))))) \leftarrow$
    $\mathsf{knows}(p, \mathsf{a2i}(r, \mathsf{ish}))$

Fig. 2. CRO trust relationship rules

says that the head of the CRO is trusted when emitting an utterance granting permission to store documents in the CRep to a principal.

Automated Analysis of Scenarios. The formal framework sketched above allows us to develop automated analysis techniques to verify the *availability* (policies suitable for scenario's execution) or the *security* (critical operations performed by trusted principals) of typical scenarios in which an ACS should operate. Both problems can be reduced to check whether, after performing a sequence of non-mechanizable activities and exchanging messages among principals, it is possible to reach a configuration of the network in which an access control query (e.g., in the CRO, "Can Ed store the citizen's request in CRep?") gets a positive or a negative answer. In other words, we want to solve *reachability problems* of the form: let the network be initially empty (formally, msg is interpreted as an empty relation), H_0 be a set of facts derived from non-mechanizable activities (e.g., (F1), (F2) and (F3) in the CRO described above), and G be a conjunction of knows-facts describing an access control query (e.g., knows(CRep, a2i(Ed, cans)) for the CRO); does there exist a sequence of n instances of the transition (1) and a sequence $H_1, ..., H_n$ of knows-facts derived from non-mechanizable activities such that G is satisfied in the final state?

Initially, we need to compute the fix-point of the facts in H_0 with the CLP rules (2), (3), (4) and those formalizing specific trust relations. This process must be repeated at each step $i = 1, ..., n$ with the facts describing the content of the network (derived by applying (3) at step $i - 1$), those in the set H_i, and the CLP rules. Since more than one transition (1) can be enabled at any given step i, it is necessary, in general, to consider several possible execution paths. Not surprisingly, the reachability problem turns out to be quite difficult. Fortunately, in scenarios with constrained message exchanging (e.g., the user-pull or the server-pull configurations considered for the CRO above), the reachability problem becomes simpler. It is possible to fix a bound n of transitions to consider and apply a reduction technique to decrease the number of different execution paths to be explored as we will see in Sections 4 and 5.

When solving the reachability problem, we will adopt a centralized approach by assuming a unique policy decision point that takes into account the union of the policies of the principals in a scenario, but note that there exist techniques that allow one to decentralize the policy decision process (e.g., [14]).

3   A Class of Access Control Schemas

According to [18], an *access control schema* ($\mathcal{ACS}$) is a transition system $(S, Q, \vdash, \Psi)$, where S is a set of states, Q is a set of queries, Ψ is a set of state-change rules, and $\vdash \subseteq S \times Q$ is the relation establishing if a query $q \in Q$ is satisfied in a given state $\gamma \in S$, written as $\gamma \vdash q$. For $s, s' \in S$ and $\psi \in \Psi$, we write $s \rightarrow_\psi s'$ when the change from s to s' is allowed by ψ. The reflexive and transitive closure of $\rightarrow_\psi$ is denoted by $\rightarrow_\psi^*$. Given an $\mathcal{ACS}$ $(S, Q, \vdash, \Psi)$, an instance (s, q, ψ) of the *reachability problem* (where $s \in S$, $q \in Q$, and $\psi \in \Psi$) consists of asking whether there exists an $s' \in S$ such that $s \rightarrow_\psi^* s'$ and $s' \vdash q$.

The Substrate Theory T_S. We define a class of $\mathcal{ACS}$s by using formulae of (many-sorted) first-order logic [11] to represent states and transitions. To do this formally, we need to introduce a *substrate* theory T_S, i.e., a set of formulae that abstractly specifies the basic data-structures and operations relevant for both access control and trust management. T_S contains a (countably) infinite set of constants of sort *Principal* to identify users, suitable operations to build *Attribute* values, and the functions a2i : *Principal* × *Attribute* → *Infon*, s2i : *Principal* × *Speech* → *Infon*, said : *Infon* → *Speech*, tdOn : *Infon* → *Attribute*, that have been already informally described in Section 2. To keep technicalities to a minimum and focus on the key notions, we do not provide here a precise definition of the T_S; full details can be found in the extended version [5]. Intuitively, T_S describes (an abstraction of) the data-structures that are relevant both for access control and trust management. T_S identifies a class of structures that are models of all formulae in T_S and say that a formula φ is satisfiable modulo T_S iff there exists a model of T_S that makes φ true.

The Set S of States. We consider the two predicate symbols uknows : $Principal \times Infon$ and msg : $Principal \times Speech \times Principal$ already introduced in Section 2. We assume the availability of a finite set Po of CLP rules, also called *policies*, of the form

$$A_0(\underline{x}) \leftarrow A_1(\underline{x}, \underline{y}) \wedge \cdots \wedge A_n(\underline{x}, \underline{y}) \wedge \xi(\underline{x}, \underline{y}), \tag{5}$$

where $\underline{x}$ and $\underline{y}$ are tuples of variables, A_0 is knows, $A_i \in \{\text{knows}, \text{uknows}\}$ for $i = 1, ..., n$, and ξ is a quantifier-free formula of the substrate theory T_S. We assume Po to always contain (2), (3), and (4). Given a set F of constrained ground facts and the set Po of policies, the set S of states contains all the constrained ground facts obtained by computing the least-fixpoint $lfp(F \cup Po)$ of the ground immediate consequence operator on $F \cup Po$ (see, e.g., [17]).

The Set Q of Queries and the Satisfaction Relation $\vdash$. A *query* is a conjunction of ground facts of the form $\text{uknows}(p, x) \leftarrow \xi(p, x)$. We define $\vdash$ to be the standard consequence relation $\models$ of first-order logic [11].

The Set Ψ of State-Change Rules. A *state-change rule* is a formula

$$\exists p, x, q. \ \text{knows}(p, x) \ \wedge \forall y, z, w. \ \text{msg}'(y, z, w) \Leftrightarrow$$
$$\text{msg}(y, z, w) \ \vee \ (y = p \wedge z = \text{said}(x) \wedge w = q) \tag{6}$$

that is usually abbreviated as (1). Intuitively, the unprimed and primed versions of msg denote the state of the network immediately before and after, respectively, of the execution of the state-change rule. Let S_1 and S_2 be two states in S and ψ be a formula of the form (6), then $S_1 \rightarrow_\psi S_2$ iff

$$S_2 := \{\text{msg}(y, z, w) \leftarrow (y = p \wedge z = \text{said}(x) \wedge w = q)\sigma \mid S_1 \cup \{\text{knows}(p, x)\sigma\} \text{ is}$$
$$\text{satisfiable modulo } T_S \text{ for } \sigma \text{ ground substitution of } p, x, q\}.$$

When $S_2 \neq \emptyset$, the state-change rule is *enabled* in S_1; otherwise (i.e., $S_2 = \emptyset$) it is *disabled in* S_1. This concludes the definition of our class of access control schema. All formal details can be found in the extended version [5].

Reachability Problems. In the class of $\mathcal{ACS}$s defined above, policies rely on conditions that are determined by the exchange of messages (cf. predicate msg and the CLP rule (3)) and non-mechanizable activities (cf. predicate uknows and the CLP rule (2)). The state-change rules in Ψ can only modify msg and leave uknows unconstrained since it is very difficult to model how humans decide to create a certain certificate. Returning to the CRO scenario, consider the assertion of fact (F3) as an example of a certificate that can be created at any time of the execution sequence of the system. To emphasize this aspect, we explicitly define the notion of (instance of) the reachability problem, although technically it can be derived from that of reachability problem given at the beginning of this section.

Definition 1. *Given a set Po of policies and a query G, an **instance of the reachability problem** amounts to establishing whether there exist an integer $n \geq 0$ and constraint facts $H_0(\mathsf{uknows}_0), ..., H_{n-1}(\mathsf{uknows}_{n-1})$ such that*

$$\mathcal{R}_n \cup \{G(\mathsf{knows}_n)\} \text{ is satisfiable modulo } T_\mathsf{S}, \tag{7}$$

where $\mathcal{R}_0 := lfp(\{H_0(\mathsf{uknows}_0)\} \cup Po(\mathsf{knows}_0))$, $\mathcal{R}_i \to_\psi \mathcal{R}_{i+1}$, $\mathcal{R}_{i+1} := lfp(\mathcal{R}_{i+1} \cup \{H_{i+1}(\mathsf{uknows}_{i+1})\} \cup Po(\mathsf{knows}_{i+1}))$, msg_i, uknows_i, and knows_i denote uniquely renamed copies of $\mathsf{msg}, \mathsf{uknows}$, and knows, respectively, and $\alpha(s_i)$ is the formula obtained from α by replacing each occurrence of the symbol s with the renamed copy s_i (for $i = 0, ..., n+1$).

Intuitively, $\mathcal{R}_0$ is the initial knowledge of the principals computed from their internal knowledge and the (exhaustive) application of the policies without any exchange of messages (recall that, initially, we assume that the network contains no messages). Then, $\mathcal{R}_1$ is obtained from $\mathcal{R}_0$ by first applying one of the available state-change rule $(\mathcal{R}_{i+1})$ followed by the exhaustive application of the policies that allows each principal to possibly derive new knowledge from both the exchanged messages and their internal knowledge. The $\mathcal{R}_i$'s for $i \geq 2$ can be similarly characterized.

When there exists a value of n such that (7) holds, we say that G is *reachable*; otherwise (i.e., when, for every $n \geq 0$, we have that (7) does not hold) we say that G is *unreachable*. If a bound $\bar{n}$ on n is known, we talk of a *bounded* reachability problem (with bound $\bar{n}$). Since the reachability problem is undecidable even without considering non-mechanizable facts (see [5] for details) in the rest of the paper, we prefer to focus on identifying restricted instances of the (bounded) reachability problem that are useful in practice and can be automatically solved.

4   Automated Analysis of Scenario-Based Specifications

Web service technology supports the development of distributed systems using services built by independent parties. Consequently, service composition and co-ordination become an important part of the web service architecture. Usually, individual specifications of web services are complemented by scenario-based specifications so that not only the intentions of individual services but also their expected interaction sequences can be documented. Interestingly, as we will show below, scenario-based specifications can be exploited to automatically and efficiently analyze security properties despite the well-known fact that unforeseen interplays among individually secure services may open security holes in their composition. The idea is to associate a scenario with an instance of a bounded reachability problem and then consider only the sequences of state-change rules that are compatible with the scenario itself.

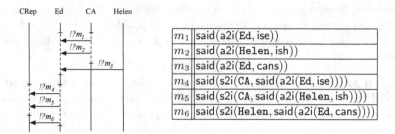

m_1	said(a2i(Ed, ise))
m_2	said(a2i(Helen, ish))
m_3	said(a2i(Ed, cans))
m_4	said(s2i(CA, said(a2i(Ed, ise))))
m_5	said(s2i(CA, said(a2i(Helen, ish))))
m_6	said(s2i(Helen, said(a2i(Ed, cans))))

Fig. 3. A user-pull scenario for the CRO: Ed sends to CRep the certificates for a positive answer to the query $G := \mathsf{knows}(\mathsf{CRep}, \mathsf{a2i}(\mathsf{Ed}, \mathsf{cans}))$

Scenarios and Bounded Reachability Problem. In our framework, a scenario is composed of a finite set of principals, some sequences of state-change rules of finite length, and a query G that encodes an availability or a security property. Since a state-change rule (1) to be enabled requires a principal to have some internal knowledge, this component of the scenario implicitly identifies a sequence $H_0(\mathsf{uknows}_0), ..., H_{n-1}(\mathsf{uknows}_{n-1})$ of non-mechanizable facts where $n \geq 0$ is the length of the longest sequence of state-change rules. An example of informal specification of a scenario is the Message Sequence Chart (MSC) for the CRO depicted on the left of Fig. 3 where the m_i's are the messages containing the utterances in the table on the right of the same figure. It is easy to find the instance of (1) that allows one to send each message m_i. The solid lines in the MSC impose an ordering on messages while dashed lines (called co-regions, see, e.g., [22]) do not. So, for example, CA can send the two certificates (in messages m_1 and m_2) about the roles of Ed and Helen to Ed in any order and these two certificates as well as the one sent by Helen about granting the permission to store documents in CRep (in message m_3) can be received in any order by Ed. For the CRO, the query $G := \mathsf{knows}(\mathsf{CRep}, \mathsf{a2i}(\mathsf{Ed}, \mathsf{cans}))$ encodes an availability property saying that the trusted user Ed can get the permission of storing the document in CRep. Since the length of the sequence of state-change rules specified by the scenario is 6, we can build an instance of the bounded reachability problem with bound $n = 6$ and the following sequence of non-mechanizable facts: $H_0 := \mathsf{uknows}(\mathsf{CA}, \mathsf{a2i}(\mathsf{Ed}, \mathsf{ise}))$, $H_1 := \mathsf{uknows}(\mathsf{CA}, \mathsf{a2i}(\mathsf{Helen}, \mathsf{ish}))$, $H_2 := \mathsf{uknows}(\mathsf{Helen}, \mathsf{a2i}(\mathsf{Ed}, \mathsf{cans}))$, and $H_i := true$ for $i = 3, 4, 5$. Other sequences are compatible with the scenario above, we just picked one. Such sequences are finitely many and can be exhaustively enumerated.

Decidability of a Class of Instances of the Reachability Problem. It would be interesting to find conditions that guarantee the decidability of this kind of instances of the bounded reachability problem with a given sequence of non-mechanizable facts. Before doing this, we need to discuss the following four technical conditions on the substrate theory T_S.

First, the fact that there is a finite and known number of principals in any scenario can be formalized by requiring the substrate theory T_S to be such that: **(C1)** $T_S \models \forall x. \bigvee_{c \in C} x = c \land \bigwedge_{c_1 \in C, c_2 \in C \setminus \{c_1\}} c_1 \neq c_2$ where C is a finite set of constants of sort *Principal*. This imposes that there are exactly $|C|$ principals. The second condition concerns the form of the policies: (**C2**) for each CLP rule in Po, all the variables in its body but not in its head range over the set C of principals. For the fix-point computation required to solve an instance of the reachability problem, variables not occurring in the head of a CLP rule but only in its body must be eliminated by a suitable (quantifier elimination) procedure (see, e.g., [17]). Assuming that such variables range only over the set C of principals—cf. condition (**C1**)—it is possible to replace each one of them with the constants in C and take the disjunction. The third and fourth conditions state respectively that: (**C3**) T_S must be closed under sub-structures and (**C4**) T_S must be locally finite, (see [5] for more details). Examples of effectively locally finite theories are the theory of an enumerated data-type or the theory of linear orders (cf., e.g., [21]). The last two (more technical) conditions allow us to reduce the satisfiability of a formula containing universal quantifiers (namely, those in the CLP rules) to the satisfiability of ground formulae by instantiating variables with finitely many (representative) terms. This implies the decidability of the satisfiability modulo T_S of (7) (in the definition of reachability problem) provided that it is decidable to check the satisfiability modulo T_S of ground formulae.

Theorem 1. *Let Po be a finite set of policies, G a query, and $H_0, \ldots, H_{n-1}$ a sequence of non-mechanizable facts ($n \geq 1$). If (**C1**), (**C2**), (**C3**), and (**C4**) are satisfied and the satisfiability modulo T_S of ground formulae is decidable, then the instance of the bounded reachability analysis problem (with bound n, sequence $H_0, \ldots, H_{n-1}$ of non-mechanizable facts, and query G) is decidable.*

The proof of this result, which is based on [21] and can be found in [5], yields the correctness of the automated analysis technique in Fig. 4. This is only a first step towards the design of a usable automated technique. In fact, at each iteration of the procedure, the solution of the bounded reachability problem (at step 1(c)) requires one to compute a fix-point and to check the satisfiability modulo the substrate theory. Such activities can be quite expensive computationally and any means of reducing their number is obviously highly desirable.

5   A Reduction Technique

The main drawback of the procedure in Fig. 4 is step 1 that forces the enumeration of all sequences in Σ. Unfortunately, Σ can be very large, e.g., there are 12 execution paths of CRO that are compatible with the MSC in Fig. 3. To overcome this problem, in the rest of this section, we design a reduction technique that allows for the parallel execution of a group of "independent" exchanges of messages so that several sequences of Σ can be considered at the same time in one iteration of step 1 in the algorithm of Fig. 4. In this way, the number of fix-point computations and satisfiability checks may be significantly reduced. The key to this refinement is a compact representation of the set Σ based on an adaptation of Lamport's *happened before* relation $\leadsto$ [16]. There are many possible choices to describe Σ, ranging from MSCs (as done in the previous section) to

Input: a substrate theory T_S, a set Po of policies, and a scenario $=$ (a finite
set C of principals, a set Σ of sequences of state-change rules of finite length,
a query G)
Output: G is reachable/unreachable
Assumptions: (**C1**), (**C2**), (**C3**), and (**C4**) are satisfied

1. For each sequence $\sigma \in \Sigma$:
   (a) Determine the sequence $H_0, ..., H_{|\sigma|}$ of non-mechanizable facts that
       enables the corresponding sequence of instances of (1).
   (b) Build an instance of the bounded reachability problem with bound
       $|\sigma|$, the non-mechanizable facts of the previous step, and G.
   (c) Try to solve the instance of the bounded reachability problem built
       at previous step.
   (d) If one of the instances at the previous step turns out to be solvable,
       return that the query G is reachable.
2. Return that the query G is unreachable (if step 1(d) is never executed).

Fig. 4. Automated Analysis of Scenario-based Specifications (interleaving semantics)

BPEL workflows for web services augmented with access control information [8].
We have chosen $\leadsto$ as a starting point because it is at the same time simple and
general, and simplifies the design of our reduction technique.

The Causality Relation. $\leadsto$ is a means of ordering L based on the potential
causal relationship of pairs of events in a concurrent system. Formally, $\leadsto$ is a
partial order on L. Two distinct events l_1 and l_2 are *concurrent* if $l_1 \not\leadsto l_2$ and
$l_2 \not\leadsto l_1$ (i.e., they cannot causally affect each other). In the usual interleaving
semantics, the set of possible executions can be seen as the set of all linear orders
that extend $\leadsto$. Formally, $\leadsto_t$ is a linear extension of $\leadsto$ if $\leadsto_t$ is a total order that
preserves $\leadsto$. Enumerating all the elements of the set $E(\leadsto)$ of linear extensions
of the partial order $\leadsto$ can be done in $O(|E(\leadsto)|)$ constant amortized time [20]
and computing $|E(\leadsto)|$ is #P-complete [9].

In our framework, L is the set of instances of the state-change rule (1) considered in a scenario-based specification. Thus, the relation $\leadsto$ must be specialized
so that: (**COMP1**) the enabledness of concurrent (according to $\leadsto$) instances of
(1) must be preserved—i.e., two such instances should not causally affect each
other by enabling (disabling) a disabled (enabled, respectively) state-change rule,
and (**COMP2**) any execution of the concurrent events in a (finite) set L, each
of which causally affects another event l not in L, results in a state in which l is
enabled. These requirements are formalized as follows.

(**COMP1**) if l_2 is enabled (disabled) in state S then it is still enabled (disabled,
respectively) in state S' for $S \to_{l_1} S'$ and the same must hold when swapping
l_1 with l_2.

(**COMP2**) $Pre(l') \subseteq L$ is such that $l \leadsto^* l'$ for each $l \in Pre(l')$ and there
is no $l'' \in L \setminus Pre(l')$ such that $l'' \leadsto^* l'$, then l' is enabled in S' where
$S \to_{l_1} \cdots \to_{l_k} S'$ and $Pre(l') = \{l_1, ..., l_k\}$.

$C := \{\texttt{Ed}, \texttt{Helen},$
$\texttt{CA}, \texttt{CRep}\}$

$L := \{SEC, SEC_2$
$SHC, SHC_2, SPC\}$

$\rightsquigarrow$ is the smallest
partial order s.t.:

- $SEC \rightsquigarrow SEC_2$
- $SHC \rightsquigarrow SHC_2$
- $SPC \rightsquigarrow SPC_2$

(SEC)	$\mathsf{knows}(\texttt{CA}, \mathsf{a2i}(\texttt{Ed}, \mathsf{ise})) \Rightarrow \oplus \mathsf{msg}(\texttt{CA}, \mathsf{said}(\mathsf{a2i}(\texttt{Ed}, \mathsf{ise})), \texttt{Ed})$
(SHC)	$\mathsf{knows}(\texttt{CA}, \mathsf{a2i}(\texttt{Helen}, \mathsf{ish})) \Rightarrow$ $\oplus \mathsf{msg}(\texttt{CA}, \mathsf{said}(\mathsf{a2i}(\texttt{Helen}, \mathsf{ish})), \texttt{Ed})$
(SPC)	$\mathsf{knows}(\texttt{Helen}, \mathsf{a2i}(\texttt{Ed}, \mathsf{cans})) \Rightarrow$ $\oplus \mathsf{msg}(\texttt{Helen}, \mathsf{said}(\mathsf{a2i}(\texttt{Ed}, \mathsf{cans})), \texttt{Ed})$
(SEC_2)	$\mathsf{knows}(\texttt{Ed}, \mathsf{s2i}(\texttt{CA}, \mathsf{said}(\mathsf{a2i}(\texttt{Ed}, \mathsf{ise})))) \Rightarrow$ $\oplus \mathsf{msg}(\texttt{Ed}, \mathsf{said}(\mathsf{s2i}(\texttt{CA}, \mathsf{said}(\mathsf{a2i}(\texttt{Ed}, \mathsf{ise})))), \texttt{CRep})$
(SHC_2)	$\mathsf{knows}(\texttt{Ed}, \mathsf{s2i}(\texttt{CA}, \mathsf{said}(\mathsf{a2i}(\texttt{Helen}, \mathsf{ish})))) \Rightarrow$ $\oplus \mathsf{msg}(\texttt{Ed}, \mathsf{said}(\mathsf{s2i}(\texttt{CA}, \mathsf{said}(\mathsf{a2i}(\texttt{Helen}, \mathsf{ish})))), \texttt{CRep})$
(SPC_2)	$\mathsf{knows}(\texttt{Ed}, \mathsf{s2i}(\texttt{Helen}, \mathsf{said}(\mathsf{a2i}(\texttt{Ed}, \mathsf{cans})))) \Rightarrow$ $\oplus \mathsf{msg}(\texttt{Ed}, \mathsf{said}(\mathsf{s2i}(\texttt{Helen}, \mathsf{said}(\mathsf{a2i}(\texttt{Ed}, \mathsf{cans})))), \texttt{CRep})$

Fig. 5. Formalization of the CRO scenario in Fig. 3

(**COMP1**) implies that the execution of either l_1 or l_2 followed by l_2 or l_1, respectively, will produce two identical states provided the two executions start from the same initial state. (**COMP2**) says that once the action of sending a message is enabled, it persists to be so; this is related to the fact that (1) can only add messages to msg. Although (**COMP2**) might seem to be restrictive, it is adequate for checking reachability (safety) properties as we do in this paper.

A partial-order relation $\rightsquigarrow$ on a finite set L of instances of (1) that satisfies (**COMP1**) and (**COMP2**) is called a *causality relation*. The tuple $(C, L, \rightsquigarrow, G)$ identifies a scenario (C, Σ, G) for C a finite set of principals, G a ground query, and Σ is the set of sequences obtained by enumerating all the linear extensions of $\rightsquigarrow$ on L. Since any linear extension of $\rightsquigarrow$ is of finite length (as $\rightsquigarrow$ is acyclic), we will also call $(C, L, \rightsquigarrow, G)$ a scenario.

We observe that when the state S is given, it is possible to show that both (**COMP1**) and (**COMP2**) are decidable (the proof is similar to that of Theorem 1). In practice, it is not difficult to argue that (**COMP1**) and (**COMP2**) hold for a given scenario. To illustrate this, we reconsider the scenario informally specified in Fig. 3 for the CRO and recast it in the formal framework developed above, as shown in Fig. 5. There is an obvious correspondence between the entries of the tables in the two figures; namely, message m_1 is the result of executing (SEC), m_2 of (SHC), m_3 of (SPC), m_4 of (SEC_2), m_5 of (SHC_2), and m_6 of (SPC_2). There is also a correspondence between the MSC in Fig. 3 and the causality relation $\rightsquigarrow$ in Fig. 5. Now, we show that (**COMP1**) holds for each pair (l_1, l_2) of concurrent rule instances in L as follows. For (SEC) and (SHC), we have that if the latter is enabled (disabled) before the execution of the first (SHC), it remains enabled (disabled, respectively) after its execution; the vice versa also holds. Similar observations hold also for the remaining pairs of concurrent events in L. Then, we show that (**COMP2**) holds for the events (SEC) and (SEC_2) that are such that $(SEC) \rightsquigarrow (SEC_2)$. When (SEC) is executed, (SEC_2) becomes enabled since the fact $\mathsf{msg}(\texttt{CA}, \mathsf{said}(\mathsf{a2i}(\texttt{Ed}, \mathsf{ise})), \texttt{Ed})$ holds as the result of executing (SEC): by the CLP rule (3) it is possible to derive $\mathsf{knows}(\texttt{Ed}, \mathsf{s2i}(\texttt{CA}, \mathsf{said}(\mathsf{a2i}(\texttt{Ed}, \mathsf{ise}))))$ that is precisely the enabling condition of (SEC_2). Similar observations hold for (SHC) and (SHC_2) as well as (SPC)

and (SPC_2). Intuitively, $\rightsquigarrow$ formalizes the obvious remark that, before Ed can forward a certificate to CRep (about his role, Helen's role, or the permission to store documents), he must have preliminarily received it regardless of the order in which he has received the certificates from CA and Helen.

A Reduction Technique Based on Causality Relations. So far, we have shown that a causality relation can be exploited to compactly specify a scenario. Here, we show how it can be used to dramatically reduce the number of fix-point computations and satisfiability checks required by the analysis technique in Fig. 4 while preserving its completeness. The key idea is the following. Since pairs of concurrent rule instances cannot causally affect each other, it is possible to execute them in *parallel*, i.e., adopt a partial-order semantics. In fact, any linearization of the parallel execution, in the usual interleaving semantics, will yield the same final state obtained from the parallel execution. This has two advantages. First, a single parallel execution of concurrent events corresponds to a (possibly large) set of linear executions. Second, the length of the parallel execution is shorter than those of the associated linear executions. The number of fix-point computations and satisfiability checks needed to solve a bounded reachability problem can be reduced depending on the degree of independence of the rule instances in the scenario. The price to pay is a modification of the definition of reachability problem (cf. the end of Section 3) to adopt a partial-order semantics. We explain these ideas in more detail below.

Definition 2. *Let Po be a (finite) set of policies and $(C, L, \rightsquigarrow, G)$ a scenario, where C is a finite set of principals, L is a finite set of rule instances of (1), $\rightsquigarrow$ is a causality relation, and G a query. An* instance of the reachability problem with partial-order semantics compatible with the causality relation $\rightsquigarrow$ *amounts to establishing whether there exist an integer $n \geq 0$ and (ground) constraint facts $H_0(\text{uknows}_0), ..., H_{n-1}(\text{uknows}_{n-1})$ such that $\mathcal{R}_n \cup \{G(\text{knows}_n)\}$ is satisfiable modulo T_S, where $\mathcal{R}_0 := lfp(\{H_0(\text{uknows}_0)\} \cup Po(\text{knows}_0))$, $\mathcal{R}_{i+1} := lfp(R_{i+1} \cup \{H_{i+1}(\text{uknows}_{i+1})\} \cup Po(\text{knows}_{i+1}))$, and $\mathcal{R}_i \rightarrow_{l_1} \cdots \rightarrow_{l_k} R_{i+1}$ for $l_1, ..., l_k \in L$ such that any pair (l_a, l_b) is of concurrent events $(a, b = 1, ..., k$ and $a \neq b)$.*

Definition 2 is almost identical to the Definition 1. The main difference is in allowing the execution of a sequence $l_1, ..., l_k$ of exchange of messages provided that these are pairwise concurrent with respect to the causality relation. Intuitively, we cumulate the effect of executing the instances $l_1, ..., l_k$ of (1) in a single step so that each principal can derive more knowledge from the exchange of several messages than the exchange of just one message as it was the case with the definition of reachability problem in Section 3.

With this new definition of reachability problem, we propose a refinement in Fig. 6 of the analysis technique in Fig. 4. The main differences between the two techniques are the following. In input, the scenario is given by using the notion of causality relation in order to exploit the new definition of reachability problem with the partial-order semantics. Then, instead of considering all the possible linear extensions of $\rightsquigarrow$ (as in Fig. 4), sets of pairwise concurrent events for parallel execution are computed by using the causality relation. The idea is to use the Hasse diagram

Input: a substrate theory T_S, a set Po of policies, and a scenario $(C, L, \rightsquigarrow, G)$= (a finite set C of principals, a finite set L of instances of (1), a causality relation $\rightsquigarrow$, a query G)
Output: G is reachable/unreachable
Assumptions: (**C1**), (**C2**), (**C3**), (**C4**), (**COMP1**), and (**COMP2**) are satisfied

1. Let $CG(\rightsquigarrow)$ be the causality graph associated to $\rightsquigarrow$.
2. Compute the set P_0 of nodes in $CG(\rightsquigarrow)$ with no incoming edges and L_{P_0} be the set of rule instances of (1) in L labeling the nodes in P_0.
3. Determine the set H_0 of non-mechanizable facts that enables all the rule instances in L_{P_0}.
4. Set $j = 0$ and while the set of nodes in $CG(\rightsquigarrow)$ is non-empty do
   (a) Delete from $CG(\rightsquigarrow)$ all the nodes in P_j and the edges whose sources are in P_j and increment j by 1.
   (b) Compute the set P_j of nodes in $CG(\rightsquigarrow)$ with no incoming edges and $L_{P_j} \subseteq L$ be the set of rule instances labeling the nodes in P_j.
5. Build an instance of the bounded reachability problem with partial-order semantics compatible with the causality relation $\rightsquigarrow$ with bound j, sequence $H_0, H_1, ..., H_j$ of non-mechanizable facts where $H_i := true$ for $i = 1, ..., j$, and the input query G. At each step i of the bounded reachability problem, the rule instances in L_{P_j} must be used for parallel execution.
6. If the instance of the bounded reachability problem is solvable, then return that the query G is reachable; otherwise, return that G is unreachable.

Fig. 6. Automated Analysis of Scenario-based Specifications (partial-order semantics)

$CG(\rightsquigarrow)$, called the *causality graph* in the following, associated to $\rightsquigarrow$, i.e. the transitive reduction of the relation $\rightsquigarrow$ seen as an oriented graph. The crucial observation is that concurrent events can be identified by looking at those nodes that are not connected by a path in the causality graph. Formally, we need the following notion. An element l is *minimal* in L with respect to $\rightsquigarrow$ iff there is no element $l' \in L$ such that $l' \rightsquigarrow l$. Since L is finite, minimal elements of $\rightsquigarrow$ must exist (this is a basic property of partial orders over finite sets). In step 2, the rule instances labeling the minimal elements in L with respect to $\rightsquigarrow$, that correspond to nodes with no incoming edges in the causality graph, are the only that require non-mechanizable facts for them to be enabled. In fact, all the rule instances labeling non-minimal elements with respect to the causality are enabled by the execution of one or more rule instances that label ancestor nodes in the causality graph, because of (**COMP2**). This is why we compute H_0 in step 3 while all the other sets of non-mechanizable facts are vacuously set to *true* in step 5. The rule instances in L_{P_0} labeling the nodes in P_0 are concurrent because of (**COMP1**). In step 4, we exploit this observation to compute the other set of concurrent rule instances that can be executed in parallel by modifying the causality graph: the nodes and the edges whose sources are in P_0 are deleted from $CG(\rightsquigarrow)$ so that the set P_1 of nodes with no incoming edges can be identified. The rule instances in L_{P_1} labeling the nodes in P_1 are the new concurrent events that can be executed in parallel and so on. The procedure eventually terminates when no more nodes are left in the causality graph. Then, in step 5, the new definition of bounded reachability problem compatible with the causality relation $\rightsquigarrow$ can be exploited by using the sets $L_{P_0}, ..., L_{P_j}$ of rules instances to be executed in parallel. If the instance is solvable, then the query G is reachable, otherwise it is unreachable. The correctness of the refined analysis in Fig. 4 stems from the fact that, by definition of causality relation, there exists an execution in the interleaving semantics for the concurrent events executed in parallel—because of (**COMP1**)—and the execution of rule instances that must happen before (with respect to $\rightsquigarrow$), enable the execution of those that happen afterwards—according to (**COMP2**).

We briefly illustrate how the refined version of the automated analysis works on the scenario in Fig. 3 of the CRO. According to the causality relation in Fig. 5, $(SEC), (SHC)$, and (SPC) are minimal elements of $\rightsquigarrow$ (step 2). Thus, the non-mechanizable fact H_0 enabling their execution is the conjunction of the following three facts: uknows(CA, a2i(Ed, ise)), uknows(CA, a2i(Helen, ish)), and uknows(Helen, a2i(Ed, cans)). Deleting the nodes labeled by $(SEC), (SHC)$, and (SPC) with the corresponding edges in the causality graph leaves us with a graph containing three isolated nodes labeled by $(SEC_2), (SHC_2)$, and (SPC_2) that can be executed in parallel. As a consequence, the bound of the reachability problem is 2 in which, initially, the parallel execution of $(SEC), (SHC)$, and (SPC) is enabled because of the non-mechanizable facts in H_0 while the parallel execution of $(SEC_2), (SHC_2)$, and (SPC_2) is enabled, in the following step, because of the three new certificates available in the net. Even in this simple example, the savings of the reduction technique are important: the two-step parallel execution corresponds to 6 interleavings executions that must be considered when using the technique in Fig. 4.

We have implemented a prototype of the procedure above in WSSMT [3]. The time taken to analyze the scenario in Fig. 5 with this prototype is negligible; larger examples are discussed in [3].

6   Discussion

We presented an automated technique to analyze scenario-based specifications of access control policies in open and distributed systems that takes into account human activities. It uses an instance of CLP to express policies and trust relationships, and reduces the analysis problem to fix-point computations and satisfiability checks. The first contribution is the decidability of the analysis of scenario-based specifications of ACSs. The second contribution is a reduction technique that allows us to make the decidability result useful in practice.

There are three main lines of research that are related to our work. First, several logic-based frameworks (e.g., [18,13,7,15,2,21]) have been proposed to specify and analyze authorization policies with conditions depending on the environment of the system in which they are enforced. In principle, it is possible to consider the conditions depending on the execution of human activities as part of the environment and then re-use the available specification and analysis techniques. The problem in doing this is that the conditions for the execution of human activities are not explicitly modeled in the system so that their applicability is unconstrained. This results in a dramatic increase of the search space that makes the application of the available technique difficult, if possible at all. We avoid this state-explosion problem by considering scenario-based specifications that allow one to focus on a small sub-set of the possible sequences of events, as explained in Section 5. It would be interesting to adapt the abduction techniques in [6,15] to identify which non-mechanizable facts need to be generated for the executability of complex scenarios in which condition (**COMP2**), about the "monotonicity" of the events (Section 5), does not hold.

The second research line is that on workflow analysis in presence of authorization policies, e.g., [8,24]. On the one hand, such works specify the workflow as a partial ordering on tasks that is similar to the causality relation introduced here. On the other hand, these works abstract away the data-flow so that there is no need to specify compatibility conditions on the causality relation (cf. (**COMP1**) and (**COMP2**)) as we do here because of the modelling of the exchange of messages among principals. Another difference is that the specification of authorization policies is reduced to a minimum in [8,24] so as to simplify the study of the completion problem, i.e., whether there exists at least one assignment of users to tasks that allow for the execution of the whole workflow. Instead, we focus on reachability problems and we model, besides authorization policies, also trust relationships among principals. It would be interesting to study the decidability of the completion problem also in our richer framework. In the related area of business process management, there is a number of simulation techniques (e.g., [1]) whose aim is to understand how non-mechanized actions influence the process run. Our work focus on (automated) analysis while [1] on simulation and it is closer to testing.

The third line of research concerns the development of (semi) formal techniques for the analysis of human interventions. In [10], the authors aim to determine how a task is executed by humans and what special factors are involved in the accomplishment of the task's goal. This work is based on informal methods to identify and analyze human actions in contrast to our framework that is based on a logical formalism. Graphs and deterministic finite state automata are used in [23] to model and analyze human behavior in critical systems. Although this approach is also formal, our framework differs for the capability to analyze systems influenced by non predictable human activities, in contrast with those predefined for industrial material-handling processes. [25,12] are interesting works in reasoning about human operators, where the analysis is based on concurrent game structures, a formalism similar to the $\mathcal{ACS}$ we used in Section 3. The accurate verification analysis and the decidability result we presented in this paper are the major differences that distinguish our work from these.

References

1. Accorsi, R.: A security-aware simulation method for generating business process event logs. In: Symp. on Data-Driven Process Discovery and Analysis (2012)
2. Alberti, F., Armando, A., Ranise, S.: Efficient Symbolic Automated Analysis of Administrative Role Based Access Control Policies. In: 6th ASIACCS. ACM (2011)
3. Barletta, M., Calvi, A., Ranise, S., Viganò, L., Zanetti, L.: WSSMT: Towards the Automated Analysis of Security-Sensitive Services and Applications. In: Proc. 12th SYNASC, pp. 417–424. IEEE Computer Society (2010)

4. Barletta, M., Ranise, S., Viganò, L.: Verifying the Interplay of Authorization Policies and Workflow in Service-Oriented Architectures. In: Proc. SecureCom 2009, pp. 289–299. IEEE CS (2009), full version at http://arxiv.org/abs/0906.4570
5. Barletta, M., Ranise, S., Viganò, L.: Automated Analysis of Scenario-based Specifications of Distributed Access Control Policies with Non-Mechanizable Activities, Extended Version (2012), http://arxiv.org/abs/1206.3180
6. Becker, M.Y., Nanz, S.: The role of abduction in declarative authorization policies. In: Hudak, P., Warren, D.S. (eds.) PADL 2008. LNCS, vol. 4902, pp. 84–99. Springer, Heidelberg (2008)
7. Becker, M.Y., Nanz, S.: A logic for state-modifying authorization policies. ACM Trans. Inf. Syst. Secur. 13(3) (2010)
8. Bertino, E., Crampton, J., Paci, F.: Access Control and Authorization Constraints for WS-BPEL. In: Proc. ICWS 2006, pp. 275–284. IEEE CS (2006)
9. Brightwell, G., Winkler, P.: Counting linear extensions is #P-complete. In: Proc. STOC, pp. 175–181. ACM (1991)
10. Diaper, D.: Task analysis for human-computer interaction. Prentice-Hall (1990)
11. Enderton, H.B.: A Mathematical Introduction to Logic. Academic Press (1972)
12. Gunter, E., Yasmeen, A., Gunter, C., Nguyen, A.: Specifying and analyzing workflows for automated identification and data capture. In: Proc. HICSS 2009, pp. 1–11. IEEE CS (2009)
13. Gurevich, Y., Neeman, I.: Dkal: Distributed-knowledge authorization language. In: Proceedings of CSF, pp. 149–162. IEEE CS (2008)
14. Gurevich, Y., Roy, A.: Operational Semantics for DKAL: Application and Analysis. In: Fischer-Hübner, S., Lambrinoudakis, C., Pernul, G. (eds.) TrustBus 2009. LNCS, vol. 5695, pp. 149–158. Springer, Heidelberg (2009)
15. Hurlin, C., Kirchner, H.: Semi-automatic synthesis of security policies by invariant-guided abduction. In: Degano, P., Etalle, S., Guttman, J. (eds.) FAST 2010. LNCS, vol. 6561, pp. 157–175. Springer, Heidelberg (2011)
16. Lamport, L., Schneider, F.B.: Pretending atomicity. Technical report. In: Research Report 44, Digital Equipment Corporation Systems Research (1989)
17. Li, N., Mitchell, J.C.: DATALOG with constraints: A foundation for trust management languages. In: Dahl, V. (ed.) PADL 2003. LNCS, vol. 2562, pp. 58–73. Springer, Heidelberg (2002)
18. Li, N., Tripunitara, M.V.: Security analysis in role-based access control. ACM Trans. Inf. Syst. Secur. 9, 391–420 (2006)
19. Li, N., Winsborough, W.H., Mitchell, J.C.: Distributed credential chain discovery in trust management. Journal of Computer Security 11(1), 35–86 (2003)
20. Pruesse, G., Ruskey, F.: Generating Linear Extensions Fast. SIAM J. Comp. 23(2), 373–386 (1994)
21. Ranise, S.: On the Verification of Security-Aware E-services. Journal of Symbolic Computation 47, 1066–1088 (2012)
22. Rudolph, E., Graubmann, P., Grabowski, J.: Tutorial on message sequence charts. Computer Networks and ISDN Systems 28(12), 1629–1641 (1996)
23. Shin, D., Wysk, R., Rothrock, L.: Formal model of human material-handling tasks for control of manufacturing systems. IEEE Transactions on Systems, Man and Cybernetics, Part A: Systems and Humans 36(4), 685–696 (2006)
24. Tan, K., Crampton, J., Gunter, C.: The consistency of task-based authorization constraints in workflow. In: Proc. CSF, pp. 155–169. IEEE CS (2004)
25. Yasmeen, A., Gunter, E.: Automated framework for formal operator task analysis. In: Proc. ISSTA 2011 (2011)

Labeled Goal-Directed Search
in Access Control Logic

Valerio Genovese[1,2], Deepak Garg[3], and Daniele Rispoli[2]

[1] University of Luxembourg, Luxembourg
[2] University of Torino, Torino, Italy
[3] MPI-SWS, Kaiserslautern and Saarbrücken, Germany

Abstract. We describe a sound, complete, and terminating procedure for goal-directed proof search in BL_{sf}^G, an expressive fragment of a recently presented access control logic, BL_{sf}. BL_{sf}^G is more expressive than many other Datalog-based access control logics that also have very efficient decision procedures, and our search procedure finds proofs of authorization quickly in practice. We also extend our search procedure to find missing credentials when a requested authorization does not hold and discuss an implementation of our techniques in an extension of the Unix file synchronization program `rsync`.

Keywords: Access control, formal logic, goal-directed search, labeled calculus.

1 Introduction

Many access control systems rely on representation of authorization policies as logical theories [11,4,5,3,16,21]. Such representation not only formalizes high-level policy intent through the logic's semantics, but also allows for direct enforcement of policies through architectures like proof-carrying authorization [11,4,5], as well as formal proofs of policy meta properties like non-interference [10,7]. In fact, a number of special modal logics, called access control logics or authorization logics, have been proposed specifically for representing, enforcing and reasoning about access policies [2,10,11,12,20,8]. Policy representation in logic and enforcement are related as follows: A requested access, represented as the logical formula φ, is authorized by a policy represented as the logical theory Γ iff Γ entails φ. Consequently, to enforce policies represented in logic through a computer system, it is important to have a method to efficiently check entailment in the logic or, equivalently, to have an efficient theorem prover for the logic. It is also useful, but not necessary, to know that the prover terminates in all cases without losing completeness (implying that the logic is decidable), so the theorem prover can be invoked in a reference monitor without having to worry about non-termination. There is a tradeoff between designing an access control logic with many useful logical connectives and one with an efficiently implementable decision procedure.

A. Jøsang, P. Samarati, and M. Petrocchi (Eds.): STM 2012, LNCS 7783, pp. 65–80, 2013.

In prior work [14] (called EW or earlier work in the sequel), we have shown that an expressive access control logic, BL_{sf}, is decidable and that its decision procedure can be used as a foundation to solve three other practical problems in access control: justifying denied access (countermodel construction), finding all consequences of a policy (saturation), and determining what additional credentials will allow a denied access (policy abduction). Although an interesting theoretical result, experimental evaluation of the EW decision procedure (explained in Section 2) indicates that it has at least exponential complexity even on very simple access policies. While this is not surprising given the generality of the decision procedure, the problem we investigate now is that of reducing this complexity in practice, albeit at the cost of sacrificing some of the decision procedure's applications.

Precisely, we argue, through theoretical and experimental results, that it is pragmatic to consider a restriction of BL_{sf} to what is called a *Hereditary-Harrop (HH) fragment* [17] and to use *goal-directed* theorem proving on it. The HH fragment of logic, first considered in λ-Prolog, is a generalization of the Horn fragment of first-order logic on which Prolog is based (and, in our case, further generalized to include access control-specific connectives of BL_{sf}). Goal-directed proof search, also called SLD resolution or top-down search in logic programming, is an efficient technique for theorem proving that prunes search very rapidly by selecting only those rules from the theory that can directly prove the goal at hand. Completeness of this pruning relies heavily on restriction to the Horn or HH fragment.

We first define the HH fragment of BL_{sf}, called BL_{sf}^{G} (the G in the superscript stands for goal-directed). We argue by examples that although only a fragment of BL_{sf}, BL_{sf}^{G} is very expressive and can represent policies that cannot be represented in other restrictions considered in literature to attain efficient proof search, e.g., the Datalog fragment. Second, we describe a goal-directed proof search procedure for BL_{sf}^{G} and prove that it is sound and complete. Following EW, our procedure is based in labeled sequent calculi [18,22], which directly use the *semantic* definitions of the logic's connectives in proof rules. Although our completeness proof follows a standard template, it is a non-trivial generalization of existing proofs to account for the labeled style and also to accommodate two access control-specific constructs of BL_{sf} — A says φ and A sf B (the latter means that principal A speaks for principal B). We then show by a careful counting of steps in our completeness proof that the termination condition of EW translates into a uniform bound on the depth of search required in BL_{sf}^{G}, thus implying that our goal-directed search procedure is a decision procedure. Although the worst-case bound of this procedure is not good in theory, we explain why goal-directed search works very efficiently in practice and confirm this explanation experimentally.

Next, we show how our goal-directed search procedure can be adapted to also find missing credentials when the policy does not allow an access. This adaptation, called an abduction procedure, mirrors a similar procedure in EW.[1] Finally, we discuss a practical application of our work: We design and implement an extension of the `rsync` software for remote file synchronization, allowing rich file access policies written in BL_{sf}^G and relying on our abduction procedure for automatically obtaining credentials from online servers when access is denied.

Besides describing and justifying the use of goal-directed proof search for BL_{sf}, we make two minor technical contributions to goal-directed search in general: (1) To the best of our knowledge, we present the first goal-directed labeled calculi for the HH fragment of a multimodal intuitionistic logic and (2) Our counting argument to establish termination bounds on goal-directed search through the completeness proof is novel and somewhat surprising in goal-directed literature.

The paper is organized as follows. In Section 2, we recall the logic BL_{sf} from EW, the method of labeled sequent calculi and EW's decision procedure, and explain by experimental evaluation the exponential behavior of the EW search procedure even on simple access policies. In Section 3, we present BL_{sf}^G together with its goal-directed search procedure. In Section 4, we present our theoretical results, showing that goal-directed search is sound and complete and deriving a depth bound on it. Section 5 presents the extension of goal-directed search to perform abduction and its implementation. Section 6 presents the extension of `rsync` with BL_{sf}^G for representing policies and abduction for finding authorization credentials on-the-fly. Section 7 discusses related work and Section 8 concludes the paper. Due to space constraints, we relegate proofs and other technical details to a technical report [13].

2   Recap of BL_{sf}: Semantics and Proof-Theory

In this section we briefly describe the logic BL_{sf} as presented in our earlier work (EW) [14]. BL_{sf} is a propositional intuitionistic logic enriched with two well-known connectives in access control logics: A says φ (principal A supports formula φ) and A sf B (principal A speaks for principal B). The former is used to represent assertions of principals and the latter is used to represent trust relationships between principals (A sf B represents that B trusts A). The syntax of BL_{sf} formulas is shown below. p denotes an atomic formula, drawn from a countable set of symbols, and A, B denote principals drawn from a different, finite set $\mathcal{I}$. The connectives $\top$ (true), $\bot$ (false), $\wedge$ (and), $\vee$ (or) and $\rightarrow$ (implication) have usual meanings from intuitionistic logic.

Formulas $\varphi, \psi ::= p \mid \top \mid \bot \mid \varphi_1 \wedge \varphi_2 \mid \varphi_1 \vee \varphi_2 \mid \varphi_1 \rightarrow \varphi_2 \mid A$ says $\varphi \mid A$ sf B

Syntactically, the logic BL_{sf} is characterized by the following axioms:

---

[1] The other two applications of BL_{sf}'s decision procedure in EW, namely counter-model construction and saturation, are fundamentally incompatible with pruning employed by goal-directed proof search. Consequently, these two applications are not considered in this paper.

(All intuitionistic propositional tautologies)

$$\vdash \varphi$$

$$\frac{}{\vdash A \text{ says } \varphi} \tag{nec}$$

$$\vdash (A \text{ says } (\varphi \to \psi)) \to ((A \text{ says } \varphi) \to (A \text{ says } \psi)) \tag{K}$$

$$\vdash (A \text{ says } \varphi) \to (B \text{ says } A \text{ says } \varphi) \tag{I}$$

$$\vdash (A \text{ sf } B) \to ((A \text{ says } \varphi) \to (B \text{ says } \varphi)) \tag{speaksfor}$$

$$\vdash A \text{ sf } A$$

$$\vdash (A \text{ sf } B) \to ((B \text{ sf } C) \to (A \text{ sf } C))$$

Rule (nec) and axiom (K) are standard in modal logic. Axiom (I) is needed to accurately model delegation in the logic [1], whereas (speaksfor) characterizes the formula A sf B: If A sf B, then any statement φ that A makes is echoed by B, so the formula A sf B means that A has authority to speak on behalf of B [2].

Kripke Semantics. The semantics of BL_{sf} are presented in the standard, Kripke style for modal logics. A model contains several points called worlds, which represent possible states of knowledge. Modalities are interpreted using binary accessibility relations on worlds, with one relation S_A for every modality (A says $\cdot$). Intuitionistic implication is modeled using a binary preorder, $\leq$. EW treats the formula A sf B as an atom in the Kripke semantics and validates axioms related to it, e.g., (speaksfor), through conditions on Kripke frames.

Definition 1 (Kripke model). *A Kripke model or, simply, model, $\mathcal{M}$ is a tuple $(W, \leq, \{S_A\}_{A \in \mathcal{I}}, h, sf)$ where: W is a set. Its elements are called worlds. $\leq$ is a preorder on W. For each principal A, S_A is a binary relation on W, called the accessibility relation of principal A. h, called the truth assignment or assignment, is a map from the set of atoms to $\mathcal{P}(W)$. For any atom p, $h(p)$ is the set of worlds where p holds. sf is a map from pairs of principals to $\mathcal{P}(W)$. For any two principals A and B, $sf(A,B)$ is the set of worlds where A sf B holds.*

Let $S_{\mathcal{I}} = \bigcup_{A \in \mathcal{I}} S_A$. For BL_{sf}, the class of models is further restricted to those that satisfy the following frame conditions.

- $\forall x.(x \leq x)$ (refl)
- $\forall x, y, z.(((x \leq y) \land (y \leq z)) \to (x \leq z))$ (trans)
- $\forall x, y, z.(((x \leq y) \land (y S_A z)) \to (x S_A z))$ (mon-S)
- $\forall x, y, z.(((x S_B y) \land (y S_A z)) \to (x S_A z))$ (I)
- If $w \in sf(A, B)$, then for all w', $w S_B w'$ implies $w S_A w'$. (basic-sf)
- For all A and w, $w \in sf(A, A)$. (refl-sf)
- If $w \in sf(A, B) \cap sf(B, C)$, then $w \in sf(A, C)$. (trans-sf)
- If $x \in h(p)$ and $x \leq y$, then $y \in h(p)$. (mon)
- If $x(\leq \cup S_{\mathcal{I}})^* y$ and $x \in sf(A, B)$, then $y \in sf(A, B)$. (mon-sf)

Properties (refl) and (trans) make $\leq$ a preorder. Property (mon-S) validates axiom (K). Property (I) corresponds to axiom (I). Property (basic-sf) corresponds to axiom (speaksfor). Properties (refl-sf) and (trans-sf) make A sf B reflexive and transitive, respectively. Property (mon) is standard in Kripke models of intuitionistic logics and forces monotonicity of satisfaction. Property (mon-sf) implies that if A sf B holds in a world, then it also holds in all future worlds.

Definition 2 (Satisfaction). *Given a model* $\mathcal{M} = (W, \leq, \{S_A\}_{A \in \mathcal{I}}, h, sf)$ *and a world* $w \in W$, *the satisfaction relation* $\mathcal{M} \models w : \alpha$, *read "the world* w *satisfies formula* α *in model* $\mathcal{M}$", *is defined by induction on* α *as follows (standard clauses for* $\top, \wedge$ *and* $\vee$ *are omitted):*

- $\mathcal{M} \models w : p$ *iff* $w \in h(p)$
- $\mathcal{M} \models w : \alpha \to \beta$ *iff for every* w' *such that* $w \leq w'$ *and* $\mathcal{M} \models w' : \alpha$, *we have* $\mathcal{M} \models w' : \beta$.
- $\mathcal{M} \models w : A$ says α *iff for every* w' *such that* wS_Aw', *we have* $\mathcal{M} \models w' : \alpha$.
- $\mathcal{M} \models w : A$ sf B *iff* $w \in sf(A, B)$.

$\mathcal{M} \not\models w : \alpha$ *if it is not the case that* $\mathcal{M} \models w : \alpha$. *A formula* α *is true in a model* $\mathcal{M}$, *written* $\mathcal{M} \models \alpha$, *if for every world* $w \in \mathcal{M}$, $\mathcal{M} \models w : \alpha$. *A formula* α *is valid in* BL_{sf}^{G}, *written* $\models \alpha$, *if* $\mathcal{M} \models \alpha$ *for every model* $\mathcal{M}$.

Labeled sequent calculus. The central technical idea in EW, on which the entire technical development of EW including BL_{sf}'s decision procedure rests, is a labeled sequent calculus for BL_{sf}. Our goal-directed search procedure is a restriction of EW's sequent calculus, so we discuss the sequent calculus is some detail here. Following standard presentations of labeled sequent calculi (also called prefixed calculi), EW's calculus, SeqC, manipulates two types of labeled formulas: *world formulas*, written $x : \varphi$, where x is a symbolic world and φ is a formula of the logic (intuitively meaning that φ holds in world x), and *relation formulas*, representing semantic relations of the form $x \leq y$ and xS_Ay between symbolic worlds.

A sequent of SeqC has the form $\Sigma; \mathbb{M}; \Gamma \Rightarrow \Delta$ where Σ is a list of world symbols, $\mathbb{M}$ is a multiset of relation formulas and Γ and Δ are multisets of world formulas. Semantically, the sequent $\Sigma; \mathbb{M}; \Gamma \Rightarrow \Delta$ means that "every model which satisfies all labeled formulas of $\Gamma \cup \mathbb{M}$ satisfies at least one labeled formula in Δ"; this is made precise in the following definition.

Definition 3 (Sequent satisfaction and validity). *A model* $\mathcal{M}$ *and a mapping* ρ *from elements of* Σ *to worlds of* $\mathcal{M}$ *satisfy a (possibly non-provable) sequent* $\Sigma; \mathbb{M}; \Gamma \Rightarrow \Delta$, *written* $\mathcal{M}, \rho \models (\Sigma; \mathbb{M}; \Gamma \Rightarrow \Delta)$, *if one of the following holds:*

- *There is an* $xRy \in \mathbb{M}$ *with* $R \in \{\leq\} \cup \{S_A \mid A \in \mathcal{I}\}$ *such that* $\rho(x) \ R \ \rho(y) \notin \mathcal{M}$.
- *There is an* $x : \alpha \in \Gamma$ *such that* $\mathcal{M} \not\models \rho(x) : \alpha$.
- *There is an* $x : \alpha \in \Delta$ *such that* $\mathcal{M} \models \rho(x) : \alpha$.

A model $\mathcal{M}$ *satisfies a sequent* $\Sigma; \mathbb{M}; \Gamma \Rightarrow \Delta$, *written* $\mathcal{M} \models (\Sigma; \mathbb{M}; \Gamma \Rightarrow \Delta)$, *if for every mapping* ρ, *we have* $\mathcal{M}, \rho \models (\Sigma; \mathbb{M}; \Gamma \Rightarrow \Delta)$. *Finally, a sequent* $\Sigma; \mathbb{M}; \Gamma \Rightarrow \Delta$ *is valid, written* $\models (\Sigma; \mathbb{M}; \Gamma \Rightarrow \Delta)$ *if for every model* $\mathcal{M}$, *we have* $\mathcal{M} \models (\Sigma; \mathbb{M}; \Gamma \Rightarrow \Delta)$.

Selected rules of SeqC are reproduced from EW in Figure 1. The first key point to observe about the calculus is that the rules of each connective (e.g., rule $\to$R for implication) mimic directly the *semantic* definition of satisfaction for the

Axiom Rules

$$\frac{}{\varSigma; \mathrm{M}, x \leq y; \varGamma, x : p \Rightarrow y : p, \varDelta}\ \text{init} \qquad \frac{}{\varSigma; \mathrm{M}; \varGamma, x : A \text{ sf } B \Rightarrow x : A \text{ sf } B, \varDelta}\ \text{sf}$$

Logical Rules

$$\frac{\varSigma, y; \mathrm{M}, x \leq y; \varGamma, y : \alpha \Rightarrow y : \beta, x : \alpha \to \beta, \varDelta}{\varSigma; \mathrm{M}; \varGamma \Rightarrow x : \alpha \to \beta, \varDelta}\ {\to}\mathrm{R}$$

$$\frac{\varSigma; \mathrm{M}, x \leq y; \varGamma, x : \alpha \to \beta \Rightarrow y : \alpha, \varDelta \qquad \varSigma; \mathrm{M}, x \leq y; \varGamma, x : \alpha \to \beta, y : \beta \Rightarrow \varDelta}{\varSigma; \mathrm{M}, x \leq y; \varGamma, x : \alpha \to \beta \Rightarrow \varDelta}\ {\to}\mathrm{L}$$

$$\frac{\varSigma, y; \mathrm{M}, x S_A y; \varGamma \Rightarrow y : \alpha, x : A \text{ says } \alpha, \varDelta}{\varSigma; \mathrm{M}; \varGamma \Rightarrow x : A \text{ says } \alpha, \varDelta}\ \text{saysR} \qquad \frac{\varSigma; \mathrm{M}, x S_A y; \varGamma, x : A \text{ says } \alpha, y : \alpha \Rightarrow \varDelta}{\varSigma; \mathrm{M}, x S_A y; \varGamma, x : A \text{ says } \alpha \Rightarrow \varDelta}\ \text{saysL}$$

Frame Rules

$$\frac{\varSigma; \mathrm{M}, x \leq y, y \leq z, x \leq z; \varGamma \Rightarrow \varDelta}{\varSigma; \mathrm{M}, x \leq y, y \leq z; \varGamma \Rightarrow \varDelta}\ \text{trans} \qquad \frac{\varSigma; \mathrm{M}, x \leq y, y S_A z, x S_A z; \varGamma \Rightarrow \varDelta}{\varSigma; \mathrm{M}, x \leq y, y S_A z; \varGamma \Rightarrow \varDelta}\ \text{mon-S}$$

$$\frac{\varSigma; \mathrm{M}, x S_B y, y S_A z, x S_A z; \varGamma \Rightarrow \varDelta}{\varSigma; \mathrm{M}, x S_B y, y S_A z; \varGamma \Rightarrow \varDelta}\ \mathrm{I} \qquad \frac{\varSigma; \mathrm{M}, x S_B y, x S_A y; \varGamma, x : A \text{ sf } B \Rightarrow \varDelta}{\varSigma; \mathrm{M}, x S_B y; \varGamma, x : A \text{ sf } B \Rightarrow \varDelta}\ \text{basic-sf}$$

Fig. 1. SeqC: EW's labeled sequent calculus for $\mathrm{BL_{sf}}$, selected rules

connective (Definition 2). Second, the frame rules enforce all conditions (refl)–(mon-sf) on models listed in Definition 1, except the condition (mon) which is implicit in the inference rule (init). We write $\vdash (\varSigma; \mathrm{M}; \varGamma \Rightarrow \varDelta)$ to mean that $\varSigma; \mathrm{M}; \varGamma \Rightarrow \varDelta$ has a proof. SeqC is sound and complete with respect to the Kripke semantics.

Theorem 4 (Soundness and Completeness [14]). $\vdash (\varSigma; \mathrm{M}; \varGamma \Rightarrow \varDelta)$ *has a proof if and only if* $\models (\varSigma; \mathrm{M}; \varGamma \Rightarrow \varDelta)$

Decision procedure. Backwards proof search in SeqC may not terminate due to potentially infinite creation of new worlds through the rules ($\to$R) and (saysR). Hence, SeqC is not a decision procedure in itself. The key insight in EW is that despite this fact, suitable (and complex) termination conditions can be imposed on backwards search to make it terminate without losing completeness, thus yielding a decision procedure for $\mathrm{BL_{sf}}$. (Further, EW describes how countermodels can be extracted when search fails.) The specific termination conditions of the decision procedure are not important for this paper. However, the following two facts about the decision procedure *are* relevant.

First, by an analysis of EW's termination proof we can show that for any sequent that we wish to prove, we can compute a number n such that backwards search in SeqC can be pruned at depth n without losing completeness. This fact was not observed in EW, but it is not difficult to prove by a careful analysis of the termination proof in EW. We use this observation to derive a similar completeness-preserving bound ($3n + 1$ to be exact) for our goal-directed proof calculus, thus implying that our calculus can also be converted to a decision procedure.

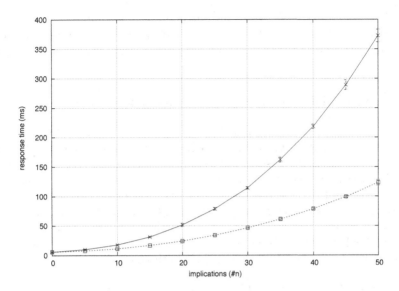

Fig. 2. Scalability of decision procedures based on SeqC and SeqG. The solid line is SeqC and the dotted line is SeqG.

Second, the number n is large — it is at least doubly exponential in the size of the sequent. Hence, the worst-case complexity of both our EW's decision procedure for BL_{sf} and ours for BL_{sf}^{G} is also quite bad. The difference is that on *practical policies*, EW's decision procedure attains at least exponential complexity, whereas our decision procedure remains polynomial (quadratic in many cases). This is a well-known fact from literature on goal-directed search and is, e.g., the reason why Prolog works efficiently in practice; here, we merely exploit this known fact for access control.

To illustrate the second point, we compare the time taken by an implementation of our decision procedure to that taken by EW's decision procedure on a simple, common policy: $\Gamma_n = \{p_1 \to q \land p_2 \to p_1 \land \ldots \land p_n \to p_{n-1}\}$. Here, $p_1, \ldots, p_n$ and q are atoms. The objective is to test the unprovable fact $\Gamma_n \Rightarrow q$. This example is representative of actual access policies, e.g., q may be a proposition representing a permission, p_1 may be condition needed for the permission, which may in turn be contingent upon p_2 and so on. The time taken by EW's procedure and our goal-directed procedures for this example are shown in Figure 2. The upper solid line, corresponding to EW, is exponential in n; the lower dotted line, corresponding to our goal-directed search, is quadratic in n. The reason for the difference is straightforward: EW's procedure works by blindly decomposing every implication in the policy using the rule ($\to$L) in every branch, which takes time exponential in n because the rule ($\to$L) has two premises. As explained in the next section, goal-directed search tries to prove the antecedents of only those implications that can help prove the goal. Thus it first tries to prove p_1, then p_2, etc. This results in an almost linear search space (the actual curve is quadratic because at each point in this search space, the procedure must try all n policy assumptions; however, all but one are immediately pruned). This simple but realistic example illustrates that goal-directed search can indeed be a pragmatic choice for theorem proving with access policies and motivates our technical work.

3 BL_{sf}^G: Goal-Directed Access Control Logic

Our main technical contribution is the development of the Hereditary-Harrop or HH fragment of BL_{sf}, which we call BL_{sf}^G, and a goal-directed proof search procedure for it, along with associated soundness, completeness and termination proofs. The HH fragment of first-order logic [17] is a generalization of the Horn fragment on which Prolog works, but still admits Prolog's top-down proof search. Our work generalizes this fragment to also include the connectives A says φ and A sf B and our proof search marries the formalism of backchaining in Prolog with labeled calculi, which we believe to be a novel contribution. The syntax of formulas in the fragment BL_{sf}^G is stratified into three categories.

$$\text{Goals} \quad G ::= p \mid A \text{ says } G \mid G_1 \wedge G_2 \mid G_1 \vee G_2 \mid N \to G \mid \top \mid \bot$$
$$\text{Clauses } D ::= p \mid G \to D \mid D_1 \wedge D_2 \mid \top \mid \bot \mid A \text{ says } D$$
$$\text{Chunks } N ::= D \mid N_1 \vee N_2 \mid N_1 \wedge N_2 \mid A \text{ sf } B$$

In our goal-directed calculus, goals can appear only on the right side in sequents, whereas clauses and chunks appear only on the left side in separate contexts. In logic programming notation, one may think of goals as the allowed queries, clauses as rules that constitute logic programs and chunks as additional constructs that combine logic programs (note that the leaf of any chunk is either a clause or A sf B). Not every connective is allowed in every category of syntax; this is necessary to guarantee completeness of goal-directed search. We do not go into the details of why this is the case as it is a standard but technically deep result in proof theory. The new interesting innovation here is deciding where to allow and disallow the new connectives A says φ and A sf B. (Interested readers are referred to existing work for details of the restriction, specifically [17] and [9, Chapter 6].)

Even though BL_{sf}^G is less expressive than BL_{sf} it is still much more expressive than Datalog-based access control languages like SecPAL[6] or DKAL[15], which also have efficient decision procedures. The main difference between a Datalog-based language and BL_{sf} is that the former will disallow disjunction altogether and also disallow implication in goals but both connectives can be useful in some cases (our next example illustrates this point). In return, Datalog-based languages have worst-case polynomial time decision procedures, which we forgo, settling for a bad worst-case execution time but efficient execution on policies of interest.

Example 1 (BL_{sf}^G Expressiveness). Suppose that *Alice* wants to share a picture *pic1* with the following policy (where $\mathcal{C}$ represents the finite domain of Alice's contacts): "Members of the group family can access *pic1* if *none* of them is a friend of a colleague of mine". Such a policy can be expressed in BL_{sf}^G as follows:

$$Alice \text{ says } (\bigwedge_{x \in \mathcal{C}} (family\_of(x, Alice) \rightarrow \bigwedge_{y \in \mathcal{C}} (colleague\_of(y, Alice) \rightarrow \neg friend\_of(y, x)))$$
$$\rightarrow (\bigwedge_{x \in \mathcal{C}} (family\_of(x, Alice) \rightarrow can\_access\_x\_pic1))$$

This example cannot be expressed in any Datalog-based access control logic because it uses left-nested implication.

3.1   SeqG: **Goal-Directed Proof Theory for** BL^G_{sf}

We now describe a goal-directed proof calculus, SeqG, for BL^G_{sf}. Following standard literature, the calculus uses more that one type of sequent; we describe each of them. A key difference from SeqC is that we allow only one formula in the right side of a sequent. This is complete because we are working in an intuitionistic logic, which has a disjunction property. Roughly, $\Sigma; \mathbb{M}; \Gamma \Rightarrow \Delta$ implies that there is some labeled formula $x : \varphi \in \Delta$ such that $\Sigma; \mathbb{M}; \Gamma \Rightarrow x : \varphi$. (We note that this is only an intuition. The precise disjunction property we need is presented in our technical report.)

It is simplest to think of the inference rules of SeqG as describing a proof search method, obtained by reading the inference rules bottom-up. Proof search starts in an *R-sequent*, which has the form $\Sigma; \mathbb{M}; \Gamma \Rightarrow x : G$. Here Γ is a multiset of labeled clauses of the form $w : D$ (no chunks are allowed in Γ in SeqG). More importantly, the rules for inferring a given R-sequent are *deterministic*: For each possible value of G, there is one rule that decomposes G into its subformulas in the premises, following the corresponding right rule in SeqC (see Figure 3). This forced decomposition of goal formulas justifies the adjective "goal-directed" for our calculus. The only exception to goal-directed decomposition is that after decomposing a goal of the form $N \rightarrow G'$, we push the chunk N into a special context denoted Ξ on the left and transition into what we call an *L-sequent*, where N is immediately decomposed with left rules (described below). After N has been decomposed completely, we return to work on G'. Eventually, in each branch, G must decompose to $\top$ (which succeeds immediately), $\bot$ (which fails immediately) or an atom p. In the last case, we backchain (through *N-sequents*), as in Prolog, by picking a suitable clause in Γ to prove p.

An L-sequent has the form $\Sigma; \mathbb{M}; \Gamma; \Xi \Leftarrow x : G$, where Ξ is a set of labeled chunks of the form $w : N$. The inference rules for an L-sequent (Figure 3) decompose the formulas in Ξ with left rules from SeqC. The results are of the form $w : D$, which are pushed into Γ (rule (pr)). Once Ξ is empty, search transitions to an R-sequent (rule (L2R)).

When a goal is reduced to an atom, search transitions from an R-sequent to an N-sequent of the form $\Sigma; \mathbb{M}; \Gamma \Leftrightarrow w : p$ (rule (atom)). There is only one rule to prove an N-sequent. This rule, called (choice), is the site of backchaining: It non-deterministically picks a clause $x : D$ from Γ (first premise), uses an *F-sequent* to determine what additional subgoals $w_1 : G_1, \ldots, w_n : G_n$, when proved, will cause $x : D$ to imply $w : p$ (second premise) and then tries to prove the subgoals (third premise).

F-sequents have the form $\Sigma; \mathbb{M}; x : D \ll w : p \mid Gl$ (here, $\ll$ replaces the sequent arrow; it is not a binary operator). The meaning of the sequent is that if all (labeled) subgoals in list Gl hold, then $x : D$ entails $w : p$. In an implementation, Gl is an output. Rules for proving F-sequents are mostly deterministic and work by decomposing D. The only exception to this determinism is the choice of rules ($\wedge L_1$) and ($\wedge L_2$) when $D = D_1 \wedge D_2$. Note that if no head in D matches p, then $\Sigma; \mathbb{M}; x : D \ll w : p \mid Gl$ cannot be established for any Gl.

There are two key points to observe about the calculus SeqG. First, unlike SeqC, there are no frame rules. Instead, the effect of all frame rules is collected into the operator $\overline{\Sigma; \mathbb{M}; \Gamma}$ in the premise of the rule (atom). This operator informally means "apply frame rules of SeqC to $\Sigma; \mathbb{M}; \Gamma$ to the extent possible". (For a formal definition, see our technical report.) Second, SeqG is largely a deterministic calculus. The *only* real source of non-determinism is in picking a clause in the first premise of the rule (choice) and in choosing between rules ($\wedge L_1$) and ($\wedge L_2$) in an F-sequent. It is because of this highly deterministic nature that proof search in SeqG works very efficiently in practice.

4 BL_{sf}^{G}: Soundness, Completeness and Termination

We prove formally that for the fragment BL_{sf}^{G}, the goal-directed calculus SeqG is sound and complete with respect to the calculus SeqC (and, hence, by Theorem 4, also with respect to the Kripke semantics). The proof of completeness (if direction of the theorem) is particularly non-trivial. We build on an earlier proof [9] for a variant of the logic BL_{sf}, but in the non-labeled setting.

Theorem 5 (Soundness and Completeness). $\vdash (\Sigma; \mathbb{M}; \Gamma \Mapsto x : \varphi)$ *in SeqG if and only if* $\vdash (\Sigma; \mathbb{M}; \Gamma \Rightarrow x : \varphi)$ *in SeqC.*

Next, we prove that SeqG can be used as a decision procedure, by bounding the maximum *depth* up to which branches need to be searched. Our argument is based on a reduction to SeqC. We first show that if a sequent has a proof of depth k in SeqC, it has a proof of depth no more than $3k + 1$ in SeqG. Second, we show that for every sequent, we can compute a number n such that if the sequent is provable, then it has a proof of depth n in SeqC. Together, the two imply that we can prune search in SeqG at depth $3n + 1$ without losing completeness. The first fact follows by a careful analysis of the proof of completeness in Theorem 5. As far as we are aware, this is a novel result for goal-directed search. The second fact follows from a combinatorial analysis of the termination proof of EW.

Lemma 6. *If* $\Sigma; \mathbb{M}; \Gamma \Rightarrow x : \varphi$ *is provable in SeqC with a derivation of depth k then* $\Sigma; \mathbb{M}; \Gamma \Mapsto x : \varphi$ *is provable in SeqG with a derivation of depth at most $3k + 1$.*

R sequents

$$\frac{\Sigma; M; \Gamma \Leftrightarrow x : p}{\Sigma; M; \Gamma \Mapsto x : p}\text{atom} \qquad \frac{\Sigma; M; \Gamma \Mapsto x : G_i}{\Sigma; M; \Gamma \Mapsto x : G_1 \vee G_2}\vee R_i \qquad \frac{\Sigma, y; M, x \leq y; \Gamma; y : N \Leftarrow y : G}{\Sigma; M; \Gamma \Mapsto x : N \to G}\to R$$

L sequents

$$\frac{\Sigma; M; \Gamma \Mapsto w : G}{\Sigma; M; \Gamma; \cdot \Leftarrow w : G}\text{L2R} \qquad \frac{\Sigma; M; \Gamma, x : D; \Xi \Leftarrow w : G}{\Sigma; M; \Gamma; \Xi, x : D \Leftarrow w : G}\text{pr} \qquad \frac{\Sigma; M; \Gamma; \Xi, x : N_1, x : N_2 \Leftarrow w : G}{\Sigma; M; \Gamma; \Xi, x : N_1 \wedge N_2 \Leftarrow w : G}\wedge L$$

$$\frac{}{\Sigma; M; \Gamma; \Xi, x : \bot \Leftarrow w : G}\bot L \qquad \frac{\Sigma; M; \Gamma; \Xi, x : N_1 \Leftarrow w : G \qquad \Sigma; M; \Gamma; \Xi, x : N_2 \Leftarrow w : G}{\Sigma; M; \Gamma; \Xi, x : N_1 \vee N_2 \Leftarrow w : G}\vee L$$

N sequents

$$\frac{x : D \in \Gamma \qquad \Sigma; M; x : D \ll w : p \mid w_1 : G_1 \dots w_n : G_n \qquad (\Sigma; M; \Gamma \Rightarrow w_i : G_i)_{i=1}^{n}}{\Sigma; M; \Gamma \Leftrightarrow w : p}\text{choice}$$

F sequents

$$\frac{}{\Sigma; M, x \leq w; x : q \ll w : p \mid \bullet}\text{init} \qquad \frac{}{\Sigma; M; x : A \text{ sf } B \ll x : A \text{ sf } B \mid \bullet}\text{sf}$$

$$\frac{\Sigma; M; x : D_i \ll w : p \mid Gl}{\Sigma; M; x : D_1 \wedge D_2 \ll w : p \mid Gl}\wedge L_i \qquad \frac{x \leq y \in M \qquad \Sigma; M; y : D \ll w : p \mid Gl}{\Sigma; M; x : G \to D \ll w : p \mid y : G, Gl}\to L$$

$$\frac{x S_A y \in M \qquad \Sigma; M; y : D \ll w : p \mid Gl}{\Sigma; M; x : A \text{ says } D \ll w : p \mid Gl}\text{saysL}$$

Fig. 3. SeqG: A goal-directed calculus for BL_{sf}^G, selected rules

Lemma 7. *For every sequent $\Sigma; M; \Gamma \Rightarrow x : \varphi$ a number n can be computed such that if $\Sigma; M; \Gamma \Rightarrow x : \varphi$ has a proof in SeqC, then it has a proof of depth less than n.*

Corollary 8 (Termination). *The rules of SeqG can be used as a decision procedure for BL_{sf}^G by pruning search in each branch at depth $3n + 1$ where n is the number from Lemma 7 for the starting sequent.*

5 SeqG^{AB}: Policy Abduction in BL_{sf}^G

We now extend the goal-directed sequent calculus SeqG to an abduction procedure. An abduction procedure, upon failure to find a proof, emits possible ways to extend the theory to complete the proof. In the context of access control, this amounts to listing additional credentials that will authorize a desired access. Our abduction calculus is directly based on a similar calculus from EW (that calculus extends SeqC). Although not a significant technical innovation, our abduction procedure works much faster in practice than that of EW, mirroring the difference between SeqC and SeqG (Section 2).

R sequents

$$\frac{\Sigma; \mathbb{M}; \Gamma \Leftrightarrow x : p \searrow_{m-1} \Theta}{\Sigma; \mathbb{M}; \Gamma \mapsto x : p \searrow_m \Theta} \text{atom}$$

$$\frac{\Sigma; \mathbb{M}; \Gamma \mapsto x : G_1 \searrow_{m-1} \Theta_1 \qquad \Sigma; \mathbb{M}; \Gamma \mapsto x : G_2 \searrow_{m-1} \Theta_2}{\Sigma; \mathbb{M}; \Gamma \mapsto x : G_1 \vee G_2 \searrow_m \Theta_1 \vee \Theta_2} \vee R$$

$$\frac{\Sigma, y; \mathbb{M}, x \leq y; \Gamma; y : N \Leftarrow y : G \searrow_{m-1} \Theta}{\Sigma; \mathbb{M}; \Gamma \mapsto x : N \to G \searrow_m \Theta} \to R$$

N sequents

$$\frac{T = \bigvee_{x : D \in \Gamma} \left\{ (\Theta_1 \wedge \ldots \wedge \Theta_n) \left| \begin{array}{l} \Sigma; \mathbb{M}, x : D \ll w : p \mid Gl \text{ and} \\ (Gl = g_1, \ldots, g_n) \text{ and} \\ (\Sigma; \mathbb{M}; \Gamma \mapsto g_i \searrow_{m-1} \Theta_i) \end{array} \right. \right\}}{\Sigma; \mathbb{M}; \Gamma \Leftrightarrow w : p \searrow_m T \vee AB(\Sigma; \mathbb{M}; \Gamma; w : p)} \text{choice}$$

$$\frac{\text{No other rule applicable or } (m - 1 = 0)}{\Sigma; \mathbb{M}; \Gamma \Leftrightarrow w : p \searrow_m AB(\Sigma; \mathbb{M}; \Gamma; w : p)} \text{AB}$$

Fig. 4. SeqG^{AB}: Abducible extraction for BL$^{G}_{sf}$, selected rules

Our abduction procedure is also presented as a calculus, SeqG^{AB}, shown in Figure 4. Judgments of the calculus have the form $\Sigma; \mathbb{M}; \Gamma \mapsto z : \varphi \searrow_m \Theta$. Here, m is a counter that decrements with each backward application of a rule. Initially, it is set to a value greater than the bound $3n + 1$ of Corollary 8. When m reaches 0 or when no other rule of SeqG can be applied, we apply rule (AB) to output an abducible Θ, which is a representation of additional credentials that could be used to prove the goal. Formally, Θ is a just a logical formula containing atoms p and formulas A says p at the leaves and only the connectives $\top, \bot, \vee$ and $\wedge$. The function $AB(\Sigma; \mathbb{M}; \Gamma; w : p)$, defined in EW, extracts such an abducible from the N-sequent. We reproduce the definition here:

$$AB(\Sigma; \mathbb{M}; \Gamma; w : p) = \left(\begin{array}{l} (\bigvee \{p \mid (\text{root}(\mathbb{M})) \leq w \in \mathbb{M}\}) \vee \\ (\bigvee \{A \text{ says } p \mid (\text{root}(\mathbb{M})) S_A w \in \mathbb{M}\}) \end{array} \right)$$

Here, root($\mathbb{M}$) is the world of $\mathbb{M}$ with which the first goal formula was labeled. Intuitively, for a given goal $w : p$, we look at the path between the root of $\mathbb{M}$ and y. Because the $\Sigma, \mathbb{M}$ and Γ are closed under backward application of rules (I), (mon-S) and (trans) (due to the closure in the premise of the rule (atom)), either $(\text{root}(\mathbb{M})) \leq y \in \mathbb{M}$ or $(\text{root}(\mathbb{M})) S_A y \in \mathbb{M}$ for some $A \in \mathcal{I}$. In the former case, it suffices to add the credential p to complete the proof and in the latter case it suffices to add the credential A says p to complete the proof. If both sets in the definition of $AB(\Sigma; \mathbb{M}; \Gamma; w : p)$ are empty, then $AB(\Sigma; \mathbb{M}; \Gamma; w : p) = \bot$.

An abducible Θ is *satisfied* by extending the current policy Γ with a set $F \subseteq \{p, A \text{ says } p \mid A \in \mathcal{I}\}$. Given such a set, we define the satisfaction relation $F \models \Theta$ in the obvious way: $F \models p$ iff $p \in F$; $F \models A$ says p iff $(A \text{ says } p) \in F$; $F \models \Theta_1 \wedge \Theta_2$ iff $F \models \Theta_1$ and $F \models \Theta_2$; etc. The following theorem states that

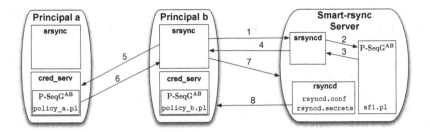

Fig. 5. The Smart-rsync Architecture

our abduction procedure is sound in the sense that if the abducible of a sequent is satisfied by F, then extending the hypotheses with F results in a provable sequent.

Theorem 9 (Soundness). *If* $\Sigma; \mathbb{M}; \Gamma \Rrightarrow w : p \searrow_m \Theta$ *and* $F \models \Theta$, *then* $\Sigma; \mathbb{M}; \Gamma \cup root(\mathbb{M}) : F \Rrightarrow w : p$.

A Prolog Implementation. We have implemented both the goal-directed calculus SeqG and its extension with abducibles, $\mathrm{SeqG}^{\mathrm{AB}}$, in Prolog and tested it with Prolog's two major interpreters, SWI-Prolog and GNUProlog. Our implementation closely mirrors the description of Sections 3.1 and 5. The implementation was used to test performance (e.g., Figure 2) and also as a black-box interpretation engine in a larger case-study with rsync that is described next.

6   Smart-rsync: Distributed File Synchronization with $\mathrm{SeqG}^{\mathrm{AB}}$

As a case study in the use of $\mathrm{BL}_{\mathrm{sf}}^{\mathsf{G}}$ and $\mathrm{SeqG}^{\mathrm{AB}}$, we extend the Unix synchronization program rsync to use $\mathrm{BL}_{\mathrm{sf}}^{\mathsf{G}}$ for representing authorization policies and $\mathrm{SeqG}^{\mathrm{AB}}$ to automatically gather credentials needed for authorization. The implementation consists of three new programs: srsyncd, srsync and cred_serv that run on different servers and clients. We also use the standard rsync server daemon, rsyncd, unmodified and a Prolog implementation of $\mathrm{SeqG}^{\mathrm{AB}}$. Figure 5 illustrates the various components of our implementation and their interaction with each other.

A client (principal b in the figure) wanting to synchronize a local file f with the server's version calls the server with our client program srsync (step 1 in the figure). This call is received by the server's daemon srsyncd. The daemon authenticates the request using a signed certificate accompanying the request, then it invokes an implementation of the calculus $\mathrm{SeqG}^{\mathrm{AB}}$ on its policy represented in $\mathrm{BL}_{\mathrm{sf}}^{\mathsf{G}}$ to determine what additional credentials, if any, are needed to authorize the access (step 2). The policy is provided to the server by an administrator through a configuration file. If no additional credentials are required to authorize the request, the server adds the permission to file f for principal b to a local permission file, rsyncd.secrets, and informs the client program of the update. The client program srsync then jumps to step 7 (described below) to synchronize the file.

If additional credentials are required, SeqG^{AB} returns to srsyncd an abducible (step 3), which srsyncd returns to the client (step 4). The client program, srsync, then communicates with the credential servers, cred_server, on various remote hosts to obtain the required credentials to satisfy the abducible. In general, to obtain a credential of the form A says p, it contacts the credential server of principal A (the principal to IP address mapping is provided to srsync in a configuration file). If there is more than one way to satisfy the abducible (because of the connective $\vee$ in the abducible), srsync tries the alternatives one at a time. In the figure, principal b contacts principal a for some credential (step 5). The contacted credential server then checks its own policy, also written in BL$^{G}_{sf}$, via a call to SeqG^{AB}, to find further abducibles needed to return the requested credentials. The client then recursively satisfies those abducibles. Eventually, this recursive process ends and the client is returned the requested credential (step 6), which it then passes to srsyncd to complete its authorization (step 7). At this point, srsyncd sets the permission to file f for the client's IP address in a special file rsyncd.secrets. The client then invokes the standard Unix program rsyncd on the server, which runs in parallel with srsyncd, to complete the synchronization (steps 7 and 8). rsyncd is configured to read permissions from rsyncd.secrets.

In our limited experience with Smart-rsync, we found it relatively easy to use. This is mainly given by two reasons. First, the proof construction process, including the recursive generation of abducibles, is totally automatic and, therefore, transparent to the user. Effort is involved in only setting the right policies, but this cannot be avoided in any case. Second, SeqG^{AB} works very efficiently (Section 2), so there isn't much visible overhead.

7   Related Work

Although BL$^{G}_{sf}$ is a fragment of BL$_{sf}$, its goal-directed proof theory is intrinsically different from the one presented in EW for BL$_{sf}$ [14]. Whereas the proof theory of BL$_{sf}$, SeqC, is a standard labeled sequent calculus, the proof theory of BL$^{G}_{sf}$, SeqG, is a marriage of labeled sequent calculi with backchaining search. SeqG works much faster in practice than SeqC but, unlike SeqC, SeqG cannot be used for policy saturation and countermodel generation.

There has also been prior work on goal-directed search in a related logic BL, presented in the second author's thesis [9, Chapter 6], but that work is based in an unlabeled sequent calculus. It does not consider the formula A sf B, but it does consider general first-order quantifiers. Without the use of labels, it is necessary to limit the nesting depth of A says φ in policies to 1 in the Hereditary Harrop fragment, so a policy like A says B says φ cannot be expressed in the goal-directed fragment of [9] (but can be expressed in BL$^{G}_{sf}$). Our proof of completeness of goal-directed search uses the same structure as that of [9].

Besides BL$_{sf}$ and BL, there is also a significant amount of work on goal-directed search in Datalog-based authorization languages. For example, the trust management language Soutei [19] is an extension of Datalog with domains that are similar to the connective A says φ and its implementation uses distributed backchaining search. The authorization policy language SecPAL [6], based on Datalog with constraints, uses tabled backchaining search to decide access policies in polynomial time. However, as discussed in Section 3, Datalog is less expressive than BL_{sf}^{G}.

8   Conclusion

We have presented BL_{sf}^{G}, a goal-directed fragment of BL_{sf} [14], and developed SeqG, a sound, complete and terminating goal-directed proof search based on it. We have explained through examples and simple experiments that although of the same worst-case complexity as BL_{sf}, BL_{sf}^{G} works much faster on realistic authorization policies. We have also modified SeqG to obtain an abduction calculus that produces missing credentials when an authorization fails and implemented it for performing automatic discovery of missing credentials in an extension of the Unix file synchronization program `rsync`.

The design space of access control logics is wide, ranging from very expressive, but intractable higher-order logics to restrictive, but efficiently decidable Datalog-based logics. We believe that goal-directed search over the Hereditary Harrop fragment, as in BL_{sf}^{G}, represents a reasonable balance of expressiveness and practical tractability.

References

1. Abadi, M.: Logic in access control. In: Proceedings of the IEEE Symposium on Logic in Computer Science (LICS), pp. 228–233 (2003)
2. Abadi, M., Burrows, M., Lampson, B., Plotkin, G.: A calculus for access control in distributed systems. ACM Transactions on Programming Languages and Systems (TOPLAS) 15(4), 706–734 (1993)
3. Avijit, K., Datta, A., Harper, R.: Distributed programming with distributed authorization. In: Proceedings of the ACM SIGPLAN Workshop on Types in Language Design and Implementation (TLDI), pp. 27–38 (2010)
4. Bauer, L.: Access Control for the Web via Proof-Carrying Authorization. Ph.D. thesis, Princeton University (2003)
5. Bauer, L., Garriss, S., McCune, J.M., Reiter, M.K., Rouse, J., Rutenbar, P.: Device-enabled authorization in the grey system. In: Zhou, J., López, J., Deng, R.H., Bao, F. (eds.) ISC 2005. LNCS, vol. 3650, pp. 431–445. Springer, Heidelberg (2005)
6. Becker, M.Y., Fournet, C., Gordon, A.D.: SecPAL: Design and semantics of a decentralized authorization language. Journal of Computer Security 18(4), 619–665 (2010)
7. Becker, M.Y., Russo, A., Sultana, N.: Foundation of logic-based trust management. In: Proceedings of the IEEE Symposium on Security and Privacy, pp. 161–175 (2012)
8. DeTreville, J.: Binder, a logic-based security language. In: Proceedings of the IEEE Symposium on Security and Privacy, pp. 105–113 (2002)

9. Garg, D.: Proof Theory for Authorization Logic and Its Application to a Practical File System. Ph.D. thesis, Carnegie Mellon University (2009)
10. Garg, D., Pfenning, F.: Non-interference in constructive authorization logic. In: Proceedings of the 19th IEEE Computer Security Foundations Workshop (CSFW), pp. 283–293 (2006)
11. Garg, D., Pfenning, F.: A proof-carrying file system. In: Proceedings of the IEEE Symposium on Security and Privacy, pp. 349–364 (2010)
12. Genovese, V., Rispoli, D., Gabbay, D.M., van der Torre, L.: Modal access control logic: Axiomatization, semantics and FOL theorem proving. In: Proceedings of the Fifth Starting AI Researchers' Symposium (STAIRS), pp. 114–126 (2010)
13. Genovese, V., Garg, D., Rispoli, D.: Labeled goal-directed search in access control logic (2012), Technical Report. Online at http://www.mpi-sws.org/~dg/
14. Genovese, V., Garg, D., Rispoli, D.: Labeled sequent calculi for access control logics: Countermodels, saturation and abduction. In: Proceedings of the 25th IEEE Symposium on Computer Security Foundations (CSF), pp. 139–153 (2012)
15. Gurevich, Y., Neeman, I.: Logic of infons: The propositional case. ACM Transactions on Programming Languages and Systems (TOPLAS) 12(2) (2011)
16. Jia, L., Vaughan, J.A., Mazurak, K., Zhao, J., Zarko, L., Schorr, J., Zdancewic, S.: Aura: A programming language for authorization and audit. In: Proceedings of the 13th ACM SIGPLAN International Conference on Functional Programming (ICFP), pp. 27–38 (2008)
17. Miller, D., Nadathur, G., Pfenning, F., Scedrov, A.: Uniform proofs as a foundation for logic programming. Annals of Pure and Applied Logic 51, 125–157 (1991)
18. Negri, S.: Proof analysis in modal logic. Journal of Philosophical Logic 34, 507–544 (2005)
19. Pimlott, A., Kiselyov, O.: Soutei, a logic-based trust-management system. In: Hagiya, M. (ed.) FLOPS 2006. LNCS, vol. 3945, pp. 130–145. Springer, Heidelberg (2006)
20. Schneider, F.B., Walsh, K., Sirer, E.G.: Nexus Authorization Logic (NAL): Design rationale and applications. ACM Transactions on Information and System Security (TISSEC) 14(1), 1–28 (2011)
21. Swamy, N., Chen, J., Fournet, C., Strub, P.Y., Bhargavan, K., Yang, J.: Secure distributed programming with value-dependent types. In: Proceedings of the 13th ACM SIGPLAN International Conference on Functional Programming (ICFP), pp. 266–278 (2011)
22. Viganò, L.: A framework for non-classical logics. Ph.D. thesis, Universität des Saarlandes (1997), also available as the book Labelled non-classical logics. Springer (2000)

A Use-Based Approach for Enhancing UCON

Christos Grompanopoulos, Antonios Gouglidis, and Ioannis Mavridis

Department of Applied Informatics, University of Macedonia,
Egnatia Street 156, 54006 Thessaloniki, Greece
`groban,agougl,mavridis@uom.gr`

Abstract. The security related characteristics of entities, the contextual information that describes them and the previous or concurrent usages exercised in the system are the criteria that the Usage CONtrol (UCON) family of models utilizes in the usage decision process. In this paper, a detailed classification of the aforementioned criteria along with a representative usage scenario for each category is presented, unveiling a number of UCON's limitations. In turn, a Use-based Usage CONtrol (UseCON) model is proposed that provides, for the creation of a usage decision, enhanced handling of information regarding context and previous or current usages exercised in the system. The enhanced capabilities of the proposed approach are demonstrated and discussed with the use of detailed application examples.

Keywords: Access control, usage control, UCON, UseCON.

1 Introduction

Controlling the access to the resources of a system is an essential requirement for every computer security system [2]. Traditional access control models utilize only a single criterion for the allowance of an access request, which is related to the security characteristics of the subject and object involved in the requested access [7]. More specifically, whenever a subject requests to access an object, the subject's clearance and the object's classification in Mandatory Access Control (MAC) models [8], the subject's identity in Discretionary Access Control (DAC) models [6] and an activated role from a set of authorized to the subject in Role Based Access Control (RBAC) models [9], are being utilized accordingly. Attribute based access control approaches [4] provide enhanced flexibility, when compared to the aforementioned access control models, by utilizing a number of subject and object security related characteristics, which are expressed in the form of attributes.

The Usage CONtrol (UCON) family of models [5] provides an integration of traditional access control, digital rights and trust management. Moreover, UCON encompasses attribute-based characteristics, along with the concepts of continuity of decision and attribute mutability. Through the utilization of continuity of decision in UCON, access control to a resource is being controlled either continuously through an ongoing rule, or only before an access is permitted through a pre rule, as in traditional access control models. Therefore the term usage is preferred to be used instead of access. Moreover, the complexity of

A. Jøsang, P. Samarati, and M. Petrocchi (Eds.): STM 2012, LNCS 7783, pp. 81–96, 2013.

modern computing environments requires the utilization of a number of criteria during the usage control decision making process. UCON, employs three criteria for the creation of a usage decision, namely, the security related characteristics (henceforth called *properties*), contextual information and information regarding previous or current usages of the system's entities. However, whenever a subject s requests the usage of an object o, the usage control decision making can be based on either information related to s and/or o, or on information related to other system entities (e.g. father's *properties* may have an influence on the son's permissions), and henceforth mentioned as *direct* and *indirect* entities of the requested usage, respectively.

Despite the fact that the usage control decision making process in UCON utilizes all the three criteria, these are commonly related only to the *direct* entities. Additionally, the attribute mutability mechanism of UCON introduces a number of limitations regarding the utilization of information about previous/current system usages. For example, no information about previous requested usages that were denied is recorded and no discrimination is done between the usages that have been revoked by the usage control system and the usages that have been terminated by a subject's request. Consequently, attribute mutability is unable to support a policy rule that is based on historical information regarding revoked usages. Moreover, modern computing environments present novel and complicated usage modes performed on objects by subjects, which are poorly supported through right entities in UCON. These complex operation modes require additional information that is essential for their execution, unlike the simple and straightforward operation modes that were previously supported by traditional access control models, e.g. read, write and execute operations in an operating system. For example, a banking transaction encompasses additional information, which is necessary for its operation, like the amount of transfer, the execution date etc.

This paper continues with a detailed categorization of the usage decision criteria utilized in UCON along with representative usage scenarios. Additionally, Sect. 2 highlights the challenging issues of utilizing the usage decision criteria in UCON. Section 3 proposes a new usage control model that extends UCON in order to provide mainly an enhanced utilization of the usage decision criteria and support for complicated usage modes. Application examples of the enhanced capabilities of the proposed model are presented in Sect. 4, and our conclusions are given in Sect. 5.

2   Utilization of Decision Criteria in UCON

UCON is a next generation access control model capable of evaluating a number of usage decision criteria for the allowance or not of a usage request. Nevertheless, a limited utilization of the aforementioned criteria, related to the *indirect* entities, is being noticed. A detailed description of the criteria's utilization, along with corresponding representative usage scenarios[1], follows.

---

[1] All the usage scenarios presented in this paper refer to pre authorization policy rules. However, the same criteria can also be applied to ongoing authorization rules.

2.1   Security Characteristics of Entities

Security characteristics of system entities in UCON, are associated with subject and object attributes. These attributes are utilized by functional predicates (authorizations) that are evaluated for the usage decision. An example of a usage scenario, where only the subject's and object's *properties* are taken into consideration during the usage decision making process, is implementation of a MAC policy in UCON as presented in [5]. More specifically, in a system that implements a MAC policy the following rules apply:

Usage Scenario 1. *A clearance attribute is assigned to all the subjects of the system. Moreover, a classification attribute that shares the same value domain with clearance, is also assigned to all the objects of the system. A relation exists between the values of clearance and classification, thus creating a form of hierarchy. Consequently, a subject can read an object only if its clearance overcomes the object's classification. In addition, an object can be written by a subject only if its classification overcomes a subject's clearance.*

Implementing the usage scenario 1 in UCON requires the utilization of authorization predicates that are evaluated on subject and object attributes. It is worth mentioning that UCON utilizes attributes for two purposes. More specifically, UCON does not only associates the entity's *properties* into the attribute values but also records into them the execution of system usages through the attribute mutability mechanism. Nevertheless, the values of the attributes that associate the *properties* of the entities are not updated automatically by the usage control system (update procedures) but only after the intervention of an administrator.

A limitation in UCON's authorizations is the fact that only the attributes from the *direct* entities are utilized. Nevertheless, in modern access control scenarios, it is possible that *properties* from *indirect* entities could also affect the authorization evaluation. A representative usage scenario that falls into the latter category is the following:

Usage Scenario 2. *Bob is a subscriber to a golf club that provides an amusement park for the children of its members. Bob's daughter, Alice is permitted to use all the available toys except from the carousel. Alice is permitted to use the carousel only if her father (Bob) is a member of the golden club category.*

When attempting to support the usage scenario 2 in UCON, Alice and carousel are considered to be the *direct* entities of the requested usage. However, during the usage decision making process, the values of Bob's attributes (e.g. his golden category membership) are also required. Due to the fact that Bob is an *indirect* entity, his attributes are not directly utilized in the corresponding authorization predicate. Nevertheless, if Alice is supported by an attribute "father" (that is assigned with the value of "Bob") then UCON is capable of resolving Bob's attribute values and consequently utilize them for the usage decision.

2.2 Contextual Information

Contextual information in UCON is associated with special system variables, which are entitled condition variables. These variables are utilized in condition predicates in order to create a usage decision. A usage scenario, as originally presented in [5], that requires the utilization of contextual information for the creation of the usage decision follows:

Usage Scenario 3. *The members of an institution are categorized into "faculty" and "student". The same categorization is also applied to the institution's areas. A member of a specific category (e.g. faculty) can exercise a right only in areas having the corresponding label (e.g. faculty areas).*

The presented approach in [5], proposes the evaluation of condition predicates that contain condition variables, which associate the location information with *direct* entities. However, in case where contextual information that is associated with the *indirect* entities is required for the usage decision, UCON seems to be incapable of resolving which condition variable represents the contextual information that is related with a particular system entity. A usage scenario where contextual information, which is associated with the *indirect* entities, is utilized for the usage decision follows:

Usage Scenario 4. *The doctors in a hospital are categorized into "seniors" and "juniors" in respect of their operational experience. Every "junior" doctor is supervised by a corresponding "senior" doctor. Whenever a "junior" doctor, named Alice, sets a request for the execution of a specialized operation, e.g. an open heart surgery, a policy directive requires the physical coexistence of Alice's "senior" doctor supervisor, named Bob.*

A policy rule in UCON that models the usage scenario 4 requires the comparison between two locations represented by two separated condition variables. The problem arises from the fact that Bob is an *indirect* entity. In such a case, specifying in UCON the particular condition variable that represents Bob's location seems to be impossible. In usage scenario 4, Alice is the *direct* entity of the usage request and only information related with her is utilized for the usage decision (condition). Even if UCON can represent with an Alice's attribute the fact that Bob is her supervisor, it is not possible to link at the same time Bob with a condition variable that represents his location. A solution could be provided by utilizing a number of condition variables that represent contextual information, which are irrelevant with the *direct* entities of the usage (e.g. "subjectsSupervisorLocation" may be the condition variable that represents the location of Bob). However, in a system with a large number of condition variables, such an implementation could result in a very complicated usage control system.

2.3 Historical Information of Usages

There are cases where historical information of previous or current usages executed by the *direct* entities, are needed to be utilized for usage decision. A usage scenario, where the previous usages of a subject may affect the allowance of a new usage requested by the same subject, is the following:

Usage Scenario 5. *An on-line collaborative educational software provides to its members the capability to post questions that can be answered by other members. However, a policy rule requires that a member is allowed to set a new question only if he had previously provided at least two answers to questions of other members.*

UCON is capable to support usage scenario 5 either through authorizations that incorporate attribute update procedures or through obligations. Specifically, if answering a question is considered to be a system usage, then each time a member provides an answer, the value of an attribute that records this usage is being updated (attribute mutability). Consequently, an authorization predicate is evaluated, based on the value of the aforementioned attribute, to allow or not to the posting of a new question. More specifically, attribute mutability in UCON actually implements a mechanism that records the allowed system usages in attributes of *direct* entities. For example, every time a user listens to a music file, a specific attribute of her is being updated. The values of these attributes do not represent security characteristics of entities and are updated automatically by the attribute mutability mechanism. As a result, information about allowed usages is utilized for usage decision. However, attribute mutability faces a number of issues. Firstly, it provides limited knowledge regarding the system usages (only the allowed ones that contain attribute updates). Secondly, attribute mutability complicates the policy administration process by adding attribute update procedures to policy rules.

Giving an answer to the question in usage scenario 5, can be considered as an obligation operation that must be executed twice as a criterion for allowing a usage request to post a new question. Obligation operations in UCON also represent usages that are exercised by subjects on objects. However, these obligation operations are discriminated from normal system usages because they are not controlled by a decision factor (Authorization, oBligation or Condition) and can be performed whenever required [10]. Nevertheless, in modern computing environments, it is possible for the usage decision to be dependent on past usages of *indirect* entities. A usage scenario that falls into this category is the following:

Usage Scenario 6. *In a research institute, a presentation room is equipped with both an interactive board and a media player. A policy rule requires that an employee is permitted to access the media player only if there is no other presentation in progress (usage of the interactive board) in the same room.*

Usage scenario 6 can be modeled only through UCON's obligations and not through authorizations that incorporate attribute mutability update procedures (as happened with usage scenario 5). Authorizations with attribute mutability fail to model scenario 6 because only the attributes of the *direct* entities of a usage are being updated. Moreover, authorizations utilize only attribute values from *direct* entities. Thus, the usage of the media player in usage scenario 6 without the utilization of obligations, seems to be impossible. However, a significant drawback of obligations is the lack of a feasible fulfillment mechanism, as it is mentioned in [3].

Therefore, we summarize the utilization of UCONs usage decision criteria in Table 1, based on the analysis performed in the aforementioned scenarios. The usage decision criteria are represented as rows on the left side of the table. These are, as identified, the *properties*, *context* (contextual information), and *history* (information regarding previous or concurrent usages) of the system entities. The far right two columns of the table represent the origin of the aforementioned criteria, which can stem from either a *direct* or an *indirect* entity. Thus, each usage decision criterion, originating from an entity, is utilized by UCONs decision factors that are expressed in the corresponding cell. Each UCON decision factor is represented by a letter (Authorization, oBligation, Condition) combined, if required, with the attribute mutability mechanism. For instance, if a usage decision criterion is based on historical information stemmed from *direct* entities, then UCON is capable of utilizing it by using either authorizations with attribute mutability (A+m) or obligations (B).

Table 1. Utilization of decision criteria in UCON

	Direct entities	Indirect entities
Properties	A	A
Context	C	-
History	A+m, B	B

3   The Proposed UseCON Model

The UCON family of models [5] is mainly characterized by fine grained control of resources, support for continuity of decision, and attribute mutability. However, as it is highlighted in the previous section, UCON presents a number of limitations regarding the utilization of criteria originating from *indirect* entities. In the rest of this section, the proposed Use-based usage CONtrol (UseCON) model is presented, as an approach to overcome the previously mentioned limitations in modern computing environments.

3.1   Elements

The UseCON model consists of three elements viz. entities, attributes and authorizations. An entity is associated with attributes and authorizations are utilized as usage decision factors.

Entities. We define the set of *entities* (E) containing all the entities $e_i, i = 1, 2, \ldots, n$, of a system, in the form of subjects (s), objects (o), actions (a) and uses (u). Subjects are entities that request to exercise operations on objects. A subject can be a human, a device or a software agent acting on behalf of a human. Objects can be physical entities, logical entities or services (e.g. a printer, a file or a database migration service). An entity operating as a subject in one usage may be the object in another usage [11]. Actions are entities that represent the operations that subjects can exercise on objects. The types of subjects or objects determine the types of the actions that can be exercised on them. For example, in case of a file, a list of possible actions could be read, write and execute.

A core entity of the UseCON model is the *use* entity. A use materializes all the characteristics of a usage that are critical for the decision making process. A use actually records the relation between the subject, object and action of a particular usage. The information contained in a use is not predetermined but is composed at the time of a usage request. The use entity that materializes the usage under consideration is the *direct* use while all the others are *indirect* uses.

Attributes. Subjects and objects are associated with security-relevant characteristics and capabilities, called attributes. In addition, contextual information, which in UCON is stored in condition variables [5], is associated in UseCON with subject or object attributes. In order to support complicated operations in modern computing systems, it is required for actions to be associated with attributes, too. An example of an action attribute in a file-related operation (e.g. write), could be an encryption key. Uses also have attributes in order to encompass information that is related to a combination of subject, object and action (e.g. the price of a service).

The set of entity attributes (EA) contains the attributes $ea_i, i = 1, 2, \ldots, m$ of all entities. A relation $\text{ATT}(e_i)$ denotes the association of an entity $e_i \in E$ with a tuple of attributes. We adopt the function notation in order to represent the value (range) that is assigned to an attribute (function) of a specific entity (domain). For example, in the expression Age(Alice) = 34, 'Alice' is an entity that has been associated with an attribute *Age* having a value of '34'. Every subject, object and action is associated with an *id* attribute, which has a unique value that remains constant during the life cycle of the usage control system [10]. When an instance of a use is created, it is associated with a tuple of attributes <*sid, oid, aid*> that have the same values with the particular *id* attributes of the *direct* entities (s, o, a) of the usage materialized by the use. Moreover, an additional *time* attribute is associated with each use [2]. The tuple <*sid, oid, aid, time*> is unique for each use (the usage of a subject on an object with an action at a specific time is also unique) and consequently operates as the identifier of the use.

---

[2] The value of the time attribute could vary from the time of usage request to the time of usage termination/completion and is left open as an implementation choice.

Each use is further associated with a *state* attribute, which embodies the accomplished status of the usage in progress, as it is described in [10] and augmented in [1]. The *state* attribute represents the current state of a usage, as depicted in Fig.1, and each time it receives one of the following values:

- Requested: On a request for a usage, appropriate attributes are associated with the use and proper values are assigned to them. The pre-authorization rules, which govern the requested usage, have not been evaluated yet.
- Activated: The requested usage has been allowed, as a result of successfully fulfilled pre-authorization rules, and is being executed.
- Denied: The requested usage has been denied, because it failed to satisfy the pre-authorization rules.
- Stopped: The allowed / ongoing usage has been terminated by the system due to a violation of an ongoing authorization rule.
- Completed: The usage that has been completed due to a subject's intervention.

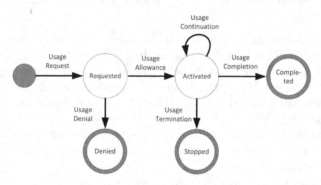

Fig. 1. Use state-transition diagram

Authorizations. UseCON's usage decision factor is authorizations. Authorizations are able to utilize all the three criteria described in the previous section, regardless they are originating from *direct* or *indirect* entities. A detailed description of authorizations follows:

- **Attribute dependent Authorizations:** AdAs are functional predicates that are evaluated on entity attributes. However, attribute values in UseCON contain both *properties* and contextual information of entities, excluding historical information of usages (as introduced by the attribute mutability mechanism in UCON).
- **Usage dependent Authorizations:** In UseCON, all the system usages are recorded with the help of the use entity. UdAs are functional predicates that are evaluated on historical information of usages. Thus, a requested usage can be permitted only if another usage has been previously exercised. For example, an UdA can model a policy rule requiring that a student can present the work of his team if and only if he has previously been registered

in the system. However, UseCON's UdAs are able to support more complicated rules. Hardening the previous example, it may be required that the
presentation of a team's work by the student is allowed if any member of his
team has already been registered. UdAs are more flexible to utilize historical
information of usages compared to UCON's authorizations combined with
attribute mutability, due to the fact that they support historical information
from both *direct* and *indirect* entities.

Associating contextual information with entity attributes, results in the replacement of UCON's conditions with authorizations. Moreover, operations required
by UCON's obligations are handled as usages in UseCON. Therefore, exercising
obligation operations in UseCON is verified by searching the history of *indirect*
use. It is worth mentioning that post obligations, which are operations that must
be fulfilled after the termination of a usage, are not supported by the proposed
model and they are considered to be an administration issue. The UseCON elements and their relations are depicted in Fig.2.

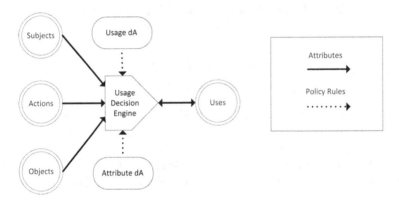

Fig. 2. UseCON usage control system

3.2   UseCON Sub-models

UseCON utilizes only AdAs and UdAs as factors for usage decision. Applying
continuity of decision results in four UseCON sub-models, as follows.

Pre-Attribute dependent Authorizations (preAdA). A subject is permitted to exercise an action on an object if a predicate preAdA is satisfied. There
is no further (ongoing) control after the usage's allowance. More specifically, a
preAda rule is defined as predicate that utilizes the attributes of the use that
materializes the requested usage as follows [3]:

---

[3]   A predicate is also able to utilize the attributes of the direct entities, by applying
the reverse id^{-1} function (e.g. $id^{-1}(sid(u)) = s$) on the id values of the entities a.
Moreover, if the value of an attribute from a direct entity is the id of an indirect
entity then a predicate can also utilize its attribute values for the evaluation. The
same applies to all UseCON's sub-models.

$$allowed(s, o, a) \Rightarrow preAdA\,(ATT(u)) \tag{1}$$

Pre-Usage dependent Authorizations (preUdA). A preUdA rule utilizes historical information of usages. More specifically, a preUdA rule is defined as a predicate that utilizes the attributes from both the *direct* use (u) and the *indirect* uses (u'). The number of the *indirect* uses that fulfill the preUdA predicate should satisfy a relational condition (less, greater or equal) with a specified natural number. The semantics of a preUdA rule is as follows:

$$allowed(s, o, a) \Rightarrow |\{u' \in U : preUdA\,(ATT(u), ATT(u'))\}| \otimes k \tag{2}$$

In the previous notation, $k \in \mathbb{N}$, the symbol $\otimes$ is replaced by a relational operator, U is the set of use entities and $|B|$ denotes the number of elements of set B.

Ongoing-Attribute Dependent Authorizations (onAdA). An onAdA rule utilizes the same elements with preAdA and is defined as follows:

$$\begin{aligned} allowed(s, o, a) &\Rightarrow true \\ stopped(s, o, a) &\Leftarrow \neg onAdA(ATT(u)) \end{aligned} \tag{3}$$

The semantics of an onAdA functional predicate are the same with a preAdA one.

Ongoing-Usage Dependent Authorizations (onUdA). An onUdA rule utilizes the same elements with preUdA and is defined as follows:

$$\begin{aligned} allowed(s, o, a) &\Rightarrow true \\ stopped(s, o, a) \Leftarrow |\{u' \in U : onUdA(ATT(u), ATT(u'))\}| &\otimes k \end{aligned} \tag{4}$$

The semantics of an onUdA functional predicate are the same with a preUdA one.

4   Examples of UseCON Enhanced Capabilities

UseCON model enhances UCON's fundamental design guidelines as continuity of decision and attribute based usage control by introducing a number of innovative modeling decisions. Specifically, UseCON directly associates entities with contextual information and also replaces UCON's rights with actions enhanced with attributes. The aforementioned decisions in combination with the augmented utilization of historical information through the support of the new *use* entity, results in enhanced capabilities, as demonstrated in the following examples.

4.1   Abstraction of Actions

In UCON, rights correspond to permissions for subjects to execute usage functions on objects. However, rights are not described with attributes. The replacement of UCON's simple rights with UseCON's actions described by attributes, provides enhanced capabilities, as follows.

Simplifying the Administration of Policy Rules. A UCON policy rule governs the allowance either for a specific right or all rights. Thus, every time a new right is introduced in the security system, the policy administrator should most likely create a corresponding policy rule that permits its usage. However, in a computing environment that encompasses a great number of rights, policy administration is becoming a complicated process. In UseCON, the description of actions by attributes provides the policy administrator with the capability to govern the allowance of a set of actions by a single policy rule, as presented in the following example.

Example 1. *A company that offers location discovery services provides the capability to its customers to require the location of an object. A customer, according to his classification, can request the location of an object with a desired accuracy level. For example, members of the "golden" category might request the location of an object with an accuracy expressed in meters, while regular users are able to request the location of an object in kilometers.*

Modeling example 1 in UCON requires the creation of a unique right entity for each accuracy level of the location discovery service. Moreover, the policy administrator must create an additional policy rule (authorization, condition or obligation) that governs the allowance of the particular right's request. Hence, it is impossible with UCON modeling to create a policy rule that governs the allowance of a subset of rights e.g. rights that model location discovery services.

However, the replacement of UCON rights with UseCON actions associated with attributes provides the capability to model the relation that possibly exists between actions. More specifically, in example 1, every action is associated with an attribute, named *type*. Actions that refer to location discovery services have a unique *type* attribute value e.g. "LocService". Thus, by utilizing the value of *type*, a policy rule is able to govern the allowance of all the actions that represent location discovery services.

The UseCON modeling of example 1 results into the following preAdA rules:

accuracy : $A \to W$ Location accuracy level supported by the service
category : $S \to C$ Customer's category. "Premium" or "Regular"
type : $A \to T$ Type of service. "LocService" for location discovery

$$allowed(s, o, a) \Rightarrow type(a) = \text{``LocService''} \land category(s) = \text{``premium''}$$
$$allowed(s, o, a) \Rightarrow type(a) = \text{``LocService''} \land category(s) = \text{``regular''}$$
$$\land\, accuracy(s) = \text{``kilometers''}$$

The first preAdA rule governs the allowance of two actions (location discovery service with accuracy level of kilometers and location discovery service with accuracy level of meters). The additional accuracy attribute utilized in the second preAdA rule represents the accuracy level of the location discovery service e.g. "kilometers" or "meters".

Negotiating Action Parameters. The use of action's attributes in UseCON does not only simplify the policy administration process, as mentioned previously, but also provides enhanced capabilities for negotiating the action parameters of a usage request.

In UCON, a subject is able to request the usage of a specific right but it is not possible to request a "generic" right, e.g. the location of an object without specifying particular accuracy requirements. However, the utilization of the attribute *type*, as introduced in UseCON modeling of example 1, is further able to provide to subjects the capability to request the execution of a usage by only specifying the type of the action. Therefore, the subject of example 1 may request the execution of any action that contains the value "LocService" in the *type* attribute. When the UseCON decision creation engine receives such a request, it evaluates the policy rules that govern the allowance of actions with the specific value in the attribute *type*. Consequently, the usage control system does not respond with a simple allow or deny message, but with a list containing all the suggested actions that the subject is permitted to exercise. Thus, if the returned list is not empty, the subject can select the action that satisfies her needs and send a new request. The sequence of messages exchanged between the subject and the UseCON usage decision engine is depicted in Fig. 3.

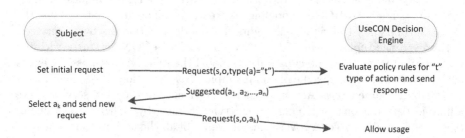

Fig. 3. Sequence of messages for action negotiation

Supporting Action Hierarchies. Relevant actions can participate in an action hierarchy. An example of action hierarchy in a hospital sector is presented in [5] where an action "a doctor writes a remedy on a patients record" is considered to be senior to the action "a doctor simply reads the patients medical history". The hierarchy of actions depends on the security policy of the particular usage control system. However, the policy rule for a senior action dominates on the policy rules for all its junior actions. A more detailed example is the following:

Example 2. *The security policy of a hospital defines that only doctors can read the medical history of a patient. However, altering a patient medical record is permitted only to doctors that have the same specialty with the category of the patient's illness.*

As UCON rights are not described with attributes, it seems impossible to model the relations between them and form a hierarchy. In UseCON, however, the classification of actions is possible through the utilization of action attributes. Consequently, both the policy administrator and the usage control mechanism are able to utilize such hierarchy information in order to enhance the expressiveness of the policy rules and to simplify the usage decision creation process, respectively. For example, whenever a subject requests the usage of two directly related actions, a proper usage control mechanism should evaluate only the policy rule that permits the senior action in the action hierarchy. In addition, in UseCON modeling of example 2, the policy administrator is capable of creating a rule that permits the execution of a read action on a medical record of a patient (a junior action), by examining if the requesting subject has previously exercised a write action on the medical record of any patient (a senior action). The modeling of example 2 with the use of a preUdA rule follows:

snr : $A \rightarrow 2^A$ The set that contains the ids of the senior actions

$$allowed(s, o, a) \Rightarrow |\ \{u' \in U : status(u') = \text{``completed''} \land sid(u') = id(s) \land$$
$$oid(u') = id(o) \land aid(u') \in snr(a)\ \}\ | \geq 1$$

4.2   Utilization of Usage Information

The introduction of the *use* entity in UseCON provides new capabilities to the policy administrator. The utilization of use entities along with their attributes values provides the capability for enhanced utilization of historical information of usages and proper association of information to the system entities, as it is presented in the following examples.

Supporting Transactions. Some *properties* are not related with a single entity (subject or object), but with a combination of them. For example, an object attribute in UCON is associating information originating either directly from the object or from the right - object combination e.g. the price of the service [5]. Thus, if different rights can be exercised on an object, a separate *price* attribute for every one of these rights should be created. In addition, a detailed analysis unveils that the price of a service is actually associating information originating form the subject - object - right combination. More specifically, different customers may be charged with different prices for the execution of the same right on the same object. Therefore, the association of *properties* in a usage control system either with a single entity or with a usage is proposed. The former kind of information is associated with the related entity attributes while the latter with the corresponding use attributes.

While the values of entity attributes are set by an administrative operation, the creation of use entities and their corresponding attribute values are not predetermined but they are accomplished during the operation of the usage control system. More specifically, a subject entity and its attribute values are determined before the execution of any usage. However, a use entity and its attribute values are created only when a subject requests the corresponding usage. The values of use attributes should be assigned with rules that are application dependent and utilize the attribute values of the other entities participating in the usage. An example of information that is associated with use attributes is related to transactions. A transaction is a complicated system process that is composed from a set of particular system usages. In the UseCON model, every usage is modeled through a use entity that is associated with a *transaction* attribute. Uses that belong to the same *transaction* can share the same value of the *transaction* attribute. By utilizing proper values of use attributes, the policy administrator is able to define usage control rules with enhanced expressiveness. An example of the transaction attribute utilization in the creation of the usage decision follows.

Example 3. *In an accounting office the whole set of usages that update the files of a specific customer are forming a transaction. All these usages can be performed by a number of different employees and may concern a number of different files. However, because all these usages belong to the same transaction, they should be covered with the same privacy statement executed once by a single employee.*

In the following preUdA rule that models example 3 in UseCON, the execution of a *consent* action by any usage of the transaction is examined:

tr $: U \to T$ The name of the transaction where the usage belongs to

$$allowed(s, o, a) \Rightarrow | \ \{u' \in U: status(u') = \text{``completed''} \land tr(u') = tr(u) \land$$
$$aid(u') = \text{``consent''} \ \} \ | \geq 1$$

Enhanced Utilization of Historical Usage Information. Attribute mutability in UCON presents a number of limitations. For example, an attribute update procedure is executed only after the allowance of a requested usage. Thus, the denied usage requests are not recorded and information regarding such facts is not utilized for subsequent usage decisions. In addition, in an UCON ongoing rule, the same attribute update procedures will be executed if either the usage has been terminated by the subject or revoked by the usage control system, due to the ongoing rule violation. Consequently, UCON is incapable to discriminate the usages terminated by the subject from those revoked by the usage control system.

The UseCON model provides with comprehensive knowledge about the previous system usages through the utilization of the use entity. More specifically, the *state* attribute of a use entity provides the ability to discriminate between requested, active, denied, revoked and terminated usages. Such information can be utilized for future usage decisions. An example, where information about previously revoked usages is used for the creation of the usage control decision follows.

Example 4. *In a Digital Rights Management (DRM) system there is an upper bound limit on the number of simultaneous usages of an object by subjects. Whenever the maximum number of usages of an object is exceeded, several revocation strategies can be applied [5]. However, as a mean of policy fairness, the execution of a usage that has been previously revoked by the system is freely permitted without the evaluation of additional policy rules.*

The corresponding preUdA rule that implements the policy described in example 4 follows:

$$allowed(s, o, a) \Rightarrow | \{u' \in U : status(u') = \text{``revoked''} \wedge sid(u') = sid(u) \wedge$$
$$aid(u') = aid(u) \wedge oid(u') = oid(u)\} | \geq 1$$

5   Conclusion

In this paper, we highlighted through representative usage scenarios the additional requirements that are posed when attempting to utilize the UCON family of models in modern computing environments. A classification of usage decision criteria, originating from either *direct* or *indirect* entities, highlighted the limitations of UCON model and spotted the necessity for a new use-based usage control model. UseCON model presented in this paper, supports complicated operations and eliminates the restrictions imposed by the attribute mutability mechanism regarding the utilization of historical information of usages. A number of examples were presented in order to demonstrate the enhanced capabilities of the UseCON model. The simplification of the policy administration process and the support of enhanced policy rules regarding their expressiveness, are included in the advantages of the proposed model. Moreover, the new characteristics of UseCON can be utilized by properly designed usage decision mechanisms in order to provide more sophisticated capabilities, as these are presented in the usage negotiation and actions hierarchy examples. The detailed investigation and analysis of the performance implications, if any, of the UseCONs modeling decisions is considered as future work.

References

1. Katt, B., Zhang, X., Breu, R., Hafner, M., Seifert, J.P.: A general obligation model and continuity: enhanced policy enforcement engine for usage control. In: Proceedings of the 13th ACM Symposium on Access Control Models and Technologies, SACMAT 2008, pp. 123–132. ACM, New York (2008)

2. Lampson, B.W.: Protection. SIGOPS Oper. Syst. Rev. 8, 18–24 (1974)
3. Lazouski, A., Martinelli, F., Mori, P.: Usage control in computer security: A survey. Computer Science Review 4(2), 81–99 (2010)
4. OASIS: Oasis extensible access control markup language (xacml) tc (2011), http://www.oasis-open.org/
5. Park, J., Sandhu, R.: The ucon abc usage control model. ACM Trans. Inf. Syst. Secur. 7, 128–174 (2004)
6. Qiu, L., Zhang, Y., Wang, F., Kyung, M., Mahajan, H.R.: Trusted computer system evaluation criteria. In: National Computer Security Center (1985)
7. Samarati, P., de Capitani di Vimercati, S.: Access control: Policies, models, and mechanisms. In: Focardi, R., Gorrieri, R. (eds.) FOSAD 2000. LNCS, vol. 2171, pp. 137–196. Springer, Heidelberg (2001)
8. Sandhu, R.S.: Lattice-based access control models (1993)
9. Sandhu, R., Coyne, E., Feinstein, H., Youman, C.: Role-based access control models. Computer 29(2), 38–47 (1996)
10. Zhang, X., Parisi-Presicce, F., Sandhu, R., Park, J.: Formal model and policy specification of usage control. ACM Trans. Inf. Syst. Secur. 8, 351–387 (2005)
11. Zhang, X., Sandhu, R., Parisi-Presicce, F.: Safety analysis of usage control authorization models. In: Proceedings of the 2006 ACM Symposium on Information, Computer and Communications Security, ASIACCS 2006, pp. 243–254. ACM, New York (2006)

Analysis of Communicating Authorization Policies

Simone Frau and Mohammad Torabi Dashti

Institute of Information Security, ETH Zürich

Abstract. We present a formal language for specifying distributed authorization policies that communicate through insecure asynchronous media. The language allows us to write declarative authorization policies; the interface between policy decisions and communication events can be specified using guards and policy updates. The attacker, who controls the communication media, is modeled as a message deduction engine. We give trace semantics to communicating authorization policies, and formulate a generic reachability problem. We show that the reachability problem is decidable for a large class of practically-relevant policies specified in our formal language.

1 Introduction

Ideally, by enforcing distributed authorization policies, the behavior of a distributed system should be constrained so that the distributed system achieves its functional goals without ever entering an insecure state. In a hospital, for example, a typical functional goal is to enable the medical personnel to access the health records of their patients; an instance of the unreachability of insecure states is: no one else can (ever) access these records. Decentralized trust management systems, or distributed authorization languages, play a pivotal role in securing distributed systems [1–5]. They allow us to formally reason about distributed authorization policies, even prior to their deployment.

We are, in this paper, concerned with policy decision points (PDPs) that communicate with each other by exchanging messages over insecure media. The policies of such PDPs change due to receive events (e.g. upon receiving a public key certificate), and they in turn constrain the communication events (e.g. access tokens are sent only to the principals whose credentials have not been revoked). As PDPs communicate over insecure media, attacks may occur when, for instance, expired certificates are replayed, certificate revocation lists are delayed, messages are tampered with, etc. We let the attacker be in direct control of the communication media. This view is motivated by the workings of security-sensitive distributed services, such as federated identity management systems (OAUTH [6], etc.). We define a formal language for specifying communicating authorization policies, and give an algorithm for deciding reachability for a large class of such policies. This builds upon our previous work on analyzing security-sensitive distributed services [7].

A. Jøsang, P. Samarati, and M. Petrocchi (Eds.): STM 2012, LNCS 7783, pp. 97–112, 2013.

In our formalism, we model *communicating authorization policies* as a finite number of *processes*. Intuitively, a process represents a PDP. Each process consists of a finite number of *threads* that share a *policy*. Threads are finite sequences of communication events; they run in parallel and exchange messages with the threads of other processes over insecure media. The policy of a process is a (declarative) program which models the shared authorization policy that the threads of the process evaluate.

Threads communicate by sending and receiving messages, as is common in asynchronous message passing environments. Each send event is constrained by a *guard*, and each receive event results in an *update* of a process' policy. Intuitively, guards and updates belong to the *policy level*, as opposed to send and receive events which constitute the *communication level*. See Figure 1. From an operational point of view, guards are statements that, if derivable from the policy of a process, allow the process to perform a corresponding send action (cf. Dijkstra's guarded command language). Updates are also statements at the policy level. When a process receives a message in one of its threads, it updates its policy correspondingly. Intuitively, updates associate meanings to the messages a process receives in terms of statements at the policy level. For example, a signed X.509 certificate sent by a certificate authority *means* that the authority endorses the public key and its owner, mentioned in the certificate.

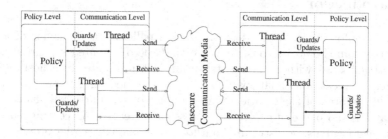

Fig. 1. Two processes (i.e. policy decision points), each with two threads

We assume an all-powerful attacker who is in direct control of the insecure communication media; see Figure 1. In fact, the messages the PDPs exchange are passed through the attacker. This is a common (worst-case scenario) assumption in the literature. The message inference capabilities of the attacker may reflect, e.g., the Dolev-Yao threat model [8]. The attacker can indirectly manipulate the policies of the participating PDPs by, e.g., sending tampered messages which affect the update statements.

Contributions. Our main contributions are: **(1)** We present a formalism for specifying communicating authorization policies, and their hostile environment. **(2)** We give an algorithm for deciding reachability of communicating authorization policies. Given a formal model of the policy decision points and the attacker, we can decide (under certain conditions, specified precisely in § 4) whether, or not, an (insecure) state is reachable. For instance, questions of the form *can the attacker learn the content of a certain file?*, or *can Ann ever be authorized to access a certain document stored at the file server?* are expressible as reachability problems. Note that communication level events, policy level computations, and the interface between the two are all taken into account when deciding reachability. This sets apart our decision algorithm from those for deciding secrecy in security protocols, and those for deciding reachability in dynamic authorization languages (see our related work, § 5).

Structure of the paper. In § 2, we introduce the main features of our formal language with a few examples. The syntax and semantics of the language are formally defined in § 3. In § 4 we identify a set of communicating authorization policies for which the reachability problem is decidable. All proofs are relegated to [9], due to space constraints. In § 5 we review the related work.

2   Examples of Communicating Authorization Policies

We introduce the main features of our formalism through three examples. The first example concerns an OAUTH 2.0 authorization endpoint that is constrained by an RBAC system with transitive attributes. The second example pertains to secure delegation of trust for distributing public key certificates. The third example discusses mechanisms for trust and permission revocation.

2.1   OAUTH, RBAC and Transitive Attributes

Suppose that Ann wants a remote print service, called RPS, to access (on her behalf) the file *brochure.pdf* stored on a file server. RPS uses OAUTH 2.0's Authorization Code Flow protocol [6] to point Ann to the file server where she can authenticate herself and grant RPS access to the file. After Ann authenticates herself to the file server, the file server needs to first check that Ann is authorized to access the file. If so, the file server sends a URI redirect message to Ann's Web browser, along with an authorization code. RPS can use the authorization code to access the file, after authenticating itself at a *token endpoint*. To keep the example simple, we do not model the entire scenario. Instead, we focus on the file server, which is an OAUTH 2.0 *authorization endpoint*.

Suppose that the file server is constrained by an RBAC policy with two roles, *user* and *admin*. The server stores two sorts of files: *public* and *confidential*. Any symbolic link to a public file is deemed public, and any link to a confidential file is deemed confidential. By transitivity, links to "links to confidential (resp. public) files" are confidential (resp. public). Users may access any public file or public link; admins may access any confidential file or link. Admins inherit all the rights attributed to users. A formalization of the file server's policy:

$$\mathcal{K}(has\_role(A, user)) \leftarrow \mathcal{K}(has\_role(A, admin))$$
$$\mathcal{K}(can\_access(A, F)) \leftarrow \mathcal{K}(has\_role(A, user)), \mathcal{K}(has\_attrib(F, public))$$
$$\mathcal{K}(can\_access(A, F)) \leftarrow \mathcal{K}(has\_role(A, admin)), \mathcal{K}(has\_attrib(F, confid))$$
$$\mathcal{K}(has\_attrib(link\_to(F), X)) \leftarrow \mathcal{K}(has\_attrib(F, X))$$

The rules above are Horn clauses. We use capital letters to denote variables, and constants are written with lower-case letters. The predicate symbol $\mathcal{K}$, standing for *knows*, denotes the knowledge of the file server's policy engine, which "knows" pieces of information; e.g. the file server's policy engine knows that Ann has the role admin. The Horn clauses thereby model the server's information inference rules. For example, the first rule states that the file server knows that if A has the role admin, then A has the role user too, due to the role hierarchy. The second (resp. the third) rule above states that users (resp. admins) can read public (resp. confidential) files. The fourth rule states that links to public (resp. confidential) objects are themselves public (resp. confidential). We will often omit $\mathcal{K}$ to avoid unnecessary cluttering.

The extensional policy (or knowledge) of the file server reflects the "current state" of the policy. For example, Ann is an admin, and *brochure.pdf* is public:

$$has\_role(ann, admin)$$
$$has\_attrib(brochure.pdf, public)$$

Now, let us consider the communication between Ann and the file server. After Ann permits RPS to access *brochure.pdf*, the file server sends back an authorization code to Ann's *user agent*, e.g. her Web browser. The following guarded send event is part of the file server's thread:

$$\{can\_access(A, F)\}\{\}^- \blacktriangleright \mathsf{snd}(auth\_code(F), R\_URI, S\_INF)$$

The send event $\{s_1, ..., s_j\}\{n_1, ..., n_k\}^- \blacktriangleright \mathsf{snd}(m)$ can be executed only if statements $s_1, \cdots, s_j$ all follow from the policy, and at least one of $n_1, \cdots, n_k$ does not. That is, if the file server's policy implies $can\_access(ann, brochure.pdf)$, then an authorization code for the file *brochure.pdf* is sent to Ann's browser. The authorization code is accompanied with a redirection URI R_URI and RPS's state information S_INFO. The user agent redirects Ann to RPS, which uses the authorization code to access the requested file after authenticating itself to a token endpoint. Note that, given the policy and extensional knowledge above, the file server can indeed derive $can\_access(ann, brochure.pdf)$.

2.2   Trust Relations

Ann knows that the root certificate authority RCA is trusted on public keys. Ann asks RCA for Piet's public key. RCA is however temporarily overloaded, and redirects Ann's request to a local certificate authority CA. RCA trusts CA on public keys. CA sends back to Ann a public key of Piet. Here, we focus on two processes: Ann and CA.

The policy of the process CA contains all public keys belonging to Piet in our scenario. CA also stores a set of revoked public keys; for example, the set $\{is\_pk\_of(pk_1, piet), is\_pk\_of(pk_2, piet), is\_pk\_of(pk_3, piet), is\_revoked(pk_2)\}$. CA signs and sends out valid public keys upon request. The following thread, which is a sequence of two events, within the CA process models this behavior:

$$\mathsf{rcv}(A, P) \blacktriangleright \{\}\{\}^\neg$$
$$\{is\_pk\_of(K, P)\}\{is\_revoked(K)\}^\neg \blacktriangleright$$
$$\mathsf{snd}(sig(ca, pk\_cert(P, K)), sig(rca, is\_pk\_certified(ca)))$$

Here CA receives a pair of names A and P: A is asking CA for a public key of P. This message could have been redirected to CA by, e.g., RCA. Receiving this message binds the variables A and P in the rest of the thread. We remark that the events of the thread are executed sequentially. The message neither adds policy statements to CA's extensional knowledge, nor retracts any policy statements; hence the sequence $\{\}\{\}^\neg$ after rcv. We come back to this point shortly. Next, the CA sends out the message $pk\_cert(P, K)$, signed by CA, denoting that CA endorses K as a valid public key of P. The endorsement is accompanied by a message signed by RCA which certifies that RCA trusts CA on public keys $(is\_pk\_certified(ca))$. CA is assumed to have obtained the RCA-signed certificate prior to this exchange.

The CA sends out this message only if:

- CA's policy entails $is\_pk\_of(K, P)$, that is K is a public key of P, and
- the policy does *not* entail $is\_revoked(K)$, i.e. K has not been revoked.

The variable K, originating in the guard $is\_pk\_of(K, P)$, allows the CA to make a non-deterministic choice. In this example, the CA may choose to send either pk_1 or pk_3 as a valid public key for Piet. The key pk_2, however, cannot be sent, because it has been revoked according to CA's policy.

We turn to Ann's process. The thread that is pertinent to this scenario is given below:

$$\{\}\{\}^\neg \blacktriangleright \mathsf{snd}(ann, piet)$$
$$\mathsf{rcv}(sig(X, pk\_cert(piet, K)), sig(rca, is\_pk\_certified(X))) \blacktriangleright$$
$$\{said(X, is\_pk\_of(K, piet)), said(rca, tdon(X, is\_pk\_of(K, piet)))\}\{\}^\neg$$
$$\{is\_pk\_of(K', piet)\}\{\}^\neg \blacktriangleright \mathsf{snd}(penc(K', payload))$$

Ann sends out a message (destined to RCA) asking for Piet's public key. The thread is tailored to handle delegation: Ann expects to receive a properly formatted message, signed by an arbitrary process X, given that X has RCA's trust on public keys. Receiving such a message affects the extensional knowledge of Ann. Ann adds two statements to her knowledge:

- $said(X, is\_pk\_of(K, piet))$ states that X endorses K as a public key of Piet. Note that is_pk_of in this process is local to Ann, i.e. it is independent of the internals of CA's policy, which happens to use the same function symbol for storing public keys and their owners.

– $said(rca, tdon(X, is\_pk\_of(K, piet)))$ states that RCA certifies that X is trusted on (denoted $tdon$) public keys; in particular, any public key associated to Piet.

In general, Ann may interpret a message either by adding policy statements to, or by retracting policy statements from, her extensional knowledge. That is, the receive event $\mathsf{rcv}(m) \blacktriangleright \{s_1, ..., s_j\}\{n_1, ..., n_k\}^\neg$ means that upon receiving message m, the statements $s_1, \cdots, s_j$ are all added to Ann's extensional knowledge, and $n_1, \cdots, n_k$ are all retracted from her extensional knowledge. Let us assume that CA sends the message $sig(ca, pk\_cert(piet, pk_3)), sig(rca, is\_pk\_certified(ca))$ to Ann. Then, Ann adds to her knowledge the following statements:

$$(s_1) \quad said(ca, is\_pk\_of(pk_3, piet))$$
$$(s_2) \quad said(rca, tdon(ca, is\_pk\_of(pk_3, piet)))$$

We remark that Ann does not retract any part of her extensional knowledge here. We come back to the notion of retraction in § 2.3.

Finally, Ann sends the message $payload$ to Piet, encrypted with K', only if Ann knows that K' is Piet's public key (asymmetric encryption is denoted $penc(\cdot, \cdot)$).

With respect to Ann's policy, we have mentioned above that Ann does not directly trust CA on public keys. She trusts RCA, who delegates its rights w.r.t. endorsing public keys to CA. We model Ann's policy below, where rules are labeled for ease of reference.

$$(tr) \quad tdon(rca, is\_pk\_of(K, U)) \leftarrow$$
$$(td) \quad tdon(P, tdon(Q, X)) \leftarrow tdon(P, X)$$
$$(ta) \quad X \leftarrow said(P, X), tdon(P, X)$$

The first rule (tr), with no preconditions, models Ann's trust relation: Ann knows that RCA is trusted on $(tdon)$ any public key. The second rule (td) is the essence of transitive trust delegation: If P is trusted on X, then P can delegate this to Q. We remark that delegation of trust need not in general be transitive; see [5] for more on transitive and non-transitive delegation. The third rule (ta) describes trust application: If Ann knows that P said X, and she knows that P is trusted on X, then Ann can infer X. Recall that the left-hand side of the last rule is in fact $\mathcal{K}(X)$; the predicate symbol $\mathcal{K}$ is suppressed.

Assuming that the statements (s_1) and (s_2) have been added to Ann's extensional knowledge, we show that Ann's policy would entail: pk_3 is Piet's public key. Thus Ann would send the message $payload$ to Piet encrypted using pk_3. The following tree, annotated with the names of rules and statements used, shows Ann's deduction steps.

$$\cfrac{(s_1) \quad \cfrac{(s_2) \quad \cfrac{\cfrac{}{tdon(rca, is\_pk\_of(pk_3, piet))}(tr)}{tdon(rca, tdon(ca, is\_pk\_of(pk_3, piet)))}(td)}{tdon(ca, is\_pk\_of(pk_3, piet))}(ta)}{is\_pk\_of(pk_3, piet)}(ta)$$

A typical security goal for this scenario is: *would Ann ever send a message encrypted with pk_2 (which has been revoked) to Piet?*. Another example: *for any key K, if Ann infers that K is Piet's public key, then Ann trusts RCA on 'K is Piet's public key'*. These goals can be expressed as reachability decision problems; cf. § 3.3. A side note: the scenario described above is susceptible to replay attacks, because there is no freshness guarantees for the certified keys received by Ann.

2.3   Retraction

Retracting policy statements is a feature often needed for modeling revocation of roles and permissions. Consider a hospital where a sensitive ward can be accessed only by the personnel who work in the ward, and have been vaccinated against a particular virus. The PDP that controls access to the ward would then contain a thread of the form:

$$\mathsf{rcv}(U, sig(ppc, is\_vaccinated(U))) \blacktriangleright \{vaccinated(U)\}\{\}^{\neg}$$
$$\{in\_ward(U), vaccinated(U)\}\{\}^{\neg} \blacktriangleright \mathsf{snd}(access\_token(U))$$

That is, an access token is sent to U only if U works in the ward (denoted $in\_ward(U)$), and U has been vaccinated. The statement that U has been vaccinated is added to the extensional knowledge of the PDP only if the hospital's personnel protection center PPC has put its signature on the message $is\_vaccinated(U)$.

Now, suppose the vaccination must be repeated every six months. The PDP would then need to inquire PPC about the status of U's vaccination: whether it is recent or not. Here is a (partial) specification of the thread in the PDP that contacts PPC:

$$\{\}\{\}^{\neg} \blacktriangleright \mathsf{snd}(v\_status(U))$$
$$\mathsf{rcv}(sig(ppc, has\_expired(X))) \blacktriangleright \{\}\{vaccinated(X)\}^{\neg}$$

That is, the PDP asks PPC about the vaccination status (v_status) of U. The PPC would send back to the PDP a signed message declaring that X's vaccination has been expired. PPC would let $X = U$ if U's vaccination has been expired; otherwise, PPC lets X be a dummy name. Then, PDP retracts the fact $vaccinated(X)$ from its policy.

Two remarks are due. First, note that the messages exchanged between PDP and PPC do not have freshness guarantees. Therefore, the attacker can replay these messages, possibly misinforming the PDP about the freshness of the vaccination of the personnel. The second, and perhaps more important, point is that the thread of the PDP that issues access tokens does not synchronize with the PDP thread that contacts the PPC. Therefore, race conditions can arise (or, can be caused by a malicious scheduler) where the access token is issued for a personnel whose vaccination is no longer effective. The first problem can be solved using the standard challenge-response message exchange patterns. The second problem can be solved, e.g., using a lock inside the PDP policy engine. This point is further discussed below.

Synchronization. In order to enforce synchronization inside the PDP, we can use a shared lock between the two threads. This can be modeled as:

Thread 1:
$$\mathsf{rcv}(U, sig(ppc, is\_vaccinated(U))) \blacktriangleright \{vaccinated(U), lock(U)\}\{\}^\neg$$
$$\{in\_ward(U), vaccinated(U)\}\{lock(U)\}^\neg \blacktriangleright \mathsf{snd}(access\_token(U))$$
Thread 2:
$$\{lock(U)\}\{\}^\neg \blacktriangleright \mathsf{snd}(v\_status(U))$$
$$\mathsf{rcv}(sig(ppc, has\_expired(X))) \blacktriangleright \{\}\{vaccinated(X), lock(U)\}^\neg$$

Upon receiving a request from U, PDP's thread 1 locks the user U internally. The lock can be released only by thread 2 of the PDP who contacts the PPC to check the status of U's vaccination. The execution of thread 1 can then resume, only if thread 2 has not retracted the statement "U is vaccinated". [1]

Propagating Revocations. As mentioned above, retracting policy statements if used without the necessary synchronization mechanisms can be futile. This point is also relevant to how revocations are propagated in distributed settings. For instance, consider the file server of § 2.1. Recall that Ann has the role *admin* in the file server. Ann may therefore access any public file. Suppose that Ann's admin role is revoked after the file server has sent out the authorization code to RPS. After the revocation, Ann does not have the role *user* in the file server, because her user role was due to her admin role, which is revoked. That is, the revocation is cascaded locally on the file server: all that followed from Ann being an admin is retracted after the revocation. The semantics of retraction in our formalism is *cascading* [11]: if a is entailed due to b, and only due to b, then retracting b would mean that a will not be entailed by the policy; see the semantics, § 3.2.

RPS may however use the authorization code issued by the file server to communicate with a token endpoint, hence accessing the file *brochure.pdf* on behalf of Ann. Meanwhile, Ann herself can no longer access the file. That is, in distributed settings, such as the scenario of § 2.1, revocations do not propagate automatically. To ensure that revocations take effect globally, synchronization mechanisms (e.g. through message passing, using shared objects) are necessary.

Careless uses, and unintentional effects, of retraction can be detected by checking reachability. For instance, in this example one could check that after the revocation Ann cannot access *brochure.pdf*, while a state in which RPS can access the file is reachable. Deciding reachability is thus crucial for understanding communicating policies.

(Un)Ambiguous Policies. A form of careless use of retraction is when the policy becomes ambiguous about rights. This point is best explained with an example:

---

[1] We do not directly address the problem of staleness in attribute-based distributed authorization systems [10]. This example however shows how we can formalize synchronization mechanisms deployed in order to prevent staleness.

Suppose that the policy of a library service states that any student can access the reading groups schedule file *schedule.pdf*, formalized as:

$$can\_access(U, schedule.pdf) \leftarrow is\_student(U).$$

Now, imagine upon receiving a complaint about Ann, who is a student, the library service retracts her permission to access *schedule.pdf*:

$$\mathsf{rcv}(complaint\_about(U)) \blacktriangleright \{\}\{can\_access(U, schedule.pdf)\}^{\neg}$$

The retraction is meant to prevent Ann from accessing the file, while the fact that she is a student implies that she may access the file. This is an ambiguity in the policy engine. In the semantics of our formalism (§ 3.2), the Horn rule trumps the retraction, because policies are seen as invariants of the process (cf. the specification language ASLan [12]). That is, Ann would be able to access the file, despite "retracting" her access. For enforcing the retraction, either the fact *is_student(U)* should be retracted (which would be too harsh a reaction to an unsigned complaint), or the guard for accessing the file should be refined to explicitly exclude those about whom a complaint has been received.

We remark that retractions in our formalism respect the semantics of Griffiths and Wade [13]: if a policy statement is added to the extensional knowledge of a process, and subsequently the same statement is retracted, the policy remains unchanged. Due to Horn rules, however, retracting policy statements that do not belong to the extensional knowledge is inconsequential, as the example above shows. Adding and retracting policy statements, through updates, indeed affect only the extensional knowledge of the processes; see § 3.2.

3   Formalizing Communicating Authorization Policies

We formally define the syntax (§ 3.1) and semantics (§ 3.2) of our language. We define the reachability problem (§ 3.3) for communicating authorization policies.

3.1   Syntax

A (first-order) *signature* is a tuple $(\Sigma, \mathcal{V}, \mathcal{P})$, where Σ is a countable set of functions, $\mathcal{V}$ is a countable set of variables, and $\mathcal{P}$ is a finite set of predicate symbols. These three sets are pairwise disjoint. We use capital letters $A, B, \ldots$ to refer to the elements of $\mathcal{V}$. The free term algebra induced by Σ, with variables in $\mathcal{V}$, is denoted $\mathcal{T}_{\Sigma(\mathcal{V})}$. A *message* is a ground term, i.e. an element of $\mathcal{T}_{\Sigma(\emptyset)}$. The set of *atoms* is defined as $\{p(t_1, \cdots, t_n) \mid p \in \mathcal{P}, t_i \in \mathcal{T}_{\Sigma(\mathcal{V})}, \text{arity of } p \text{ is } n\}$. A *fact* is an atom with no variables. In the following we fix a signature $(\Sigma, \mathcal{V}, \mathcal{P})$.

An *event* is either a *send event* or a *receive event*. A send event is of the form $g \blacktriangleright \mathsf{snd}(m)$, where g is a *guard* and m is a term. A receive event is of the form $\mathsf{rcv}(m) \blacktriangleright u$, where m is a term and u is an *update*. A guard g is of the form $g_\exists \; g_{\not\exists}$, where $g_\exists$ and $g_{\not\exists}$ are disjoint finite sets of atoms. An update u is of the form $u_+ \; u_-$, where u_+ and u_- are disjoint finite sets of atoms. We refer to $g_\exists$

(resp. u_+) as a positive guard (resp. update), and to $g_{\nexists}$ (resp. u_-) as a negative guard (resp. update). In the examples of § 2 we have superscripted negative guards and negative updates with $\neg$ to improve readability.

A thread t is a finite sequence of events $t = e_1, \cdots, e_n, n \geq 0$. For a variable v appearing in thread t, we say the event e_i, with $1 \leq i \leq n$, is the origin of v in t iff i is the smallest index of the events in which v appears. In the remainder of the paper we only consider threads t that satisfy the *origination property*: for any variable v appearing in t the following holds.

- if the origin of v is the event $\mathsf{rcv}(m) \blacktriangleright u_+ \; u_-$, then either v appears in m, or v appears in u_- and v does not appear elsewhere in the thread;
- if the origin of v is the event $g_{\exists} \; g_{\nexists} \blacktriangleright \mathsf{snd}(m)$, then either v appears in $g_{\exists}$, or v appears in $g_{\nexists}$ and v does not appear elsewhere in the thread.

A *process* π is a tuple $(\eta_\pi, \Omega_\pi, \mathbf{I}_\pi)$, where η_π is a finite set of threads, Ω_π is a finite set of facts, called the *extensional knowledge* or *extensional policy* of π, and $\mathbf{I}_\pi$ is a finite set of *Horn clauses*, called the *policy* of π. A Horn clause is of the form $a \leftarrow a_1, \cdots, a_n$, with $n \geq 0$ and $a, a_1, \cdots, a_n$ being atoms.

An *attacker model* $\mathbb{A}$ is a pair $(\Omega_{\mathbb{A}}, \vdash^{\mathbb{A}})$, where $\Omega_{\mathbb{A}}$ is a finite set of messages, called the extensional knowledge of the attacker, and $\vdash^{\mathbb{A}}$, referred to as the policy of the attacker, is a subset of $2^{\mathcal{T}_{\Sigma(\emptyset)}} \times \mathcal{T}_{\Sigma(\emptyset)}$; intuitively, $M \vdash^{\mathbb{A}} m$ means that the attacker can derive message m, given the finite set M of messages. The attacker is thus identified in our model with her extensional knowledge (which stores the set of the messages observed by the attacker) and her policy (which encodes the deduction capabilities of the attacker). Moreover, the attacker is able to send and receive messages; these capabilities are reflected in the execution model § 3.2.

We are now ready to define communicating authorization policies, hereafter referred to as CAPs. A CAP is a tuple $((\Sigma, \mathcal{V}, \mathcal{P}), \pi_1, \cdots, \pi_\ell, \mathbb{A})$, where $(\Sigma, \mathcal{V}, \mathcal{P})$ is a signature, $\pi_1, \cdots, \pi_\ell$ are (honest) processes and $\mathbb{A}$ is an attacker model, all defined using the signature $(\Sigma, \mathcal{V}, \mathcal{P})$. To avoid trivial name clashes, variables appearing in different threads are assumed to be distinct.

3.2 Semantics

For a finite set H of Horn clauses, a fact a and a finite set T of facts, we write $T \vdash^H a$ iff a belongs to the closure of T under H. We write $T \vdash^H T'$, for a finite set of facts T', iff $T \vdash^H a$ for all $a \in T'$. Let A be a set of atoms. Define $A\downarrow$ as the set of all facts, i.e. ground atoms, that can be obtained by applying a substitution to the elements of A.

Given a process $\pi = (\eta_\pi, \Omega_\pi, \mathbf{I}_\pi)$, we use $\vdash^\pi$ as a shorthand for $\vdash^{\mathbf{I}_\pi}$, and we refer to the set $\{a \mid \Omega_\pi \vdash^\pi a\}$ as the *knowledge* of π. That is, the knowledge of π is the set of facts that can be inferred from the extensional knowledge of π using its policy. The knowledge of the attacker $(\Omega_{\mathbb{A}}, \vdash^{\mathbb{A}})$ is the set $\{m \mid \Omega_{\mathbb{A}} \vdash^{\mathbb{A}} m\}$.

A *configuration* of $\mathsf{cap} = ((\Sigma, \mathcal{V}, \mathcal{P}), \pi_1^0, \cdots, \pi_\ell^0, \mathbb{A}^0)$ is an $\ell + 1$ tuple where the first ℓ elements are processes, and the last element is an attacker model. The *initial* configuration of cap is the tuple $(\pi_1^0, \cdots, \pi_\ell^0, \mathbb{A}^0)$. We define trace semantics for CAPs. Let Z be the set of all configurations of cap, i.e. the set of all tuples of the form $z = (\pi_1, \cdots, \pi_\ell, \mathbb{A})$. We define the relation $\rightarrow \subseteq Z \times E \times Z$ as: $(z, e, z') \in \rightarrow$ iff $z = (\pi_1, \cdots, \pi_i, \cdots, \pi_\ell, \mathbb{A})$, $z' = (\pi_1, \cdots, \pi_i', \cdots, \pi_\ell, \mathbb{A}')$, $\mathbb{A} = (\Omega_\mathbb{A}, \vdash^\mathbb{A})$, $\pi_i = (\eta, \Omega, \mathbf{I})$ and $p = e \cdot p' \in \eta$ for some thread p' and $1 \leq i \leq \ell$, and one of the following conditions hold:

- $e = g_\exists \; g_{\overline{\exists}} \blacktriangleright \mathsf{snd}(t)$, $\mathbb{A}' = (\Omega_\mathbb{A} \cup \{t\sigma\}, \vdash^\mathbb{A})$ and $\pi_i' = (\eta \setminus \{p\} \cup \{p'\sigma\}, \Omega, \mathbf{I})$, for some substitution σ that satisfies the following conditions:
  - $g_\exists \sigma$ is a set of facts and $\Omega \vdash^{\pi_i} g_\exists \sigma$.
  - If $g_{\overline{\exists}}$ is non-empty, then there exists no substitution σ' s.t. $\Omega \vdash^{\pi_i} g_{\overline{\exists}} \sigma \sigma'$.
- $e = \mathsf{rcv}(t) \blacktriangleright u_+ \; u_-$, $\mathbb{A}' = \mathbb{A}$ and $\pi_i' = (\eta \setminus \{p\} \cup \{p'\sigma\}, \Omega \setminus u_-\sigma \downarrow \cup u_+\sigma, \mathbf{I})$, for some substitution σ such that $t\sigma$ is a message and $\Omega_\mathbb{A} \vdash^\mathbb{A} t\sigma$.

We write $z \xrightarrow{e} z'$ for $(z, e, z') \in \rightarrow$. A *trace* of cap is an alternating sequence of configurations and events of the form $z_0 e_1 z_1 \cdots z_{n-1} e_n z_n$, with $n \geq 0$, such that z_0 is the initial configuration of cap and $z_{i-1} \xrightarrow{e_i} z_i$ for all $i \in [1, n]$. The *semantics* of the cap is defined as the set of all its traces. We say that configuration z is *reachable* in cap iff there exists a trace $z_0 e_1 z_1 \cdots e_n z_n$ in the semantics of cap with $n \geq 0$ and $z = z_n$.

Note that the extensional knowledge of the processes and the attacker in any reachable configuration of cap are indeed sets of facts (i.e. they do not contain variables). This is due to the origination property and the conditions the semantics enforces on substitutions.

An important feature of our formalism, not covered in § 2, is the variables that originate in negative guards or updates. This is described below.

Variables originating in negative guards or updates, and SoD. Consider a hospital data center HDC that receives a message from the hospital's human resources department HR stating that a doctor has retired. The following thread of HDC models this event:

$$\mathsf{rcv}(sig(hr, retired(D))) \blacktriangleright \{\}\{patient\_of(P, D)\}^\neg$$

That is, after receiving the message, HDC retracts the statements $patient\_of(P, D)$ for *all* patients P. In other words, after D has retired, no patient can be considered as his/her patient. That is, the variables that originate in negative updates are interpreted universally (see the semantics). It is therefore natural that such variables cannot be referred to in the rest of the thread; see the origination property. We remark that variables cannot originate in positive updates.

Now we turn to the variables that originate in negative guards. Suppose that HDC receives a report R from a medical personnel P. To review the report, the report may be forwarded to any doctor D who does not work in the same ward as P. The following thread models this scenario.

$$\mathsf{rcv}(penc(pk(hdc), sig(P, report(R)))) \blacktriangleright \{\}\{\}^\neg$$
$$\{is\_doctor(D)\}\{in\_ward(P, W), in\_ward(D, W)\}^\neg \blacktriangleright$$
$$\mathsf{snd}(penc(pk(D), please\_review(R)))$$

Here, $in\_ward(X, W)$ means that X works in ward W, $pk(X)$ is a public key of process X. The variable W originates in a negative guard. Therefore, according to the semantics given above, this guard is satisfied for any D such that: (as in § 2, we omit the predicate symbol $\mathcal{K}$, i.e. *knows*, around these terms to simplify the presentation)

$$is\_doctor(D) \wedge \not\exists W.\ in\_ward(P, W) \wedge in\_ward(D, W)$$

The guard is satisfied for D only when there is *no* instantiation for W where both D and P work in ward W. Variables originating in negative guards can therefore not be referred to elsewhere in the thread; see the origination property.

Similarly, separation of duty (SoD) can be expressed in our formalism. Two tasks T_1 and T_2 are constrained under an SoD relation iff no single principal is allowed to perform them both. In general, SoD relations must be anti-reflexive and symmetric. Consider the following guarded send event:

$$\{can\_do(A, T_1)\}\{has\_done(A, T_2), in\_sod(T_1, T_2)\}^\neg \blacktriangleright \mathsf{snd}(auth\_token(A, T_1))$$

An authorization token to perform task T_1 is issued for A only if

- A is allowed to perform T_1, denoted $can\_do(A, T_1)$.
- There exists no task T_2 such that T_2 has been performed by A, denoted $has\_done(A, T_2)$, and there is a SoD constraint on tasks T_1 and T_2, denoted $is\_sod(T_1, T_2)$. That is,

$$can\_do(A, T_1) \wedge \not\exists T_2.\ has\_done(A, T_2) \wedge in\_sod(T_1, T_2)$$

In case the authorization code to perform T_1 is sent to A, the fact $has\_done(A, T_1)$ should be added (via update statements) to the extensional knowledge of the process that enforces SoD, after A has performed the task. This is necessary to keep a complete record of the tasks that have been performed.

Note that, if needed, changes in the SoD relation can be expressed using positive and negative updates in our formalism.

3.3   The Reachability Decision Problem

Fix a CAP, defined as $\mathsf{cap} = ((\Sigma, \mathcal{V}, \mathcal{P}), \pi_1, \cdots, \pi_\ell, \mathbb{A})$. A *goal* G for cap is an $\ell + 1$ tuple $G = (f_1, \cdots, f_\ell, m)$, where $f_i \in \mathcal{A}_{\Sigma(\emptyset)}$ and $m \in \mathcal{T}_{\Sigma_{msg}(\emptyset)}$. Intuitively, goals are conditions on the knowledge of the processes and the attacker: the knowledge of π_i must entail f_i, and m should belong to the knowledge of the attacker. The *reachability* problem $\mathrm{REACH}\langle\mathsf{cap}, G\rangle$ asks whether, or not, there exists a reachable configuration $((\eta_1, \Omega_1), \cdots, (\eta_\ell, \Omega_\ell), \Omega_\mathbb{A})$ in cap such that

$$\forall i \in [1, \ell].\ \Omega_i \vdash^i f_i \bigwedge \Omega_\mathbb{A} \vdash^\mathbb{A} m$$

These cases are, resp., denoted by $\mathrm{REACH}\langle\mathsf{cap}, G\rangle = \mathsf{T}$ and $\mathrm{REACH}\langle\mathsf{cap}, G\rangle = \mathsf{F}$. As a convention, we may write $\mathrm{REACH}\langle\mathsf{cap}, \pi : f\rangle$ or $\mathrm{REACH}\langle\mathsf{cap}, \mathbb{A} : m\rangle$ when we are interested only in the knowledge of process π, or the knowledge of the attacker $\mathbb{A}$. This can be obviously reduced to the reachability problem defined above, by adding dummy facts/messages to the knowledge of the processes/attacker whose knowledge is of no interest to us. Similarly, reachability for generic guards can be reduced to REACH; see [9].

Due to the semi-decidability of Horn clauses, REACH is in general undecidable. In § 4 we identify a set of CAPs for which REACH is decidable.

4 Decidable Communicating Authorization Policies

In this section, we identify a set of CAPs specified in our formal language for which REACH is decidable. We refer to this set as **DC**. Intuitively, a CAP belongs to **DC** iff the following conditions hold: (1) The policies of honest processes are written in a fragment of Horn theories, hereafter called **AL**, formally defined below. **AL** stands for *authorization logic*. (2) The attacker has the capabilities of the standard Dolev-Yao (DY) attacker [8]. The Dolev-Yao attacker intercepts and remembers all transmitted messages, it can encrypt, decrypt and sign messages if it knows the corresponding keys, it can compose and send new messages using the messages it has observed, and can remove or delay messages in favor of others being communicated.

First, we introduce the notion of *infons*, adopted from [5]. Infons are pieces of information, e.g. *can_read(piet, file12)* stipulating that Piet can read a certain *file12*. An infon does not admit a truth value, i.e. it is never false or true. Instead, infons are the interface between the communication level and policy level for honest processes. The simplest form of an infon is constructed by applying *wrappers* to message terms. For example, if the message term n is a nonce, then the wrapper *is_fresh* can be used to construct the piece of information *is_fresh(n)*, denoting that the nonce n is fresh. More interesting infons are constructed by applying *infon constructor* functions to other infons (and messages). For example, $said(\pi, is\_fresh(n))$ is an infon that states that process π said that n is a fresh nonce. Then, $said(\pi', said(\pi, is\_fresh(n)))$ is the infon that states that process π' said that: process π said that n is fresh.

In the following, for any signature $(\Sigma, \mathcal{V}, \mathcal{P})$ we assume $\Sigma = \Sigma_{msg} \sqcup \Sigma_{infon}$ and $\mathcal{V} = \mathcal{V}_{msg} \sqcup \mathcal{V}_{infon}$, where Σ_{msg} is the set of message constructor functions, and Σ_{infon} is the set of infon constructors. The notation $\sqcup$ stands for the union of disjoint sets. Two types of terms are generated by Σ: message terms, and infons (defined formally below). We assume that the elements of Σ_{infon} are associated with types: each function symbol $f \in \Sigma_{infon}$ of arity n specifies the types of its n arguments. Formally, the elements of $\mathcal{T}_{\Sigma_{msg}(\mathcal{V}_{msg})}$ are called message terms, and have the type msg. The set *Infons* is the smallest set that contains $\mathcal{V}_{infon}$ and s.t. $f(t_1, \cdots, t_n) \in Infons$ for any $f \in \Sigma_{infon}$ of arity n, and t_i being of the correct type. The elements of *Infons* have the type infon. An infon constructor function whose arguments are all of type msg is called a wrapper function. the types msg and infon are disjoint. Any element of $\mathcal{T}_{\Sigma(\mathcal{V})}$ that is not a message or infon is considered ill-typed, hence ignored in our study.

We introduce the **AL** theories in order to model the policies of honest processes. [2] In **AL**, the policy statements for honest processes (i.e. facts derived from the processes' policies) are predicates over infons.

Definition 1. *Let T be a finite set of Horn clauses, where any clause in T is of the form $p(t) \leftarrow p_1(t_1), \cdots, p_\ell(t_\ell)$, with $\ell \geq 0$, $p, p_1, \cdots, p_\ell \in \mathcal{P}$, and $t, t_1, \cdots, t_\ell \in Infons$. T is an **AL** theory iff $T = T_\leftarrow \sqcup T_\rightarrow$ where*

(a) *The set rewrite system $\mathfrak{R}_{T_\leftarrow} = \{a \Rightarrow a_1 \cdots a_n \mid a \leftarrow a_1, \cdots, a_n \in T_\leftarrow\}$ induced by $T_\leftarrow$ is terminating, i.e. it does not admit reduction sequences of infinite length.*

(b) *For each clause $p(t) \leftarrow p_1(t_1), \cdots, p_\ell(t_\ell)$ in $T_\rightarrow$, at least one of the t_j, with $j \in [1, \ell]$, is an anchor for the clause; that is:*
   - *$var(t_j)$ contains all the variables appearing in the clause, and*
   - *all the variables in t_j are infon variables (i.e. elements of $\mathcal{V}_{infon}$), and*
   - *$p_j(t_j)$ unifies with no atom in T, except for itself and $p(t)$, and*
   - *the term rewriting system $\{t_j \Rightarrow t\}$ induced by the clause is terminating.*

It is easy to observe that all the policies defined in § 2 belong to **AL**; for instance, for the the example of § 2.2, T is partitioned into $T_\leftarrow = \{tr, td\}$ and $T_\rightarrow = \{ta\}$. For more detail, see [9].

Below, we define a set **DC** of CAPs for which we prove REACH is decidable.

Definition 2. *The set **DC** consists of all the CAPs $((\Sigma, \mathcal{V}, \mathcal{P}), \pi_1, \cdots, \pi_\ell, \mathbb{A})$ that satisfy the following conditions:*

- *$(\Sigma, \mathcal{V}, \mathcal{P})$ is a signature, with $\Sigma = \Sigma_{msg} \sqcup \Sigma_{infon}$, and:*
  - *Σ_{msg} contains the functions $penc(\cdot, \cdot)$, $\{\cdot\}\cdot$, $sig(\cdot, \cdot)$, $pk(\cdot)$, $sk(\cdot)$, $h(\cdot)$, $(\cdot, \cdot)$, representing the usual cryptographic primitives. Namely, they represent respectively asymmetric and symmetric encryption, digital signature, public key and private key constructors, hash and pairing functions.*
- *For any process $\pi = (\eta_\pi^0, \Omega_\pi^0, \mathbf{I}_\pi)$:*
  - *$\mathbf{I}_\pi$ is an **AL** theory.*
  - *Atoms in Ω_π^0, in guards and in updates are of the form $p(i)$, where $p \in \mathcal{P}$ and i is an infon; i.e. the knowledge of the process ranges over infons.*
  - *Variables in the guards and updates range over messages, i.e. they are always under the application of a wrapper function symbol.*
  - *In all the events $g \blacktriangleright snd(m)$ and $rcv(m) \blacktriangleright u$, $m \in \mathcal{T}_{\Sigma_{msg}}(\mathcal{V})$; i.e. participants send and receive message terms, as opposed to infons.*
- *$\mathbb{A} = (\Omega_\mathbb{A}^0, \vdash^\mathbb{A})$, where $\Omega_\mathbb{A}^0$ is a finite subset of $\mathcal{T}_{\Sigma_{msg}}(\emptyset)$, and $\vdash^\mathbb{A}$ reflects the capabilities of the standard Dolev-Yao attacker, defined, e.g., in [14].*

The proof of the following theorem can be found in [9].

Theorem 1. REACH⟨cap, G⟩ *is decidable for any* cap *in* **DC**, *and any goal G.*

---

[2] In contrast to Datalog, **AL** allows for nested function symbols and variables that only appear in rules' heads.

5 Related Work

The closest related works are (1) dynamic authorization logics, and (2) security protocols annotated with authorization constraints.

(1) Dynamic authorization logics. Existing distributed authorization logics, such as [1–5], cannot express the dynamic aspects of distributed policies. We, in contrast, model communicating authorization policies which change due to communication events. Our formalism allows therefore for modeling the dynamic aspects of distributed (i.e. communicating) authorization policies. This is the fundamental difference between our formalism and the dynamic authorization logics that confine their analysis to a centralized policy decision point, such as [15–18].

We decide reachability in communicating authorization policies by taking into account the "low-level" cryptographic protocols that implement the policies, and also the interface between the low-level protocols and the policies. This is in contrast to the dynamic authorization logics that model the causes and effects of policy changes at the same level of abstraction as the policy, such as [19,20]. These logics hence abstract away the mechanisms through which policy decision points communicate and possibly influence each other. For instance, the notion of updates in our language is close to the notion of *effects* in [19,20]. We however do not associate effects to policy decisions; rather, effects (or updates) are associated with receiving messages. What we call a guarded send event in our formalism has no counterpart in [19,20]. In our decision algorithm, we not only take into account the asynchronous communications among the policy decision points, but also we can explicitly model the capabilities of the hostile entity (e.g. the Dolev-Yao [8] attacker) that controls their communications.

(2) Security protocols annotated with authorization constraints. Our formalism is related to the body of research on annotating security protocols with authorization constraints [7, 12, 21–24]. None of these works (except for [7]) give an algorithm for deciding reachability. In contrast, we can decide reachability for a large class of authorization policies. We extend the decidability result of [7] in two directions: (a) We have negative statements in guards, and we allow the policy statements to be retracted from the extensional policies of the processes. These features enable us to naturally model non-monotonic behaviors, such as revocation of rights. (b) We give a decision algorithm for a rich set of policies **AL**, which strictly subsumes the *type-1* policy theories of [7].

Acknowledgements. We are grateful to Jorge Cuéllar, Srdjan Marinovic, and Petar Tsankov for their comments on the paper. This work is partially supported by NESSoS: the EU FP7-ICT-2009.1.4 Project No. 256980.

References

1. Abadi, M., Burrows, M., Lampson, B., Plotkin, G.: A calculus for access control in distributed systems. ACM Trans. Program. Lang. Syst. 15(4), 706–734 (1993)
2. Blaze, M., Feigenbaum, J., Lacy, J.: Decentralized trust management. In: IEEE Symposium on Security and Privacy, pp. 164–173. IEEE CS (1996)
3. DeTreville, J.: Binder, a logic-based security language. In: IEEE S&P, p. 105 (2002)

4. Becker, M., Fournet, C., Gordon, A.: Design and semantics of a decentralized authorization language. In: CSF 2007, pp. 3–15. IEEE Computer Society (2007)
5. Gurevich, Y., Neeman, I.: DKAL: Distributed-knowledge authorization language. In: CSF 2008, pp. 149–162. IEEE Computer Society (2008)
6. Hammer, E., et al.: The OAuth 2.0 authorization framework (2012); IETF
7. Frau, S., Torabi Dashti, M.: Integrated specification and verification of security protocols and policies. In: CSF, pp. 18–32. IEEE CS (2011)
8. Dolev, D., Yao, A.: On the security of public key protocols. IEEE Trans. on Information Theory IT-29(2), 198–208 (1983)
9. Frau, S.: Analysis of Reachability Properties in Communicating Authorization Policies. PhD Thesis, ETH Zürich (November 2012)
10. Krishnan, R., Niu, J., Sandhu, R.S., Winsborough, W.H.: Stale-safe security properties for group-based secure information sharing. In: FMSE 2008, pp. 53–62 (2008)
11. Bertino, E., Samarati, P., Jajodia, S.: An extended authorization model for relational databases. IEEE Trans. Knowl. Data Eng. 9(1), 85–101 (1997)
12. Armando, A., Arsac, W., Avanesov, T., Barletta, M., Calvi, A., Cappai, A., Carbone, R., Chevalier, Y., Compagna, L., Cuéllar, J., Erzse, G., Frau, S., Minea, M., Mödersheim, S., von Oheimb, D., Pellegrino, G., Ponta, S.E., Rocchetto, M., Rusinowitch, M., Torabi Dashti, M., Turuani, M., Viganò, L.: The AVANTSSAR platform for the automated validation of trust and security of service-oriented architectures. In: Flanagan, C., König, B. (eds.) TACAS 2012. LNCS, vol. 7214, pp. 267–282. Springer, Heidelberg (2012)
13. Griffiths, P., Wade, B.: An authorization mechanism for a relational database system. ACM Trans. Database Syst. 1(3), 242–255 (1976)
14. Rusinowitch, M., Turuani, M.: Protocol insecurity with finite number of sessions is NP-complete. In: CSFW 2001, p. 174. IEEE CS (2001)
15. Chaudhuri, A., Naldurg, P., Rajamani, S., Ramalingam, G., Velaga, L.: EON: modeling and analyzing dynamic access control systems with logic programs. In: ACM CCS 2008, pp. 381–390. ACM (2008)
16. Dougherty, D., Fisler, K., Krishnamurthi, S.: Specifying and reasoning about dynamic access-control policies. In: Furbach, U., Shankar, N. (eds.) IJCAR 2006. LNCS (LNAI), vol. 4130, pp. 632–646. Springer, Heidelberg (2006)
17. Garg, D., Pfenning, F.: Stateful authorization logic: In: Cuellar, J., Lopez, J., Barthe, G., Pretschner, A. (eds.) STM 2010. LNCS, vol. 6710, pp. 210–225. Springer, Heidelberg (2011)
18. Li, N., Tripunitara, M.V.: Security analysis in role-based access control. ACM Trans. Inf. Syst. Secur. 9(4), 391–420 (2006)
19. Becker, M., Nanz, S.: A logic for state-modifying authorization policies. ACM Trans. Inf. Syst. Secur. 13(3) (2010)
20. Becker, M.Y.: Specification and analysis of dynamic authorisation policies. In: CSF, pp. 203–217. IEEE Computer Society (2009)
21. Guttman, J.D., Thayer, F.J., Carlson, J.A., Herzog, J.C., Ramsdell, J.D., Sniffen, B.T.: Trust management in strand spaces: A rely-guarantee method. In: Schmidt, D. (ed.) ESOP 2004. LNCS, vol. 2986, pp. 325–339. Springer, Heidelberg (2004)
22. Fournet, C., Gordon, A., Maffeis, S.: A type discipline for authorization policies. ACM Trans. Program. Lang. Syst. 29(5) (2007)
23. Barletta, M., Ranise, S., Viganò, L.: A declarative two-level framework to specify and verify workflow and authorization policies in service-oriented architectures. Service Oriented Computing and Applications 5(2), 105–137 (2011)
24. Bansal, C., Bhargavan, K., Maffeis, S.: Discovering concrete attacks on website authorization by formal analysis (2012); to appear in CSF 2012

Building Trust and Reputation In: A Development Framework for Trust Models Implementation

Francisco Moyano, Carmen Fernandez-Gago, and Javier Lopez

Network, Information and Computer Security Lab
University of Malaga, 29071 Malaga, Spain
{moyano,mcgago,jlm}@lcc.uma.es

Abstract. During the last years, many trust and reputation models have been proposed, each one targeting different contexts and purposes, and with their own particularities. While most contributions focus on defining ever-increasing complex models, little attention has been paid to the process of building these models inside applications during their implementation. The result is that models have traditionally considered as ad-hoc and after-the-fact solutions that do not always fit with the design of the application. To overcome this, we propose an object-oriented development framework onto which it is possible to build applications that require functionalities provided by trust and reputation models. The framework is extensible and flexible enough to allow implementing an important variety of trust models. This paper presents the framework, describes its main components, and gives examples on how to use it in order to implement three different trust models.

1 Introduction

There is not a standard definition of trust, although it is agreed that it is of paramount importance when considering systems security, as a tool to leverage decision-making processes. The concept of trust spans across several areas beyond computer science, such as psychology, sociology or economy.

The concept and implications of trust are embodied in the so-called trust models, which define the rules to process trust in an automatic or semi-automatic way in a computational setting. There are different types of trust models, each one considering trust in different ways and for different purposes. The origins of trust management date back to the nineties, when Marsh [10] proposed the first comprehensive computational model of trust based on social and psychological factors. Two years later, Blaze [2] identified trust management as a way to enhance the problem of authorization, which up to that date was separated into authentication and access control.

These two seminal contributions reveal the two main branches or categories of trust models that have been followed until today, and which we classified in a previous work [13]. On the one hand, and following Marsh's approach, we find evaluation models, where factors that have an influence on trust are identified, quantified and then aggregated into a final trust score. Uncertainty and evaluation play an important role in these models, as one entity is never completely sure whether it should trust another entity, and a decision process is required after evaluating the degree of trust placed in the entity.

A. Jøsang, P. Samarati, and M. Petrocchi (Eds.): STM 2012, LNCS 7783, pp. 113–128, 2013.

On the other hand and following Blaze's approach, we find decision models, which are tightly related to authorization. An entity holds credentials and a policy verify whether these credentials are enough to permit access to certain resources. Here, trust evaluation is not so important in the sense that there are no degrees of trust (and as a consequence, there is not uncertainty), and the outcome of the process is a binary answer: yes (access granted) or no (access denied). In this paper, we lay aside these models and focus only on evaluation models.

Both categories, evaluation and decision models, evolved, leading to ever-complex models. One of the branches of evaluation models with higher impact has been reputation models, in which a reputation score about a given entity is derived from other entities' opinions about it. Reputation and trust are related concepts, and as stated by [8], reputation can be used to determine whether an entity can trust another entity.

One issue with trust models is that they are very context-dependent, and are often designed as ad-hoc mechanisms to work in a limited range of applications. Actually, the standard is to plug a trust model into an existing, already-built application after-the-fact. This might lead to architectural mismatches between the application and the model, and the reusability of the model could also be damaged. Moreover, it is not possible for the model to exploit all the information available to the application, since there is not any systematic procedure to include the model as a holistic part of the application. As a consequence, there are no mechanisms to consider trust requirements from the very beginning of the software development lifecycle or to align the design of the model with the design of the application.

To overcome these shortcomings, we propose an object-oriented development framework that allows implementing trust evaluation models as a core part of the applications themselves. Our aim is to assist developers during the development of applications that might require using evaluation models. The contributions of this paper are (i) a domain analysis for trust evaluation models; (ii) the elicitation of the requirements that the framework should meet; (iii) a first design of the framework architecture; (iv) and guidelines to implement three different trust evaluation models using the framework.

The rest of the paper is organized as follows. Section 2 reviews several contributions that are related to ours. A conceptual model of trust, which constitutes the domain analysis for the framework, is presented in Section 3. This analysis is used as an input to elicit the requirements and the design of the framework architecture, described in Section 4, whereas Section 5 explains how the framework can be used to implement three evaluation models. Finally, the conclusion and future work are presented in Section 6.

2   Related Work

SECURE project [3] proposes a trust model to formally reason about trust, and a framework to provide applications with trust functionalities. Trust decisions rely on cost-PDFs that compare the benefits of a given interaction with the cost of such interaction. Thus, although the authors propose an interesting framework, we do not find it general enough to implement other types of trust or reputation models found in the literature.

Kiefhaber et al. [16] present the Trust-Enabling Middleware, which provides applications running on top of it with methods to save, interpret and query trust related information. The middleware uses built-in functions to measure the reliability of nodes by considering packets losses. Although rather complete, it lacks a framework-oriented approach since it does not make explicit the process of implementing existing or new trust models, and its focus is on distributed, message-oriented applications.

Huynh [6] proposes the Personalized Trust Framework (PTF), a rule-based system that makes use of semantic technologies for, given a domain, to apply the most suitable trust model. In a similar direction, Suryanarayana et al. [18] present PACE (Practical Architectural approach for Composing Egocentric trust), an architectural style for composing different trust models into the architecture of a decentralized peer in a P2P architecture. The first contribution is a user framework that assists users in determining the trustworthiness of resources, but it is not a development framework. The second contribution is an architectural style. Thus, its purpose is helping the architect of the application with a style to compose trust models, but like the PTF, it is not a framework, in the sense that it does not provide developers with mechanisms to implement trust models, nor to use them in their own applications.

Har Yew [5] presents a computational trust model and a middleware called SCOUT, made up of three services that implement the model: the evidence gathering service, the belief formation service and the emotional trust service. Regardless being a comprehensive model, it is not designed as an extensible framework and it is not clear, if possible at all, how a developer could implement existing trust models.

Finally, Lee and Winslett present TrustBuilder2 [9], where they propose an extensible framework that supports the adoption of different negotiation-based trust models. Although this is indeed a development framework, they focus on decision models, laying aside the evaluation models we are considering in this paper.

3   Trust and Reputation: A Domain Analysis

The aim of this section is to shed light on concepts related to trust and reputation. First, in Section 3.1, we discuss some definitions of trust that are often found in the literature, whereas in Section 3.2 we put forward a conceptual model in the form of knowledge graphs that constitutes a domain analysis of trust and reputation models. This analysis is required for identifying the concepts that are likely to be part of the framework, as well as their relationships.

3.1   Definitions

Many definitions of trust have been provided along the years. This is due to the complexity of this concept, which spans across several areas such as psychology, sociology, economics, law, and more recently, computer science. The vagueness of this term is well represented by the statement "trust is less confident than know, but also more confident than hope" [12].

Gambetta [4] defines trust as "a particular level of the subjective probability with which an agent will perform a particular action [. . .] in a context in which it affects our own action". McKnight and Chervany [11] explain that trust is "the extent to which one party is willing to depend on the other party in a given situation with a feeling of relative security, even though negative consequences are possible". For Olmedilla et al. [14], "trust of a party A to a party B for a service X is the measurable belief of A in that B behaves dependably for a specified period within a specified context (in relation to service X)". Ruohomaa and Kutvonen [17] state that trust is "the extent to which one party is willing to participate in a given action with a given partner, considering the risks and incentives involved". Finally, Har Yew [5] defines trust as "a particular level of subjective assessment of whether a trustee will exhibit characteristics consistent with the role of the trustee, both before the trustor can monitor such characteristics (or independently of the trustor's capacity ever to be able to monitor it) and in a context in which it affects the trustor's own behavior".

We propose the following definition : *trust is a subjective, context-dependent property that is required when (i) two entities need to collaborate (i.e. there is a dependence relationship between them and there exists the willingness to collaborate), but they do not know each other beforehand, (ii) and when the outcome of this collaboration is uncertain (i.e. entities do not know if they will perform as expected) and risky (i.e. negative outcomes are possible).* In this situation, trust acts as a mechanism to reduce the uncertainty in the collaboration and to mitigate the risk. As risk increases (either the probability or the impact of negative outcomes), trust becomes more crucial.

The concept of reputation is more objective than the concept of trust. According to the Concise Oxford dictionary, reputation is "what is generally said or believed about a person or the character or standing of a thing". Although the exact relationship between trust and reputation remains fuzzy, we think that Jøsang [8] linked these two terms appropriately with the following two statements: "I trust you because of your good reputation" and "I trust you despite your bad reputation". Thus, reputation can be considered as a building block, or indicator, to determine trust, although it does not have the final say.

3.2 Conceptual Model

This section presents the most important concepts related to evaluation trust models. These concepts were identified surveying relevant literature and finding commonalities and variations in the definition of different models. This conceptual model constitutes a domain analysis and the starting point for the framework requirements elicitation and for the architecture design, as some concepts and relationships can map to object-oriented components. The conceptual framework is graphically described by means of knowledge graphs and using a UML notation, as depicted in Figures 1 and 2. Due to space limitations, we concentrate on those concepts that have a higher impact for the requirements and architecture of the framework.

A trust model aims to compute trust in a given setting. This setting should have, at least, two entities that need to interact. An entity might play a role or even several ones. The basic roles are trustor (the entity that places trust) and trustee (the entity on which trust is placed). Once there is a trustor and a trustee, we claim that a trust relationship has been established. A trust relationship has a purpose, which can be for example controlling the access to a resource, the provision of a resource or the identity of an entity. It might also serve to set trust in the infrastructure (devices, hardware, etc). In the very end, the purpose of a trust model is to aid making a decision. At the higher level, it is a trust decision in the sense of answering the question: would this entity behave as expected under this context? At a lower level, an entity trusts a property of another entity. For instance its capability to provide a good quality of service. A trust model also makes some assumptions, such as "entities will provide only fair ratings" or "initial trust values are assumed to exist", and might follow different modeling methods.

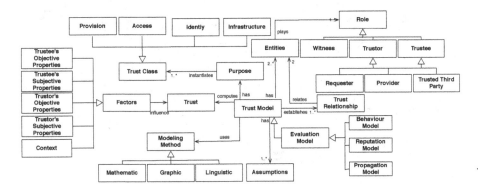

Fig. 1. Concepts for Evaluation Models (i)

There are three types of evaluation models, namely reputation models, behaviour models and propagation models.

Behaviour models often follow a trust lifecycle with three phases. In the bootstrapping phase, initial trust values are assigned to the entities of the system. Then, some monitoring is performed to observe a variable or set of variables. Finally, a trust assessment process is done in order to assign values to these variables and to aggregate them into a final trust evaluation.

In these models, trust relationships are tagged with a trust value that describe to what extent the trustor trusts the trustee. This trust value has semantics and dimension, which might be simple or a tuple. Trust values are assigned during trust assessment through trust metrics, which receive a set of variables as input and produce a measure of one or several attributes using a computation engine. There are several computation engines used in the literature, ranging from the most simple ones such as summation engines, to complex ones that entail probability distributions or fuzzy logic.

There are several sources of information that might feed a trust metric. The most common one is the direct interaction of the entity with the trustee. Other possible sources of information, although less frequent, are sociological information (e.g. considering the roles of entities or their membership to a group) and psychological information (e.g. prejudice).

Reputation models can be, in turn, another source of information where opinions of a given trustee by different entities are made public and are used to compute a score. Reputation can be centralized or distributed, depending on whether reputation scores are stored in a central location or are saved by each individual entity.

Propagation models aim to create new trust relationships from existing ones. Some of them assume that trust is transitive and exploit this property. New trust values are often computed by means of operators, and in several models, we find two of them:

a concatenator and an aggregator. The former is used to compute trust along a trust path or chain, whereas the latter aggregates the trust values computed for each path into a final trust value.

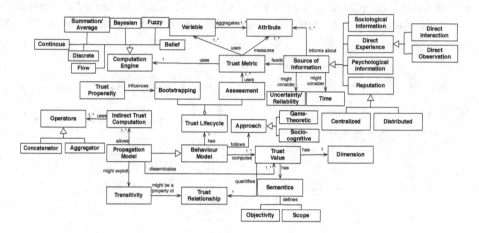

Fig. 2. Concepts for Evaluation Models (ii)

4   Trust and Reputation Development Framework

In this section, the object-oriented development framework for trust is presented. Both the requirements and the design are influenced by the domain analysis presented in the previous section. Section 4.1 describes the requirements that the framework should fulfil, whereas Section 4.2 presents the first version of the framework architecture.

4.1   Framework Requirements

This section summarizes the requirements that the framework must meet. At a high-level, the framework has to support the implementation of three types of evaluation models, namely reputation models, behaviour models and propagation models. Although these models have commonalities, they also pose subtle differences that the framework must support.

The primary goal of reputation models is to compute reputation scores for entities. These scores must be stored (centrally or distributively) and entities should be able to access this information before interacting with other entities. On the other hand, behaviour models establish relationships between entities, and their main goal is to compute trust values for these relationships. Finally, propagation models also build on trust relationships, and their primary goal is to disseminate trust information to establish new trust relationships.

The following list of requirements describes the coarse-grained functionality that the framework should provide to developers:

- Entities management: entities hold trust values in other entities. The framework must allow the creation, binding and naming of entities.

- Trust relationships management: trust relationships might change along time. New trust relationships might be created (e.g. by propagation models), other relationships might be deleted, and it is likely that trust values change as well.
- Trust metrics definition: although the framework can provide some default built-in metrics implementations, it is important to let developers to define their own trust metrics, as they are the core concept in evaluation models.
- Variables management: a trust metric is composed of variables. It is important to let developers to create new variables, which can be used by user-defined metrics.
- Computation engines management: an engine implements a trust metric. This engine uses variables according to certain rules. Engines range from simple summation or average functions to complex fuzzy and probability distributions.
- Indirect trust computation: the framework should provide ways to determine the value of an undefined trust relationship based on defined ones by propagating trust information.
- Operators definition: indirect trust computation relies on operators that take trust paths as input and return trust values as output (and thus, a new trust relationship). Although several operators should be provided by default, the framework should allow developers to define new operators.

The ultimate goal of the framework is to allow developers to implement both existing evaluation models and new ones. Next section describes the architecture that supports these requirements.

4.2   Framework Architecture

This section describes a first version of the framework architecture. The structural view of the architecture is depicted as a class diagram in Figure 3. Note that some classes have been mapped directly from the conceptual model described in Section 3, such as *Entity* and *TrustRelationship* among others.

The architecture follows a layered design, where each layer uses the services provided by the lower layer. Likewise, the framework follows a grey-box approach, where the developer can use several functionalities in a black-box fashion as well as define new functionalities based on his needs. Next we describe the classes and relationships for each of the layers.

Model Layer. In this layer we find the models that the developer can implement, namely reputation models, behaviour models, and propagation models. More information about each type of model is provided in Section 5. *ReputationModel, BehaviourModel* and *PropagationModel* are inherited classes from *EvaluationModels* and as such, they share a context (a string describing the context under which the model operates) and a list of entities that take part in the model. *EvaluationModel* also provides other methods, and their functionality will be delegated to lower layer classes, depending on the model type.

A reputation model adds a connector to an external database system to store reputation scores, and it holds the type of reputation model, which might be centralized or distributed. Moreover, this class exposes the method *updateReputation* which, in addition to computing the reputation score, it saves it in the trust database.

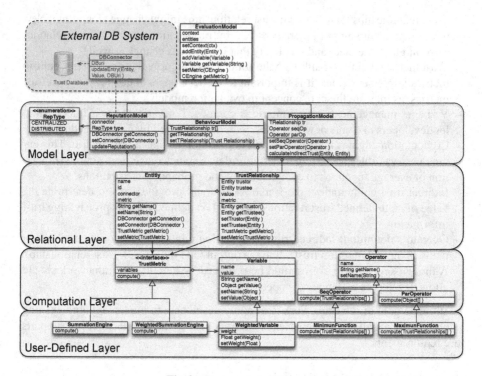

Fig. 3. Framework Architecture

A behaviour model contains a list of trust relationships and exposes methods to get and set these relationships. Finally, a propagation model, in addition to containing a list of trust relationships, it also contains a sequential operator and a parallel operator [1]. It exposes methods to set them and to calculate indirect trust relationships.

Relational Layer. This layer contains the basic building blocks onto which the models of the upper layer are developed: entities and trust relationships.

Entities have a name, an automatically-generated identifier, a database connector and a trust metric. The fact that each entity holds a database connector enables distributed reputation systems, where each entity must store the reputation information regarding another entity in a personal database. Likewise, as each entity holds a trust metric instance, we allow each entity in the model to use a different trust metric to compute other entities' reputation.

Regarding trust relationships, they consist on a tuple that specify which is the entity that places trust (trustor), the entity on which trust is placed (trustee), the extent to which the trustor trusts the trustee (value), and the trust metric used to derive this value. Again, having the metric as an instance variable in this class improves flexibility as each trust relationship could be measured with different metrics.

---

[1] In the conceptual model we called them *concatenator* and *aggregator* operators. However, as we later implement a model where they are called *sequential* and *parallel*, we have adopted this notation for the architecture.

The decision that both an entity and a trust relationship may define their metrics supports the implementation of more advanced trust models where the final trust value that a trustor places on a given trustee might be determined by both the reputation of the trustee and the trust relationship between the trustor and the trustee.

Computation Layer. Evaluation models rely on trust metrics to perform trust values calculations. This is the layer in charge of such computation.

Basically, *TrustMetric* is an interface that a developer should implement to override the *compute()* method, where the trust calculation takes place. Trust metrics use variables, through the class *Variable*, which have a name and a value, as well as methods to get and set these parameters. Operators for propagation models belong also to this layer.

Note that trust metrics contain instances of variables. As entities and trust relationships hold in turn instances of trust metrics, each entity or relationship might use different variables, increasing the flexibility of the framework to accommodate complex models.

User-Defined Layer. This layer is created as users extend the computation layer to accommodate their own definitions. As we explain in the next section, users can create new computation engines (implementations of the *TrustMetric* interface) and new variables to implement an important range of models. For illustration purposes, the architecture includes a summation engine (that basically sums up the variables that it contains) and a weighted summation engine (that adds a weight to each variable). The latter requires creating a specialized variable class that adds the weight to its internal state.

Up to now, we have described the framework from a structural point of view. The behavioural view of the architecture is further analyzed in the following section, where the framework is used to implement three evaluation models.

5   Instantiations of the Framework

In this section, we describe how the framework presented in Section 4 could address the implementation of three simple evaluation models. These models have been chosen because they are well-known as well as representative of the three types of evaluation models discussed earlier. In the first part of this section, we briefly describe the models to be implemented. In the second part, we actually use the framework to implement the models. The goal of this section is to analyze the feasibility of the framework to implement different evaluation models.

5.1   Models Description

Ebay Reputation Model [15]. Ebay [2] is probably the most famous auction-based online marketplace where buyers and sellers interact. Once a transaction has finished, buyers can evaluate sellers, expressing their satisfaction with regard to the transaction outcome. This evaluation is made by providing positive or negative feedbacks. The reputation score of a seller is computed by subtracting the negative feedbacks from the

---

[2] www.ebay.com

positive feedbacks. This model has its shortcomings, as expressed by Jøsang et al. [8], since people are usually reluctant to provide a negative evaluation and prefer to solve their problems off-line. Thus, the reputation score of a person is not very representative, since a person with 50 positive feedbacks and 10 negative feedbacks should be considered rather more untrustworthy than another one with only 40 positive feedbacks (although they would have the same reputation score under the model). On the other hand, it is a simple, easy-to-understand model, and that is why we have chosen it for illustration purposes.

Risk and Utility-based Behaviour Model. In this made-up model a trustor determines his trust in a trustee by means of two factors: the risk and utility of the interaction. The higher the risk (as perceived by the trustor), the lower the trust. Likewise, the higher the utility (as perceived by the trustor), the higher the trust. This model can be considered an oversimplification of Marsh's computational model [10], where the author identifies many parameters that influence trust and combine them into different formulas. In the simplified version that we propose, the trustor performs the division between the utility and the risk to calculate the trust in the trustee.

Propagation Model. Agudo et al. [1] present a graph-based propagation model that allows to compute indirect trust relationships from direct ones. Let us suppose, in the context of the previous model, that an entity e_1 does not know the risk and utility values of interacting with an entity e_3. In this setting, there is not an explicit trust relationship between these two entities. However, let us suppose that we know the risk and utility values that e_1 hold for e_2, and the ones that e_2 hold for e_3 (that is, there is a trust relationship between e_1 and e_2, and between e_2 and e_3). Then, we could use the propagation model to compute the final trust value from e_1 to e_3, establishing a new trust relationship.

5.2   Using the Framework

Ebay Reputation Model. Let us suppose a distributed setting in which three entities (which do not know each other beforehand) have to perform several works. These entities can choose whether to execute a given work by themselves or to delegate it to the entity with the higher reputation. Each time an entity delegates a work, it registers a listener through which the delegatee informs about the outcome of the work (e.g. success or failure, time consumed, etc). Depending on these parameters, the delegator decides whether to place a positive feedback or a negative feedback on the delegatee. Thus, we are implementing the eBay reputation model onto another kind of application.

```
ReputationModel rm = new ReputationModel("Work Dispatching",
              3, CENTRALIZED, SUMMATION);
rm.addVariable("Positive Feedback", 0);
rm.addVariable("Negative Feedback", 0);
```

This simple code snippet creates a reputation model under the context "Work Dispatching". The next parameter represents the number of entities (three in our example).

Next, we specify that the reputation model is centralized (and not distributed), and this creates a database connector that acts as the interface to the reputation database (where reputation scores for the entities are stored). If the reputation model was distributed, there would be required to create a database connector for each entity created. The final parameter is the computation engine, which in this case is a simple built-in summation engine. As mentioned earlier, the framework is designed to allow different computation engines for different entities. By default, however, all entities share the same computation engines and the same variables.

After initializing the reputation model, we add the variables required, namely the positive and negative feedbacks, specifying their default values. The code that adds the variables is shown next:

```
public class ReputationModel {

  //If no entity is specified, when we add a
  //variable, it is added to the computation
  //engine of every entity
  public void addVariable(String name, Object value) {
      for (int i = 0; i < entities.size(); i++) {
              entities.get(i).getComputationEngine().
                addVariable(name, f);
      }
  }

  // ... (Other methods)
}
```

From this point onwards, the developer accesses the framework functionalities through the reputation model instance variable. The following code snippet shows the method to execute when the listener is triggered.

```
//This is the method the listener invokes when a work is finished
public void onWorkFinished(Work w, Entity delegatee, Message m,
        Time tConsumed) {

        Variable nFeedback = rm.
                getVariable("Negative Feedback", delegatee);
        Variable pFeedback = rm.
                getVariable("Positive Feedback", delegatee);

        if (m.isError() || tConsumed > threshold) {
                rm.setVariable("Negative Feedback", delegatee,
                        -(++nFeedback.getValue()));
        } else {
                rm.setVariable("Positive Feedback", delegatee,
                        ++pFeedback.getValue());
        }

        rm.updateReputation(delegatee);
}
```

Variables are updated depending on the outcome of the work dispatching, and there is a call to *updateReputation*. The code for this method is very simple, as shown next:

```
public class ReputationModel {

  public void updateReputation (Entity e) {
    //connector is an instance variable of reputation
        // model that allows accessing a persistent
        // database for storing reputation scores
        connector.updateEntry(e,
                e.getComputationEngine().compute());
    }

    // ...(Other methods)
}
```

The *updateReputation* method will perform the computation of the reputation score according to the summation computation engine and the variables defined. Furthermore, it will update the central reputation database.

The summation engine overrides the *compute()* method of *TrustMetric*. This way, the framework provides enough flexibility to easily implement different metrics. Another metric could use weights to give a higher relevance to negative feedbacks, for instance. The developer would need to define two new classes: one extending *TrustMetric*, namely *WeightedSummation*, and another one extending *Variable*, namely *WeightedVariable*. The latter must contain the weight associated to the variable, whereas the former should override the method *compute()* of *TrustMetric*, as depicted in Figure 4.

In the code snippets from Figure 4., *variables.size()* equals two, since there are two variables (positive and negative feedbacks). The upper code represents the computation of the traditional eBay reputation model, whereas the other one describes a weighted version of it.

Risk and Utility-Based Behaviour Model. In reputation models, according to the framework design, variables and computation engines belong to entities. That is, each entity has its own variables and computation engines. Now, an entity might hold a different risk and utility values for any other entity in the system. In order to support this, the framework introduces the class *TrustRelationship*, which encapsulates the information regarding a trust relationship, namely the trustor, the trustee, the trust value, and the computation engine used to calculate the trust value. Thus, any trust relationship remains perfectly specified by an instance of this class.

Let us assume a setting with three entities again. The code snippet that the developer has to write is the following:

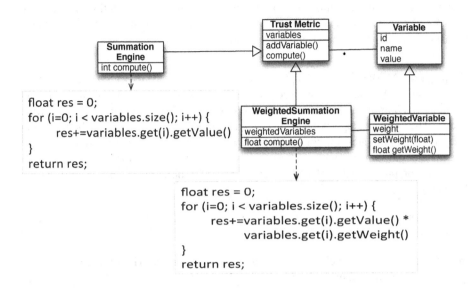

Fig. 4. Creation of Metrics and Variables

```
BehaviourModel bm = new BehaviourModel("Work Dispatching");

//If entities do not exist, they are created in the
//addTrustRelationship method. This process is
//tedious and could better done through
//configuration files or GUIs
bm.addVariable(bm.addTrustRelationship("e1", "e2"),
        "Risk", 0,3);
bm.addVariable(bm.addTrustRelationship("e1", "e2"),
        "Utility", 0,9);
bm.addVariable(bm.addTrustRelationship("e2", "e3"),
        "Risk", 0,6);
bm.addVariable(bm.addTrustRelationship("e2", "e3"),
        "Utility", 0,4);

// Set engine for all trust relationships
bm.setComputationEngine(riskUtilityEngine);
bm.compute(bm.getTrustRelationship("e1", "e2"));
bm.compute(bm.getTrustRelationship("e2", "e3"));
```

The computation engine that implements the trust metric, namely *riskUtilityEngine* must be defined by the developer, overriding the *compute()* method of *TrustMetric*. In our example, the engine would only need to retrieve the variable named *Risk* and divide it by the variable *Utility*.

Note that after the execution of the previous code, there is a trust relationship between e_1 and e_2, and between e_2 and e_3. We now proceed to use a propagation model to create a trust relationship between e_1 and e_3, as described next.

Propagation Model. The model proposed by Agudo et al. [1] uses a *sequential operator* to compute the trust value between two entities in a given trust chain, and a *parallel operator* to compute a global trust value between two entities linked by multiple trust chains. The same concepts are used in other trust models, such as Jøsang's belief model [7], which disseminates opinions through *discounting* and *consensus* operators.

Consider the same example of the previous model. Let us assume that the developer wants to compute a trust value between e_1 and e_3. The code he should write is the following:

```
PropagationModel pm = new PropagationModel(bm, MIN, MAX);
pm.calculateIndirectTrust("e1", "e3");
```

In this example, we have chosen the built-in minimun and maximum functions as sequential and parallel operators, respectively. However, as there is only one trust path from e_1 to e_3, the parallel operator is not necessary and will not be applied.

Also note that the first argument of the constructor is the instance of the previous model (*bm*), since the propagation model needs access to the trust relationships previously defined.

The method *calculateIndirectTrust* is described next:

```
public void calculateIndirectTrust(Entity e1, Entity e3) {
    float[] values;
    TrustRelationship[] trustChains =
            retrieveTrustChains(tr, e1, e3);
    for (int i = 0; i < trustChains.size(); i++) {
            values[i] = sequentialOp.compute(trustChains[i]);
    }
    tr.addTrustRelationship (e1, e3,
            parallelOp.compute(values));
}
```

The *sequentialOp* and *parallelOp* are instance variables that store an instance of the operators, which might be defined by the user extending the corresponding abstract classes. Basically, the method retrieves all the trust paths between e_1 and e_3. Then, it applies the sequential operator to every path, and finally, it applies the parallel operator to the obtained values.

6   Conclusion and Future Work

There is a huge amount of different trust models proposed in the literature. These models, however, are often designed to work in ad-hoc environments, and to be plugged into already-existing applications. In this paper, we have presented an object-oriented development framework to assist developers during the implementation of applications that might require support from trust or reputation models. As the application is developed using the framework, trust models are aligned with the design of the application and they can exploit all the data available to the application.

In order to achieve this, we have classified the knowledge about trust models by means of knowledge graphs in a domain analysis. This analysis has helped us to elicit the requirements that the framework should meet, and also to identify several classes, attributes and methods, from which we designed a first version of the architecture. Finally, we have proved the feasibility of the framework by giving guidelines on the implementation of three different evaluation models: the eBay reputation model, an oversimplified version of Marsh's model, and a propagation model.

As future work, we intend to extend the framework in order to accommodate several models features that are often found in the literature. First, we are interested in supporting the implementation of models where the trust values are represented by a tuple of values (multiple dimensions) rather than by a single value. We intend to allow defining a different metric for each dimension in order to provide greater flexibility.

Some trust models yield an uncertainty value together with the trust value, in order to inform other entities about how certain the trust value should be considered. We plan to add support for this feature as well. Also, roles played by entities or the membership of entities to a given group are factors taken into account in other models to determine trust, and therefore we intend to include this feature in the near future too.

Finally, we aim to add more complex built-in computation engines, including beta-probability distributions and fuzzy engines.

Acknowledgements. This work has been partially funded by the European Commission through the FP7 project NESSoS under grant agreement number 256980, and by the Spanish Ministry of Science and Innovation through the research projects ARES (CSD2007-00004) and SPRINT (TIN2009-09237). The first author is funded by the Spanish Ministry of Education through the National F.P.U. Program.

References

1. Agudo, I., Fernandez-Gago, C., Lopez, J.: A model for trust metrics analysis. In: Furnell, S.M., Katsikas, S.K., Lioy, A. (eds.) TrustBus 2008. LNCS, vol. 5185, pp. 28–37. Springer, Heidelberg (2008)
2. Blaze, M., Feigenbaum, J., Lacy, J.: Decentralized trust management. In: IEEE Symposium on Security and Privacy, pp. 164–173 (1996)
3. Cahill, V., Gray, E., Seigneur, J.-M., Jensen, C.D., Chen, Y., Shand, B., Dimmock, N., Twigg, A., Bacon, J., English, C., Wagealla, W., Terzis, S., Nixon, P., di Marzo Serugendo, G., Bryce, C., Carbone, M., Krukow, K., Nielsen, M.: Using trust for secure collaboration in uncertain environments. IEEE Pervasive Computing 2(3), 52–61 (2003)
4. Gambetta, D.: Can we trust trust? In: Trust: Making and Breaking Cooperative Relations, pp. 213–237. Basil Blackwell (1988)
5. Har Yew, C.: Architecture Supporting Computational Trust Formation. PhD thesis, University of Western Ontario, London, Ontario (2011)

6. Huynh, T.D.: A Personalized Framework for Trust Assessment. In: ACM Symposioum on Applied Computing - Trust, Reputation, Evidence and other Collaboration Know-how Track, vol. 2, pp. 1302–1307 (December 2008)

7. Jøsang, A.: A logic for uncertain probabilities. International Journal of Uncertainty, Fuzziness and Knowledge-Based Systems 9(3), 279–311 (2001)

8. Jøsang, A., Ismail, R., Boyd, C.: A survey of trust and reputation systems for online service provision. Decision Support Systems 43(2), 618–644 (2007)

9. Lee, A.J., Winslett, M., Perano, K.J.: TrustBuilder2: A reconfigurable framework for trust negotiation. In: Ferrari, E., Li, N., Bertino, E., Karabulut, Y. (eds.) IFIPTM 2009. IFIP AICT, vol. 300, pp. 176–195. Springer, Heidelberg (2009)

10. Marsh, S.: Formalising Trust as a Computational Concept. PhD thesis, University of Stirling (April 1994)

11. Harrison McKnight, D., Chervany, N.L.: The meanings of trust. Technical report, University of Minnesota, Management Information Systems Research Center (1996)

12. Miller, K.W., Voas, J., Laplante, P.: In Trust We Trust. Computer 43, 85–87 (2010)

13. Moyano, F., Fernandez-Gago, C., Lopez, J.: A conceptual framework for trust models. In: Fischer-Hübner, S., Katsikas, S., Quirchmayr, G. (eds.) TrustBus 2012. LNCS, vol. 7449, pp. 93–104. Springer, Heidelberg (2012)

14. Olmedilla, D., Rana, O.F., Matthews, B., Nejdl, W.: Security and trust issues in semantic grids. In: Proceedings of the Dagsthul Seminar, Semantic Grid: The Convergence of Technologies, vol. 5271 (2005)

15. Resnick, P., Zeckhauser, R.: Trust among strangers in Internet transactions: Empirical analysis of eBay's reputation system. In: Baye, M.R. (ed.) The Economics of the Internet and E-Commerce. Advances in Applied Microeconomics, vol. 11, pp. 127–157. Elsevier Science (2002)

16. Siefert, F., Anders, G., Ungerer, T., Reif, W., Kiefhaber, R.: The Trust-Enabling Middleware: Introduction and Application. Technical report, Institut fur Informatik Universitat Augsburg (March 2011)

17. Ruohomaa, S., Kutvonen, L.: Trust management survey. In: Herrmann, P., Issarny, V., Shiu, S.C.K. (eds.) iTrust 2005. LNCS, vol. 3477, pp. 77–92. Springer, Heidelberg (2005)

18. Suryanarayana, G., Diallo, M.H., Erenkrantz, J.R., Taylor, R.N.: Architectural Support for Trust Models in Decentralized Applications. In: Proceeding of the 28th International Conference on Software Engineering, pp. 52–61. ACM Press, New York (2006)

Matrix Powers Algorithms
for Trust Evaluation in Public-Key
Infrastructures

Jean-Guillaume Dumas[1] and Hicham Hossayni[2]

[1] Laboratoire J. Kuntzmann, Université de Grenoble. 51, rue des Mathématiques,
umr CNRS 5224, bp 53X, F38041 Grenoble, France
`Jean-Guillaume.Dumas@imag.fr`
[2] CEA/Léti, 17, rue des Martyrs, 38000 Grenoble
`Hicham.Hossayni@cea.fr`

Abstract. This paper deals with the evaluation of trust in public-key infrastructures. Different trust models have been proposed to interconnect the various PKI components in order to propagate the trust between them. In this paper we provide a new polynomial algorithm using linear algebra to assess trust relationships in a network using different trust evaluation schemes. The advantages are twofold: first the use of matrix computations instead of graph algorithms provides an optimized computational solution; second, our algorithm can be used for generic graphs, even in the presence of cycles. Our algorithm is designed to evaluate the trust using all existing (finite) trust paths between entities as a preliminary to any exchanges between PKIs. This can give a precise evaluation of trust, and accelerate for instance cross-certificate validation.

Keywords: Trust evaluation, Matrix powers, Spectral analysis of networks, Distributed PKI trust model.

1 Introduction

The principle of a Public Keys Infrastructure (PKI) is to establish (using certificates) a trust environment between network entities and thus guarantee some security of communications.

For instance companies can establish hierarchical PKI's with a certification authority (CA) signing all the certificates of their employees. In such a setting there is a full trust between employees and their CA. Now if entities with different PKI structures want to communicate, either they find a fully certified path between them or they don't. In the latter case some degree of trust has to be established between some disjoint entities.

Ellison and Schneier identified a risk of PKIs to be "Who do we trust, and for what?" which emphasizes the doubts about the trust relationship between the different PKI components [4]. Several incidents, including the one in which VeriSign issued to a fraudulent two certificates associated with Microsoft [8], or even the recent fraudulent certificates for Google emitted by DigiNotar [1], confirm the importance of the trust relationship in the trust models, see also [14]. This leads to

A. Jøsang, P. Samarati, and M. Petrocchi (Eds.): STM 2012, LNCS 7783, pp. 129–144, 2013.

the need of a precise and a global evaluation of trust in PKI architectures. Another approach would be to use some fully trusted keys or authorities, like the Sovereign Keys or the Convergence project[1], or e.g. trust lists [20].

For example in a cross-certification PKI, an entity called Alice can establish a communication with another entity called Bob only after validating Bob's certificate. For this, Alice must verify the existence of a certification path between her trust anchor and Bob's certification authority (CA). This certificate validation policy imposes that each entity must have a complete trust in their trust anchors, and that this trust anchor has a complete (direct or indirect) trust relationship with other CAs.

In e.g. [11–13, 6] algorithms are proposed to quantify the trust relationship between two entities in a network, using transitivity. Some of them evaluate trust throughout a single path, while others consider more than one path to give a better approximation of trust between entities. However to the best of our knowledge they are restricted to simple network *trees*. In this paper we choose the last approach and use transitivity to efficiently approximate global trust degree. Our idea is to use an adapted power of the adjacency matrix (used e.g. to verify the graph connectivity or to compute the number of *finite* paths between nodes). This spectral approach is similar to that used also e.g. for community detection in graphs [5] and we use it to produce a centralized or distributed quantification of trust in a network. Moreover it allows to deal with *any kind of graphs, without any restrictions to trees nor dags*.

More generally, the aim of this paper is to propose a generic solution for trust evaluation adapted to different trust models. The advantage of spectral analysis is twofold : first the use of matrix computations instead of graph algorithms provides an optimized computational solution in which the matrix memory management is more adapted to the memory hierarchy; second, our algorithm can be used for generic graphs, even in the presence of cycles. Moreover, our algorithm is iterative so that a good approximation of the global trust degrees can be quickly computed: this is done by fixing the maximum length of the trust paths that are considered. The complexity of this algorithm is $O(n^3 \cdot \varphi \cdot \ell)$ in the worst case, polynomial in n, the number of entities (nodes of the graph), φ, the number of trust relationships (edges), and ℓ, the size of the longest path between entities. For instance the algorithm proposed in [12] worked only for directed acyclic graphs (DAG) and required the approximate resolution of the Bounded Disjoint Paths problem, known to be NP-Hard [19]. In case of DAGs the complexity of our algorithm even reduces to $O(n \cdot \varphi \cdot \ell)$.

Our algorithm is designed to evaluate the trust using all existing (finite) trust paths between entities as a preliminary to any exchanges between PKIs. This can give a precise evaluation of trust, and optimize the certificate validation time. These computations can be made, in a centralized manner by a trusty independent entity, like Wotsap for a web of trust networks[2], by CAs in the case of cross-certification PKI (e.g. via PKI Resource Query Protocols [18]), or by the

---

[1] https://www.eff.org/sovereign-keys, http://convergence.io
[2] http://www.lysator.liu.se/~jc/wotsap/index.html

users themselves in the case of PGP web of trust. The latter can even happen in a distributed manner [3] or with collaborations [17].

Our algorithm works for generic trust metrics but can be more efficient when the metrics form a ring so that block matrix algorithms can be used. We thus present in section 2 different possible trust metrics and their aggregation in trust network. We then present the transformation of DAG algorithms for the computation of the aggregation into matrix algorithms in section 3. We do this in the most generic setting, i.e. when even the dotproducts have to be modified, and with the most generic trust metric (i.e. including trust, uncertainty *and* *verified distrust*). Finally, in section 4, we present our new polynomial algorithm for generic graphs.

2   Transitive Trust Metrics

2.1   The Calculus of Trust

There are several schemes for evaluating the (transitive) trust in a network. Some present the trust degree as a single value representing the probability that the expected action will happen. The complementary probability being an uncertainty on the trust.

Others include the *distrust* degree indicating the probability that the opposite of the expected action will happen [11]. More complete schemes can be introduced to evaluate trust: Jøsang [15] for instance introduced the Subjective Logic notion which expresses subjective beliefs about the truth of propositions with degrees of "uncertainty".

[12, 13] also introduced a quite similar scheme with a formal, semantics based, calculus of trust and applied it to public key infrastructures (PKI). We chose to present this metric for its generality and include in this section some definitions and theorems taken from [12]. The idea is to represent trust by a triplet, (trust, distrust, uncertainty). Trust is the proportion of experiences proved, or believed, positive. Distrust is the proportion of experiences *proved negative*. Uncertainty is the proportion of experiences with unknown character.

Definition 1 ([12, §5.1]). *Let d be a trustor entity and e a trustee. Let m be the total number of encounters between d and e in a given context. Let n (resp. l) be the number of positive (resp. negative) experiences among all encounters between d and e.*

- **The trust degree** *is defined as the frequency rate of the trustor's positive experience among all encounters with the trustee. That is, $td(d,e) = \frac{n}{m}$.*
- **The distrust degree***: similarly we have $dtd(d,e) = \frac{l}{m}$.*
- **The uncertainty***: denoted by ud is defined by: $ud(d,e) = 1 - td(d,e) - dtd(d,e)$.*

In the following we will denote the **trust relationship** by a triple $tr(a,b) = \langle td(a,b),\ dtd(a,b),\ ud(a,b)\rangle$ or simply $tr(a,b) = \langle td(a,b), dtd(a,b)\rangle$ since the uncertainty is completely determined by the trust and distrust degrees.

In these definitions, the trust depends on the kind of expectancy, the context of the experiences, type of trust (trust in belief, trust in performance), ..., see e.g. [13]. For simplicity, we only consider in the next sections the above generic concept of trust.

2.2   Aggregation of Trust

The main property we would like to express is *transitivity*. Indeed in that case keys trusted by many entities, themselves highly trusted, will induce a larger confidence. In the following we will consider a trust graph representing the trust relationships as triplets between entities in a network.

Definition 2 (Trust graph). *Let $\mathcal{T} \subset [0,1]^3$ be a set of trust relationships. Let V be a set of entities of a trust network. Let E be a set of directed edges with weight in $\mathcal{T}$. Then $G = (V, E, \mathcal{T})$ is called a* trust graph *and there is an edge between two vertices whenever there exist a nonzero trust relationship between its entities.*

Next we define the transitivity over a path between entities and using parallel path between them as sequential and parallel aggregations. We first need to define a trust path:

Definition 3 (Trust path). *Let $G = (V, E, \mathcal{T})$ be a trust graph. A trust path between two entities $A_1 \in V$ and $A_n \in V$ is defined as the chain, $A_1 \xrightarrow{t_1} A_2 \xrightarrow{t_2} ...A_{n-1} \xrightarrow{t_{n-1}} A_n$, where A_i are entities in V and $t_i \in \mathcal{T}$ are respectively the trust degrees associated to each trust relation $(A_i \xrightarrow{t_i} A_{i+1}) \in E$.*

The need of the sequential aggregation is shown by the following example. Consider, as shown on figure 1, Alice trusting Bob with a certain degree, and Bob trusting Charlie with a certain trust degree. Now, if Alice wishes to communicate with Charlie, how can she evaluate her trust degree toward him? For this, we use the sequential aggregation of trust to help Alice to make a decision, and that is based on Bob's opinion about Charlie.

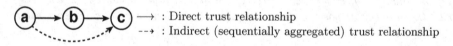

$\longrightarrow$: Direct trust relationship

$--\rightarrow$: Indirect (sequentially aggregated) trust relationship

Fig. 1. Simple sequential trust aggregation

Definition 4 (Sequential aggregation of trust [12, Theorem UT-1]). *Let $G = (V, E, \mathcal{T})$ be a trust graph. Let a, b and c be three entities in V and $tr(a, b) \in \mathcal{T}, tr(b, c) \in \mathcal{T}$ be respectively the trust degrees associated to the entity pairs (a, b)*

and (b, c). The sequential aggregation of trust between a and c is a function f, that calculates the trust degree over the trust path $a \to b \to c$. It is defined by :

$$f : \mathcal{T} \times \mathcal{T} \to \mathcal{T} \text{ with } \quad f(tr(a, b), tr(b, c)) = tr_f(a, c) = \langle td_f(a, c), dtd_f(a, c) \rangle$$

$$\text{where} \quad td_f(a, c) = td(a, b).td(b, c) + dtd(a, b).dtd(b, c)$$

$$dtd_f(a, c) = dtd(a, b).td(b, c) + td(a, b).dtd(b, c)$$

Lemma 1. *Definition 4 is sound.*

Proof. We consider the trust path $a \xrightarrow{x} b \xrightarrow{y} c$ and let $x = \langle x_t, x_d, x_u \rangle$, $y = \langle y_t, y_d, y_u \rangle$ and $z = \langle z_t, z_d, z_u \rangle = f(x, y)$. Then $z_u = 1 - x_t y_t - x_d y_d - x_t y_d - x_d y_t = 1 - x_t(y_t + y_d) - x_d(y_t + y_d) = 1 - (x_t + x_d)(y_t + y_d) = 1 - (1 - x_u)(1 - y_u)$. Since $0 \leq x_u \leq 1$ and $0 < leq y_u \leq 1$, we have that $0 \leq (1 - x_u)(1 - y_u) \leq 1$ so that $0 \leq z_u = x_u + y_u \leq 1$. Since x_u and y_u are positive by definition, it follows that $f(x, y)$ *is* a trust relationship.

From the definition we also for instance immediately get the following properties.

Lemma 2. *f (Sequential aggregation) increases uncertainty.*

Proof. As in the proof of lemma 1, we let $x = \langle x_t, x_d, x_u \rangle$, $y = \langle y_t, y_d, y_u \rangle$ and $z = f(x, y)$. From $z_u = 1 - (1 - x_u)(1 - y_u)$ we have that $z_u = x_u + y_u(1 - x_u)$. Therefore as y_u and $1 - x_u$ are positive we in turn have that $z_u \geq x_u$. We also have $z_u = y_u + x_u(1 - y_u)$ and therefore also $z_u \geq y_u$. Moreover we see that if both uncertainties are non zero, then the uncertainty of $f(x, y)$ is strictly increasing.

Lemma 3 ([13, Property 2]). *f (Sequential aggregation) is associative*

Proof. We consider the trust path $a \xrightarrow{x} b \xrightarrow{y} c \xrightarrow{z} d$ and let $x = \langle x_t, x_d \rangle$, $y = \langle y_t, y_d \rangle$, $z = \langle z_t, z_d \rangle$. Then $f(x, y) = \langle x_t y_t + x_d y_d, x_d y_t + x_t y_d \rangle$ and $f(y, z) = \langle y_t z_t + y_d z_d, y_d z_t + y_t z_d \rangle$, so that $f(f(x, y), z) = \langle (x_t y_t + x_d y_d) z_t + (x_d y_t + x_t y_d) z_d, (x_d y_t + x_t y_d) z_t + (x_t y_t + x_d y_d) z_d \rangle$. In other words, $f(f(x, y), z) = \langle x_t(y_t z_t + y_d z_d) + x_d(y_d z_t + y_t z_d), x_d(y_t z_t + y_d z_d) + x_t(y_d z_t + y_d z_d) \rangle = f(x, f(y, z))$.

From this associativity, this sequential aggregation function can be applied recursively to any tuple of values of $\mathcal{T}$, to evaluate the sequential aggregation of trust over any trust path with any length ≥ 2, for instance as follows: $f(t_1, ..., t_n) = f(f(t_1, ..., t_{n-1}), t_n)$.

Now, the following definition of the parallel aggregation function can also be found in [13, § 7.2.2], it is clearly associative and is illustrated on figure 2.

Definition 5 (Parallel aggregation of trust [12, §6.2]). *Let $G = (V, E, \mathcal{T})$ be a trust graph. Let $a, b_1, \ldots, b_n, c$ be entities in V and $tr_i(a, c) \in \mathcal{T}$ be the trust degree over the trust path $a \to b_i \to c$ for all $i \in 1..n$. The parallel aggregation* *of trust is a function g, that calculates the trust degree associated to a set of disjoint trust paths connecting the entity a to the entity c. It is defined by:*

$$g : \mathcal{T}^n \to \mathcal{T} \text{ with } g([tr_1, tr_2, \ldots, tr_n](a, c)) = tr_g(a, c) = \langle td_g(a, c), dtd_g(a, c)\rangle$$

$$\text{where } td_g(a, c) = 1 - \prod_{i=1..n}(1 - td_i) \text{ and } dtd_g(a, c) = \prod_{i=1..n} dtd_i$$

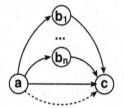

$\longrightarrow$: Direct trust relationship

$\dashrightarrow$: Indirect (parallely aggregated) trust relationship

Fig. 2. Parallel aggregation of trust for multiple trust

Lemma 4. *Definition 5 is sound.*

Proof. We start by proving it for two paths of length 1. Let $x = \langle x_t, x_d\rangle$ and $y = \langle y_t, y_d\rangle$. Then $g(x, y) = \langle 1 - (1 - x_t)(1 - y_t), x_d y_d\rangle$. It is clear that td_g and dtd_g are non negative. Now from the definition of trust relationship we know that $x_t + x_d \leq 1$ and $y_t + y_d \leq 1$ so that $x_d \leq 1 - x_t$ and $y_d \leq y_t - 1$. Therefore $x_d y_d \leq (1 - x_t)(1 - y_t)$ and $td_g(x, y) + dtd_g(x, y) \leq 1$. This generalizes smoothly to any number of paths by induction.

Definition 6 (Trust evaluation). *Let $G(V, E, \mathcal{T})$ be a directed acyclic trust graph, and let a and b be two nodes in V. The trust evaluation between a and b is the trust aggregation over all paths connecting a to b. It is computed recursively by aggregating (evaluating) the trust between the entity a and the predecessors of b (except, potentially, a). Denote by $Pred(b)$ the predecessors of b and by p_i the elements of $Pred(b) \setminus \{a\}$. The trust evaluation between a and b consists in first recursively evaluating the trust over all paths $a \to \ldots \to p_i$, then applying the sequential aggregation over the paths $a \to p_i \to b$ and finally the parallel aggregation to the results (and $(a \to b)$, if $(a \to b) \in E$).*

Remark 1. Note that since the predecessors of b are distinct, after the sequential aggregations all the resulting edges from a to b are distinct. They are thus disjoint paths between a and b and parallel aggregation applies.

Remark 2. In the above definition of trust evaluation we favor the evaluation from right to left. As shown on the example below this gives in some sense prominence to nodes close to the beginning of the path, that is nodes closer to the one asking for an evaluation. This is illustrated on figure 3 where to different strategies for the evaluation of trust are shown: on the left, one with parallel, then sequential, aggregation; the other one with sequential, then parallel, aggregation. Would f be distributive over g we would get the same evaluation. As we will see in section 4, this choice of evaluation can has an important impact in the presence of cycles.

From left to right, we get
$f(a, g(f(b,c), d))$

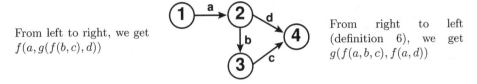

From right to left
(definition 6), we get
$g(f(a,b,c), f(a,d))$

Fig. 3. Two strategies for trust evaluation between node 1 and 4

The graph theoretic method proposed by [12, §6.3] for evaluating trust between two nodes in a DAG requires the approximate solution of the Bounded Disjoint Paths problem, known to be NP-Hard [19]. This algorithm has two steps: first an elimination of cycles via BDP, then a composition of sequential and then parallel aggregation. We will show in the next section that our matrix algorithm produces the same output on acyclic graphs. Moreover, in section 4, we will present a variant of this algorithm, still with polynomial time bound, that directly deals with generic graphs.

By storing the already evaluated relationships, the aggregation part of [12, §6.3] can for instance compute the global trust in a graph with 1000 vertices and 250 000 edges in about 1 minute on a standard laptop. In the following, we propose to rewrite this algorithm in terms of linear algebra [16]. Using sparse linear algebra the overall complexity will not change, and the analysis will be eased. Now if the graph is close to complete, the trust matrix will be close to dense and cache aware linear algebra block algorithms will be more suited.

In both cases, the linear algorithm will decompose the evaluation into converging iterations which could be stopped before exact convergence in order to get a good approximation faster.

Furthermore, using this linear algebra point of view, we will we able to generalize the algorithm to any directed graph.

3   Matrix Powers Algorithm For Directed Acyclic Graphs

In the previous section, we presented the trust propagation scheme introduced by [12], which consists of using the parallel and sequential trust aggregations for evaluating the trust between a network's entities. Indeed, our matrix powers algorithm can be implemented with different trust propagation schemes under one necessary condition: the transitivity property of the (sequential and parallel) trust propagation formulas. In this section, we propose a new algorithm for evaluating trust in a network using the powers of the matrix of trust. This algorithm uses techniques from graph connectivity and communicability in networks [5].

3.1   Matrix and Monoids of Trust

Definition 7. *Let* $G = (V, E, \mathcal{T})$ *be a trust graph, the* matrix of trust *of* G, *denoted by* C, *is the adjacency matrix containing, for each node of the graph ,G the trust degrees of a node toward its neighbors,* $C_{ij} = \langle td(i,j), dtd(i,j), ud(i,j) \rangle$.

When there is no edge between i and j, we choose $C_{ij} = \langle 0, 0, 1 \rangle$ and, since every entity is fully confident in itself, we also choose for all i: $C_{ii} = \langle 1, 0, 0 \rangle$.

Definition 8. *Let $\mathcal{T}$ be the set $\mathcal{T} = \{\langle x, y, z \rangle \in [0,1]^3, x + y + z = 1\}$, equipped with two operations "+" and "." such that $\forall (\langle a, b, u \rangle, \langle c, d, v \rangle) \in \mathcal{T}^2$ we have: $\langle a, b, u \rangle . \langle c, d, v \rangle = \langle ac + bd, ad + bc, 1 - ac - ad - bd - bc \rangle$, and $\langle a, b, u \rangle + \langle c, d, v \rangle = \langle a + c - ac, bd, (1-a)(1-c) - bd \rangle$. We define as the monoids of trust the monoids $(\mathcal{T}, +, \langle 0, 1, 0 \rangle)$ and $(\mathcal{T}, ., \langle 1, 0, 0 \rangle)$.*

$\langle 0, 0, 1 \rangle$ is the absorbing element of "." in $\mathcal{T}$. This justifies a posteriori our choice of representation for the absence of an edge between two nodes in definition 7.

We can also see that the set $\mathcal{T}$ corresponds to trust degrees $\langle td, dtd, ud \rangle$. In addition, the operations "." and "+" represent respectively the sequential and parallel aggregations of trust, denoted f and g in definitions 4 and 5.

Remark 3. Note that "." is *not* distributive over "+". This fact can prevent the use of block algorithms and fast matrix methods. Now if the simpler metric without distrust is used (i.e. distrust is fixed to zero for every entity in the graph, and *will remain zero* all along our trust algorithms), then "." becomes distributive over "+". Thus in the following section we will present timings with or without taking distrust into consideration.

3.2 d-Aggregation of Trust

Definition 9 (d-aggregation of trust). *For $d \in \mathbb{N}$, the d-aggregation of trust between two nodes A and B, in an acyclic trust graph, is the trust evaluation over all paths of length at most d, connecting A to B. It is denoted $d\text{-agg}_{A,B}$.*

Definition 10 (Trust vectors product). *Consider the directed trust graph $G = (V, E, \mathcal{T})$ with trust matrix C. Let $\overrightarrow{C_{i*}}$ be the i-th row vector and $\overrightarrow{C_{*j}}$ be the j-th column vector. We define the product of $\overrightarrow{C_{i*}}$ by $\overrightarrow{C_{*j}}$ by:*

$$\overrightarrow{C_{i*}}.\overrightarrow{C_{*j}} = \sum_{\substack{k \in V}}^{k \neq j} C_{ik}.C_{kj}$$

Note that $C_{ii} = C_{jj} = \langle 1, 0, 0 \rangle$ is the neutral element for ".". Therefore, our definition differs from the classical dot product as we have removed one of the $C_{ij} = C_{ii} \cdot C_{ij} = C_{ij} \cdot C_{jj}$, but then it matches the 2-aggregation:

Lemma 5. *The product $\overrightarrow{C_{i*}}.\overrightarrow{C_{*j}}$ is the 2-aggregated trust between i and j.*

Proof. We prove first that $C_{ik}.C_{kj}$ is the sequential aggregation of trust between i and j throughout all the paths (of length ≤ 2) $i \to k \to j$ with $k \in V$. Let k be an entity in the network. There are two cases: whether k is one of the boundaries of the path or not. The first case is: $k = i$ or $k = j$:

- if $k = i$, then from the trust matrix definition 7, $C_{ii} = \langle 1, 0, 0 \rangle \forall i$, thus we have $C_{ik}.C_{kj} = C_{ii}.C_{ij} = \langle 1, 0, 0 \rangle . C_{ij} = C_{ij}$.

– if $k = j$, then similarly $C_{ik}.C_{kj} = C_{ij}.C_{jj} = C_{ij}.\langle 1, 0, 0 \rangle = C_{ij}$

Therefore $C_{ik}.C_{kj}$ corresponds to the [sequential aggregation of] trust between i and j throughout the path (i, j) of length 1. This is why in the product, we added the constraint $k \neq j$ in the sum to avoid taking C_{ij} twice into account. Now the second case is: $k \neq i$ and $k \neq j$:

– if k belongs to a path of length 2 connecting i to j, then: i trusts k with degree $C_{ik} \neq \langle 0, 0, 1 \rangle$, and k trusts j with degree $C_{kj} \neq \langle 0, 0, 1 \rangle$. From definition 4, $C_{ik}.C_{kj}$ corresponds to the sequential aggregation of trust between i and i throughout the path $i \rightarrow k \rightarrow j$.

– If there is no path of length 2 between i and j containing k, then we have $C_{ik} = \langle 0, 0, 1 \rangle$ or $C_{kj} = \langle 0, 0, 1 \rangle$, and thus $C_{ik}.C_{kj} = \langle 0, 0, 1 \rangle$ is also the aggregation of trust between i and j on the path traversing the node k.

Finally, we can deduce that $\overrightarrow{C_{i*}}.\overrightarrow{C_{*j}} = \sum_{k \in V}^{k \neq j} C_{ik}.C_{kj}$ corresponds to the parallel aggregation of trust between i and j using all paths of length ≤ 2, which is the 2-aggregated trust between i and j. Note that the latter is equivalent to $\overrightarrow{C_{i*}}.\overrightarrow{C_{*j}} = \sum_{k \in Pred.(j) \setminus \{i\}} C_{ik}.C_{kj} + C_{ij}$.

Definition 11 (Trust matrix product). *Let $C_{(ij)}$ and $M_{(ij)}$ be two trust matrices. We define the matrix product $N = C * M$ by: $\forall i, j \in \{1..n\}$*

$$N_{ij} = \begin{cases} \overrightarrow{C_{i*}}.\overrightarrow{M_{*j}} = \sum_{k \in V}^{k \neq j} C_{ik}.M_{kj} & if \; i \neq j \\ \langle 1, 0, 0 \rangle & otherwise \end{cases}$$

Lemma 6. *Let (C_{ij}) be the trust matrix of a network of entities, whose elements belong to a trust graph G. The matrix M defined by: $M = C^2 = C * C$ represents the 2-aggregated trust between all distinct entity pairs and the total trust of entities for themselves.*

Proof. From definition 11, we have: $M_{ij} = \begin{cases} \overrightarrow{C_{i*}}.\overrightarrow{C_{*j}} = \sum_{k \in V}^{k \neq j} C_{ik}.C_{kj} & if \; i \neq j \\ \langle 1, 0, 0 \rangle & otherwise \end{cases}$.

Thus, if $i = j$, then $M_{ii} = \langle 1, 0, 0 \rangle$ as claimed. Otherwise, $i \neq j$ and according to lemma 5, M_{ij} the 2-aggregated trust between i and j.

Now, according to definition 6 of the trust evaluation in a network, we can generalize lemma 6 to evaluate trust using all paths of a given length:

Theorem 1. *Let $G = (V, E, \mathcal{T})$ be an acyclic trust graph with matrix of trust C. Then C^d represents the d-aggregated trust between all entity pairs in V.*

Proof. We proceed by induction. Let $HR(d)$ be the hypothesis that C^d represents the d-aggregated trust between all entity pairs in V. Then $HR(2)$ is true from lemma 6. Now let us suppose that $HR(d)$ is true. First if $i = j$, then $(d + 1)$-$\text{agg}_{i,i} = \langle 1, 0, 0 \rangle = C_{i,i}^{d+1}$ from definition 11. Second, definition 6, gives:

$$(d+1)\text{-agg}_{i,j} = \sum_{k \in Pred.(j)\backslash\{i\}} d\text{-agg}_{ik}.C_{kj} + C_{ij} \qquad \text{by def. 6}$$

$$= \sum_{k \in Pred.(j)\backslash\{i\}} C_{ik}^d.C_{kj} + C_{ij} \qquad \text{by } HR(d)$$

$$= \sum_{k \in Pred.(j)} C_{ik}^d.C_{kj} \qquad \text{since } C_{ii} = \langle 1, 0, 0 \rangle$$

$$= \sum_{\substack{k \in V \\ k \neq j}} C_{ik}^d.C_{kj} \qquad \text{if } (ik) \notin E,\ C_{ik} = \langle 0, 0, 1 \rangle$$

Overall, $HR(d + 1)$ is proven and induction proves the theorem.

From this theorem, we immediately have that in an acyclic graph the matrix powers must converge to a fixed point.

Corollary 1. *Let $G = (V, E, \mathcal{T})$ be an acyclic trust graph with trust matrix C. The successive application of the matrix powers of C converges to a matrix C^ℓ, where ℓ is the size of the longest path in G. Which means that C^ℓ is a fixed point for the matrix powers:*

$$\lim_{n \to \infty} C^n = C^l$$

For the proof of this corollary, we need the following lemma.

Lemma 7. *Let $\lambda_{i,j}$ be the length of the largest path between i and j. Then either $\lambda_{i,j} = 1$ or $\lambda_{i,j} = max_{k \in Pred.(j)\backslash\{i\}}(\lambda_{i,k}) + 1$.*

Proof (Proof of corollary 1). We prove the result by induction and consider the hypothesis $HR(d)$ with $d \geq 1$:

$$\forall i, j \in V, \text{ such that } \lambda_{i,j} \leq d \text{ and } \forall t \geq \lambda_{ij}, \text{ then } C_{ij}^t = C_{ij}^{\lambda_{i,j}}$$

We first prove the hypothesis for $d = 1$: Let i and j be such that the longest path between them is of length 1. This means that in this acyclic directed graph, there is only one path between i and j, the edge $i \to j$. Now from definition 6, we have that $\forall t, C_{ij}^t = \sum_{k \in Pred.(j)\backslash\{i\}} C_{ik}^{t-1}.C_{kj} + C_{ij}$. However, $Pred.(j) \backslash \{i\} = \emptyset$ so that $C_{ij}^t = C_{ij}$, for all t. This proves $HR(1)$.

Now suppose that $HR(d)$ is true. Let i and j be two vertices in $G(V, E, \mathcal{T})$. We have two cases. First case: $\lambda_{ij} \leq d$. Then $\lambda_{i,j} \leq d + 1$ and from the induction hypothesis, we have that $C_{ij}^t = C_{ij}^{\lambda_{ij}} \forall t \geq \lambda_{ij}$. Therefore $HR(d + 1)$ is true for i and j. Second case: $\lambda_{ij} = d + 1 \geq 2$. Then we have $\forall u \geq 0$ $C_{ij}^{d+1+u} = \sum_{k \in Pred.(j)} C_{ik}^{d+u}.C_{kj}$. Now, from lemma 7, the maximum length of any path between i and a predecessor of j is $\lambda_{i,j} - 1 = d$. Therefore, from the induction hypothesis, we have that $C_{ik}^{d+u} = C_{ik}^{\lambda_{ik}} = C_{ik}^d$ for all $k \in Pred.(j)$. Then $C_{ij}^{d+1+u} = \sum_{k \in Pred.(j)} C_{ik}^d.C_{kj} = C_{ij}^{d+1}$ which proves the induction and thus the corollary.

From the latter corollary, we now have an algorithm to compute the trust evaluation between all the nodes in an acyclic trust network: perform the trust matrix powering with the monoids laws up to the longest path in the graph.

Theorem 2. *Let (C_{ij}) be the trust matrix corresponding to an acyclic graph with n vertices and φ edges whose longest path is of size ℓ. The complexity of the evaluation of the aggregated trust between all entity pairs represented by this trust matrix is bounded by $O(n \cdot \varphi \cdot \ell)$ operations.*

Proof. C is sparse with φ non zero element. Thus multiplying C by a vector requires $O(\varphi)$ operations and computing $C \times C^i$ requires $O(n\varphi)$ operations. Then, theorem 1 shows that C^j for $j \geq \ell$ is the j-aggregated trust between any entity pair. Finally, corollary 1 shows that $C^j = C^\ell$ as soon as $j \geq \ell$.

The implementation of this algorithm took less than 1 second to perform an iteration (C^2) on the graph of section 2 with 1000 vertices and $250K$ edges. And it needed less than 6 seconds to return the final trust degrees.

4   Evaluation of Trust in the Presence of Cycles

The algorithm induced by theorem 1 works only for directed acyclic graphs. Its advantage is thus restricted to the case when the distrust is *not* taken into consideration: then block or sparse algorithms can provide the BLAS[3] linear algebra performance to trust evaluation.

Now, in the presence of cycles in a network, the matrix powers algorithm will add the contribution of each edge of a cycle indefinitely.

Consider the graph of figure 4, with a, b, c, d the trust degrees corresponding to the links $1 \xrightarrow{a} 2 \xrightarrow{b} 3 \xrightarrow{c} 4 \xrightarrow{d} 2$. Its trust matrix C and applications of the matrix powers algorithm on this matrix are shown on figure 4, right.

For instance, the value:

$$C_{1,3}^5 = 0 + C_{1,2}^4 C_{2,3} + 0 = (C_{1,2} + C_{1,4}^3 C_{4,2})C_{2,3}$$
$$= (C_{1,2} + (C_{1,3}^2 C_{3,4})C_{4,2})C_{2,3} = (C_{1,2} + (C_{1,2}C_{2,3})C_{3,4})C_{4,2})C_{2,3}$$
$$= (a + a.b.c.d).b,$$

corresponds to the aggregation on the paths $1 \to 2 \to 3$ and $1 \to 2 \to 3 \to 4 \to 2 \to 3$ linking 1 to 3. If we continue iterations for $n > 5$, we find that the algorithm re-evaluates infinitely the trust on the loop $3 \to 4 \to 2 \to 3$ to yield $C_{1,3}^{2+3k} = (a + C_{1,3}^{2+3k-1}.b.c.d).b$ with most probably an increase in uncertainty (e.g. from the many sequential aggregations and lemma 2).

4.1   Convergent Iteration

To solve this issue, we propose to change the matrix multiplication procedure, so that *each edge will be used only once in the assessment of a trust relationship.*

---
[3] e.g. ATLAS [23], GotoBLAS [9], MUMPS http://graal.ens-lyon.fr/MUMPS etc.

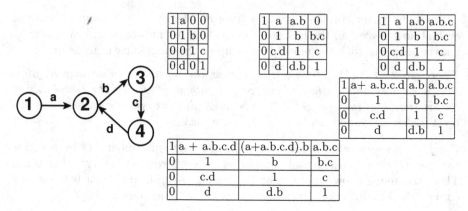

$$
C^2=\begin{bmatrix}1&a&0&0\\0&1&b&0\\0&0&1&c\\0&d&0&1\end{bmatrix}\quad
C^3=\begin{bmatrix}1&a&a.b&0\\0&1&b&b.c\\0&c.d&1&c\\0&d&d.b&1\end{bmatrix}\quad
C^4=\begin{bmatrix}1&a&a.b&a.b.c\\0&1&b&b.c\\0&c.d&1&c\\0&d&d.b&1\end{bmatrix}
$$

$$
\begin{bmatrix}1&a+\,a.b.c.d&a.b&a.b.c\\0&1&b&b.c\\0&c.d&1&c\\0&d&d.b&1\end{bmatrix}
$$

$$
C^5=\begin{bmatrix}1&a+a.b.c.d&(a+a.b.c.d).b&a.b.c\\0&1&b&b.c\\0&c.d&1&c\\0&d&d.b&1\end{bmatrix}
$$

Fig. 4. Graph with one cycle and its trust matrix C with C^2, C^3, C^4 and C^5.

For this, we use a memory matrix R_{ij}. This stores, for each pair of nodes, all edges traversed to evaluate their trust degree. Only the paths containing an edge not already traversed to evaluate the trust degree are taken into account at the following iteration. Therefore, the computation of C_{ij}^ℓ for $n \geq 1$, becomes that given in algorithm 1.

Algorithm 1. Matrix powers for generic network graphs

Input An $n \times n$ matrix of trust C of a generic directed trust graph.
Output Global trust in the network.
1: $\ell = 2$;
2: **Repeat**
3:    **For all** $(i,j) \in [1..n]^2$ with $i \neq j$ **do**
4:        $C_{ij}^\ell = \langle 0,0,1 \rangle$;
5:        $R_{ij}^\ell = \emptyset$;
6:        **For** $k = 1$ **to** n **do**
7:            $t = C_{ik}^{\ell-1}.C_{kj}$;
8:            **If** $(t \neq \langle 0,0,1 \rangle)$ **then**
9:                $C_{ij}^\ell = C_{ij}^\ell + t$;
10:               $R_{ij}^\ell = R_{ij}^\ell \bigcup R_{ik}^{\ell-1} \bigcup (k \to j)$; // using a sorted list union
11:           **End If**
12:       **End For**
13:       **If** $\left(\#R_{ij}^\ell \subset \#R_{ij}^{\ell-1}\right)$ **then** $C_{ij}^\ell = C_{ij}^{\ell-1}; R_{ij}^\ell = R_{ij}^{\ell-1};$ **End If**
14:   **End For**
15: **Until** $C^\ell == C^{\ell-1}$; $++\ell$;
16: **return** C^ℓ;

By doing this modification of the matrix multiplication we will obtain a different trust evaluation. We have no guarantee that this new evaluation is somewhat more accurate but intuitively as in any path an edge is considered only once, cycles will not have a preponderate effect. Furthermore, we recover an interesting fixed point.

Theorem 3. *Let C be the trust matrix corresponding to a generic trust graph. Algorithm 1 converges to the matrix C^ℓ where ℓ is the longest acyclic path between vertices.*

Proof. Let C^ℓ be the evaluation of the ℓ-aggregated trust between all entity pairs after ℓ iterations where ℓ is the longest acyclic path between vertices. At this stage, for each pair i, j, all the edges belonging to a path between i and j will be marked in R_{ij}^ℓ. Therefore, no new $t = C_{ik}^\ell . C_{kj}$ will be added to $C_{ij}^{\ell+1}$. Conversely, at iteration $x < \ell$, if there exist an acyclic path between a pair i, j of length greater than x, then it means that there exists at least one edge e not yet considered on a sub-path from, say, u to v, of length x: $i \dashrightarrow u \dashrightarrow \overset{e}{\rightarrow} \dashrightarrow v \dashrightarrow j$. Then R_{uv}^x will be different from R_{uv}^{x-1} and so will be C_{uv}^x from C_{uv}^{x-1}. $\quad\square$

Theorem 4. *Let C be the trust matrix corresponding to a generic trust graph with n vertices and φ edges whose longest path between vertices is of size ℓ. The complexity of the global evaluation of all the paths between any entity is bounded by $O(n^3 \cdot \varphi \cdot \ell)$ operations.*

Proof. Using algorithm 1, we see that the triple loop induces n^3 monoid operations and n^3 merge of the sorted lists of edges. A merge of sorted lists is linear in the number of edges, φ. Then the overall iteration is performed at most ℓ times from theorem 3. $\quad\square$

By applying the new algorithm on the example of figure 4, we still obtain $C_{1,3}^5 = (a + a.b.c.d).b$, but now $R_{1,3}^5 = \{a, b, c, d\}$ and thus no more contribution can be added to $C_{1,3}^{5+i}$.

A first naive dense implementation of this algorithm took about 1.3 seconds to perform the first iteration (C^2) on the graph of section 2 with 1000 vertices and $250K$ edges. And it needed only 7 iterations to return the final trust degrees with high precision.

Remark 4. More generally, the convergence will naturally be linked to the ratio of the dominant and subdominant eigenvalues of the matrix. For instance on some random matrices it can be shown that this ratio is $O(\sqrt{n})$ [7, Remark 2.19], and this is what we had experimentally. Of course, for, e.g., PKI trust graphs, more studies on the structure of the typical network would have to be conducted.

4.2   Bounded Evaluation of Trust

In practice, the evaluation of trust between two nodes A and B need not consider all trust paths connecting A to B for two reasons:

- First, the mitigation is one of the trust properties, i.e. the trust throughout trust paths decreases with the length of the latter. Therefore after a certain length L, the trust on paths becomes weak and thus should have a low contribution in improving the trust degree after their parallel aggregation.

- Second, if at some iteration $n \geq 1$, we already obtained a high trust degree, then contributions of other paths will only be minor.

Therefore, it is possible to use the matrix powers algorithm with less iterations and e.g. a threshold for the trust degree, in order to rapidly compute a good approximation of the trust in a network. To determine the optimal threshold, we have conducted hundreds of comparisons between results of each iterations of our algorithm and the final trust degrees computed with Algorithm 1. We found that on average on $1K$-vertices random matrices, we needed 6 iterations to get an approximation of the trust degrees at 0.01, and only 7 iterations[4] (in 97% of the cases) to achieve an error rate less than 10^{-6}.

5   Conclusion and Remarks

The actual public-key infrastructure models assume that the relationships between the PKI entities are based on an absolute trust. However, several risks are related to these assumptions when using PKI procedures.

In this paper, we have reduced the evaluation of trust between entities of a DAG network to linear algebra. This gives a polynomial algorithm to asses the global trust evaluation in a network. Moreover, depending on the sparsity of the considered graphs, this enables to use adapted linear algebra methods. Also the linear algebra algorithm decomposes the evaluation into converging iterations. These iterations can be terminated earlier than convergence in order to get a good approximation faster. Finally this enabled us also to generalize the trust evaluation to any directed graph, i.e. not necessarily acyclic, still with a polynomial complexity.

Further work include the determination of the optimal number of iterations necessary to get a good approximation of trust in minimal time. Small-world theory for instance could be of help [22, 2].

Also, there is a restriction in the current trust models, which imposes that Alice cannot communicate with Bob if there is no trust path between them. However, this limitation can be overcome by using the reputation notion jointly with the trust notion. If Alice can be sure that Bob has a good reputation in its friends circle and vice versa, then they can extend their trusty network and communicate safely [21].

Finally, the choice of the implementation model is a crucial subject. One approach is to adopt a centralized model, where all computation are done by a unique trusty entity. Then the reliability of the system depends entirely on the reliability of the trusted entity. This would typically be achieved by CAs. Another approach is a distributed model, where the entities must contact each others to share some trust degrees. This will enable each entity to evaluate the (at least *local*) trust in its neighborhood. On the one hand, this can be

---

[4] From remark 4, we see that would the product be a classical matrix product, $\sqrt{n}$ being about 32, to get an approximation at 10^{-6} we would have needed on the order of $6/log_{10}32 \approx 3.98 \leq 4$ iterations to converge.

applied to large networks while preserving for each entity a low computational cost. On the other hand, each entity might have only a limited view of the whole network. Therefore, a dedicated Network Discovery Mechanism (NDM) is needed to expand the entities trust sub-network. This NDM can be crucial to determine the trust model safety [10]. Besides, the trust degrees could be a sensitive information. Therefore, the join use of trust matrices and homomorphic cryptosystems enabling a private computation of shared secret could be useful.

References

1. Adkins, H.: An update on attempted man-in-the-middle attacks. Technical report, Google Online Security Blog (August 2011),
   http://googleonlinesecurity.blogspot.com/2011/
   08/update-on-attempted-man-in-middle.html
2. Albert, R., Jeong, H., Barabasi, A.-L.: Diameter of the world-wide web. Nature 401, 130–131 (1999)
3. Dolev, S., Gilboa, N., Kopeetsky, M.: Computing multi-party trust privately: in O(n) time units sending one (possibly large) message at a time. In: Proceedings of the ACM Symposium on Applied Computing, SAC 2010, pp. 1460–1465. ACM, New York (2010)
4. Ellison, C., Schneier, B.: Ten risks of PKI: What you're not being told about Public Key Infrastructure. Computer Security Journal 16(1), 1–7 (2000),
   http://www.counterpane.com/pki-risks.pdf
5. Estrada, E., Hatano, N.: Communicability graph and community structures in complex networks. Applied Mathematics and Computation 214(2), 500–511 (2009)
6. Foley, S.N., Adams, W.M., O'Sullivan, B.: Aggregating trust using triangular norms in the keyNote trust management system. In: Cuellar, J., Lopez, J., Barthe, G., Pretschner, A. (eds.) STM 2010. LNCS, vol. 6710, pp. 100–115. Springer, Heidelberg (2011)
7. Goldberg, G., Okunev, P., Neumann, M., Schneider, H.: Distribution of subdominant eigenvalues of random matrices. Methodology and Computing in Applied Probability 2, 137–151 (2000)
8. Gomes, F.: Security alert: Fraudulent digital certificates. Technical report, SANS Institute InfoSec Reading Room (June 2001),
   http://www.sans.org/reading_room/whitepapers/certificates/
   security-alert-fraudulent-digital-certificates_679
9. Goto, K., van de Geijn, R.A.: High-performance implementation of the level-3 BLAS. ACM Transactions on Mathematical Software 35(1), 4:1–4:14 (2008)
10. Govindan, K., Mohapatra, P.: Trust computations and trust dynamics in mobile adhoc networks: A survey. IEEE Communications Surveys and Tutorials 14(2), 279–298 (2012)
11. Guha, R., Kumar, R., Raghavan, P., Tomkins, A.: Propagation of trust and distrust. In: Proceedings of the 13th International Conference on World Wide Web, WWW 2004, pp. 403–412. ACM, New York (2004)
12. Huang, J., Nicol, D.: A calculus of trust and its application to PKI and identity management. In: Proceedings of the 8th Symposium on Identity and Trust on the Internet, IDTRUST 2009, pp. 23–37. ACM, New York (2009)
13. Huang, J., Nicol, D.: A formal-semantics-based calculus of trust. IEEE Internet Computing 14, 38–46 (2010)

14. Jøsang, A.: Trust extortion on the internet. In: Meadows, C., Fernandez-Gago, C. (eds.) STM 2011. LNCS, vol. 7170, pp. 6–21. Springer, Heidelberg (2012)
15. Jøsang, A.: Probabilistic logic under uncertainty. In: Proceedings of Computing: The Australian Theory Symposium (CATS 2007) (January 2007)
16. Orman, L.V.: Transitivity and aggregation in trust networks. In: Proc. of the 21st Workshop on Information Technologies and Systems (WITS 2010) (December 2010)
17. Pala, M.: A proposal for collaborative internet-scale trust infrastructures deployment: the public key system (pks). In: Proceedings of the 9th Symposium on Identity and Trust on the Internet, IDTRUST 2010, pp. 108–116. ACM, New York (2010)
18. Pala, M., Smith, S.W.: Peaches and peers. In: Mjølsnes, S.F., Mauw, S., Katsikas, S.K. (eds.) EuroPKI 2008. LNCS, vol. 5057, pp. 223–238. Springer, Heidelberg (2008)
19. Reiter, M.K., Stubblebine, S.G.: Resilient authentication using path independence. IEEE Trans. Comput. 47, 1351–1362 (1998)
20. Rifà-Pous, H., Herrera-Joancomartí, J.: An interdomain PKI model based on trust lists. In: López, J., Samarati, P., Ferrer, J.L. (eds.) EuroPKI 2007. LNCS, vol. 4582, pp. 49–64. Springer, Heidelberg (2007)
21. Schiffner, S., Clauß, S., Steinbrecher, S.: Privacy and liveliness for reputation systems. In: Martinelli, F., Preneel, B. (eds.) EuroPKI 2009. LNCS, vol. 6391, pp. 209–224. Springer, Heidelberg (2010)
22. Schnettler, S.: A structured overview of 50 years of small-world research. Social Networks 31(3), 165–178 (2009)
23. Whaley, R.C., Petitet, A., Dongarra, J.J.: Automated empirical optimizations of software and the ATLAS project. Parallel Computing 27(1–2), 3–35 (2001), http://www.netlib.org/utk/people/JackDongarra/PAPERS/atlas_pub.pdf

Formal Modelling of (De)Pseudonymisation:
A Case Study in Health Care Privacy

Meilof Veeningen, Benne de Weger, and Nicola Zannone

Eindhoven University of Technology, The Netherlands
{m.veeningen,b.m.m.d.weger,n.zannone}@tue.nl

Abstract. In recent years, a number of infrastructures have been proposed for the collection and distribution of medical data for research purposes. The design of such infrastructures is challenging: on the one hand, they should link patient data collected from different hospitals; on the other hand, they can only use anonymised data because of privacy regulations. In addition, they should allow data depseudonymisation in case research results provide information relevant for patients' health. The privacy analysis of such infrastructures can be seen as a problem of data minimisation. In this work, we introduce coalition graphs, a graphical representation of knowledge of personal information to study data minimisation. We show how this representation allows identification of privacy issues in existing infrastructures. To validate our approach, we use coalition graphs to formally analyse data minimisation in two (de)-pseudonymisation infrastructures proposed by the Parelsnoer initiative.

1 Introduction

The quality of medical research benefits from the collection of patient data from different health care organisations. By analysing data from different sources, researchers are able to study treatments from several angles, which can lead to new insights. To facilitate the collection and dissemination of medical data, several initiatives like the Dutch Parelsnoer initiative have developed data management infrastructures [11–13]. Such infrastructures store patient data collected from health care organisations into a central medical research database and then distribute such data to researchers. Besides providing data to researchers, they should also allow the sharing of findings about patients' conditions made by researchers to hospitals in order to provide treatments to patients.

When distributing patient data, these infrastructures should protect the patient's privacy by making sure that data are properly anonymised.In particular, researchers should not be able to link data to a particular patient, or data from different research projects to each other. However, it is not possible to just remove all identifiers from the data: the need to share findings with the patient's hospital implies that the data may need to be deanonymised. Thus, there is a need to supplement data management infrastructures for medical research with (de)pseudonymisation functionality. Depseudonymisation should be possible only following a rigorous process involving a coalition of several different

A. Jøsang, P. Samarati, and M. Petrocchi (Eds.): STM 2012, LNCS 7783, pp. 145–160, 2013.

parties; the infrastructure should technically ensure that other coalitions do not have anough knowledge to correlate patient data.

The problem of depseudonymisation exemplifies the broader concept of data minimisation [9], which is nowadays imposed by privacy regulations (e.g., EU Directive 95/46/EC, HIPAA). Data minimisation decreases both the risk of abuse by insiders [8] and the impact of information theft by outsiders. The concept is gaining relevance as the increase in personal information exchanged on-line has raised privacy issues not only about health care data, but also search data, data on shopping habits, etc. However, comprehensive analyses of data minimisation in these different settings are usually lacking. In discussions on (de)pseudonymisation of health care data and proposed infrastructures (e.g., [3, 10, 13]), the aim is usually to prevent knowledge of *particular* links by *particular* actors; however, a full analysis of data minimisation that considers *all* possible correlations allowed by a system and checks whether they are inherent to the setting or preventable, is usually missing.

In [19], we presented a formal model that, given the information exchanged between actors, analyses the knowledge of personal information that actors learn. This model makes it possible to verify privacy requirements by checking whether a particular coalition of actors can correlate particular pieces of information. However, it neither provides a general comparison of all knowledge of all coalitions in different infrastructures, nor discusses the concept of minimality.

In this work, we study data minimisation in the Parelsnoer infrastructure for health care data (de)pseudonymisation. We discuss general requirements for such infrastructures, but focus our analysis on Parelsnoer (we briefly discuss related proposals in Section 7). We introduce a novel formalism, called *coalition graphs*, to express the profiles of personal information that can be compiled by coalitions of actors within a system. We show how coalition graphs can be used to comprehensively model data minimisation, identify possible privacy improvements, and verify their effect. Specifically:

- We capture different privacy risks by considering actors that only store what they should store and actors that remember all information they observe;
- We show how coalition graphs can be derived automatically from a formal model describing actors' communication [19] ;
- By formalising requirements for distributing medical data for research, and privacy consequences of using a central database, we model the "optimal" situation in terms of data minimisation achievable by (de)pseudonymisation infrastructures;
- Using coalition graphs, we analyse two (de)pseudonymisation infrastructures proposed by the Parelsnoer initiative, and propose privacy improvements.

The paper is structured as follows. We first describe the setting of distributing patient data for research, and two infrastructures proposed by Parelsnoer (§2). We then introduce coalition graphs (§3). We derive an optimal coalition graph for the Parelsnoer setting (§4), use it to analyse data minimisation in the proposed infrastructures (§5), and analyse possible improvements (§6). Finally, we discuss related work and conclude by providing directions for future work (§7).

2   Pseudonymisation Infrastructure

In this section, we discuss the requirements for (de)pseudonymisation infrastructures for medical research databases. In particular, we consider the privacy requirements defined within the Dutch legal framework regarding the processing of medical data. We then present two (de)pseudonymisation infrastructures developed as a result of the Parelsnoer initiative (http://www.parelsnoer.org/): one based on hashing, and one based on a trusted "pseudonymisation service".

2.1   Setting

For medical research, data about a patient collected from different health care organisations have to be linked together into a single dataset. Data integration, however, is challenging because of the stringent constraints imposed by data protection regulations. We now discuss the functional (**FR**) and privacy (**PR**) requirements for the handling of medical data within the Dutch legal framework.

The Dutch legal framework constrains the identification of medical data. For treatment, health care organisations are obliged to use the "burgerservicenummer" (BSN: the Dutch social security number) (**FR1**); for other purposes, they (and others) are forbidden to do so (**PR1**). Medical data may be used for research (**FR2**) if anonymised so that association to the BSN or (indirectly) to the patient is impossible, and different projects' datasets cannot be linked (**PR2**).

However, in certain circumstances, this anonymisation needs to be reversed. In case of a discovery beneficial for the patient (a so-called *coincidental finding*), the health care organisations which collected the data should be notified so they can provide treatment: *full depseudonymisation* (**FR3**). Moreover, if additional patient data is needed for a certain research project, it should be possible to link together data about the same patient: *partial depseudonymisation* (**FR4**).

To facilitate the provision of medical data to researchers, data collected from different health care organisations can be stored into a single database [11–13], hereafter called *Central Infrastructure* (CI). We describe the operation of systems with a CI by enumerating the main design decisions (**DD**) that cover the handling of personal information. The CI stores the data about one patient from different hospitals in one profile (**DD1**). It obtains this data directly from the different hospitals (**DD2**). When a researcher needs a dataset, the CI compiles it from its database and sends it to the researcher (**DD3**), who is not otherwise involved in the pseudonymisation process. For extension of a dataset (i.e., partial depseudonymisation), the researcher contacts the CI, which then compiles the extended dataset without involving the original hospital (**DD4**). Finally, depseudonymisation should be performed via a trusted third party to ensure that it is only possible under strictly defined conditions (**DD5**).

2.2   Parelsnoer Initiative

This section presents two infrastructures for (de)pseudonymisation developed by the Parelsnoer initiative [11, 12]. This initiative is a collaboration between eight university medical centres in the Netherlands.

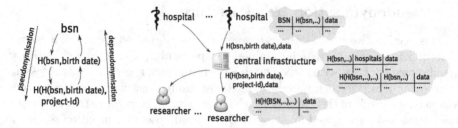

Fig. 1. Parelsnoer Hash-Based Pseudonymisation Infrastructure (H-PI): pseudonyms (left) and operation (right)

Hash-Based Pseudonymisation Infrastructure (H-PI). The first Parelsnoer proposal for (de)pseudonymisation [11] uses pseudonyms for the storage and transmission of medical data that are constructed using hash functions (Figure 1). In particular, when providing data to the CI, hospitals use a hash h_1 of a patient's BSN and birth date as pseudonym. This allows the CI to link data from different hospitals without learning the BSN. Each research project has a separate identifier; when the CI distributes data for a research project, the project identifier is hashed along with the pseudonym h_1 into a new pseudonym h_2. For partial depseudonymisation, the CI needs a table containing the links (h_1, h_2) for all distributed datasets. For full depseudonymisation, the CI additionally needs a table containing the identities of hospitals for all patient pseudonyms h_1. Each hospital stores a table containing the links (bsn, h_1) for its own patients.

One drawback of this approach is that an attacker who learns a pseudonym, can try to depseudonymise it using a dictionary attack: this is feasible because the entropy in the combination of BSN and birth date is at most 42 bits [11]. In addition, the fact that hospitals and CI need to keep pseudonym translation tables poses significant risks of data breaches. Note that H-PI does not use a TTP to control depseudonymisation; as shown later, this makes it non-optimal in terms of data minimisation.

Pseudonymisation Service Infrastructure (PS-PI). Parelsnoer's Pseudonymisation Service Infrastructure [12] addresses the limitations of the hash-based approach using a TTP called *pseudonymisation service* (PS). The pseudonyms used in the system are called "pseudocodes". These pseudocodes are unique given a BSN and a "domain" (i.e., the CI, hospitals, and research projects) in which patient data should be linked. The mapping between BSNs and pseudocodes and between pseudocodes from different domains is calculated using a domain-specific secret known only by the PS.

Figure 2 shows the translation steps (left) and the information that is exchanged and stored (right). First, the PS translates the BSN into a pseudocode in the hospital domain, which the hospital uses to send medical data to the CI. The CI requests the PS to re-translate the pseudocode to its own domain so it can link data from different hospitals together. When data are distributed to a researcher, the pseudocode is translated to the project domain. For depseudonymisation,

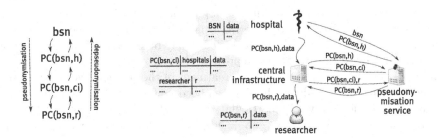

Fig. 2. Parelsnoer Infrastructure with Pseudonymisation Service (PS-PI): pseudonyms (left) and operation (right)

pseudocodes are translated back to the BSN in exactly the opposite order. For partial depseudonymisation, the researcher provides the research pseudocode to the CI, which requests the PS to translate it to its own domain. The CI remembers which research domain belongs to which researcher; it includes the research domain in the depseudonymisation request to the PS, which compares it to the actual domain within the pseudocode. For full depseudonymisation, the CI then requests the PS to translate the pseudocode from the CI domain to the hospital domain based on the list of hospitals that have provided data.

This infrastructure solves the drawbacks of the hash-based infrastructure. Since pseudocodes are calculated using a secret known only by the PS, this infrastructure is not subject to dictionary attacks. Moreover, the hospital and CI no longer store tables to translate pseudocodes to BSNs. Indeed, depseudonymisation is not possible without the PS, reducing privacy impact when data of hospitals and the CI are compromised.

2.3   Scenario

We introduce a scenario that is general enough to capture all aspects we are interested in yet small enough to allow a clear visualisation. We consider (coalitions of) six different actors: three hospitals umc_1, umc_2, and umc_3; one researcher r; and CI ci and TTP ttp (in PS-PI: the PS). These actors exchange information about a particular patient. Two of the three hospitals have medical data about the patient: umc_1 knows three pieces of information d_1, d_2, and d_3; umc_2 knows d_4, d_5, and d_6. The items d_i are non-identifying; i.e., they represent attributes for which different patients may have a common value. The hospitals identify their patient records by BSN bsn. The third hospital umc_3 does not know the patient. Researcher r needs data about the patient for two different research projects: d_1 and d_4 for one project, and d_2 and d_5 for a second project. By considering two hospitals with patient data and one without, we can consider correlation between these two types of hospitals and other actors, and between two different hospitals that both know the patient. Verifying privacy with respect to data of one single researcher from two different projects is sufficient: if she cannot link the data, then neither can two different researchers from two different projects.

Our scenario has three steps. First, umc_1 and umc_2 provide their patient data to ci. Second, r receives patient data from the ci in two different datasets for the two different projects. In both steps, the TTP may be involved. Third, as part of the investigation in the first research project, the researcher learns a coincidental finding d_7 that may be important for treatment of the patient. We consider the moment when the coincidental finding has been made, but depseudonymisation has not been performed yet. In particular, the hospitals do not know d_7 yet, so we can reason about coalitions that enable hospitals to link d_7 to the corresponding patient.

3   Coalition Graphs

In this section, we introduce coalition graphs as a graphical way of studying data minimisation. First, we phrase the data minimisation problem in terms of profiles derivable by coalitions of actors. We then introduce coalition graphs as a way to compare infrastructures. Finally, we show how to obtain coalition graphs automatically, and how to use them for data minimisation analysis.

3.1   Data Minimisation, Coalition Knowledge, and Forgetting

The data minimisation principle aims to prevent abuse of personal information by restricting the information an actor can collect to what is strictly necessary to carry out assigned duties. The adherence of actors to data minimisation can be analysed with respect to their behaviours. *Honest* actors store only the information the system allows them to store. However, actors may observe other information. We call actors who store all the information they observe *honest-but-curious*. As an example, the PS-PI architecture aims to ensure that depseudonymisation can only happen though the PS. However, this data minimisation goal can only be achieved when the other actors are honest: if hospitals and the CI are honest-but-curious, they can link data by remembering pseudocodes and thus bypass the PS. We analyse data minimisation with respect to arbitrary coalitions of honest and honest-but-curious actors, thus clarifying the assumptions under which privacy properties hold. Although honest and honest-but-curious actors differ in what they remember, they both only obtain the information that they are supposed to obtain. Privacy protection against actors who actively try to obtain information they should not know, is out of our scope (but could be captured by coalition graphs).

In [18], we proposed personal information models as a representation of actors' knowledge of personal information. A personal information model consists of items of interest (i.e., data items, identifiers, and entities) and linkability relations between them. *Data items* and *identifiers* are pieces of information that characterise an *entity*. Differently from data items, identifiers uniquely identify an entity (e.g., social security number). The set $\mathcal{O}$ denotes the items of interest, i.e., sensitive information to be protected. In our scenario, $\mathcal{O} = \{bsn, d_1, ..., d_7\}$, where bsn is an identifier and $d_1, \ldots, d_7$ are data items. This set does not contain pseudonyms because their knowledge in itself is not relevant; the fact that they can be used to link different pieces of data together is accounted for by the linkability relation. A *profile* is a set $O \subset \mathcal{O}$ of items of interest characterising the same entity; e.g., $\{bsn, d_1, d_2, d_3\}$ represents the patient's profile at umc_1.

Actors have partial knowledge of the personal information model. Set $\mathcal{A}$ denotes the set of actors involved in the system (in our scenario, $\mathcal{A} = \{umc_1, umc_2, umc_3, ci, ttp, r\}$). These actors are honest; we denote their honest-but-curious counterparts with a *, e.g., $ci^* \in \mathcal{A}^*$ is the honest-but-curious counterpart of ci. A *coalition* of actors is any subset of $\mathcal{A} \cup \mathcal{A}^*$ in which actors can be either honest or honest-but-curious. For instance, $\{umc_1, ci^*\}$ is a coalition formed by a honest umc_1 and a honest-but-curious ci. Coalition A can be *extended* to coalition B, denoted $A \sqsubseteq B$, if any honest actor in A is also in B (either honest-but-curious or honest), and any honest-but-curious actor in A is also honest-but-curious in B. For instance, $\{umc_1\} \sqsubseteq \{umc_1, ci\} \sqsubseteq \{umc_1, ci^*\}$ but $\{umc_1^*\} \not\sqsubseteq \{umc_1, ci^*\}$.

The knowledge of coalitions is captured by the *profile detectability* relation $\vDash$. Given a coalition A and a set $O \subset \mathcal{O}$ of pieces of information, $A \vDash O$ expresses that coalition A knows: 1) the items in O (detectability); and 2) the fact that the items in O are about one single person (linkability). For instance, $\{umc_1\} \vDash \{bsn, d_1, d_2, d_3\}$ indicates that umc_1 knows bsn, d_1, d_2, and d_3 and it knows that these items of interest belong to the same patient. Similarly, $\{r\} \not\vDash \{d_1, d_2\}$ indicates that r is not able to link d_1 and d_2. Profile detectability $\vDash$ satisfies two properties: 1) if $A \vDash O$ and $A \sqsubseteq B$, then $B \vDash O$; and 2) if $A \vDash O$ and $P \subseteq O$, then $A \vDash P$. We say that $A \vDash O$ *implies* $B \vDash P$ if $A \sqsubseteq B$ and $P \subseteq O$.

3.2   Coalition Graphs, Comparison, and Reduction

The information known by coalitions of actors can be visually represented as a directed graph. Nodes are pairs (A, O) such that $A \vDash O$. Edges are defined by the partial order $\leq$ on nodes that combines the partial orders on coalitions and profiles. $(A_1, O_1) \leq (A_2, O_2)$ expresses that coalition A_2 is an extension of coalition A_1, and profile O_2 is a superset of profile O_1. Formally:

Definition 1. *The* coalition graph *for relation* $\vDash$ *is the graph* $(V, \leq)$ *with:*

- $V = \{(A, O) \mid A \sqsubseteq \mathcal{A}^*;\ O \subset \mathcal{O};\ A \vDash O\}$
- $(A_1, O_1) \leq (A_2, O_2)$ *iff* $A_1 \sqsubseteq A_2 \wedge O_1 \subseteq O_2$.

Infrastructures can be compared wrt data minimisation by means of their coalition graph. If in infrastructure X every coalition can derive at least the same information that it can in infrastructure Y, then the coalition graph of X includes all nodes of the coalition graph of Y. Moreover, $\leq$ is defined independently from $\vDash$, so if the two coalition graphs share two nodes and these nodes are connected in one graph, then they are also connected in the second graph. Based on these observations, we introduce the notion of achieving better privacy.

Definition 2. *Let X and Y be two infrastructures with coalition graphs G_X, G_Y, respectively. We say that X achieves (strictly) better privacy than Y if G_X is a (proper) subgraph of G_Y.*

For visualisation purposes, we introduce the *reduced coalition graph* $(V', \preceq)$ of a coalition graph $(V, \leq)$. In reduced graphs, redundant information from coalition graphs is eliminated: V' is the set of minimal nodes in V, i.e., nodes that are not implied by any other nodes in V; $\preceq$ is the non-reflexive, transitive reduction of $\leq$ on V'. The reduced coalition graph of an infrastructure can be determined automatically by enumerating the knowledge of all coalitions.

To verify whether infrastructure X achieves better privacy than infrastructure Y, we compare their reduced coalition graphs $(V_X, \preceq_X)$, $(V_Y, \preceq_Y)$. However, this comparison cannot be done by checking whether $(V_X, \preceq_X)$ is a subgraph of $(V_Y, \preceq_Y)$. This is because nodes that are minimal in one graph may not be minimal in the other graph. For instance, suppose $(\{a, b\}, \{d_1, d_2\}) \in V_X$ and $(\{a\}, \{d_1, d_2\}) \in V_Y$. In such a case, $(\{a, b\}, \{d_1, d_2\}) \notin V_Y$ because the node is not minimal in Y: it is implied by $(\{a\}, \{d_1, d_2\})$. Instead, in order to compare two infrastructure, we visualise their reduced coalition graphs in a single graph. The nodes of the new graph are $V_X \cup V_Y$; for each node, we indicate if it is implied in X, Y, or both. Edges are the non-reflexive, transitive reduction of $\leq$ on $V_X \cup V_Y$. Infrastructure X then satisfies better privacy than infrastructure Y if all nodes in $V_X \cup V_Y$ are implied by the nodes in V_Y.

3.3   Studying Data Minimisation by Coalition Graphs

Data minimisation analysis using coalition graphs is performed as follows. First, requirements and design decisions are formalised and represented in an "optimal" coalition graph. Then, an infrastructure is analysed through an iterative process: 1) determine the coalition graph of the infrastructure; 2) compare this graph to the optimal graph to detect design drawbacks; 3) propose enhancements.

The optimal graph is based on functional requirements and design decisions that specify the information that actors should know. They are modelled as profile detectability statements $A \vDash O$; the statement $A \vDash O$ and any statement it implies hold in all infrastructures providing the required functionality. Privacy requirements state that certain actors should *not* know certain information. These are formalised by profile undetectability statements $A \nvDash O$; the statement $A \vDash O$ and any statement implying it should not hold in well-designed infrastructures. Section 4.2 shows how to determine the optimal graph from $\vDash$.

The coalition graph of the system is computed using the formal analysis method in [19]. Given a description of initial knowledge and communication, the method determines which copies of items of interest (coalitions of) actors can detect, and which items they can link. Intuitively, actors can link items through identifiers (e.g., BSNs, pseudocodes, and session identifiers). Profile detectability $\vDash$ holds if there are detectable and mutually linkable copies of all items in the profile. We developed a tool (see http://www.mobiman.me/downloads/) that automatically generates the coalition graph by running the implementation of [19] on all coalitions, eliminating implied nodes, and visualising using GraphViz. The method in [19] only considers honest-but-curious actors. To represent honest actors, we have extended it by introducing a Store operation that describes what information actors should store. Intuitively, a data item is added to the

Table 1. Privacy consequences of functional (**FR**) and privacy (**PR**) requirements and design decisions (**DD**)

Requirement/Decision	Privacy consequences
(**FR1**) Hospitals store data using BSN	$\{umc_1\} \vDash \{bsn, d_1, d_2, d_3\}$, $\{umc_2\} \vDash \{bsn, d_4, d_5, d_6\}$
(**FR2**) Researchers obtain dataset	$\{r\} \vDash \{d_1, d_4, d_7\}$, $\{r\} \vDash \{d_2, d_5\}$
(**FR3**) Full depseudonymisation	$\{umc_1, ci, ttp, r\} \vDash \{bsn, d_7\}$, $\{umc_2, ci, ttp, r\} \vDash \{bsn, d_7\}$
(**FR4**) Partial depseudonymisation	$\{umc_1, ci, ttp, r\} \vDash \{d_1, d_2, d_3, d_7\}$, $\{umc_2, ci, ttp, r\} \vDash \{d_4, d_5, d_6, d_7\}$
(**PR1**) BSN not for research purposes	$\{r^*, ci^*, ttp^*\} \nvDash \{bsn\}$
(**PR2**) Researcher cannot link datasets	$\{r^*\} \nvDash \{d_1, d_2\}$, $\{r^*\} \nvDash \{d_1, d_5\}$, $\{r^*\} \nvDash \{d_2, d_4\}$, $\{r^*\} \nvDash \{d_4, d_5\}$
(**DD1**) CI collects data	$\{ci\} \vDash \{d_1, d_2, d_3, d_4, d_5, d_6\}$ $\{umc_1, ci, ttp\} \vDash \{bsn, d_1, d_2, d_3, d_4, d_5, d_6\}$ $\{umc_2, ci, ttp\} \vDash \{bsn, d_1, d_2, d_3, d_4, d_5, d_6\}$
(**DD2**) Data transfer between UMC, CI	$\{umc_1{}^*, ci^*\} \vDash \{bsn, d_1, d_2, d_3, d_4, d_5, d_6\}$, $\{umc_2{}^*, ci^*\} \vDash \{bsn, d_1, d_2, d_3, d_4, d_5, d_6\}$
(**DD3**) Dataset from CI to researcher	$\{ci^*, r\} \vDash \{d_1, d_2, d_3, d_4, d_5, d_6, d_7\}$
(**DD4**) Partial depseudo w/o hospital	$\{ci, ttp, r\} \vDash \{d_1, d_2, d_3, d_4, d_5, d_6, d_7\}$
(**DD5**) (De)pseudonymisation by TTP	(See consequences of (**FR**), (**PR**), (**DD**))

knowledge base of an actor only if he is allowed to store it. For instance, in the model of PS-PI, Store does not store BSNs in the knowledge base of PS.

We compare the coalition graph to the optimal graph by visualising both in one picture. Non-optimal nodes highlight privacy drawbacks in the system design. The analysis of why these nodes exist may raise enhancements, which are then analysed to verify whether the drawbacks have been addressed.

4 Privacy-Optimal Graph

In this section, we analyse the optimal privacy achievable in (de)pseudonymisation infrastructures for medical research databases. An "optimal" coalition graph formalises the privacy consequences of functional requirements and design decisions. We also formalise privacy requirements defining the information a given actor should not know.

4.1 Formalisation of Requirements and Design Decisions

Table 1 formalises the privacy consequences of the functional requirements, privacy requirements, and design decisions described in Section 2.1. Actors' knowledge is taken after the CI has distributed the datasets to the researcher and she has made a coincidental finding, but before depseudonymisation has taken place.

Functional requirements (**FR1**) and (**FR2**) directly translate to the fact that hospitals and researchers know certain data about the patient. Functional requirements (**FR3**) and (**FR4**) state that full/partial depseudonymisation should be possible. In particular, a hospital, the TTP, the CI, and the researcher together should be able to perform full depseudonymisation, i.e., they should be able to link d_7 to bsn. Similarly, for partial depseudonymisation, they should be able to link d_7 to the patient data.

Privacy requirement (**PR1**) states that BSNs cannot be used for research purposes. Thus, even if the CI, TTP, and researcher are curious and combine their knowledge, they should not be able to derive the patient's BSN. For (**PR2**), the researcher should not be able to link any information from his first dataset to any information from his second dataset, even if he is curious.

Introducing the medical research database CI has several privacy consequences. Design decision (**DD1**) states that the task of the CI is to collect and link the data from different hospitals; it has two consequences. First, the CI knows the medical data from the two hospitals in one profile. Second, if a hospital, CI and TTP combine their knowledge, they can link the BSN to the full patient record at the CI (by definition of the collection process). By design decision (**DD2**), we consider systems where the CI and UMC communicate directly during the collection process. At the time of this communication, the hospital knew the BSN, and the CI knew the link to the full patient record. Therefore, if both have remembered some details of the communication such as the session identifier (i.e., they were curious), they can link the BSN to the full patient record without the PS. Design decision (**DD3**) states that the researcher is involved in (de)pseudonymisation merely as the passive recipient of the datasets. During the provision of such a dataset, the CI knew the link between records in the distributed dataset and the full patient records. If the CI is curious and remembers this link, and the researcher discovers an accidental finding related to some record, then together they can link the finding to the record. Design decision (**DD4**) states that hospitals are not involved in partial depseudonymisation; instead, it is performed by linking the incidental finding of the researcher to the patient record at the CI using the TTP. Finally, design decision (**DD5**) is the introduction of the TTP. This design decision is reflected by the fact that TTP is needed for data collection (**DD1**) and full (**FR3**) and partial (**FR4**), (**DD4**) depseudonymisation, as well as by the fact that the TTP is introduced for research purposes and therefore should not know BSNs (**PR1**).

4.2   Privacy-Optimal Graph

Figure 3 combines the privacy consequences in Table 1 into a coalition graph. Intuitively, it is the coalition graph of a hypothetical infrastructure O-PI which satisfies all requirements and design decisions, and whose design is optimal in terms of data minimisation. Nodes represent unavoidable disclosures.

The graph is obtained from Table 1 by considering which consequences apply to any particular coalition. Given a coalition A, we consider which profile detectability statements $A \vDash O$ are implied by the entries in the table. For instance, for coalition $A = \{umc_1\}$, the table implies detectability of profile $\{bsn, d_1, d_2, d_3\}$, which corresponds to a node in the graph. Coalition $A = \{r\}$ can detect two profiles $\{d_1, d_4, d_7\}$ and $\{d_2, d_5\}$ but it should not be able to

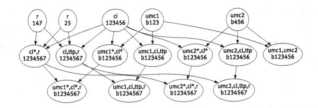

Fig. 3. Reduced coalition graph in optimal situation (O-PI). Node captions represent coalitions A and profiles O, respectively, with $A \vDash O$; 'b' means bsn, '1' means d_1, etc.

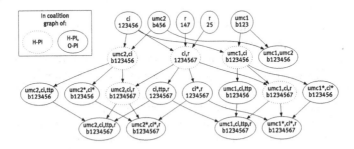

Fig. 4. Comparison between reduced coalition graphs of Parelsnoer hash-based pseudonymisation infrastructure (H-PI) and optimal situation (O-PI)

link them together, so the two profiles occur as two nodes in the graph. On the other hand, for coalition $A = \{umc_1, umc_2\}$, $A \vDash \{bsn, d_1, d_2, d_3\}$ is implied by $\{umc_1\} \vDash \{bsn, d_1, d_2, d_3\}$, and $A \vDash \{bsn, d_4, d_5, d_6\}$ is implied by $\{umc_2\} \vDash \{bsn, d_4, d_5, d_6\}$. These two profiles can be linked together because they both contain the BSN; therefore, they are represented by node $A \vDash \{bsn, d_1, \ldots, d_6\}$. Informally, coalitions of honest actors can link profiles if they have stored a shared identifier; coalitions of honest-but-curious actors can additionally link profiles if they have exchanged personal information from the profiles. These conclusions can be formally derived using the method in [19].

The reduced coalition graph of the optimal situation O-PI makes it possible to assess the extent to which existing infrastructures satisfy data minimisation. Namely, we can compare the reduced coalition graph of an existing infrastructure to the reduced coalition graph of O-PI, as described in Section 3. If the two graphs are the same, the infrastructure achieves optimal privacy. Otherwise, the privacy issues of the analysed infrastructure can be identified by analysing non-optimal nodes in the graph.

5   Coalition Graphs for Parelsnoer Infrastructures

In this section, we analyse data minimisation in the Parelsnoer infrastructures by comparing their reduced coalition graphs to the optimal one.

Hash-Based Infrastructure. Figure 4 compares the reduced coalition graph of the hash-based Parelsnoer infrastructure (H-PI) to the optimal situation (O-PI). The dotted nodes represent nodes that only occur in H-PI's coalition graph and thus point to violations of data minimisation. The solid nodes are also in O-PI's coalition graph and thus unavoidable. (H-PI does not use the TTP; it occurs in this graph because we compare it to the optimal situation, in which the TTP is needed for (de)pseudonymisation.)

The non-optimal nodes can be explained by the use of translation tables for depseudonymisation, as opposed to using the services of the TTP. Hospitals need to remember the pseudocode sent to the CI for full depseudonymisation, which implies $\{umc_i, ci\} \vDash \{bsn, d_1, \ldots, d_6\}$. The CI needs to remember the pseudocode sent to the researcher, implying $\{ci, r\} \vDash \{d_1, \ldots, d_7\}$. Combining the translation tables gives $\{umc_i, ci, r\} \vDash \{bsn, d_1, \ldots, d_7\}$.

The privacy difference between using translation tables and using a TTP can be observed from the coalition extensions needed to make non-optimal nodes optimal. First, for any non-optimal node $A \vDash O$, node $A \cup \{ttp\} \vDash O$ is optimal. This expresses that actors A are in fact allowed to compile profile O; the problem is that H-PI does not ensure that this only happens through a rigorous process involving the TTP. Second, for any non-optimal node $A \vDash O$, node $A' \vDash O$ is optimal in which hospitals and CI in A are made curious. This expresses that these actors are allowed to store more data than is desirable. Such data are needed to overcome the absence of the TTP.

Finally, H-PI satisfies the privacy requirements from Table 1. Indeed, the BSN itself never leaves the hospitals; however, the model does not capture that the BSN can be determined from its hash using a dictionary attack.

Pseudonymisation Service. We now discuss privacy in the Pseudonymisation Service infrastructure. We compare it to the hash-based infrastructure (Figure 5(a)) and to the optimal situation (Figure 5(b)).

Figure 5(a) shows that all non-optimal nodes of H-PI (shown dotted) are eliminated in PS-PI; however, PS-PI introduces new non-optimal nodes (shown dashed) which reflect two new privacy problems. The first problem is that the PS ttp learns the patient's BSN in the pseudonymisation process, and can contribute this information to coalitions that should not know it. This is reflected by nodes $\{ttp^*\} \vDash \{bsn\}$, $\{ci, ttp\} \vDash \{bsn, d_1, \ldots, d_6\}$, and $\{ci, ttp, r\} \vDash \{bsn, d_1, \ldots, d_7\}$ (in H-PI, these actors know the same data, but without the BSN). The second problem is that the PS is able to link profiles of researchers and hospitals without involving the CI. This problem, combined with the first problem, is reflected by nodes $\{ttp, r\} \vDash \{bsn, d_1, d_2, d_4, d_5, d_7\}$ (linking profiles from different research projects); $\{umc_1, ttp, r\} \vDash \{bsn, d_1, d_2, d_3, d_4, d_5, d_7\}$ and $\{umc_2, ttp, r,\} \vDash \{bsn, d_1, d_2, d_4, d_5, d_6, d_7\}$ (linking profiles from researcher and hospital); and $\{umc_1, umc_2, ttp, r\} \vDash \{bsn, d_1, \ldots, d_7\}$ (combination of the two). As Figure 5(b) shows, these nodes, which all include the PS, are exactly PS-PI's non-optimal nodes.

The analysis shows how privacy protection in PS-PI crucially depends on the trustworthiness of the PS. If we assume that the PS is never involved in privacy

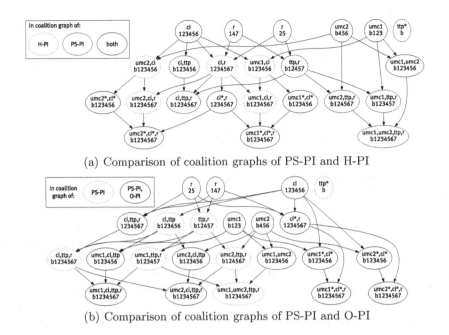

(a) Comparison of coalition graphs of PS-PI and H-PI

(b) Comparison of coalition graphs of PS-PI and O-PI

Fig. 5. Coalition graph comparison of the Pseudonymisation Service infrastructure (PS-PI) with the hash-based infrastructure (H-PI) and the optimal situation (O-PI)

breaches, then coalitions including the PS are not relevant; in this case, PS-PI is optimal. However, without this assumption, PS-PI provides worse privacy than H-PI by offering additional ways to establish links and find out the patient's BSN. In particular, the fact that a curious PS can find out the BSN violates privacy requirement **(PR1)**. To mitigate this, measures should be taken to make sure that the PS cannot use the BSN, e.g., by carrying out all computations on the BSN using trusted hardware (as done by Parelsnoer).

6   From Pseudonymisation Service to Optimal System

In the previous section, we have identified the privacy issues in the PS-PI infrastructure. We now discuss solutions, and then consider a hypothetical infrastructure incorporating these solutions and analyse it using coalition graphs.

The first privacy problem is that the PS learns the patient's BSN. Although it may be mitigated using trusted hardware, it is desirable to technically ensure that the BSN does not leave the hospitals, i.e., that requirement **(PR1)** is fully satisfied. The main challenge in achieving **(PR1)** is that the CI needs to link records from different hospitals. In particular, all hospitals should use the same pseudonym of a patient when communicating with the PS. Intuitively, all hospitals should use a shared secret to generate pseudonyms, or in case they do not share any secret, they should use the same procedure to generate pseudonyms, for instance hashing BSNs as in H-PI. The drawback of the first solution is that

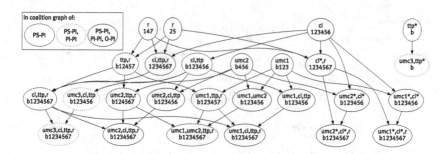

Fig. 6. Comparison of reduced coalition graphs of the improved PS infrastructure (PI-PI) with the original PS infrastructure (PS-PI) and the optimal situation (O-PI)

depseudonymisation can also be performed by hospitals that do not have a record of the patient (e.g., umc_3 in our scenario). On the other hand, if the pseudonyms are generated using one procedure, they may be vulnerable to dictionary attacks as in H-PI. We leave further analysis of this issue as future work.

The second problem is that the PS can help researchers link their data to hospitals or other researchers, bypassing the CI. To solve this, the PS should not be able to link pseudonymisation requests for different domains. This means that when the CI compiles a dataset for distribution, it should modify its linkable pseudocode before requesting the PS to repseudonymise it. The CI may either use the same secret for all datasets, or use different secrets for different datasets or records: both approaches seem possible.

To evaluate the privacy impact of the discussed solutions on PS-PI, we analyse an infrastructure PI-PI that incorporates the solutions in PS-PI. The order of the messages exchanged in PI-PI is as in Figure 2, but the information transmitted is changed. To make sure the BSN does not leave the hospitals, all hospitals share a symmetric key; instead of providing the BSN to the PS, they provide an encryption of the BSN under this key. To prevent linking of distributed datasets by the PS, the CI has a symmetric key for each research domain; when compiling a dataset for distribution, it sends to the PS not his pseudocode itself, but an encryption of the pseudocode under this symmetric key. Instead of re-translating the pseudocode from the CI's domain, the PS simply constructs a new pseudocode using this encryption as pseudonym.

Figure 6 compares PI-PI with the original infrastructure PS-PI and the optimal situation O-PI. As the figure shows, PI-PI indeed solves the privacy problems in PS-PI; however, one problem remains. Namely, besides umc_1 and umc_2, umc_3 can also help in depseudonymisation although it does not know the patient. Note that H-PI does not have this problem because umc_3 does not know the BSN and birth date of the patient. Hence, the privacy of H-PI and PI-PI is formally incomparable. In practice, we have a choice between depseudonymisation by any hospital knowing a secret (PI-PI), or by any third party able to perform a dictionary attack (H-PI).

7   Related Work and Conclusions

In this work, we formally analysed privacy by data minimisation in the setting of (de)pseudonymisation infrastructures for centralised medical research databases. We discussed the unavoidable privacy consequences of the requirements of this setting, and used them to analyse two infrastructures proposed by the Dutch Parelsnoer initiative. In the first, depseudonymisation is performed using tables, introducing privacy risks when data of hospitals or the CI are compromised. In addition, the use of hashes makes it vulnerable to a dictionary attack. The second solves these issues, but lets a TTP learn more information than necessary: it learns the BSN and can link distributed datasets. We discussed solutions to these issues and analysed a hypothetical infrastructure incorporating them.

Apart from Parelsnoer, there are several other proposals for (de)pseudonymisation of patient data for medical research. Serveral proposals [13] in the German legal framework are similar to H-PI and PS-PI, so we expect the findings of our analysis to also apply there. A model from Belgium [3] uses not central storage but a pseudonymisation service which also distributes the data (though encrypted so that the PS cannot read it). In such models, the pseudonymisation service can also be split into two parties [14] which separately do not learn any information. More general approaches for the exchange of medical data between health care providers [6, 15, 20] or pseudoynmised data in general [17] may also be adapted for pseudonymisation for research purposes. To our knowledge, there are no studies that analyse or compare privacy characteristics of these systems; this is an interesting direction for future work. Ultimately, the question is whether optimal data minimisation in this setting is (practically) achievable.

To formally analyse data minimisation, we introduced a novel representation of actor knowledge called coalition graphs. This graph shows which coalitions of actors in a system can compile which profiles of personal information. Honest and honest-but-curious actors capture different assumptions on their behaviour. An "optimal" coalition graph captures unavoidable knowledge; by comparing it to the coalition graph of an existing system, areas for privacy improvement can be identified. We have developed tools to automatically obtain a coalition graph from a formal model of communication.

Other formal methods, e.g. [1, 2, 4, 5, 7, 19], analyse knowledge of communicating actors. These methods verify that *particular* information cannot be derived by *particular* actors. In contrast, we express *all* relevant knowledge of *all* coalitions of actors in one single representation. These methods also do not usually distinguish between honest and honest-but-curious actors. In BAN-style [2] belief logics, a "Forget" operation has been proposed [16] usable for privacy analysis of honest actors [1]. Our work is more similar to state exploration techniques (e.g., [4, 5, 7, 19]). These only consider an (outside) attacker who may be passive or active, but always remembers everything he observes. The operation of honest actors could be simulated indirectly using these techniques; instead, our framework captures their operation explicitly.

Two issues not considered in our model are interesting for future work: first, linking medical data using statistical methods rather than by pseudonyms;

second, deriving implicit knowledge [19], for instance whether a researcher knows at which hospital the medical data in his dataset have been collected.

Acknowledgements. We are grateful for comments received from several people involved with Parelsnoer: Evert Jan Evers, Hans Maring, and Léon Haszing. This work is funded by the Dutch Sentinel Mobile IDM project (#10522), by the Dutch national program COMMIT through the THeCS project, and by the EU Seventh Framework Programme under grant agreement no. 295261 (MEALS).

References

1. Alcaide, A., Abdallah, A.E., González–Tablas, A.I., de Fuentes, J.M.: L–PEP: A logic to reason about privacy–enhancing cryptography protocols. In: Garcia-Alfaro, J., Navarro-Arribas, G., Cavalli, A., Leneutre, J. (eds.) DPM 2010 and SETOP 2010. LNCS, vol. 6514, pp. 108–122. Springer, Heidelberg (2011)
2. Burrows, M., Abadi, M., Needham, R.: A logic of authentication. ACM Trans. Comput. Syst. 8, 18–36 (1990)
3. Claerhout, B., DeMoor, G.J.E.: Privacy protection for clinical and genomic data: The use of privacy-enhancing techniques in medicine. IJMI 74(2-4), 257–265 (2005)
4. Dahl, M., Delaune, S., Steel, G.: Formal analysis of privacy for anonymous location based services. In: Mödersheim, S., Palamidessi, C. (eds.) TOSCA 2011. LNCS, vol. 6993, pp. 98–112. Springer, Heidelberg (2012)
5. Delaune, S., Kremer, S., Ryan, M.: Verifying privacy-type properties of electronic voting protocols. Comput. Secur. 17(4), 435–487 (2009)
6. Deng, M., Cock, D.D., Preneel, B.: Towards a cross-context identity management framework in e-health. Online Information Review 33(3), 422–442 (2009)
7. Dreier, J., Lafourcade, P., Lakhnech, Y.: A formal taxonomy of privacy in voting protocols. In: Proc. of SFCS 2012. IEEE (2012)
8. Fyffe, G.: Addressing the insider threat. Netw. Secur. 2008(3), 11–14 (2008)
9. Guarda, P., Zannone, N.: Towards the Development of Privacy-Aware Systems. Information and Software Technology 51(2), 337–350 (2009)
10. Lo Iacono, L.: Multi-centric universal pseudonymisation for secondary use of the EHR. Stud. Health Technol. Inform. 126, 239–247 (2007)
11. Parelsnoer Initiatief: Programma van eisen intstellingen. Tech Report v.1.2 (2008)
12. Parelsnoer Initiatief: Architecture Central Infrastructure. Tech Report v.1.0 (2009)
13. Pommerening, K., Reng, M.: Secondary use of the EHR via pseudonymisation. Stud. Health Technol. Inform. 103, 441–446 (2004)
14. Quantin, C., et al.: Medical record search engines, using pseudonymised patient identity: An alternative to centralised medical records. IJMI 80(2), 6–11 (2011)
15. Riedl, B., et al.: A secure architecture for the pseudonymization of medical data. In: Proc. of ARES 2007, pp. 318–324. IEEE (April 2007)
16. Rubin, A.D.: Nonmonotonic cryptographic protocols. In: Proceedings of Computer Security Foundations Workshop, pp. 100–116. IEEE (1994)
17. Teepe, W.: Integrity and dissemination control in administrative applications through information designators. Comput. Syst. Sci. Eng. 20(5) (2005)
18. Veeningen, M., de Weger, B., Zannone, N.: Modeling identity-related properties and their privacy strength. In: Degano, P., Etalle, S., Guttman, J. (eds.) FAST 2010. LNCS, vol. 6561, pp. 126–140. Springer, Heidelberg (2011)
19. Veeningen, M., de Weger, B., Zannone, N.: Formal privacy analysis of communication protocols for identity management. In: Jajodia, S., Mazumdar, C. (eds.) ICISS 2011. LNCS, vol. 7093, pp. 235–249. Springer, Heidelberg (2011)
20. Zhang, N., et al.: A linkable identity privacy algorithm for HealthGrid. In: Studies in Health Technology and Informatics, vol. 112, pp. 234–245. IOS Press (2005)

Switchwall: Automated Topology Fingerprinting and Behavior Deviation Identification

Nelson Nazzicari, Javier Almillategui, Angelos Stavrou, and Sushil Jajodia

George Mason University, Fairfax VA, 22030-4444, USA
http://csis.gmu.edu/

Abstract. The continuous improvement of bandwidth, pervasiveness, and functionality of network switching technologies is deeply changing the Internet landscape. Indeed, it has become tedious and sometimes infeasible to manually assure the network integrity on a regular basis: existing hardware and software can be tampered with and new devices can be connected or become nonoperational without any notification. Moreover, changes in the network topology can be introduced by human error, by hardware or software failures, or even by a malicious adversary (e.g. rogue systems).

In this paper, we introduce Switchwall, an Ethernet-based network fingerprinting technique that detects unauthorized changes to the L2/L3 network topology, the active devices, and the availability of an Enterprise network. The network map is generated at an initial known state and is then periodically verified to detect deviations in a fully automated manner. Switchwall leverages a single vantage point and uses only very common protocols (PING and ARP) without any requirements for new software or hardware. Moreover, no previous knowledge of the topology is required, and our approach works on mixed speed, mixed vendors networks. Switchwall is able to identify a wide-range of changes which are validated by our experimental results on both real and simulated networks.

1 Introduction

Due[1] to its capacity and ubiquitous nature, Future Internet is bound to exacerbate the management requirements and issues faced by current networks. Networked systems are becoming increasingly complex and growing to the point where the sheer volume of configurations that need to be managed and maintained on a regular basis becomes simply too much to manually inspect for administrators [1].

IT managers are in charge of bringing the system back to the normal state [2]. In this scenario, changes to topology [3, 4] are a critical factor, but they are often noticed only when they create disruption in functionality. On the othe hand detecting and managing changes ensure quality of service and reduces

---

[1] This material is based upon work supported by the Army Research Office under MURI grant W911NF-09-1-0525 and DURIP grant W911NF-11-1-0340.

A. Jøsang, P. Samarati, and M. Petrocchi (Eds.): STM 2012, LNCS 7783, pp. 161–176, 2013.

operational risks. Changes are due to either by human errors, or have a malicious origin, e.g. cheap wireless access points are illegally connected to the network borders, or devices are moved or substituted without notifying administrators.

To address this, we propose a new-generation network management tool aiming to offer administrators some degree of network self-awareness. With almost no initial configuration necessary, Switchwall is able to measure several aspects of the network state and produce a topological fingerprint called *Network Snapshot*. Detecting changes becomes then a matter of simple statistical analysis, with the administrator being alerted when the system deviates from the normal state. Switchwall is Ethernet based and targets L2/L3 topology. It cyclically produces a new network snapshot, which is automatically compared with a database of stored states. When changes or deviations are detected the system can present the operator a warning and pinpoint the change. All operations are performed by a *Probe*, i.e. a normal workstation leveraging a single vantage point sending crafted network packets that inspect the state of the system.

Switchwall performs two types of inspections. The first one, based on round-trip-time (RTT) statistical analysis, is host-based: each reachable host is pinged and the obtained frequency distribution is correlated to the stored one. Thus the system gets information on the crossed nodes, even in case of unmanaged, transparent component (e.g. layer-1 hubs). The second set of measures is more topology focused and measures, for any two hosts, how the paths connecting them to the *Probe* relate to each other. Two streams of ARP [5] packets are conveniently crafted and used to sample the network behavior. For each host several sets of measures are then saved and become part of the network snapshot.

Network administrators are involved only during the setup phase. Routine checks can be performed periodically, and be limited or not to a subnetwork. Moreover, if the network behavior depends on the time of the day (e.g. because of traffic) several snapshot can be stored, creating a time-dependent profile of the network state. To experimentally validate our approach in real-world scenarios we implemented a prototype system in our lab environment, where we were able to construct and test topologies spanning multiple network segments and end-hosts. Furthermore, we tested our system against large scale topologies and systems using virtual topologies created using Mininet [6]. In all of our experiments, Switchwall was able to successfully detect deviations in network topology and capacity.

2   Related Works

Network topology monitoring is often considered a subcategory of topology discovery, on which a rich body of research exists [7–9].

A very common approach to topology discovery relies on Simple Network Management Protocol (SNMP) to discover the network layout [10–14]. However, SNMP protocol requires inherent support from the underlying devices making it infeasible to identify devices that do not provide explicit support or are not properly configured. In particular, cheap network devices that are added to network periphery often do not support SNMP, thus compromising this kind of approach. Moreover, SNMP is fairly insecure: numerous vulnerabilities have been reported in multiple vendors' SNMP implementations. These vulnerabilities may allow unauthorized privileged access, denial-of-service attacks, or cause unstable network behavior [15, 16].

Other studies have introduced the concept of network tomography to infer the physical network topology without SNMP management information base support. In [17] Rabbat et al. describe a collaborative framework for performing network tomography on topologies with multiple sources and multiple destinations. Our approach differs in that we consider only a single vantage point, thus minimizing traffic overhead and simplifying maintenance. Moreover, we don't need support for any special crafted multicast protocols.

In [18] and [19] active end-to-end measurements are used to infer the distance between end-hosts. However, these works do not aim to characterize the internal network, and the distance maps they produce do not retrieve path characteristics for different pairs of hosts.

Other existing solutions work under the hypothesis that homogeneous technologies are chosen to implement the network: [20] requires OS support, i.e. pre-installed Windows services running on almost every host; [21] relies on the CISCO CDP proprietary protocol, supported mainly by CISCO products and oblivious of those portions of the network not supporting it. We do not require any software support on the network devices. Instead, we measure physical characteristics of different properties of the network without any management protocol support. Moreover, comparing the measured and the expected answering times, we are able to detect the presence of hidden layer-2 (switches) or layer-1 (hubs) devices, even if they are completely transparent to all protocols.

3   Definitions

In this section we introduce some standard terminology and a few definitions that will be consistently used along the whole paper.

Hosts, Addresses and Paths. An Ethernet network is, from the topological point of view, a tree graph [22]. Redundant links are eliminated by wiring rules or through STP protocol. Each leaf of the tree is a *Host*, a network device characterized by its distinct *MAC address*. A computer with multiple network interfaces is treated as multiple hosts. A packet travels from a source host to a destination host. The list of the crossed network devices is called a *Path*.

Switches and Hubs. A *Switch* is a layer-2 network device that can dynamically learn which address are on each port, and filter packets accordingly. A *Hub* is a layer-1 stateless network device: each packet received from a port is broadcast on all other ports. From the topological point of view Switches and Hubs are connecting nodes and never leaf nodes.

   Probe: a workstation running the Switchwall algorithm.

   Snapshot: a set of measures describing the network connectivity and topology in a specific time.

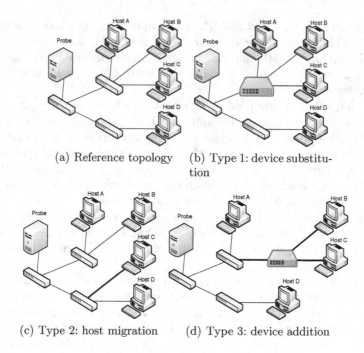

(a) Reference topology   (b) Type 1: device substitution

(c) Type 2: host migration   (d) Type 3: device addition

Fig. 1. Examples of possible topology changes

Topological change - type 1 - device substitution: a network device is phisically substituted with another one. (see Figure 1(b)). From the topological point of view the connectivity does not change.

Topological change - type 2 - host migration: a host is unplugged from its usual position and plugged in another place, (see Figure 1(c))

Topological change - type 3 - device addition: a device is added to the network. A typical scenario see host users adding a Hub at the network periphery to gain connectivity. This kind of change is exemplified in Figure 1(d)

4   System Overview

The Switchwall system periodically measures several aspect of the network behavior, and compares the measured values with a set of stored ones to detect any difference. Each measure is obtained generating a small amount of traffic from the Probe, a single vantage point that also packs the results in a compact data structure called Network Snapshot. After a new Snapshot is obtained the Probe compares it with a stored one. The stored Snapshot acts as a reference point for standard network behavior.

A Snapshot contains two types of data: non numerical (the list of active hosts) and numerical (the reply times statistics and the list of Triangular Samplings). The details for these data are exposed in Section 5. All numerical values must differ for less than a fixed threshold from the stored reference Snapshot, or an alarm is triggered. To properly analyze the system performance in Section 6 we detail a set of experiments where the thresholds are changed and the change detection rates are measured.

The list of active hosts can vary, too. Switchwall can therefore be configured to implement different reaction policies, ranging from a silent update of the reference Snapshot to a specific alarm triggered by host appearance or disappearance. More details on this topic are found in Section 5.1

Finally, Switchwall detection capability is limited by the frequency at which it is allowed to measure new snapshots. Bigger networks require longer times to be measured, thus imposing an upper bound to the system efficiency. To mitigate this aspect more than one probe can work together in the same network, each one testing only a piece of it. More details on this topic are found in Section 8

5 Network Snapshots

Switchwall combines two different techniques to create a *Network Snapshot*, i.e. a set of measures describing the current network connectivity and topology. A Snapshot contains the list of active hosts, and for each host the average reply time. Moreover, the Snapshot contains a matrix with the Triangular Samplings, a set of measures describing the current topological state of the network. The Probe periodically measures the network behavior and produced a new Snapshot.

In the next sections we illustrate how the measures are obtained and how they can be compared to the stored ones to detect topology modifications.

5.1 Active Hosts Acquisition

Several tools allow to list active hosts in a network, typically leveraging ICMP or TCP packets [23–25]

Switchwall uses the tool of choice to retrieve and store the list of active hosts, and to periodically verify its consistency (i.e. Switchwall looks for new host appearing on the network or known hosts disappearing from it). This is the initial step of topology fingerprinting, and also covers topological changes of type 3 relatively to host addition: if the retrieved list does not exactly match the stored one an alarm can be raised. In particular, Switchwall can be configured to react to the following cases:

- *a new host is detected*: in this case the event is logged. Switchwall can be configured to ignore the new host or store new statistics about it, thus updating the reference Snapshot;
- *a known host disappears*: in this case Switchwall can be configured to raise an alarm, or simply log the event, or delete the host from the reference Snapshot.

Different configurations can be chosen to implement the preferred policy, depending also on the frequency on which the active host list changes. Errors in the initial reference Snapshot would cause alarms and then be rapidly solved. Switchwall can be set to ignore missing hosts to avoid false positives due to switched off computers and focus only on new hosts showing up.

5.2   Reply Times Analysis

Round Trip Time (RTT) is a measure of the time needed for a packet to travel from a source host to a destination host, plus the time for the packet ACK to travel back to the source. In our analysis scenario the source host is always the Probe. Every active host is cyclically targeted, and a statistical analysis of RTT is performed. Because of the nature of networks, RTT is not constant but depends on several variables: traffic, intermediate switches state, and packet size among others. However, a statistical analysis reveals that the frequency distribution of RTT follows a consistent model.

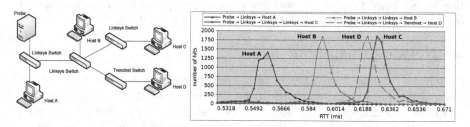

Fig. 2. A simple topology and the resulting RTTs histograms

Figure 2 shows how the RTT values depend on the topology. For the sake of example, the host machines are considered identical, and only their topological distance from the Probe varies. The biggest changes happen when the topological distance between the Probe and the host varies, because a different number of network devices is elaborating the packet. However, differences between device brands can lead as well to different RTT distributions even with the same topological distance. The cited example uses two different switch brands, and the RTT histograms reflect the network device heterogeneity.

The desired level of precision in changes detection depends on two parameters: the number of measures and the alarm threshold. Our standard RTT estimation uses 10,000 measures, with an effective confidence interval ($\alpha = 99.9\%$) usually in the order of nanoseconds. This level of precision allows Switchwall to intercept those changes that modify the topological distance between Probe and target host. When a new Snapshot is measured, each RTT is compared with the stored ones, and if the absolute difference between the old and the new values is bigger than a fixed threshold an alarm is raised. We analyze the effects of threshold selection in Section 6.

RTT statistical analysis is useful to detect changes of all three types. When changes of Type 1 happens, different device models will produce different contribution to RTT [26]. Thus, all hosts involved in the change will fail the test, allowing the administrator to investigate the cause. Obviously if a device is substituted with another of the exact same brand and model no change will be observed. However in this case it is arguable if an actual network modification happened. Note that this approach can detect a change also in the host network card, since a different harware will likely produce different response times.

Regarding Type 2 changes, when a host is moved to a different location the resulting RTT will reflect the event, since the path connecting it to the Probe changes. The only case not covered by this test is when the new location is topologically at the same distance from the Probe, and the new path traverse the same type of hardware. In this case another type of analysis is required.

Changes of type 3 are the most disruptive from the topological point of view and will be reflected in several alarms being raised.

5.3   Triangular Sampling

The second set of measures injects ARP streams in the network to evaluate the topological status between the Probe and each active host. The atomic operation performed is called Triangular Sampling and investigates the paths connecting the Probe to other two hosts of the newtork. For every active host T (target), the system will perform a series of Triangular Sampling between T, the Probe, and a third host H. The host H varies between all other active hosts (or a subset of all active hosts). For each target host T the results of all Triangular Samplings are stored. Together with the RTT analysis exposed in Section 5.2, they completes the Network Snapshot relatively to host T.

To perform a single Triangular Sampling two ARP streams are injected in the network: one is broadcast and performs an ARP manipulation technique focused on target host T, the other one is directed to a single host H and is used to sample the status of the network.

To better illustrate the techinque, the following subsections refer to the topology shown in Figure 3, and detail how to perform a Triangular Sampling between the Probe, the Target Host, and Host 1.

ARP Stream 1: Diversion Windows. With reference to Table 1 (left), the first ARP stream is a broadcast request containing, as sender MAC, the address of the Target Host. As sender IP the Probe uses its own real IP address, and as receiver IP the address of the Target Host. Since the network is based on layer-2 or layer-3 switches, only the Ethernet header will be used for forwarding and to update forwarding tables.

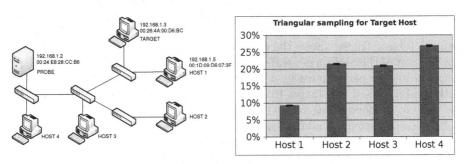

Fig. 3. A simple topology and the Triangular Samplings for TARGET host. The black ticks on top of histograms bars are confidence intervals.

Table 1. Triangular Sampling ARP streams

Stream 1			Stream 2		
Probe ARP broadcast request			**Probe ARP direct request**		
Ethernet	from MAC	00:26:4A:00:D6:BC	Ethernet	from MAC	00:24:E8:28:CC:B6
	to MAC	broadcast		to MAC	00:1D:09:D6:07:3F
ARP	from MAC	00:26:4A:00:D6:BC	ARP	from MAC	00:26:4A:00:D6:BC
	IP	192.168.1.2		IP	192.168.1.2
	to MAC	broadcast		to MAC	00:1D:09:D6:07:3F
	IP	192.168.1.3		IP	192.168.1.5
answer from Target Host			**answer from Host 1**		
Ethernet	from MAC	00:26:4A:00:D6:BC	Ethernet	from MAC	00:1D:09:D6:07:3F
	to MAC	00:26:4A:00:D6:BC		to MAC	00:26:4A:00:D6:BC
ARP	from MAC	00:26:4A:00:D6:BC	ARP	from MAC	00:1D:09:D6:07:3F
	IP	192.168.1.3		IP	192.168.1.5
	to MAC	00:26:4A:00:D6:BC		to MAC	00:26:4A:00:D6:BC
	IP	192.168.1.2		IP	192.168.1.2

When the stream propagates through the network all the crossed switches update their forwarding tables to redirect the traffic addressed to the Target Host to the Probe, coherently with the broadcast Ethernet header. That change actually affects only the switches along the path between the two hosts, since all other hosts need to pass through the connecting path anyway. When the Target host is reached by the stream it creates a stream of answers directed to a host that has its same MAC address, but a different IP. This stream of answers travels back to the Probe, and forces all the switches to update again their forwarding tables, restoring the initial condition. The effect of the streams is shown in Figure 4: each switch along the path, for a certain period of time, will forward the packets directed to the Target Host to the Probe. This Diversion Window (DW) is minimal for the switch directly connected to the Target Host, and grows when getting closer to the Probe.

ARP stream 2: Windows Sampling. The second stream is used to sample the size of the DW created by the Stream 1. It consists of a series of direct ARP requests to another host, using the Target Host MAC address as sender address for the ARP protocol, and using the real Probe MAC address in the Ethernet header. Table 1 (right) shows the configuration of the stream aimed to Host 1. Each packet of this stream generates an answer packet coming back from Host 1. Since the answer packet must be delivered to a MAC address which is shared by both the Probe and the Target Host, its actual forwarding path will depend on the state of the forwarding tables of the intermediate switches.

If the second stream is addressed to a host direct neighbour of the Target Host (e.g. Host 1), the vast majority of the answers will be forwarded to the Target Host, since the DW on the last switch is minimal. If the second stream targets a host closer to the Probe (e.g. Host 2), a bigger number of packets will be diverted to the Probe. Figure 3 reports also the percentage of packets from the

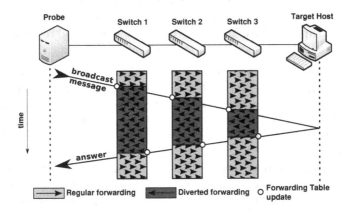

Fig. 4. The effects of Stream 1 on the forwarding tables of the switches between the Probe and the Target Host

second stream that has been diverted to the Probe for the discussed topology. Note that Host 2 and Host 3 produce similar values: switches outside the path connecting the Probe to Target Host are transparent to this kind of measure (and their forwarding tables are not touched). This results confirm that Triangular Samplings wields information on the current topology status. In particular, it can be used to infer how much the paths connecting the Probe to any two other hosts overlaps. Thus, Switchwall is able to intercept topology changes of Type 2 not covered by RTT analysis, as confirmed by experiments exposed in Section 6.

6   Experimental Results

We tested Switchwall on both physical and simulated networks. All experiments started with the definition of an initial network topology acting as reference state. We then introduced several topology modifications and measured Switchwall detection rate.

Physical Networks. The first testbed was assembled in our laboratory using physical network devices. We used a mix of Trendet eight port switches (model no. TEG-S80g) and Linksys five port switches (model no. EG005W v3) to compose several up to 7-hops deep topologies. We completed the topologies with up to eleven mixed-vendors, mixed-operating system hosts. Once a topology was assembled, the modifications were introduced by phisically rewiring hosts and switches, thus reproducing host migration, device substitution, and device additions.

Testing Switchwall on a completely controlled physical network allowed to highlight differences in the timing behaviour of different switch brands, as showed in Figure 2. The algorithm behaved exactly as expected, and we easily achieved 100% detection rate toward all the introduced changes, with a running time of about three minutes (184 seconds).

However, the scope of these experiments was intrinsically limited. In fact it is not feasable to test thousands of configurations if it is necessary to physically plug and unplug cables. To explore bigger topologies and reach statistically meaningfull numbers we thus moved to a simulated environment.

Mininet Environment. The second set of experiments used Mininet [6] on a Dell PowerEdge R715 server with 128 GB of Ram and two 12 cores CPUs. Mininet environment exploits Linux kernel name-spaces to simulate hosts with their own network stack. In order to simulate the switches, Mininet supports the reference implementation of openflow switch [27] and open vSwitch [28].

To obtain a network behavior as close as possible to real world scenarios we faced the need to modify one of Mininet modules. NOX [29] has been thus partially rewrited to match real switched behavior. Furthermore, in order to simulate bandwidth limitations typical of real networks, we combined Mininet to the Linux Traffic Control facilities [30]. In this way we added to Mininet the capability to differentiate single switches behavior, thus effectively implementing heterogeneous networks support. Current Mininet official release lacks these features. In this upgraded test bed we simulated topologies with up to 30 switches and up to 90 hosts.

6.1   Device Substitution Detection

To systematically measure Switchwall device substitution detection capability we varied the elaboration times of Mininet simulated switches. During the experiments Switchwall recorded all active hosts RTTs on an initial reference topology. A switch was then randomly selected and its speed modified using the Traffic Control tool. This approach allowed us to introduce an arbitrary delay D in the selected device, thus simulating a substitution.

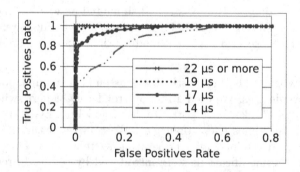

Fig. 5. Device substitution detection: ROC curves for different values of D

We measured the system precision using the very well known ROC curve. The following cases where defined: a **False Negative** happens when a switch is modified to expose a different elaboration time, but Switchwall does not detect the change; a **True Positive** happens if Switchwall detects the change; a **True**

Negative happens when no change is introduced, and no alarm is raised; a **False Positive** happens if an alarm is raised even if no modification has been introduced in the reference topology.

A change is detected when the measured RTT differs from the reference one for more than a fixed threshold. Very low thresholds minimize the number of False Negatives, but raise the number of False Positives. A higher threshold produce the opposite behavior. Moreover, the amount of introduced delay D determines how effective is Switchwall in detecting device substitution. Figure 5 shows ROC curves for several values of D. An introduced delay of 22 μs resulted in an almost 100% detection rate, with an effective 0% False Positives rate and an Area Under Curve (AUC) value of 0.998

Switchwall is exposing a reasonable behavior even with values of D as small as 14 μs, with an effective 0.902 AUC. All experiments used a standard set of 10,000 RTT measures.

6.2   Host Migration Detection

To test host migration detection rate we defined a reference Mininet topology. A host was then randomly choosen and moved to different positions. We measured Switchwall accuracy through the definition of the following cases: a **False Negative** happens when a host is moved to a different location, but Switchwall does not detect the chage; a **True Positive** happens if Switchwall detects the change; a **True Negative** happens when no change is introduced, and no alarm is raised; a **False Positive** happens if an alarm is raised even if no modification has been introduced in the reference topology.

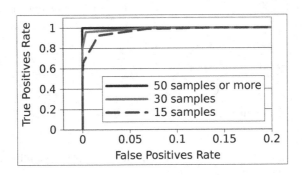

Fig. 6. Host Migration: ROC curves for different amount of samples

RTT analysis allowed to intercept when the topological distance of the migrating host new position was different from the original one. In other words, if the path connecting the probe to the new position was shorter or longer than the old one, RTT analysis would raise an alarm. Since in our experiments each crossed switch added about a hundred microseconds to the RTT, Switchwall was able to easily achieve a perfect score (100% detection rate with 0% False

Positives rate). Ence, to further test the limits of the implemented system, we decided to reduce the number of RTT measures performed. With reference to Figure 6, we found that with as low as 50 RTT samples the system performs with an effective 0.983 AUC, and when the samples are reduced to 15 the AUC drops only to 0.966, thus proving the high capacity of Switchwall to detect host migration events. In this case, too, the ROC curves were obtained varying the alarm threshold.

6.3 Device Addition Detection

Device addition can be easily intercepted by RTT analysis, since it modifies the topological distance between the probe and the active hosts, producing a precision similar to what exposed in Section 6.2. The only changes not detected by RTT analysis are the ones conservative toward topological distances, exemplified in Figure 7(a), 7(b), and 7(c). The figures refer to an experiment implemented in our laboratory using physical devices.

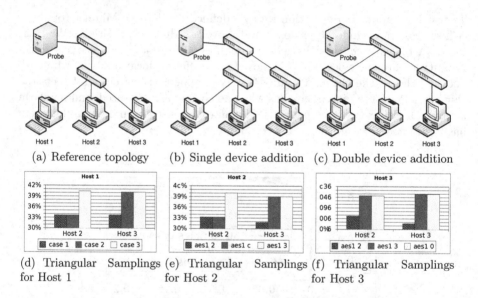

(a) Reference topology   (b) Single device addition   (c) Double device addition

(d) Triangular Samplings for Host 1   (e) Triangular Samplings for Host 2   (f) Triangular Samplings for Host 3

Fig. 7. The consequences of device addition on Triangular Samplings. Experiment implemented on physical networks (not simulated).

A Triangular Sampling can be used to detect this kind of network modification, as well as to detect host migrations that do not modify the topological distances. Figure 7 reports also the Triangular Samplings for each host. In the discussed example low values (30-33%) indicate that the hosts are connected to the same switch, while higher values (38-40%) mean that the hosts are connected to different switches. Because of differences in host hardware, topologically equivalent hosts expose different Triangular Samplings. The confidence intervals ($\alpha = 99.9\%$), not reported in the charts for clarity, are all below the 0.02% threshold.

To systematically measure Switchwall ability to detect device additions not intercepted by RTT analysis we implemented several networks in Mininet environment. Each active host maintained the same topological distance across all experiments, even if the switch wiring changed. We then defined False Positives and True Positives rates in a way similar to what exposed in the previous sections, and proceeded to trace the system ROC. However, given the level of precision reachable, Switchwall was always able to achieve a perfect score (100% detection rate, with 0% false positives rate) for all the tested topologies. These results completely support the proposed algorithm capability to intercept network modifications.

7   Impact on Network

Network Disruption. Triangular Samplings modify network connectivity for a brief amount of time. The actual damage is very limited, especially when related to guaranteed delivery protocols such as TCP. A single Triangular Sampling lasts for a RTT between Probe and Target host. Of that time, only a fraction sees an actual connectivity disruption.

We however decided to implement an extra safeguard to limit disruption: if the Probe starts receiving regular traffic addressed to the Target Host it immediately stops the tests. With the safeguard up and running the connectivity disruption was not measurable: all bandwidth tests between several parts of the network produced exactly the same results (less than 0.1% difference) with or without Switchwall being activated.

Overhead. On the average, on a network working at 1 Gbps, we have observed a generated network traffic of ~4 Mbps per host for the RTT estimation mechanism, and a network traffic of ~16 Kbps for Triangular Sampling mechanism. From the network point of view both mechanisms used by our probe caused negligible overhead on the monitored infrastructure.

8   Limitations and Future Works

Some specific network condition can limit Switchwall effectiveness, and several new capabilities are currently being developed. This section lists the most important topics relatively to Switchwall edges.

ICMP and Firewalls: RTT analysis leverages PING, an ICMP based utility, but ICMP packets can be blocked by Firewalls for security reasons. However, several measures can be taken to overcome this limitation:

- ARP PING [31] can be used instead of regular PING. ARP PING is limited to the local network, but since Switchwall works at local level this does not limit its application. Preliminary experiments shows that ARP PING can be used to achieve the same level of precision at the cost of longer samplings;

- similarly, TCP SYN packets could be used to obtain a functionality similar to regular PING. This approach is sometimes called TCP (port) Ping, and several implementations are freely available [32] [33];
- since Switchwall produces legitimate traffic, firewalls could be reconfigured to allow ICMP traffic from and to the Probe.

Moreover, firewalls usually lay on the network borders. Since Switchwall targets internal topology, a switch/hub based netwtork with firewalls on its borders creates no limitations to our tool.

Rapidly changing networks, with host frequently connecting and disconnecting (e.g. wireless hotspots), could limit Switchwall detection capability. However, a dedicated Probe can be configured to monitor the evolving parts with a higher frequency. Since the topology of hotspots is tipically very simple, the Probe could even be configured to simply track the active hosts and skip RTT analysis, Triangular Samplings, or both, thus gaining speed.

Non-tree networks limit Switchwall effectiveness. Non-tree topologies often exist in large networks with controlled redundancy, or can happen because misconfigurations in the Spanning Tree Protocol (STP) generate duplicated links. In the first case Switchwall could still operate using different probes configured to control tree subnetworks, each probe being oblivious of the redundancy and still able to operate.

In case of STP configuration errors Switchwall is not able to operate, and would continuously indicate large portions of the network being moved. Ence, even if correcting STP errors is beyond the scope of the presented tool, Switchwall can help to highlight network misconfigurations.

Finally, we are working on **efficiency improvement**. Several experiments suggest that hosts close to the probe could be monitored with fewer samplings, thus reducing the analysis time. Host farther from the probe tend to expose more unstable reaction times and require longer sampling to achieve statistical stability. The current Switchwall implementation follows the most conservative approach and uses the same configuration for all hosts. A more context-aware approach that dynamically minimizes the amount of samplings would thus reduce the time required to get a Network Snapshot and avoid duplicate analysis.

9   Conclusions

In this paper we presented Switchwall, a tool for automatic network fingerprinting able to detect topology changes like device substitution, host migration, and device addition. Switchwall does not require any special protocol, special hardware or the support of expensive management interfaces. In fact, Switchwall leverages a single vantage point to inject ARP and PING packets and test network responsivity and behavior. Our system can also detect changes involving transparent, unmanaged network devices.

To verify the accuracy of our approach, we formally defined three types of modifications to the network connectivity, and experimentally measured the system detection efficiency. We deployed our prototype implementation to both real and simulated environments, using well known and recognized testing tools. Drawing from our experimental results, we show that Switchwall can correctly detect changes at the cost of only minimal overhead and network disruption.

References

1. Towards the future internet - a european research perspective, Amsterdam (2009), http://oro.open.ac.uk/24440/
2. Haibo, B., Sohraby, L., Wang, C.: Future internet services and applications. IEEE Network 24(4), 4–5 (2010)
3. Lin, H.-C., Lai, H.-L., Lai, S.-C.: Automatic link layer topology discovery of ip networks. In: 1999 IEEE International Conference on Communications, ICC 1999, vol. 2, pp. 1034–1038 (1999)
4. Gobjuka, H., Breitbart, Y.: Ethernet topology discovery for networks with incomplete information. IEEE/ACM Transactions on Networking 18(4), 1220–1233 (2010)
5. Plummer, D.: Ethernet Address Resolution Protocol: Or Converting Network Protocol Addresses to 48.bit Ethernet Address for Transmission on Ethernet Hardware. RFC 826 (Standard). Updated by RFCs 5227, 5494 (November 1982), http://www.ietf.org/rfc/rfc826.txt
6. Mininet, http://yuba.stanford.edu/foswiki/bin/view/OpenFlow/Mininet
7. Donnet, B., Friedman, T.: Internet topology discovery: a survey. IEEE Communications Surveys and Tutorials 9(4), 2–15 (2007)
8. Rahman, M.A., Paktas, A., Wang, F.Z.: Network topology generation and discovery tools
9. Ahmat, K.: Ethernet topology discovery: A survey. CoRR, abs/0907.3095 (2009)
10. Breibart, Y., Garofalakis, M., Jai, B., Martin, C., Rastogi, R., Silberschatz, A.: Topology discovery in heterogeneous ip networks: The netinventory system. IEEE Transactions on Networking 12(3), 401–414 (2004)
11. Uzair, U., Ahmad, H., Ali, A., Suguri, H.: An efficient algorithm for ethernet topology discovery in large multi-subnet networks. In: IEEE International Conference on System of Systems Engineering, SoSE 2007, pp. 1–7 (April 2007)
12. Jia, B.: Research of physical topology discovery in heterogeneous ip networks with vlan. In: Innovative Computing Communication, 2010 Intl. Conf. on and Information Technology Ocean Engineering, 2010 Asia-Pacific Conf. on (CICC-ITOE), pp. 244–247 (January 2010)
13. Bejerano, Y.: Taking the skeletons out of the closets: a simple and efficient topology discovery scheme for large ethernet lans. IEEE/ACM Trans. Netw. 17(5), 1385–1398 (2009)
14. Mukhtar, H., Ahmad, H., Ki-Hyung Kimand Ali, A., Suguri, H.: Autonomous network topology discovery of large multi-subnet networks using lightweight probing. In: Network Operations and Management Symposium Workshops, NOMS Workshops 2008, pp. 351–356. IEEE (2008)
15. Cert advisory on snmp vulnerabilities, http://www.cert.org/advisories/CA-2002-03.html
16. Cert faqs on snmp vulnerabilities, http://www.cert.org/techtips/snmpfaq.html
17. Rabbat, M., Nowak, R.: Multiple source, multiple destination network tomography. In: Proc. of IEEE Infocom (2004)

18. Francis, P., Jamin, S., Jin, C., Jin, Y., Raz, D., Shavitt, Y., Zhang, L.: Idmaps: a global internet host distance estimation service. IEEE/ACM Trans. Netw. 9(5), 525–540 (2001)
19. Ng, T.S.E., Zhang, H.: Predicting internet network distance with coordinates-based approaches. In: INFOCOM, pp. 170–179 (2001)
20. Black, R., Donnelly, A., Fournet, C.: Ethernet topology discovery without network assistance. In: ICNP (2004)
21. Cisco catalyst series switches, http://www.cisco.com/en/US/products/hw/switches/ps663/ productstechnote09186a0080094713.shtml#cdp
22. IEEE-Computer-Society. 802.1d ieee standard for local and metropolitan area networks. Technical report, IEEE Computer Society (2004)
23. Nmap tool for host discovery, http://nmap.org/book/man-host-discovery.html
24. Hping packet assembler/analyzer tool, http://www.hping.org/
25. Oissg on network fingerprinting, http://www.oissg.org/wiki/index.php?title=Network_Mapping_%28Scanning %2C_OS_Fingerprinting_and_Enumeration%29#Identify_Live_Hosts
26. Pgmag switches benchmark, http://www.pcmag.com/imagepopup/0,1871,iid=5847,00.asp
27. Openflow network research framework, http://www.openow.org/wp/research/
28. Pfaff, B., Pettit, J., Koponen, T., Amidon, K., Casado, M., Shenker, S.: Extending networking into the virtualization layer. In: Proc. HotNets (October 2009)
29. Gude, N., Koponen, T., Pettit, J., Pfaff, B., Casado, M., McKeown, N., Shenker, S.: NOX: towards an operating system for networks. ACM SIGCOMM Computer Communication Review 38(3), 105–110 (2008)
30. Linux tc tool for traffic shaping, http://linux.die.net/man/8/tc
31. Thomas habets' arping tool, http://www.habets.pp.se/synscan/programs.php?prog=arping
32. Eli fulkerson's tcping for windows, http://www.elifulkerson.com/projects/tcping.php
33. Richard van den berg's tcpping tool for gnu/linux, http://www.vdberg.org/~richard/tcpping.html

DOT-COM:
Decentralized Online Trading and COMmerce*

Moti Geva and Amir Herzberg

CS Department, Bar Ilan University
{moti.geva,amir.herzberg}@gmail.com

Abstract. Current financial markets rely on direct trust between trading parties or a common trusted third party (TTP). The Internet enables practically any two possible traders around the world to locate each other, but payments and trading mechanisms are still centralized, inefficient, and require direct trust or trusted intermediaries. We present *DOT-COM*, a financial trading protocol that supports trades between any trading parties, even when no trust or common TTP exist between them. The proposed system makes sure that the traded financial products are exchanged by both sides while ensuring that neither side is exposed to fraud, default or settlement risks. Trade execution is carried out within a predefined time frame, and may be subject to arbitrary conditions defined by the traders. *DOT-COM* design allows such trades to be conducted over the Internet, automatically, efficiently, securely and cheaply.

1 Introduction

The global economy grew substantially as a result of the improvements in transportation and communication over the last couple of centuries, enabling trades with remote partners around the world. Trading nowadays is facilitated by the existence of secure, decentralized and (relatively) efficient payment mechanisms, such as fund transfer networks, and charge-card networks. Efficient financial markets, supported by stock exchanges and financial trading networks, play key role in the economy. Currently, financial instruments are traded mostly using trusted intermediaries - brokers and escrow services. Brokers trade financial instruments on behalf of their customers, with other customers, brokers or via markets, ensuring that each party will receive the agreed-upon compensation. Escrow services commonly perform fair-exchange of (digital or other) goods deposited in the escrow service by the counterparties.

The Internet, with its global, ubiquitous and computerized connectivity, provided yet another boost to global economy. Providers and customers, around the world use Internet applications to locate each other, compare between alternative offers, and to deliver services and digital goods. One important family of 'digital goods' consists of financial products - stocks, bonds, currencies, derivatives,

* This research was supported by grant 1354/11 from the Israeli Science Foundation (ISF).

A. Jøsang, P. Samarati, and M. Petrocchi (Eds.): STM 2012, LNCS 7783, pp. 177–192, 2013.

structured products and more. The Internet is also used to improve efficiency of payment and trading networks, however, so far, there was no wide-spread adoption of new payment or trading systems designed specifically to enable secure and efficient trading and payments among distant entities, avoiding and minimizing assumptions of direct trust or overhead and restrictions of trusted intermediaries.

In this paper we present Decentralized Online Trading and COMmerce (*DOT-COM*), a secure protocol for trading financial instruments, designed for the Internet. *DOT-COM* incorporates mechanisms to allow secure and efficient trading and payments of financial instruments, even between extremely remote parties who share no trust. *DOT-COM* minimizes the assumptions and costs due to dependencies on intermediaries, allowing to improve efficiencies and reduce overhead, in terms of cost, speed, and risks mitigation. To bridge the trust gap between traders, *DOT-COM* uses a *chain-of-trust* based on existing trust-relations between financial-service-providers (FSP), such as banks and brokers.

To better explain the contribution, consider the following scenario. Two companies require to exchange currencies. Company A wishes to sell USD and buy Euro, whereas company B wishes to sell Euro and buy USD. Traditionally, both companies would go to their banks and receive a quote with a bid/ask spread. Had trust relation pre-existed between A and B, both companies would probably prefer to directly exchange the currencies around mid-spread, earning profit to both. However, currently the required trust relations probably do not exist, and ad-hoc trust relations are hard and expensive to form, hence are not cost-effective. Figure 1 depicts such an exchange scenario, comparing the current status and proposed. Our solution (right figure) is aimed at enabling A and B to directly negotiate the trade terms, and securely exchange the assets. The FSPs do not provide quotes, and merely supply the means for the secure clearing and settlement of the trade. The *non-binding negotiations* resemble real life negotiations, which are only made legally binding when signing a legally binding contract at a later stage.

The main goal of *DOT-COM* is to enable secure transactions between mistrusting traders, where the trade conditions are negotiated directly but settled securely, thereby eliminating much of the current middlemen role of *FSPs*. Adding the fact that the customers themselves provide the assets switching hands, leaving the FSP to invest its assets elsewhere, should improve trade conditions. Transaction costs should be relatively low as compensation to FSPs is reduced for the credit usage and settlement risk. In addition, *DOT-COM* can become facilitator for new types of digital assets, such as Bitcoin[17], by making it more accessible and exchangeable, as long as route of FSPs supporting the digital asset can be found.

DOT-COM presents a disruptive model to the traditional banking model, in which financial institutions profit from quoting, clearing and settlement processes. However, we trust that numerous financial institutions which take part in the existing financial infrastructure are potential adopters of our new model. Potential companies include credit companies, brokerage companies, and possibly

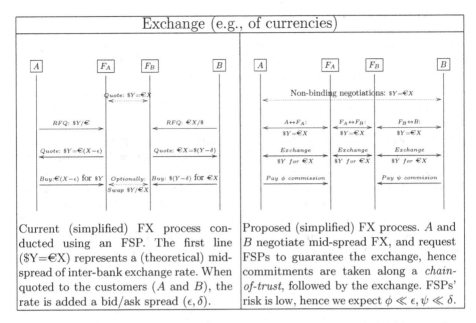

Fig. 1. Simplified comparison of exchange between current state and proposed

insurance companies and other medium scaled financial institutions, which can lawfully provide credit and handle credit risks, but are commonly not referred to for trade quotes.

Figure 4 depicts a *DOT-COM* system architecture. Due to space limitations, in this paper we only discuss the system protocol (*DOT-COM*), and refer to related work when justifying the feasibility of the other subsystems.

2   Background and Model

Any trade requires trust and risk taking. Whenever two parties make a transaction they give some asset in hope of being compensated with another. However, trades might fail, and more specifically they might fail after one party has given away his asset, commonly referred as *counterparty risk*. To make a trade, each trader needs to trust that the transaction will complete successfully, and should be willing to take the counterparty risk involved.

Trust relations usually mean that a legally binding contract exists between the parties which states their rights and obligations. In many cases, the parties give credit to one another, that is, one party – the creditor – provides the other party – the borrower – with an asset without being immediately compensated. Credit is involved with *credit risk*, that is, the risk that the borrower would not repay the creditor. Credit is usually provided based on the borrower's reputation and credit history, and in many cases involves collaterals. Forming new trust and credit relations is not trivial.

2.1   Trade and Trust Models

In the majority of trades, direct trust does not exist between the trading parties, hence a trusted third party (TTP) is commonly used. The TTP may assume the counterparties' risk upon himself, or assure fair-exchange, e.g. by assuring delivery-versus-payment (DVP) or payment-versus-payment (PVP). If either
party fails to deliver its asset, the transaction is aborted, and the assets are returned to their original owner.

In the credit-card trust model a customer has trust relations with a credit-
card *issuer*, e.g. his bank. The issuer issues the customer with a credit-card,
which is later used by the customer for making payments. A merchant receiving
the payment from the customer is not required to have trust relations with the
issuer, instead it has trust relations with a credit-card clearing company – the
acquirer. The acquirer in turn does have trust relation with the issuer thereby
enabling the payment to take place and transfer money from the customer's
account into the merchant's account. Figure 2 depicts the above common trust
relations between trading parties.

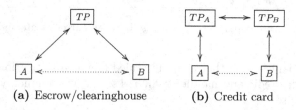

(a) Escrow/clearinghouse   (b) Credit card

Fig. 2. A and B are trading parties, and TP is a trusted party. Solid lines represent
direct trust relations whereas dotted lines represent trust via a TP. Figure 2a depicts
a model in which a TP, such as escrow or clearinghouse, is used to clear and settle
trades; this model is commonly used in stock exchanges and OTC markets. Figure 2b
depicts a model in which TP_A (A's trusted party) trusts TP_B (B's trusted party); this
model is commonly used for credit card clearing, e.g. TP_A is the issuer and TP_B is an
acquirer.

In a brokerage trading model the broker is a trusted party which takes the
responsibility for finding a counterparty for the trade, possibly acting as a TTP,
or as a mediator on behalf of the trader in markets such as a stock exchange[18]
or over-the-counter (OTC) markets[19]. In some cases the broker may also be
used to anonymize the parties and hide their identity. Generally, a broker can
profit by charging commission or by widening the bid/ask spread when quoting
to the trader. Moreover, when two of the broker's customers make a matching
bid and ask, the broker can settle trades directly without actually performing
any market orders, thereby earning the spread directly.

In some transactions an actual chain-of-trust is used, e.g. in foreign exchange
(FOREX or FX) between two "third party institutions" in CLS[1]. Another
example is cashing of foreign checks, which is usually expensive and takes long

time to clear. These examples imply that a chain-of-trust exists between most FSPs, however it is not automated, and cannot be exploited by end-traders as proposed in this paper.

2.2 Mitigating Settlement Risk

Settlement refers to the delivery of the traded assets and constitute finalization of the trade. *Settlement risk* is the counterparty risk or credit risk that the debtor would not honor its settlement obligations. As the time between trade and its settlement might take a while, and in order to mitigate the settlement risk, clearing processes usually take place post-trade and pre-settlement. To further alleviate settlement risk, (trusted) clearinghouses play an important role, commonly by assuming the counterparty risk from the trading parties, and assuring the trade execution. A clearinghouse can assure DVP (e.g., in securities) or PVP (e.g., in FX), which means that an asset is delivered only upon payment, or currencies are exchanged when both sides deliver their payments. Other ways include requiring collaterals or by employing other financial operations. Technological advances produced automated clearinghouse (ACH) and real-time gross-settlement (RTGS) systems which speedup the clearing process and assure settlement in real-time. Clearing costs, and especially automated settlement costs, are (very) low and help reduce both risks as well as transaction costs[3].

2.3 *DOT-COM* Model

DOT-COM model is based on the *network-of-trust* model, since many real-life financial networks can be modeled in a similar way, e.g. FOREX between two third-parties relying on two members performed in the CLS Bank[1]. Hence, our model assumes a directed *trust graph* $G = (V, E)$, in which edges represent trust. All (trust) edges in the graph are associated with two weights: *credit* and *latency*.

For edge $e = (v_1, v_2) \in E$, $Credit(e)$ is the maximum amount of money, that v_1 is willing to risk as a result of commitments made by v_2, i.e., v_1 maximal loss due to v_2's default (or fraud) is bounded by $Credit(e)$. $Latency(e)$ is the time which takes v_1 to deliver messages to v_2 over a communication channel.

For simplicity, in this paper we assume that the communication channel between trusting peers is reliable and delivers timestamped non-repudiated messages within $Latency(e)$. This assumption is justified as in many trust relations, such as a customer and its bank, one side (the bank) is fully trusted by the other (the customer), and commonly a standard Internet connection can provide the required reliability. For less trusting peers, non-repudiation can be achieved using digital signatures, in which legally binding messages are delivered along with a digital signature. For timely delivery attestation, stronger properties are required, and are commonly implemented using a TTP to attest for the message time of delivery. Prior work, such as the attestation layer in [16] and real-world systems such as SWIFT Messaging Service[6], present such channels, which are commonly required for inter-FSP communication. Further discussion of secure communication channels is out of the scope of this paper. We emphasize that in the *DOT-COM* model, *trusted channels are only required between trusting peers* and not between the mistrusting counterparties.

Finally, all messages delivered over the trust graph are legally binding, whereas all other messages are not. Hence, communication between mistrusting trade parties is never legally binding, whereas communication between adjacent trusting peers is legally binding.

3   *DOT-COM* Design

In a typical scenario, Alice (A) holds a financial asset, denoted $asset_A$, deposited at some FSP which A trusts, denoted F_A; similarly, Bob (B) holds $asset_B$ at F_B. The goal of *DOT-COM* is to assure the exchange of assets between A and B, resulting in A holding $asset_B$ at F_A, and B holding $asset_A$ at F_B.

DOT-COM provides a secure settlement protocols, protecting the interests of all trading parties against settlement risk such as fraud, default, and other counterparty risks. There are a few challenges *DOT-COM* must handle. First, *DOT-COM* is required to use only existing trust and credit relations. This isn't trivial as we assume that A and B do not share a common trusted party, or some existing trust relations as in Figure 2b. Second, *DOT-COM* must mitigate counterparty risks and prevent situations where one party sends its asset but does not receive the counterparty's asset, e.g., Alice sends $asset_A$ but does not receive $asset_B$ as agreed.

3.1   Definitions

Commitment $Commit(e, a, t_a, c, t_c)$, is a *legally binding obligation* over an edge $e = (v_1, v_2) \in E$, made by v_2 to deliver an asset a to v_1 by time t_a if condition c is met by time t_c, where $t_c < t_a$. Hence, if a commitment is made by v_2, and the condition c is met by t_c, v_2 is in debt of a to v_1, otherwise the commitment is nullified.

Default commitment is a commitment $Commit(e, a, t_a, c, t_c)$, s.t., v_2 did not deliver a, current time $t > t_a$, and c was met before t_c.

Unmet commitment is $Commit(e, a, t_a, c, t_c)$, s.t., v_2 did not deliver a and current time $t < t_c$ or $t < t_a$ and c became True before t_c.

Contract $Contract(cmts, c)$ is a set of commitments $cmts$ and conditions (terms) c, s.t., the commitments are valid iff the conditions are met. Common contract conditions are the timely agreement of both counterparties to the set of commitments described in the contract.

3.2   Protocol Requirements

We now describe the requirements from *DOT-COM* protocol. The protocol, described later, is built incrementally, hence initially it meets only part of the requirements.

1. **Credit overuse prevention.** When more than one commitment is made over an edge, the overall sum of *defaulted commitments* and *unmet commitments* should not exceed the *credit* allocated on each edge $e \in E$.
2. **Timely transactions.** End-to-end settlement of transactions must be finalized within a pre-defined time frame.
3. **Quote hijacking prevention.** FSPs along the route should not be able to complete the trade without compensating the trading parties.[1]
4. **Future transactions.** The protocol should support transaction of *futures* (future contracts), in which commitments should be exchanged within a (short) pre-defined time frame, and the exchange of assets occurs at a (distant) future time.
5. **Misconduct Compensation.** The protocol should support penalizing misconducting parties, that is, in case a counterparty didn't stand up to its contractual obligations, it could be penalized, therefore compensating the other counterparty for its misconduct.
6. **Transaction details hiding.** Trading parties should be able to conceal transaction details from FSPs along the clearing route, before the commitments are made legally binding.

3.3 Trust and Credit: Constructing a Clearing-Route

Figure 3 depicts a network of trust, in which (directed) edges represent trust relations between adjacent FSP nodes. In order to construct ad-hoc trust between A and B, without making any party add new trust relations, *DOT-COM* finds a *chain-of-trust* between A to B, and construct a trusted *clearing-route*, e.g. $A \leftrightarrow F_A \leftrightarrow F_I \leftrightarrow F_K \leftrightarrow F_B \leftrightarrow B$. The clearing-route is like a "virtual-circuit" which is allocated before trade execution. We assume that in real-life, a similar network of trust exist between FSPs, and it can be utilized to provide secure trading infrastructure, i.e. a clearing route, between almost any two arbitrary

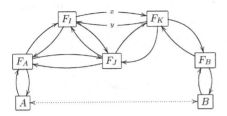

Fig. 3. Network of trust

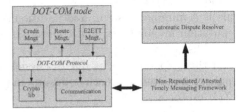

Fig. 4. *DOT-COM* Architecture

---

[1] This is an important requirement, as without it, FSPs could take over (i.e., hijack) the "profitable trades", making the system worthless and not cost-effective to use.

mistrusting traders. For example, any two banks around the world are likely to be able to find a route of banks which can deliver financial assets between them.

Constructing a chain-of-trust resembles searching data in unstructured peer-to-peer networks[8], in which there's no need for a global name space, and searching is performed in various ways, such as flooding, BFS, DFS etc. These brute-force searches can possibly be optimized by using various techniques, such as caching. Another possibility is to use a global name space with unique routable addresses, such as IP addresses, structured P2P[8], or BIC and IBAN used by SWIFT[2]. Whereas in P2P networks, locating data is often sufficient, in *DOT-COM* we want to mark and use the route which led to the destination.

In the *DOT-COM* model, trust relations mean that credit is allocated to peers. Credit allocation is based on risk-management performed by each node, and usually backed by collaterals and legal contracts. For example, in Figure 3 the edge $F_I \rightarrow F_K$ (denoted by x) implies that F_I trusts F_K and that F_I is willing to provide F_K with some credit, i.e. F_I is willing to take a credit risk that F_K will not repay its debt. Similar relations (may) exist vice versa (edge y in Figure 3). *DOT-COM* does not require any special risk-management, and does not require any change to the way risks are currently being managed. We assume each node manages its risks based solely on its own discretion. When constructing a route, we require that enough credit should be available for executing the transaction between any two peering nodes along the route.

Once a route of trust and credit is available, *DOT-COM* utilizes the chain of trusting peers for trade execution, hence it becomes the trade's *clearing route*. Credit is utilized by exchanging contracts between adjacent peers along the clearing route, therefore, each node remains in full control over the credit it gives its peers. Credit is never given to any peer which is not already trusted, and the node should not allow for any credit overuse, consequently it should never get exposed any more than it was initially willing to.

3.4   System Architecture

Figure 4 depicts the system architecture for a *DOT-COM* node, and additional (optional) sub-systems used for interactions with trusted-peer nodes. Note that this is a minimal system, and additional functionalities and modules, such as reputation management and counterparty selection, are also relevant within a wider discussion scope.

In this paper we focus our discussion on the *DOT-COM node*, that is, the application running at each node, and implements the functionality of the *DOT-COM* protocol.

Credit Management module is in charge of the node's credit allocation to trusted peers and the credit's usage. The module uses the node's risk- and credit-management policies.

Route Management module performs a routing-like functionality required for constructing and destructing a *clearing-route* (or *chain-of-trust*) between two trading parties. Due to space limitations, in this paper we assume this module exists and provides *DOT-COM* a valid-route when required.

End-to-End Transaction Terms (E2ETT) Management module provides the E2ETT required for construction of Peer-to-Peer Contracts (P2PC) along the clearing-route (see Section 3.5).

Cryptographic Library provides one-way functions, PKI, and shared key primitives.

Communication module is used for communication between nodes, both trusted and untrusted.

Due to space limitations, in this paper we focus on the *DOT-COM* Protocol and assume that all other modules exist. Specifically, we assume that the clearing-route, which should be constructed with the help of the *Route Management* module, is provided as input.

3.5 Transaction Terms and Contracts

To implement the required functionality we construct two types of messages as described in Table 1. The first type is an End-to-End Transaction Terms (E2ETT) message. E2ETT are the *non-binding transaction terms* agreed upon between two *mistrusting parties* – A and B. E2ETT contains the following fields:

E2ETT ID is a unique identifier.

Assets the parties wish to exchange.

Clearing-route or a corresponding identifier (see Section 3.3)

Trade hijack prevention are one-way-function images ($\mathcal{OWF}$), e.g. SHA-1, calculated over random preimages (PI) selected by the end-traders respectively. The preimages are required for the settlement process (see Section 3.6

Table 1. End-to-End Transaction Terms (E2ETT) are non-binding transaction terms negotiated directly between two mistrusting traders (A and B) and constitute the infrastructure for the legally binding Peer-to-Peer Contracts (P2PC) constructed and signed by two trusting parties (T and S), e.g. A and F_A respectively

Transaction Terms (End-to-End)	Contract (Peer-to-Peer)

1. E2ETT unique ID
2. Transaction Assets
  (a) $A \overset{asset_A}{\rightarrow} B$
  (b) $B \overset{asset_B}{\rightarrow} A$
3. Clearing-route
4. Trade hijack prevention
  (a) $Val_A = \mathcal{OWF}(PI_A)$
  (b) $Val_B = \mathcal{OWF}(PI_B)$
5. Deadlines
  (a) P2P commitments completion
  (b) Preimages delivery completion
	1. P2PC unique ID
	2. Transaction Terms (E2ETT)
	  (a) $T \equiv A$
	  (b) $S \equiv B$
	3. Deadlines for
	  (a) T's and S's contract consent
	  (b) PI_A and PI_B delivery
	4. Contract valid *iff*
	  (a) T consents to the P2PC
	  (b) S consents to the P2PC

for details). Only the creators of the random PI can provide them, which prevents FSPs along the route to complete the transaction without the initiating nodes involvement.

P2P commitments deadline for completing the P2P contracts across the clearing route. If this deadline is not met then the E2ETT expires. This field is used for limiting the time in which all commitments must take place.

Preimages delivery deadline of the images in Section 4 of the E2ETT. This is used for limiting the time for the transaction execution (settlement) (see Section 3.6 for details).

Since E2ETT is agreed upon between *mistrusting nodes* who share no trust and/or credit, it only describes the transaction terms and deadlines, but does not imply any commitment. To that end a second type of message is constructed: Peer-to-Peer Contract (P2PC), which contains *legally binding commitments* created between any two *trusting peers* along the clearing-route. P2PCs are based on the *non-binding E2ETT* as agreed between the trading parties A and B. P2PC consists of the following fields:

P2PC ID is a unique identifier.

Transaction Terms (E2ETT) is the E2ETT upon which the current contract is based. This section in the P2PC should also map between the P2PC counterparties and the E2ETT counterparties, hence clearly defining which assets should be delivered by which counterparty, when etc.

Deadlines for both delivering an agreement to the contract, and to the delivery of the preimages, which act as the settlement enablers.

Contract validation the delivery of the contract to the peer over a reliable channel (see Section 2.3) implies consent to the contract (if PKI is used between the peers, this can mean to digitally sign the contract).

P2PC timestamps are used to assure that each peer has enough time to reach the end of the route by the E2ETT deadlines, considering edges latencies. Hence, each node along the clearing-route should know the latencies between itself and the last host in the route, and require at least that amount of time before the E2ETT deadlines. Hence, every node along the route will decrease the time it requires from its previous node, and increase the whole clearing time.

E2ETT and P2PCs are used by the exchange protocol as described in Section 3.6. Note that additional conditions can be added to the described terms and commitments, for example, the commission charged by the FSP can added to the P2PC transaction details.

3.6   The *DOT-COM* Protocol

We now present a protocol using E2ETT and P2PC messages, to assure assets exchange between mistrusting parties A and B. Figure 5 depicts the protocol in high-level. For simplicity the figure depicts a sequential order of messages, however the messages should actually be initiated by both sides simultaneously.

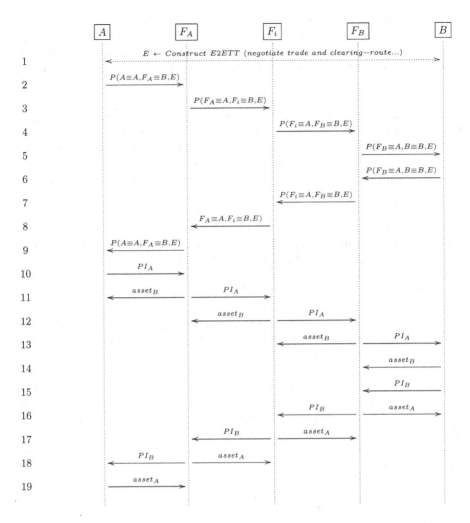

Fig. 5. Spot exchange protocol. A and B are mistrusting trading parties. F_A and F_B are A's and B's FSPs respectively. F_i represent additional FSPs which may exist between F_A and F_B. E is the non-binding End-to-End Transaction Terms (E2ETT) message agreed upon by A and B, containing the clearing route: $A \leftrightarrow F_A \leftrightarrow F_i \leftrightarrow F_B \leftrightarrow B$ (or a route ID). P are legally binding Peer-to-Peer Contracts (P2PC) between all pairs of trusting peers, along the clearing-route. Delivering a contract implies agreement. $asset_A$ and $asset_B$ are the exchanged assets.

Initially, A and B perform negotiation and agree on non-binding End-to-End Transaction Terms (E2ETT) which includes the clearing-route, known onward as E (line 1 of Figure 5). Next, A creates a legally binding P2PC between itself and its trusted FSP – F_A – based on the agreed E2ETT, and send it to F_A. F_A creates a *new* P2PC between itself and F_i (the next *trusted peer* in the clearing-route), in which F_A acts as A, and F_i acts as B, and so on until a corresponding

P2PC is created between F_B and B. B should also initiate the same process, hence when it does we get B's agreement on the contract between B and F_B, in which point both F_B and B are committed to the transaction. F_B will then deliver an agreement to F_i (legally binding F_B and F_i to the contract) and so on, until A is reached.

Once both A or B have contracts with their trusted FSP (i.e. after line 9), they can safely send PI_A and PI_B, the preimages of the $\mathcal{OWF}$, appearing in Section 4 of the E2ETT, thus validating that they are indeed executing the trade. Once an FSP receives a valid preimage it compensates the preimage sender and forwards the preimage to the next peer in the clearing-route, which should similarly compensate it. E.g., in line 10 F_A receives PI_A from A, provides it with $asset_B$ and forwards PI_A to F_i and so on until PI_A reaches B and vice versa. Note that without receiving PI_A from A, F_A cannot execute the trade by itself. Hence since A only reveals PI_A *after* F_A is committed to the P2PC, then F_A is obliged to compensate A. This use of preimages, prevents quote hijacking and meets Requirement 3. Once committed to the contract, each rational node has an incentive to forward its consent to the contract, as otherwise it won't be able to supply the preimage and hence won't be compensated.

B's processes of P2PC initiation, as well as supplying its preimage is completely independent of A's, and is not necessarily sequential as depicted in the figure; it should actually be simultaneous due to the time limitations set in the contracts, which would most probably make both sides deliver their agreements roughly at the same time.

Finally, we can see that *1)* the assets were safely exchanged between the mistrusting A and B. *2)* During the exchange period no node was exposed to credit risk other than it was willing to take in respect to its trusted-peers, and *3)* commitments are made only when compensation was assured to A and B, otherwise this implies that an FSP was able to find a PI collision, which contradicts the $\mathcal{OWF}$ assumption.

3.7   Node Functionality

Algorithm 1 presents pseudo-code for a simplified node functionality. In order to describe the functionality executed by each node, we assume the following functions are implemented.

Prev(P2PC)/Next(P2PC) returns the previous/next node in the clearing-route.

PrevAst(P2PC)/NextAst(P2PC) returns the *Asset* which should be provided by $Prev(P2PC)/Next(P2PC)$.

In addition the following function are assumed to be implemented by the node's *Credit Management Module*.

ChkCrdt(P2PC) checks whether we can credit $Prev(P2PC)$ with $PrevAst(P2PC)$.

AllocCrdt(P2PC) deduces the *PrevAst(P2PC)* from *Prev(P2PC)*'s credit until *DeallocCrdt(P2PC)* is called.

DeallocCrdt(P2PC) reinstates *PrevAst(P2PC)* to *Prev(P2PC)*'s credit.

Algorithm 1. Node Functionalities

```
Function OnP2PC(p) /* p: P2PC                              */
/* Called upon receiving a new P2PC                        */
begin
```
  if $p.agreementDeadline < now()$ *or* $ChkCrdt(p) = False$ **then**
  | **return** Fail;
  end
  AllocCrdt(p);
  Construct p' based on p (acting as A) send it to $Next(p)$;
  Wait until p' is received from $Next(p)$ or
  $p.agreementDeadline < now()$;
  if p' *not received from* $Next(p)$ **then**
  | **return** Fail;
  end
  Send p to $Prev(p)$;
```
  /* Consent to contract                                   */
```
  return Success;
end

```
Function OnPreimage(p, pi) /* p: P2PC, pi: preimage        */
/* Called when Prev(p) delivers the preimage for p         */
begin
```
  if $p.piDeliveryDeadline < now()$ **or** $\mathcal{OWF}(pi) \neq p.E2ETT.preimage$
  then
  | **return** Fail;
  end
  Send (p', pi) to $Next(p)$;
  Deliver $NextAst(p)$ to $Prev(p)$;
  Wait until $NextAst(p)$ is received from $Next(p)$;
  DeallocCrdt(p);
  return Success;
end

3.8   Advanced Requirements

To support Requirements 4-6 some changes should be made to the E2ETT and P2PC, as follows.

Future Contracts (Requirement 4). we can add two date fields to the *Deadlines*, Section 5 of the E2ETT, as follows

4. Deadlines
   (a) A will deliver $asset_A$ by $timestamp_A$
   (b) B will deliver $asset_A$ by $timestamp_B$

The delivery date does not change the expiry date of E2ETT and P2PC, which means that the commitments should still be exchanged in a relatively short time. However, the allocated credit should be preserved until the assets have been exchanged or the transaction was timed out.

Future transactions can support financial tools such as loans and forwards. For example, A lends money now ($timestamp_A$) to B, and B repays the money (with interest) at a future time ($timestamp_B$). Installments can be implemented by duplicating Section 4b, each describing a payment and its timestamp.

Misconduct Compensation (Requirement 5). Misconduct compensation can be used, for example, if a party fails to deliver an asset or a PI. The penalty can be added as the following condition:

1. A pays B $penalty_A$, unless A provide $asset_A/PI_A$ by $timestamp_A$.

Note that if $timestamp_A$ has expired and A hasn't provided $asset_A/PI_A$, then A now uses $penalty_A$ of its credit. FSPs in turn are likely to assure that they are compensated by the next node for such failures, which implies that both A and B should eventually commit to misconduct penalties.

Transaction Details Hiding (Requirement 6). We can hide transaction details by providing an $\mathcal{OWF}$ image, such as a SHA-1, on the Transaction Assets of the E2ETT (Section 2), instead of the actual section (adding a nonce to avoid guessing the correct values). The details are revealed by providing the preimage when required. However, hiding transaction details poses a credit management problem, as the FSP does not know its exposure. Therefore, one can provide a transaction "spread", according to which the FSP would consider the worst case. For example, assuming A and B decided to exchange \$D and €E. In the E2ETT A and B would announce that A delivers B \$($\delta_0 < D < \delta_1$) and B delivers A €($\epsilon_0 < E < \epsilon_1$). Another way is by using the penalty mechanism, that is, the FSP can always choose to pay the penalty instead of the asset, hence it is exposed up to the penalty and can therefore mange its credit exposure based on the penalty, disregarding the actual obligations.

4   Related Work

Traditional fair exchange protocols, e.g [10,12], commonly require a TTP which we assume does not exist. Moreover, legally binding signatures imply global public key infrastructure, which is not required by our solution. Furthermore, the contract should also include a legal authority (and venue) for resolving disputes – which will probably prove cost-ineffective, esp. for international transactions. Additionally, even if contracts could be drafted and fairly signed, we would still require a clearing/settlement route, which is slow and costly based on existing FSPs, hence are unusable for our settings.

Extensive research has been done in the area of payment systems in the past decades, however, the prevailing method for online payments still remains the giving of one's credit-card details, hopefully over SSL/TLS, which offers limited security. We note that *DOT-COM* is essentially different from payment systems as it is a designed for trading and exchange in which payments constitute a private case where only one party delivers money to the other.

Payment systems[9], such as Paypal[4] and iKP/SET[11,7], are aimed at providing a secure Internet version of existing payment methods such as credit card or account-based payments. Micropayments[15], such as [21,22] focus on making small-amount payments cost-effective, as traditional credit-card clearing is usually high. Digital cash, such as Bitcoin[17] and PPay[22] are used as low-cost traceable digital coins, whereas other digital cash schemes[13] are concerned with anonymity.

Decentralized payment systems come in many forms. Some perform secure decentralization of processing resources[20]. In [15,14], the authors suggested a decentralized payment system, in which payment-routing messages are propagated within a payment-service-provider (PSP) network. By propagating payment-routing messages the PSP states that is willing to honor a signed payment-order (PO) by other PSPs appearing in the payment-routing message. *DOT-COM* constructs a different network decentralization, as it does not trust or accepts signatures from any FSP other than its trusted-peers. This makes payment-routing messages, which may contain confidential business information, unnecessary.

The Ripple Project[5] uses a social network to construct a payment network, in which members are willing to give credit to people they know in real life. To perform payment, the system forwards a debt, in the form of "IOU" (I owe you) messages, along a chain of social connections. Unlike *DOT-COM* Ripple is not an exchange network and is not designed to integrate within a banking-like system. Ripple is designed for small-volume credit, which can be allocated amongst friends without binding contracts. Moreover, Ripple is uses a centralized server to maintain accounts and calculate routes for IOUs.

5   Conclusions

In this paper we have presented *DOT-COM*, a system and protocol allowing distant mistrusting traders to perform online trades and securely exchange financial assets. *DOT-COM* uses only existing trust and credit relations, and requires no special risk management changes or additional trust. Using a chain-of-trust *DOT-COM* builds a clearing-route, and maintain commitments between all nodes along the route up to the allowed credit. *DOT-COM* prevents trades from being hijacked by nodes along the clearing-route. *DOT-COM* consists of mechanisms which enable construction of future contracts such as loans and forwards, as well as other complex financial tools and commitments.

References

1. About CLS, http://www.cls-group.com/Publications/CLS%20About%20Us.pdf
2. Business Identifier Code (BIC),
   http://www.swift.com/products/bic_registration
3. CLS: The Missing Link in Foreign Exchange Settlements,
   http://www.cls-group.com/ForYou/CLSFunds/fundcasestudies/Pages/
   CLSTheMissingLink.aspx
4. PayPal, https://www.paypal.com/
5. Ripple Project, http://ripple-project.org/
6. SWIFT FIN Messaging System, http://www.swift.com/products/fin
7. Agnew, G.: Secure electronic transactions: Overview, capabilities, and current status, ch. 10 (2003) ISBN 3-540-44007-0
8. Androutsellis-Theotokis, S., Spinellis, D.: A survey of peer-to-peer content distribution technologies. ACM Comput. Surv. 36(4), 335–371 (2004),
   http://doi.acm.org/10.1145/1041680.1041681
9. Asokan, N., Janson, P.A., Steiner, M., Waidner, M.: The state of the art in electronic payment systems. COMPUTER: IEEE Computer 30 (1997)
10. Asokan, N., Shoup, V., Waidner, M.: Optimistic fair exchange of digital signatures. IEEE Journal on Selected Areas in Communications 18(4), 593–610 (2000)
11. Bellare, M., Garay, J.A., Hauser, R., Herzberg, A., Krawczyk, H., Steiner, M., Tsudik, G., Herreweghen, E.V., Waidner, M.: Design, implementation, and deployment of the iKP secure electronic payment system. IEEE Journal of Selected Area in Communications 18(4), 611–627 (2000)
12. Ben-Or, M., Goldreich, O., Micali, S., Rivest, R.: A fair protocol for signing contracts. IEEE Transactions on Information Theory 36(1), 40–46 (1990)
13. Chaum, D.: Blind signatures for untraceable payments. In: Advances in Cryptology: Proceedings of Crypto, vol. 82, pp. 199–203 (1983)
14. Herzberg, A., Shai, E., Zisser, I.: Decentralized electronic certified payment, uS Patent 7546275 (2009)
15. Herzberg, A.: Micropayments. In: Kou, W. (ed.) Payment Technologies for E-Commerce, ch. 12, pp. 245–280. Springer (2003) ISBN 3-540-44007-0
16. Herzberg, A., Yoffe, I.: Layered architecture for secure e-commerce applications. In: SECRYPT, pp. 118–125 (2006)
17. Nakamoto, S.: Bitcoin: A peer-to-peer electronic cash system (2009),
    http://bitcoin.org/bitcoin.pdf
18. New York Stock Exchange: How Do Stocks Work?
    http://nyse.nyx.com/en/learningcenter/allaboutinvesting/stocks/how-do-stocks-work
19. OTC Markets Group Inc: OTC 101: Learn - Part 2 - Trading,
    http://www.otcmarkets.com/otc-101/trading
20. Serban, C., Chen, Y., Zhang, W., Minsky, N.: The concept of decentralized and secure electronic marketplace. Electronic Commerce Research 8(1), 79–101 (2008)
21. Sirbu, M., Tygar, J.: Netbill: An internet commerce system optimized for network-delivered services. IEEE Personal Communications 2(4), 34–39 (1995)
22. Yang, B., Garcia-Molina, H.: Ppay: micropayments for peer-to-peer systems. In: Proceedings of the 10th ACM Conference on Computer and Communications Security, pp. 300–310. ACM (2003)

Formalizing Physical Security Procedures

Catherine Meadows[1] and Dusko Pavlovic[2]

[1] Naval Research Laboratory, Washington, DC, USA
meadows@itd.nrl.navy.mil
[2] Royal Holloway, Oxford and Twente
dusko.pavlovic@rhul.ac.uk

Abstract. Although the problems of physical security emerged more than 10,000 years before the problems of computer security, no formal methods have been developed for them, and the solutions have been evolving slowly, mostly through social procedures. But as the traffic on physical and social networks is now increasingly expedited by computers, the problems of physical and social security are becoming technical problems. From various directions, many security researchers and practitioners have come to a realization that the areas such as transportation security, public and private space protection, or critical infrastructure defense, are in need of formalized engineering methodologies. Following this lead, we extended Protocol Derivation Logic (PDL) to Procedure Derivation Logic (still PDL). In contrast with a protocol, where some principals send and receive some messages, in a procedure they can also exchange and move some objects. For simplicity, in the present paper we actually focus on the security issues arising from traffic of objects, and leave the data flows, and the phenomena emerging from the interaction of data and objects, for future work. We illustrate our approach by applying it to a flawed airport security procedure described by Schneier.

Keywords: formal security protocol analysis, physical procedure analysis, physical security, security policies.

1 Introduction

It is well known that the use of security protocols goes well beyond their application to communication between electronic devices. Any procedure that gives rules for interaction between a set of principals in order to provide security against misbehavior can be considered a security protocol in a broader since, whether the principals are human beings, computers, hand-held or embedded devices, or some mixture. Thus Ellison [10] proposed the idea of "ceremonies", which extend the notion of computer-to-computer security protocols to the human end users who interact with them. In [2] Blaze proposes an even further extension of the notion of security protocols: those that cover scripted interactions in general, for example, interactions between passengers and authorities in airports, railroad seat checks, and denial of service in burglar alarms.

Blaze's example of a flawed airport security procedure gives an idea of the kind of things that can go wrong. It arose from the fact that passengers arriving in the

A. Jøsang, P. Samarati, and M. Petrocchi (Eds.): STM 2012, LNCS 7783, pp. 193–208, 2013.
© Springer-Verlag Berlin Heidelberg 2013

US from overseas must clear their luggage through customs at their first point of entry, even if they are connecting to another flight within the US. Originally, passengers were not required to be checked through security again after clearing customs. They simply re-checked their luggage. This caused a problem when rules changed shortly after September 11, 2001, after which passengers could no longer carry knives aboard planes, but were allowed to put them in checked luggage. Until the rules were modified to require another security check, a passenger could circumvent the new policy by packing knives in his checked luggage, picking it up upon arrival in the US, transferring the knives to his person, passing through customs, dropping off his now knifeless luggage, and catching the next flight.

Another flawed airport security procedure was documented by Bruce Schneier in [20].Shortly after the "shoe bomber" incident, a new policy went into effect in many locations requiring shoes to be screened, but many airport security scanners could not screen passengers' feet. For a short while the following policy was implemented at Heathrow Terminal 3. A passenger would go through security, handing his carry-on to be scanned and himself passing through a security scanner, and pick it up upon emerging from the other end. Then he would pass to another station in which he would hand over his shoes to be scanned. Schneier points out that that a passenger could easily circumvent this procedure by hiding contraband items in his shoes, and packing another pair of shoes in his carry-on. After passing through the body scanner, the passenger could then switch shoes and proceed to the shoe scanning station, where his now innocent shoes would be given a clean bill of health.

These procedures, and the class of airport security procedures in general, belong to a larger class of procedures that govern the motion and location of principals and objects. Any procedure governing the access to a secure facility such as an airport or an office building falls into this category. As we see from the above examples, it is as easy for flaws to creep in as it is for cyber security protocols, especially when, as is often the case, new procedures are hastily implemented in response to a changed security situation.

In this paper we show how the logical framework we developed in [19] can be extended to reasoning about physical access procedures. This framework, called the Procedure Derivation Logic (PDL), extends our Protocol Derivation Logic (also PDL) [13,3,16,1,14,18,17], and the earlier ideas of Protocol Composition Logic (PCL) [9,5,4], to reason about the network interactions where principals may control complex network configurations, consisting of multiple nodes representing diverse devices, objects and data, with different channels between them, providing different security guarantees. Such a network configuration, as a concrete realization of the capabilities of a principal, is what we call an *actor*, with a respectful nod to Actor Network Theory [12], in an attempt to take into account some social interactions in security.

In [19] we formalized and analyzed some multi-factor, multi-channel authentication and key agreement procedures, one involving smart cards and card readers, and the other biometric devices and physical sources of randomness, together with the humans and the standard internet nodes. Both procedures involved some authentic visual and social channels, together with the standard, insecure internet links. In the present work, we focus on the procedures where the humans control hierarchical configurations of physical objects, such as those that arise when we travel, packing our luggage, tickets and documents to satisfy complex security and safety requirements. Such procedures are effectively described as interactions between the actors, which include not only the passengers with their luggage, but also the various authorities and service providers, with their control devices, used for screening and transportation.

There are several important issues that these procedures bring forward. The first one is the *dynamics* of actors' configurations: e.g., during the check-in procedure, a passenger divests himself of some luggage, which becomes a part of another configuration; during security check, the passenger passes his carry-on luggage, and in some case his shoes, under the control of the screeners, who may or may not return these objects later on in the procedure. The next important issue is the *compositionality* of security procedures: e.g., the airport procedures usually come about as combinations of several simpler procedures, previously introduced to address different security concerns. A passenger interacts with various other actors in stages, where he receives his boarding pass at one stage, checks his luggage at another, then enters the screening area where he hands his carry-on over to the screener, and passes through a body scanning device with a certain probability, and so on. The problems with the airport security procedures tend to arise not because their individual components are implemented incorrectly, but because the properties that they guarantee are not adequate for the composite contexts into which they are introduced. Thus, the task of procedure design is often inseparable from the problem of procedure composition. While the same problem is familiar from protocol design, and the incremental approach of Protocol Derivation Logic usefully extends to Procedure Derivation Logic, the reasoning templates developed for security protocols do not suffice for analyzing the complex interactions of the heterogenous security components in networks of actors. The question then arises: at what level should we specify and reason about their compositions?

The answer to this question becomes clearer when we take a closer look at what airport security procedures and policies are regulating. They are concerned not only with authenticating a passenger's identity, and the integrity of his luggage, but also with constraining his movements, depending on the configuration of the objects and data that he controls. Moreover, the passenger's interactions with the airport authorities largely consist of movements: handing over luggage and ID, proceeding from one place to another when indicated. Finally, the breaches and circumventions of the procedures consist of movements as well, if a passenger finds a way to bring a weapon or a prohibited object into a secure area by finding a way to move them from one place to another along an unforeseen path. This situation, in which an attacker is deemed capable of performing any combination of a relatively small number of actions, should be familiar to those acquainted with the formal protocol analysis literature. It is exactly the kind of approach taken in the Dolev-Yao model [8,7] in which the attacker is assumed to be able to read, alter, and redirect traffic, as well as perform a small number of operations such as concatenation, deconcatenation, encryption, and decryption. This gives a regular structure to the attacker model which makes security protocols amenable to both logical analysis and model checking.

In this paper we show how we use these insights to develop a logical system for the analysis of policies on of moves, with an application to airport security procedures. In Section 2 we extend the notion of a network configuration, that endowed principals with the structure of actors in [19], into the notion of *box configuration*, that describes how some objects contain other objects. This turns out to be convenient for expressing the basic goals and methods of, e.g., airport security procedures, since the complex configurations of objects controlled by the participating actors are usually enclosed into physical box configurations. In Section 3 we provide an overview of a *box configuration logic* in which conditions and consequences of moves can be reasoned about. In Section 4 we apply the logic to airport security procedures, by specifying two different airport security procedures in terms of the constraints on passenger movements imposed a a result of the various subprocedures a passenger must engage in order to pass into the secured area. We also use the logic to analyze the procedures, and show how, in the case of the shoe procedure, the attempt that prove that the security goals are satisfied fails. In Section 5 we discuss related work. In Section 6 we conclude the paper and discuss future directions, in particular our plans for extending our work to include the analysis of interactions and data flows between principals.

2   Configurations and Box Configurations

In this section we introduce the basic notion of configurations and box configurations. A configuration is a recursively defined set of sets. A box configuration is a recursively defined set of possibly labeled sets. Both configurations and box configurations may also be thought of as unordered trees.

2.1   Basic Definitions

A configuration is a collection of nodes that operate jointly in the execution of a procedure. A *box configuration* is a special case of a slightly expanded notion of the definition of configuration introduced in [19]. There we defined a configuration over a set S to be either a subset of S or a set of configurations over S. For box configurations, we find it convenient to allow sets made up of both elements of S and configurations. Thus we use the following definition:

Definition 1. *A configuration over a set S is either an element of S or a finite set of configurations over S, i.e. $C ::= s \mid \{\} \mid \{C_0, C_1, \ldots, C_n\}$, where $s \in S$ and $n \geq 0$. The empty configuration is $\{\} = \emptyset$. The set of S-configurations is $\mathcal{C}(S)$.*

Configurations are thus the elements of what set theorists would call a *cumulative hierarchy of finite sets*, generated by a set of *atoms* S. It is easy to see that each S-configuration corresponds to a unique finite tree where the leaves may be labelled by the elements of S or the empty label (i.e., the empty set). The subconfigurations of a configuration are those corresponding to the subtrees of its tree representation.

Now we introduce the notion of a box configuration:

Definition 2. *A* box configuration *over a set S, or an S-box configuration, is either an S-configuration, or an S-box configuration in a box b, i.e. $F ::= s \mid \{\} \mid \{F_0, \ldots, F_n\} \mid \{F_0, \ldots, F_n\}_b$ where the boxes b are distinguished elements of S. For simplicity, we assume that all elements of S can be boxes. The set of S-box configurations is written $\mathcal{F}(S)$. The element relation is generated by the clauses $F_0, \ldots, F_n \in \{F_0, \ldots, F_n\}$ and $b, F_0, \ldots, F_n \in \{F_0, \ldots, F_n\}_b$. We say that $\{F_0, \ldots, F_n\}_b$ is rooted in b. We use the notation X_b to denote an arbitrary box configuration rooted in b.*

Example 1. A box configuration describing a passenger pa with a newspaper np, a phone ph and sunglasses sg in his pocket, and a suitcase sc containing a knife kn and an explosive device ex can be written as $\{np, \{ph, sg\}, \{kn, ex\}_{sc}\}_{pa}$.

Definition 3. *We say that a box configuration A is* contained *in a box configuration C, or that A is a* part of *C's contents, and write*

$$A \sqsubseteq C \iff A = C \vee \exists B. A \sqsubseteq B \in C \text{ and } A \sqsubset C \iff A \sqsubseteq C \wedge A \neq C$$

Example 2. In Example 1 above, both $kn \sqsubset \{np, \{ph, sg\}, \{kn, ex\}_{sc}\}_{pa}$ and $\{kn, ex\}_{sc} \sqsubset \{np, \{ph, sg\}, \{kn, ex\}_{sc}\}_{pa}$ hold.

Configurations and Box Configurations as Trees

Proposition 1. *The set $\mathcal{C}(S)$ of S-configuration is in bijective correspondence with the set of finite unordered irredundant trees with whose leaves labelled by elements of S or the empty label. (A tree is irredundant if no two child trees of any node are identical (see [15], Sec. 5.2 for a discussion).) The set $\mathcal{F}(S)$ of S-box configurations is in bijective correspondence with the set of finite unordered irredundant trees whose nodes are labelled by elements of S or the empty label.*

For reasons of space the proof is omitted. We note in particular that if A and B are two box configurations, then $A \sqsubseteq B$ only if the tree associated with A is a subtree of the tree associated with B.

We will be particularly interested in box configurations whose labels are all different; i. e. each labelled node corresponds to a unique object.

Definition 4. *A box configuration C is* normal *if no two nodes of the corresponding tree are labelled by the same atom from S.*

Example 3. Example 1 can also be depicted as the following labelled tree

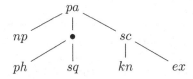

2.2   Types and Constraining Set Membership

We put a typing structure on S, where a type is simply a subset of S. Types are partially ordered by the subset relation. The typing is also applied to box configurations of the form X_s; if $s \in S$ is of type $\mathbf{t}$, then so is X_s.

One important application of types is in the expression of restrictions on what can box configurations can be elements of what other box configurations. For example, we may want to specify that an passenger can be inside an airplane, but an airplane can't be inside a passenger. We define a relation $\ltimes$ on box configuration types, where $\mathbf{a} \ltimes \mathbf{b}$ if and only if box configurations of type $\mathbf{a}$ can be elements of box configurations of type $\mathbf{b}$.

Example 4. Let $\mathbf{pa}$ be the type passenger, $\mathbf{su}$ be the type suitcase, $\mathbf{kn}$ be the type knife, and let $\mathbf{ex}$ be the type explosive. Then $\mathbf{su}, \mathbf{kn}, \mathbf{ex} \ltimes \mathbf{pa}$ and $\mathbf{kn}, \mathbf{ex} \ltimes \mathbf{su}$.

We note that, although the $\ltimes$ relation defined in Example 4 is transitive, this is not always the case. For example, if we have box configurations of the type principal, room, and building, it may make sense to say that a principal may be an element of a room, and a room may be an element of a building, but the principal can't be an element of a building. That is, a principal can't be contained in a building unless he is in a room in the building.

Definition 5. *We define the* multiplicity *of a type $\mathbf{t}$ in a box configuration C, denoted by $mult(C, \mathbf{t})$ as follows: 1) $mult(\emptyset, \mathbf{t}) = 0$, 2) $mult(s, \mathbf{t}) = 1$ if $s \in \mathbf{t}$, else $mult(s, \mathbf{t}) = 0$. 3) $mult(\{F_1, \ldots F_n\}, \mathbf{t}) = \sum_{i=0}^{n} mult(F_i, \mathbf{t})$, and 4) $mult(X_s, \mathbf{t}) = mult(X, \mathbf{t}) + mult(s, \mathbf{t})$.*

We also use $mult(b, \mathbf{t})$ to refer to the multiplicity of $\mathbf{t}$ in the box configuration rooted in b, when we can avoid confusion.

Example 5. Let $PA = \{\{kn_1, kn_2, ex_1\}_{su_1}, su_2\}_{pa}$ where $pa \in \mathbf{pa}$, $su_1, su_2 \in \mathbf{su}$, $kn_1, kn_2 \in \mathbf{kn}$, and $ex_1 \in \mathbf{ex}$. Then $mult(PA, \mathbf{kn}) = 2, mult(PA, \mathbf{su}) = 2$, and $mult(PA, \mathbf{ex}) = 1$.

The following property of multiplicities, which follows straightforwardly from the properties of trees, will also be useful to us.

Proposition 2. *Let X and Y be box configurations, and let $\mathbf{t}$ be a type. Then if $X \sqsubseteq Y$, then $mult(X, \mathbf{t}) \le mult(Y, \mathbf{t})$.*

Example 6. Let X_{pa} be a passenger in the secure area sa of an airport, i. e. $X_{pa} \sqsubset Y_{sa}$. Suppose that it is known that the secure area contains no explosives, that is $mult(sa, \mathbf{ex}) = 0$. Then we can conclude that $mult(pa, \mathbf{ex}) = 0$.

2.3   Displacing Subtrees

A key feature of our logical system is the ability to reason about what occurs when a box subconfiguration moves from one part of a box configuration to another. In order to capture what happens in these circumstances, we define the notion of box subconfiguration displacement. We first introduce some notation.

Definition 6. *Suppose that X, Y, and Z are box configurations such that $X \in Y$ and $X \notin Z$. We denote $Y \setminus \{X\}$ by $Y \ominus X$ and $Z \cup \{X\}$ by $Z \oplus X$. If $Y, Z \sqsubseteq W$, we denote the result of replacing Y in W with $Y \ominus X$ by $W[Y \ominus X]$, and the result of replacing Z in W with $Z \oplus X$ by $W[Z \oplus X]$.*

Definition 7. *Suppose that $X \in Z \sqsubseteq U$ and $Y \sqsubseteq U$ where U is normal and $Y \not\sqsubseteq X$. We define a* displacement *of X from under Z to under Y in U , denoted by $U[Y \xrightarrow{X} Z]$, as follows. If $Y \not\sqsubseteq Z$ replace Z with $Z \ominus X$, otherwise leave it unchanged. If $Z \not\sqsubseteq Y$ replace Y with $Z \oplus X$, otherwise leave it unchanged.*

Example 7. Suppose that two passengers pa_1 and pa_2 are in an airport ap. Suppose that one passenger is carrying a suitcase, in which there is a knife, and hands the knife to the other passenger. The original box configuration is $U = \{\{\{kn\}_{sc}\}_{pa_1}, pa_2\}_{ap}$. The new one is is $\{\{sc\}_{pa_1}, \{kn\}_{pa_2}\}_{ap}$.

The next proposition follows directly from the properties of normal trees.

Proposition 3. *Suppose U is normal, and that $X \sqsubseteq U$ and $Y \sqsubseteq U$. Then*

1. *If $X \in Z \sqsubseteq Q \sqsubseteq U \wedge Q \cap Y = \emptyset$ then Q is replaced in $U[Y \xrightarrow{X} Z]$ with $Q[Z \ominus X]$ and $mult(Q[Z \ominus X], \mathbf{m}) = mult(Q, \mathbf{m}) - mult(X, \mathbf{m})$.*
2. *If $Z \sqsubseteq Q \sqsubseteq U \wedge X \cap Q = \emptyset \wedge Y \sqsubseteq Q$ then Q is replaced in $U[Y \xrightarrow{X} Z]$ with $Q[Y \oplus X]$ and $mult(Q[Y \oplus X], \mathbf{m}) = mult(Q, \mathbf{m}) + mult(X, \mathbf{m})$*
3. *If $X \in Z \sqsubseteq Q \sqsubseteq U \wedge Y \sqsubseteq Q$ then Q is replaced in $U[Y \xrightarrow{X} Z]$ with $Q[Y \xrightarrow{X} Z]$ and $mult(Q[Y \xrightarrow{X} Z], \mathbf{m}) = mult(Q, \mathbf{m})$.*

3   A Logic of Moves

In this section we present our logic of moves. In Section 3.1 we give the semantic underpinnings of the logic, in Section 3.2, a policy language for moves, and in Section 3.3, a logical system for proving that a policy specified in the policy language implements a policy defined in terms of state invariants on runs.

3.1   States, Runs, and Processes

We consider a process $\mathcal{P}$ made up of nondeterministic concurrent processes P, each associated to a unique principal p, that act upon a single state variable $\mathbf{U}$ whose value is a normal box configuration called the *universe* U. P acts on $\mathbf{U}$ by assigning to it a new version of the universe $U[X \xrightarrow{O} Y]$ for some O, X, and Y in U. We refer to such actions as *move actions*.

We make use of the following notation:

Definition 8. *A* move action *of O from under Y to under X executed by principal p is a state transition in which the preceding state U satisfies $O \in Y \sqsubseteq U$ and the succeeding state is $U[Y \xrightarrow{X} O]$. It is denoted by $p : X \xrightarrow[\in]{O} Y$. A move* action of O from X to Y executed by p *is an action* $p : R \xrightarrow{O}{}_{\in} Q$ *in which* U *satisfies* $O \in R \sqsubseteq X \sqsubseteq U$ *and* $Q \sqsubseteq Y \sqsubseteq U$ *for some* R, Q *immediately before the transition. It is denoted by* $p : X \xrightarrow{O} Y$.

We note that $p : X \xrightarrow{O}{}_{\in} Y$ denotes a unique action, while $p : X \xrightarrow{O} Y$ denotes one of a possible set of actions. We define $p : X \xrightarrow{O} Y$ in this way because in many cases we do not care whether an object is an element of another as long as it is a box subconfiguration of the other. For example, if A puts a knife into B's suitcase, she can be considered as having given it to B.

Move actions are assumed to be *atomic*, so that a condition that holds when a move action begins to execute continues to hold until it is finished.

Example 8. The action in Example 7 can be represented as

$$pa_1 : \{\{\{kn\}_{sc}\}_{pa_1}, pa_2\}_{ap} \xrightarrow{kn} pa_2$$

Moves can describe a number of different actions. Let Z_p and W_q be box configurations of type principal, and let X, Y, O be of some other type. Then,

1. $p : X \xrightarrow{Z_p} Y$ describes a principal p moving from X to Y.
2. $p : Z_p \xrightarrow{O} W_q$ describes one principal p giving O to another, q.
3. $p : W_q \xrightarrow{O} Z_p$ describes one principal taking O from another.
4. $p : Z_p \xrightarrow{O} Y$ describes a principal putting O in Y.
5. $p : X \xrightarrow{O} Z_p$ describes a principal removing O from X.
6. $p : X \xrightarrow{O} Y$ describes a principal p moving O from X to Y.

Move polices are conditions on what moves may be taken and under what conditions. Move polices are defined locally, but the intended consequences are global, defined in terms of runs, as follows.

Definition 9. *A run is an alternating sequence of states and moves*

$$U_1, p_1 : X_1 \xrightarrow{O_1} Y_1, U_2, \ldots, U_i, p_i : X_i \xrightarrow{O_i} Y_i, U_{i+1}, \ldots$$

A *policy* $\mathcal{R}$ defines a set of legal runs. For example, the legal runs of the airport policy are those in which, in every state, the multiplicity of knives and explosives in the secure area is zero.

3.2 Syntax of Move Policies

For practical reasons, one enforces a policy, not by controlling the states, but by controlling the actions. We make this more precise below.

Definition 10. *Let $\mathcal{P}$ be a policy, and $\mathcal{R}$ be the set of runs satisfying that policy, let a be an action, and let f be a predicate on states. We say that f guards a, written as $f \Rightarrow a$ if, for every run $R \in \mathcal{R}$, if S immediately precedes a in $\mathcal{R}$, then $f(S)$ holds.*

Definition 11. *A* move policy *is a set of statements describing under what conditions an action may take place. The syntax of move policies is given below, where X is a variable representing a boxconfiguration, and p, $\mathbf{t}$, and n, are each a variable or constant representing respectively a principal, type, and integer.*

$$C ::= X \mid b \mid p \mid \{C\} \mid C_b \mid C_1[C_2 \ominus C_3] \mid C_1[C_2 \oplus C_3] \mid \{C|R\} \mid$$
$$C_1[C_3 \xrightarrow{C_2} C_4] \mid \{C_1, \ldots, C_k\}$$
$$E ::= n \mid mult(C, \mathbf{t}) \mid mult(b, \mathbf{t}) \mid E_1 \times E_2 \mid E_1 - E_2 \mid E_1 + E_2$$
$$R ::= E_1 = E_2 \mid E_1 \le E_2 \mid E_1 < E_2 \mid C_1 \sqsubset C_2 \mid C_1 \sqsubseteq C_2 \mid C_1 = C_2 \mid$$
$$\mathbf{t_1} \ltimes \mathbf{t_2} \mid b \in \mathbf{t} \mid R_1 \Rightarrow R_2 \mid not(R) \mid R_1 \vee R_2 \mid R_1 \wedge R_2 \mid \exists X.R \mid \perp \mid \top$$
$$A ::= p : C_1 \xrightarrow{C_3} C_2 \mid p : C_1 \xrightarrow[\in]{C_3} C_2$$
$$G ::= R \Rightarrow A$$

Variables are assumed to be universally quantified unless bound by $\exists$.

Example 9. Given two locations, the unsecured area ua, and the secure area sa, such that no object or person containing a knife may enter sa, we write the move policy as $mult(Z, \mathbf{kn}) = 0 \Rightarrow p : O_{ua} \xrightarrow{O} Y_{sa}$.

3.3 Move Logic

In this section we give the logic of moves that will be used to show that a move policy enforces a policy on runs that is described in terms of state invariants.

Statements in the move logic are of two forms. They can be Hoare triples, which say that if a state satisfies predicate f_1 before an action, then it satisfies predicate f_2 after that action:

$$\{f_1\}p : X \xrightarrow[\in]{O} Y\{f_2\} \quad \text{or} \quad \{f_1\}p : X \xrightarrow{O} Y\{f_2\}$$

Statements can also be expressed in terms of move policy statements as defined in Section 11. If no policy statement exists for an action a, then $\perp \Rightarrow a$ holds.

The idea is to specify a safety policy in terms of invariants on states that are preserved in all possible runs. A move policy is then specified as in Definition 11. One then uses the Hoare logic to determine the result of enforcing the policy. This is done by finding, for each move action a, and each invariant g specified by the policy, a guard f such that $\{f \wedge g\}a\{g\}$ holds.

We use the standard inference rules in Hoare logic (e.g. as presented in [11]), with the exception of the while rules and the rule for composition, which are not sound with respect to our concurrent semantics. We also use the inference rules for first-order logic and the following rule governing guards:

$$\frac{f_1 \Rightarrow a \qquad f_2 \Rightarrow a}{f_1 \wedge f_2 \Rightarrow a}$$

We also give the following axioms describing results of moves, which follow directly from the definitions given in Section 3.1.

$$\{\mathbf{U} = U\}p \overset{\cdot}{:} X \xrightarrow[\in]{O} Y \{\mathbf{U} := U[X \xrightarrow{O} Y]\} \tag{1}$$

$$O \in X \sqsubseteq U \Rrightarrow p : X \xrightarrow[\in]{O} Y \tag{2}$$

$$\{\mathbf{U} = U\}p : X \xrightarrow{O} Y \{\exists Q, R. Q \sqsubseteq X \wedge R \sqsubseteq Y \wedge \mathbf{U} := U[Q \xrightarrow{O} R]\} \tag{3}$$

$$O \sqsubseteq X \sqsubseteq U \Rrightarrow p : X \xrightarrow{O} Y \tag{4}$$

4 Airport Security Procedure

We develop the airport security procedure in an incremental fashion. We begin with the simplest case, with only spatial constraints on passenger movements. We then add a step in which passengers are checked for forbidden items. We next add the step in which passenger carry-ons are checked separately. We finish with an insecure procedure in which the passenger's shoes are checked separately.

4.1 Locations, Passengers and the Items Passengers may Carry

In this section we specify the various types used in the procedure, and the subtype relation between them. First is the passenger type **pa**: a subtype of principal. Next is the type **su** for suitcase. The type **su** has three subtypes, large suitcase **ls**, small suitcase **ss**, and personal item **pi**. We also have type disallowed, or **da**, with subtypes knives **kn** and explosives **ex**. We also have the types **ft** for foot and **sh** for shoes. Finally, we have the type location **lo** and the universe **u**.

We give the relation ⋉ defining what box configurations may contain others:

lo ⋉ **u**	**ls** ⋉ **t.t** ∈ {**pa**, **lo**}	**pi** ⋉ **t.t** ∈ {**ss**, **ls**, **pa**, **lo**}	**pa** ⋉ **lo**
sh ⋉ **ft**	**ss** ⋉ **t.t** ∈ {**ls**, **pa**, **lo**}	**da** ⋉ **t.t** ∈ {**sh**, **pi**, **ss**, **ls**, **pa**, **lo**}	

Our goal is to prove that all actions maintain the invariant $mult(sa, \mathbf{da}) = 0$.

4.2 Procedure with Spatial Constraints Only

We begin with just three locations: outside the airport, or os, the unsecured area inside the airport, or ua, and the secure area inside the airport, or sa.

At this point, the security controls are minimal. We do make a few restrictions however: the only thing a passenger can move from one location to another is himself, and there are restrictions on the areas he can move between. This can be expressed in the move logic syntax as the disjunction of atomic conditions, but for the sake of conciseness and readability we express it using a relation $\mathcal{R}_1 = \{(os, ua), (ua, os), (ua, sa)(sa, ua)\}$. We specify the permitted move actions:

$$(\ell_1, \ell_2) \in \mathcal{R}_1 \Rightarrow pa : X_{\ell_1} \xrightarrow{Z_{pa}} Y_{\ell_2} \tag{5}$$

$$lo \in \mathbf{lo} \wedge Z \sqsubseteq X \wedge U_{pa} \sqsubseteq V_{lo} \wedge X \sqsubseteq V_{lo} \wedge Y \sqsubseteq V_{lo} \Rightarrow pa : X \xrightarrow{Z} Y \tag{6}$$

Axiom 5 tells us that a passenger can move from one location ℓ_1 to another location ℓ_2 only if $(\ell_1, \ell_2) \in \mathcal{R}_1$. Axiom 6 tells us that a passenger can move a box configuration (other than himself) from X to Y only if X, Y, and the passenger are in the same location.

By applying Proposition 3, we see that the only way a disallowed item can pass into the secured area sa is by a passenger carrying it passing from the unsecured area ua into sa. Thus one way to prevent disallowed items from entering sa is to prevent passengers carrying them from moving from ua to sa.

4.3   Adding Passenger Screening

In order to add passenger screening, we add the location it will take place in: the passenger screening area, psa. We replace the passage between ua and sa in $\mathcal{R}_1$ with passages between ua and psa and between psa and sa:

$$\mathcal{R}_2 = (\mathcal{R}_1 / \{(ua, sa)\}) \cup \{(ua, psa), (psa, ua), (psa, sa)\}$$

We now replace Axiom 5 with

$$(lo_1, lo_2) \in \mathcal{R}_2 \Rightarrow pa : X_{lo_1} \xrightarrow{Z_{pa}} Y_{lo_2} \tag{7}$$

We next need to include a condition saying that the passenger can be carrying no large suitcases, and only one small suitcase and one personal item. However, we note that it is not enough to count multiplicities in the passenger, since a passenger can carry more than one personal item as long as all but one are in the small suitcase. That is, the multiplicity of personal items in the box configuration formed by deleting the small suitcase box configuration (if one exists) from the passenger box configuration should be no more than one. We write this as follows.

$$Z_{pa} \sqsubseteq X_{sl} \wedge mult(Z_{pa}, \mathbf{ls}) = 0 \wedge mult(Z_{pa}, \mathbf{ss}) \leq 1 \wedge$$

$$mult(Z_{pa}, \mathbf{pi}) - mult(\{W_{ss} | W_{ss} \sqsubseteq Z_{pa}\}, \mathbf{pi}) \leq 1 \Rightarrow pa : X_{sl} \xrightarrow{Z_{pa}} Y_{psa} \tag{8}$$

Axiom 6 remains the same.

We now add an axiom saying that the passenger can move from the passenger screening area to the secure area only if he is carrying no disallowed items.

$$Z_{pa} \sqsubseteq X_{psa} \wedge mult(pa, \mathbf{da}) = 0 \Rightarrow pa : X_{psa} \xrightarrow{Z_{pa}} Y_{sa} \tag{9}$$

Proposition 4. *Suppose that Axioms 6, 7, 8, and 9 hold. Then any permitted action a preserves the invariant.*

Proof. (Sketch) By Proposition 3 the only actions permitted by the policy that we need to consider are those of the form $a = pa : X_{psa} \xrightarrow{Z_{pa}} Y_{sa}$, guarded by $mult(pa, \mathbf{da}) = 0$. Since, according to Axiom 9, a is guarded by $mult(pa, \mathbf{da}) = 0$, it remains to prove that $\{mult(pa, \mathbf{da}) = 0 \wedge mult(sa, \mathbf{da}) = 0\} a \{mult(sa, \mathbf{da}) = 0\}$. But this again follows directly from Proposition 3.

4.4 Removing Carry-On

In the above procedure, we specified a single screening step. But the passenger screener actually consists of two screeners, one for the passenger, and one for the carry-on. We refine the screening step by introducing two new locations: the carry-on screener cs, and the passenger screener ps. The passenger now goes from pa to ps to sa, and before he goes through ps, he is expected to deposit any carry-on in cs. Thus we begin by defining a new relation $\mathcal{R}_4$ on locations.

$$\mathcal{R}_3 = (\mathcal{R}_2/\{(psa, sa)\}) \cup \{(psa, ps), (ps, psa), (ps, sa)\}$$

Axiom 7 is replaced with:

$$(lo_1, lo_2) \in \mathcal{R}_3 \Rightarrow Z_{pa} : X_{lo_1} \xrightarrow{Z_{pa}} Y_{lo_2} \tag{10}$$

We also introduce an exception to the rule not allowing passengers to move items from one location to another by allowing passengers in the passenger screening area to place any item they are is carrying in the carry-on screener. Thus Axiom 6 is replaced by the following:

$$(Z_{pa} \sqsubseteq W_{lo} \wedge X \sqsubseteq W_{lo} \wedge Y \sqsubseteq W_{lo}) \vee (Z_{pa} \sqsubseteq U_{psa} \wedge T \sqsubseteq Z_{pa} \wedge Y \sqsubseteq V_{ca})$$
$$\Rightarrow Z_{pa} : X \xrightarrow{T} Y \tag{11}$$

Furthermore, a passenger moving from the passenger screening area to the passenger screener must not be carrying any small suitcases or personal items:

$$mult(pa, \mathbf{ss}) = mult(pa, \mathbf{pi}) = 0 \Rightarrow pa : X_{psa} \xrightarrow{Z_{pa}} Y_{psa} \tag{12}$$

Axiom 9 is replaced by the following, which applies the same conditions to the passenger's movement from the passenger screener to the secure area.

$$Z_{pa} \sqsubseteq X_{ps} \wedge mult(Z_{pa}, \mathbf{da}) = 0 \Rightarrow pa : X_{ps} \xrightarrow{Z_{pa}} Y_{sa} \tag{13}$$

To get the carry-on into the secure area, we introduce another type of principal: the airport authority **aa**, and a subtype of this principal, the carry-on screening authority **csaa**. The responsibility of **csaa** is to remove carry-ons from the carry-on screener to the secure area if they are free of disallowed items. Thus:

$$Z_{ca} \sqsubseteq X_{cs} \wedge mult(ca, \mathbf{da}) = 0 \Rightarrow csaa : X_{cs} \xrightarrow{Z_{ca}} Y_{sa} \tag{14}$$

Proposition 5. *Let SA denote the secure area. Suppose that Axioms 11, 13, 10, 8, ,12 and 14 hold. Then any permitted action a preserves the invariant.*

Proof. The proof is similar to that of Proposition 4 and we omit it.

4.5   Screening Shoes

To reproduce the Heathrow solution, we introduce two new locations : the post-passenger screening area $ppsa$, and the shoe screener shs. The passenger now goes from psa to $ppsa$ to the shs, and finally to the secure area sa. Likewise, the carry-on screener authority puts cleared carry-on in $ppsa$, not in the sa. The check done in psa is on all of the passenger except his feet:

$$\mathcal{R}_4 = (\mathcal{R}_3/\{(ps, sa)\}) \cup \{(ps, ppsa), (ppsa, ps), (ppsa, shs), (shs, ppsa), (shs, sa)\}$$

$$(lo_1, lo_2) \in \mathcal{R}_4 \Rightarrow ps : X_{lo_1} \xrightarrow{Z_{pa}} Y_{lo_2} \tag{15}$$

$$mult(Z_{pa}, \mathbf{da}) - mult(\{W_{ft}|W_{ft} \sqsubseteq Z_{pa}\}, \mathbf{da}) = 0 \Rightarrow pa : X_{ps} \xrightarrow{Z_{pa}} Y_{sa} \tag{16}$$

$$Z_{ca} \sqsubseteq X_{cs} \wedge mult(Z_{ca}, \mathbf{da}) = 0 \Rightarrow csaa : X_{cs} \xrightarrow{contZca} Y_{ppsa} \tag{17}$$

We also include an axiom describing conditions in which the passenger passes from the shoe screener to the secure area. If the passenger has one or more feet then each foot must have a shoe, a shoe that is free of disallowed items:[1]

$$(W_{ft} \sqsubseteq Z_{pa} \Rightarrow V_{sh} \sqsubseteq W_{ft}) \wedge mult(sh, \mathbf{da}) = 0) \Rightarrow pa : X_{ssh} \xrightarrow{Z_{pa}} Y_{sa} \tag{18}$$

The relevant axioms are now Axioms 8, 12 , 15, 16, 18 and 17.

We now try to prove that the procedure still satisfies the security policy. There is no longer a guard requiring passengers moving to sa to be free of disallowed items, so we cannot apply Proposition 3 directly as before. However, all box configurations entering sa do so through the shoe screener. Thus, if we can show that for any action a, $\{mult(ssh, \mathbf{da}) = 0\}a\{mult(ssh, \mathbf{da}) = 0\}$, we can use Proposition 2 to obtain that any box configuration within ssh contains no disallowed items, and thus use Proposition 3(1) to prove that for any action a moving a box configuration from ssh to sa, $\{mult(SA, \mathbf{da}) = 0\}a\{mult(SA, \mathbf{da}) = 0\}$.

But this is not the case, because shoes are not checked before being moved from $ppsa$ to ssh. Moreover, passengers and shoes are together in the $ppsa$, and, according to Axiom 6, passengers can move disallowed objects from their shoes to their persons when both passengers and shoes are both in the same location. Thus, we can show that the procedure does not satisfy the security property by constructing a scenario in which a passenger moves a disallowed item from his shoes to his person (or, to give Schneier's example, to his carry-on).

5   Related Work

There has been a substantial amount of work on the logical modeling of location and movement. Much of it is motivated by the desire to give as accurate picture

---

[1] We note that the policy does not take into account the existence of socks, and the fact that a passenger, could, e.g., hide a knife in his socks. This reflects the Heathrow policy, which in our experience did not require passengers to remove their socks.

of the relevant details of the world as possible (e.g. for modeling transmission in wireless networks), and is thus beyond the scope of what we are attempting to achieve. Another area that has been extensively studied is the security of mobile processes, in which, although location is relevant and included in the model, is still focused on cyber networks, not human or mixed cyber and human security procedures. However, as we have noted, there has been increasing awareness of the need to extend the concept of network security, and with it its formal analysis beyond cyberspace. We discuss some closely related work below.

Portunes [6] models the physical, social, and digital interactions that take place in order to defend against or execute a cyber attack. Portunes covers a wide range of attacks, including social engineering; however the writer of a Portunes specification needs to specify the individual steps (although not the attack sequence) taken by the intruder. Thus, if an attacker needs to attach a dongle to a computer to load a rootkit, one can write that the attacker can offer a dongle to an employee. In our approach, one would write an axiom governing the deposition of items in the computer box configuration. The application of our logic would uncover what the permissible flows are (that is, whether objects not supplied by the company can be deposited on a computer in a secure room), but not the specific attack. This difference arises from the somewhat different goals of Portunes, which is designed to generate attack scenarios for further analysis, and ours, which is designed for proving (or disproving) security properties.

In [22] Srivatanakul applies different techniques developed for assessing system safety to the analysis of security policies involving authorization and containment, including that used by the Bangkok International Airport's baggage handling system. The techniques used included methods such as hazard analysis, fault tree analysis, and mutation testing of formal specifications. In the case of the baggage handling study, they were particularly useful in identifying potential consequences of the security assumptions not being satisfied. These results are complementary to ours, and we can see Srivatanakul's and our techniques being applied iteratively in tandem, with the safety analysis techniques used to identify risks, and ours used to evaluate mitigations.

In [21] Scott presents a language for specifying concerning location and movement. His model and ours have some features in common, as they both involve nested box configurations and conditions on moves, but it provides only a method for specifying policies, not reasoning about them. However, he discusses the possibility of analysis as well as specification, and it possible that an approach such as ours to reasoning about moves might be realizable within his framework.

6   Conclusion

We have given a logical framework for reasoning about permitted and required movements, and have shown how it can be applied for reasoning about the security of procedures that govern the movement of human beings, such as airport security procedures. It should be clear though that there is still much relevant material that is left out. This is everything covering the passenger's interactions with the airport authorities. It is not enough, for example, that a passenger's carry-on must not contain disallowed items. Instead an airport security agent, or rather, a configuration consisting of the agent and the screening device, must observe that the bag is free of disallowed items, and that the passenger has appropriate authorization and documents.

We have avoided these issues in this paper in order to have as clean a model as possible of the properties that need to be checked for, as opposed to the process of checking. But in [19] we developed a framework for reasoning about interactions between configurations across channels that is intended to capture just those types of procedures, and the framework set forth in this paper is designed to be complementary to it. In future work we plan to combine these two approaches to obtain a comprehensive methodology for reasoning about procedures that govern movement.

We also see this work as having potential for application in many other areas. There has been a substantial interest in security policies and procedures involving location, including location-based access control, secure verification of location, and location privacy. However, movement is usually only considered as a means of hiding or tracking location. We believe that the including policies about movement and logical methods for reasoning about it, can lead, for example, to richer and more meaningful location-based access control policies. For example, a passenger in a secure area could be granted certain privileges *because* he or she has been verified to be free of knives and explosives. A method of reasoning about the procedure by which that conclusion was reached would help in ascertaining the safety of such a policy.

References

1. Anlauff, M., Pavlovic, D., Waldinger, R., Westfold, S.: Proving authentication properties in the Protocol Derivation Assistant. In: Proc. of FCS-ARSPA 2006. ACM (2006)
2. Blaze, M.: Toward a broader view of security protocols. In: Christianson, B., Crispo, B., Malcolm, J.A., Roe, M. (eds.) Security Protocols 2004. LNCS, vol. 3957, pp. 106–120. Springer, Heidelberg (2006)
3. Cervesato, I., Meadows, C., Pavlovic, D.: An encapsulated authentication logic for reasoning about key distribution protocols. In: Proc. of CSFW 2005. IEEE (2005)
4. Datta, A., Derek, A., Mitchell, J., Roy, A.: Protocol composition logic (PCL). Electron. Notes Theor. Comput. Sci. 172, 311–358 (2007)
5. Datta, A., Derek, A., Mitchell, J., Pavlovic, D.: A derivation system and compositional logic for security protocols. J. of Comp. Security 13, 423–482 (2005)
6. Dimkov, T., Pieters, W., Hartel, P.H.: Portunes: Representing attack scenarios spanning through the physical, digital and social domain. In: Armando, A., Lowe, G. (eds.) ARSPA-WITS 2010. LNCS, vol. 6186, pp. 112–129. Springer, Heidelberg (2010)
7. Dolev, D., Even, S., Karp, R.M.: On the security of ping-pong protocols. Information and Control 55(1-3), 57–68 (1982)
8. Dolev, D., Yao, A.C.-C.: On the security of public key protocols. IEEE Transactions on Information Theory 29(2), 198–207 (1983)

9. Durgin, N., Mitchell, J., Pavlovic, D.: A compositional logic for proving security properties of protocols. J. of Comp. Security 11(4), 677–721 (2004)
10. Ellison, C.: Ceremony design and analysis. Cryptology ePrint Archive. Report 2007/399 (October 2007)
11. Gries, D.: The Science of Programming. Springer (1981)
12. Latour, B.: Reassembling the Social: An Introduction to Actor-Network Theory. Oxford University Press (2005)
13. Meadows, C., Pavlovic, D.: Deriving, attacking and defending the GDOI protocol. In: Samarati, P., Ryan, P.Y.A., Gollmann, D., Molva, R. (eds.) ESORICS 2004. LNCS, vol. 3193, pp. 53–72. Springer, Heidelberg (2004)
14. Meadows, C., Poovendran, R., Pavlovic, D., Chang, L., Syverson, P.: Distance bounding protocols: authentication logic analysis and collusion attacks. In: Poovendran, R., Wang, C., Roy, S. (eds.) Secure Localization and Time Synchronization in Wireless Ad Hoc and Sensor Networks. Advances in Information Security, vol. 30, pp. 279–298. Springer, Heidelberg (2006)
15. Pavlovic, D.: Categorical logic of concurrency and interaction I. synchronous processes. In: Theory and Formal Methods of Computing 1994, pp. 105–141. World Scientific (1995)
16. Pavlovic, D., Meadows, C.: Deriving secrecy in key establishment protocols. In: Gollmann, D., Meier, J., Sabelfeld, A. (eds.) ESORICS 2006. LNCS, vol. 4189, pp. 384–403. Springer, Heidelberg (2006)
17. Pavlovic, D., Meadows, C.: Bayesian authentication: Quantifying security of the Hancke-Kuhn protocol. E. Notes in Theor. Comp. Sci. 265, 97–122 (2010)
18. Pavlovic, D., Meadows, C.: Deriving ephemeral authentication using channel axioms. In: Christianson, B., Malcolm, J.A., Matyáš, V., Roe, M. (eds.) Security Protocols 2009. LNCS, vol. 7028, pp. 262–268. Springer, Heidelberg (2013)
19. Pavlovic, D., Meadows, C.: Actor-network procedures (extended abstract). In: Ramanujam, R., Ramaswamy, S. (eds.) ICDCIT 2012. LNCS, vol. 7154, pp. 7–26. Springer, Heidelberg (2012)
20. Schneier, B.: Defeating the shoe scanning machine at Heathrow Airport. Schneier on Security, December 14 (2007)
21. Scott, D.J.: Abstracting application-level security policy for ubiquitous computing. PhD thesis, University of Cambridge (2004), ISSN 1476-2986, UCAM-CL-TR-613
22. Srivatanakul, T.: Security Analysis with Deviational Techniques. PhD thesis, University of York (2005), YCST-2005-12

A PUF-Based Authentication Protocol to Address Ticket-Switching of RFID-Tagged Items

Sjouke Mauw[1] and Selwyn Piramuthu[2,3,⋆]

[1] Computer Science and Communications, University of Luxembourg, Luxembourg
[2] Information Systems and Operations Management, University of Florida, USA
[3] RFID European Lab, Paris, France
selwyn@ufl.edu

Abstract. Ticket-switching incidents where customers switch the price tag or bar code in order to pay a lower amount for their 'purchased item' is not uncommon in retail stores. Since the item has to pass through a check-out counter before leaving the store, it has a (even if miniscule) positive probability of being identified. However, when item-level RFID tags are used in an automated check-out environment, the probability of such incidents coming to light is estimated to be almost zero. We propose an authentication protocol for this scenario using a pair of item-level RFID tags, one of which is PUF-enabled to resist cloning attacks.

Keywords: RFID authentication protocol, ticket-switching, PUF.

1 Introduction

Incidents where a customer switches the price tag on an expensive item with that from a relatively 'cheap' item are not new. It is generally assumed that only a small fraction of such incidents are identified. With the advent and widespread use of bar codes, this same behavior has translated to switching bar codes between items or affixing a bar code from a relatively inexpensive item on an expensive item. For example, recently (May 8, 2012), a customer at a San Francisco Bay Area Target store was caught affixing false (home-printed) bar codes (i.e., "ticket switching") to packages of LEGOs that allowed him to purchase expensive sets at substantial discounts ([20], [21]). Similar incidents have occurred in other countries where items at retail stores have been the subject of such attacks. In May 2011, a 23-year-old was caught in a Leclerc supermarket in Trélisssac, Dordogne, for replacing the labels on two €2,300 bottles of *Petrus* with €2.50 labels[23]. In a majority of such incidences, the person involved is caught by a vigilant (usually, check-out) person at the store. The increase in the number of cases where item-level RFID tags are used in retail stores (e.g., Trasluz, American Apparel) and related automation of processes such as inventory management, check-out, among others has the potential to exacerbate this situation due to reduced human interaction in the process.

⋆ Corresponding author.

A. Jøsang, P. Samarati, and M. Petrocchi (Eds.): STM 2012, LNCS 7783, pp. 209–224, 2013.
© Springer-Verlag Berlin Heidelberg 2013

Since bar codes represent information only at the class-level, it is relatively easy to get away with a switch of bar codes between two items or replace bar code on expensive item with a 'home-made' bar code corresponding to a cheaper item. However, with instance-level information stored in item-level RFID tags, it becomes somewhat difficult since 'home-made' RFID tags need to contain an extensive set of information that is read and authenticated by the store check-out system. The ticket-switcher also needs to ensure (perhaps, with an RFID-shield) that the tag does not trigger an alarm (e.g., by RFID gates at the store entrance) when it is brought into the store. Moreover, unlike *physically* switching price tags or bar codes that are affixed or printed on the item, it is relatively difficult for the ticket-switcher to deal with RFID tags since these tags could be embedded in the item. When the RFID tag is affixed on the item (possibly under a bar code sticker), it is relatively physically easy to replace it with another tag given necessary skills and resources. With sufficient effort, it is not impossible to replace RFID tag(s) in/on an expensive item with that from a 'cheap' item in the retail store. Even worse, it is not inconceivable to destroy the RFID tag(s) in/on an item and just walk away with this item in an automated check-out retail store environment. However, RFID tags can be used in combination with existing loss-prevention measures (e.g., ink tags) to ensure that this eventuality does not occur or at least significantly reduce its occurrence probability. In an automated check-out retail store setting, the damage is done once the RFID tag "ticket-switching" has occurred. There is, therefore, a need to address this vulnerability before item-level RFID tags become ubiquitous in retail settings.

There is an extensive set of literature that deals with the counterfeiting prevention, in applications that involve expensive or critical item as well as those that involve pharmaceuticals, through RFID tags. There is also a growing set of literature on tampering of RFID tags. For example, Gandino et al. [8] provide an overview of risks and defenses of tampered RFID tags. Researchers have proposed several means to address tampering RFID tags, including watermarking and the use of Physically Unclonable Functions (PUFs). In general, watermarking RFID tags involves placing unique identification information in the Object Class (OC) and/or the EPC Manager (EM) fields. The watermark information thus stored are retrieved later for physical authentication. PUFs, on the other hand, are hardware-dependent and are generated using variations that are introduced during manufacture of the RFID device.

To summarize, related challenges in a retail store check-out environment include the ability to (a) flag an item that has never been on sale at this retail store (i.e., identify 'home-made' tags or tags that are not from this retail store), (b) identify duplicates (i.e., when an item's RFID tag is cloned or when an item with this tag was already 'checked-out' from this store), and (c) recognize when an item has a false tag (i.e., mismatch between item and its tag). Among these, (a) can be addressed through item authentication, (b) can be addressed through authentication as well as records from the store's information system (e.g., inventory, check-out), and (c) can be addressed through random physical checks for matching of item and its entry in the receipt or through cloning-prevention. Cloning or tag-impersonation, its lighter version, can sometimes be easily accomplished by communicating with the tag and capturing necessary responses and appropriately replaying them to the system. We use PUF-enabled manufacturer-placed tag as part of the mechanism to dissuade cloning attacks.

To our knowledge, no published authentication protocol addresses the issue of "ticket-switching" item-level RFID tags in a retail setting. We attempt to fill this gap by considering watermarking-based and PUF-based RFID tags as possible contenders for this purpose. There are instances (e.g., Target stores in the U.S.) where the retail store is known to use its own bar code information that is different from that generated by the item's manufacturer. Unlike this scenario, we use *both* the manufacturer- and retailer- generated information to authenticate an item. Our rationale for two tags is two-fold: (1) a manufacturer-placed RFID tag inside the sealed item package would render it difficult to counterfeit the item as well as tamper with the tag and (2) the retailer-placed tag would allow for more retailer flexibility since this would be independent of any constraints (e.g., storage space, write-protection) in the manufacturer-placed tag. Moreover, since we are interested in RFID-tagged items, we assume the presence of a manufacturer-placed PUF-enabled RFID tag embedded in the item to prevent *cloning* and a retailer-placed passive RFID tag placed on the item. We authenticate the *simultaneous* presence of both these tags with the item of interest. Although the general idea for ensuring the simultaneous presence of two tags in the field of the reader is similar to that of *yoking proof* [11] and its variants, our protocol is structurally different and we consider a PUF-enabled manufacturer-placed RFID tag to decrease the opportunity for tampering/switching.

The rest of the paper is organized as follows: We first review a few selected related publications on watermarking and PUF-based RFID tags in the next section. We briefly discuss our system model in Section 3. We then present our PUF-based authentication protocol in Section 4 and evaluate its security properties in Section 5. We conclude the paper with a brief discussion in Section 6.

2   Related Literature

We first discuss a few related publications on watermarking RFID tags followed by those on PUF-enabled RFID tags.

2.1   Watermarking RFID Tags

Digital watermarking, a form of steganography, is a passive protection tool that helps hide information that is meant to be accessible only to authorized parties. The 'watermark' thus placed are robust against modification and are generally not encrypted - securing information about its very existence is therefore of paramount importance. The non-volatile location in an RFID tag where watermarking information is placed is known only to legitimate readers and back-end systems since these are generally not password-protected. Since not all RFID tags have watermark information, even its very existence is known only to legitimate entities that are validated to have access to this information. When the existence and location of this information is exactly known, an adversary can easily have access to this information. There are also constraints on the length of the watermarks due to the extremely limited non-volatile space in low-cost RFID tags that are generally used in retail applications.

Potdar and Chang [16] propose TamDetect, an 8-bit watermark and a parity bit, which is a one-way hash generated from data stored in the EPC Manager (EM) and Object Class (OC) partitions. The watermark is generated by the RFID reader or RFID middleware and is embedded in the serial number partition. This can then be used to detect if data tampering has occurred in the RFID tag. Since the proposed watermarking is based on a secret function, Gandino et al. [8] claim that revelation of this function, either through an *insider attack* or otherwise, would necessitate a major modification of the system. External entities that later own this RFID-tagged entity cannot identify a tampered tag.

Noman et al. [14] develop a 32-bit watermark that they place in the reserve memory of the 32-bit *Kill* password. They claim that this can be used in applications where this *Kill* function is unused. Similar to Potdar and Chang, Noman et al. use padded values from EM and OC partitions to generate the watermark.

Yamamoto et al. [27] propose another means to watermark RFID tags. However, Gandino et al. [8] observe that this method has several drawbacks including the requirement of large memory, long transmission time for tamper checking, and its limited applicability.

Curran et al. [4] use a one-dimensional chaotic map, called the Skew Tent map, to randomly choose 6 bit positions from the OC (24-bit) field and the SN (36-bit) field to embed the watermark for the EM and the OC fields respectively.

While watermarking can be used to identify the occurrence of tampering, it is of not much help when other types of attacks (tag switching) occur.

2.2   PUF-Based RFID Tags

After extensive review of existing literature on PUFs, Maes and Verbauwhede [13] conclude that PUF is not a "rigorously defined concept, but a collection of functional constructions which meet a number of naturally identifiable qualities such as uniqueness, physical unclonability and possibly tamper evidence." The implementation or use of PUFs involve the generation of a set of challenge-response pairs (CRPs) where a *challenge* to the PUF results in a *response* from the PUF. Several such CRPs are generated during the *enrollment* phase and stored in a CRP database. At a later point in time, during *verification*, the response from the PUF for a chosen challenge from this CRP database is compared with the corresponding response in the CRP database. Due to variations related to ambient conditions (e.g., temperature) as well as hardware, the response from the PUF may not exactly match that in the CRP database. However, a match within acceptable tolerance level is deemed to be sufficient.

A majority of PUF-based authentication schemes of RFID tags (e.g., [3], [5]) are not scalable since they use a pre-recorded set of challenge-response pairs which run out after a deterministic number of authentication protocol runs. A given challenge-response pair cannot be reused since this facilitates denial-of-service attack. Another issue with PUF-generated challenge-response is that a given challenge does not result in the exact same response due to noise or hardware-related variations. This inconsistent behavior renders it difficult for the response from a PUF-enabled device to be directly used for authentication purposes. To alleviate problems associated with these issues, some researchers (e.g., [6]) use output from PUF along with *helper data* to generate keys.

Several types of PUFs have been studied by researchers including optical PUF (e.g., [15]), coating and acoustic PUFs (e.g., [22], [24]), silicon PUFs (e.g., [5]), among others. Maes and Verbauwhede [13] and Armknecht et al. [1] provide excellent overviews of PUFs.

Bolotnyy and Robins [3] propose a hardware-based approach to RFID security that relies on PUFs. They develop algorithms for key generation, tagging, and verification using PUFs and discuss the benefits of PUFs vs. hash functions for low-cost RFID tags. They note that PUFs are more resistant to side-channel attacks and physical tampering while being difficult to quantify since PUFs rely on physical characteristics that are also difficult to replicate. Bolotnyy and Robins claim that PUFs require about an order of magnitude less in terms of the number of gates required for computing hash functions. However, they require a sequence of PUF values to be stored on the already space-constrained tag.

Bassil et al. [2] propose a PUF-based mutual authentication protocol. However, their protocol is vulnerable and has several errors. For example, the secret value of the tag (SVT) is generated by the tag as PUF(random number) and the secret value of the reader (SVR) is generated by the reader as PUF(SVT). However, SVT, which is a *secret* is sent in the open. Moreover, the other terms that are *encrypted* can be easily recovered by an adversary. For example, they derive $A \leftarrow SVT \oplus SVR \oplus n_1$, $B \leftarrow Rot(SVR \oplus n_2, SVT)$, and $C \leftarrow Rot(SVT \oplus SVR \oplus n_1, n_2)$ and send $A\|B\|C$ from reader to tag. Now, using A and C, it is easy to know n_2; knowing n_2 and SVT, it is easy to know SVR using B; knowing SVT, SVR, and A, it is easy to solve for n_1. With this knowledge, the rest of the *secret* terms (i.e., SVT_{new}, SVR_{new}) can be determined. What is not mentioned in the paper is that the reproducibility of response, $PUF(x)$, may not be reliable for a given x on multiple invocations (e.g., [3]) and this could render authentication difficult.

Rührmair et al. [18] study challenge-response pairs for a few different (e.g., standard Arbiter, Ring Oscillator of arbitrary size, XOR Arbiter, Lightweight Secure, Feed-Forward Arbiter) PUFs and show using machine learning techniques that these PUFs can be impersonated and, therefore, cloned. Their results indicate that nonlinearities and larger bit-lengths as well as optical strong PUFs add mode complexity and are difficult to clone.

Sadeghi et al. [19] propose an authentication protocol using a PUF-enabled device which was later shown by Kardas et al. [12] to be vulnerable to a *cold boot attack* [9]. Kardas et al. [12] then present a means to thwart this attack with two keys that are consecutively generated by the same PUF-enabled device with the claim that only one of these will be revealed in a cold boot attack scenario. However, they do not present any details of their modified protocol. The destructive-private PUF-based RFID protocol presented in Sadeghi et al. [19] is also vulnerable to impersonation of the reader to the tag by an adversary. The adversary can observe a round of the protocol for a given tag of interest and note its ID, which is sent in the open when the tag is authenticated. Later, when the adversary wants to authenticate itself as a reader to this tag, a random number (i.e., a) can be sent to the tag, which replies with (b, c) and the adversary can reply to this with the tag's ID.

Kardas et al. [12] also present a distance bounding protocol based on PUFs with a fast and a slow phase and use three registers (v_1, v_2, v_3) to accomplish the fast phase. Since these three registers do not include any prover-specific information that can be replayed or used to retrieve any prover-specific information, they are easily shared by a dishonest prover with an accomplice to carry out a *terrorist fraud attack* [17].

Van Herrewege et al. [26] propose a PUF-enabled lightweight mutual authentication protocol using reverse fuzzy extractors for compact and fast implementations of secure sketches and fuzzy extractors. As opposed to the typical use of fuzzy extractors where the computationally intensive *reproduction phase* is implemented in the PUF-enabled device, they implement the *helper data generation phase* on the PUF-enabled device and move the reproduction phase to the verifier. In their mutual authentication protocol, they send the tag's identifier (i.e., ID) in the open and this can be used by an adversary to *track* the tag. The adversary can begin this protocol by sending *auth* to the tag, which will reply with its ID. The adversary does not have to continue with the rest of the protocol since the tag is now uniquely identified to be present at that location.

Based on our review of existing literature, we observe the absence of published research that specifically addresses ticket-switching. Resistance to ticket-switching requires rendering it difficult to (a) remove the price tag, bar code, or RFID tag from the 'cheap' item and (b) somehow affix/embed this (or a cloned) price tag, bar code, or RFID tag on the desired item, while ensuring that (a) the items or their packaging are not damaged and (b) their identification by the retail store 'system' (e.g., store check-out person or automated check-out system) is not compromised in the process. Although there are publications that are tangentially related such as those on yoking-proof and its variants and those that address tampering tags, we are unaware of any that directly attempts to address ticket-switching.

3 System Model

3.1 Principals

Our system comprises the following four principals: *customers, RFID-tagged items, manufacturers,* and *retailer* (Figure 1).

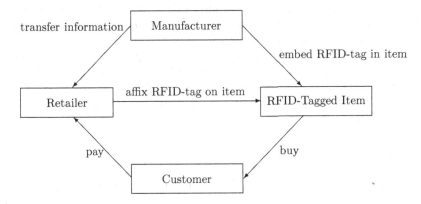

Fig. 1. The relationship among principals

The RFID-tagged item contains two RFID tags: a PUF-enabled passive tag that is embedded in the item by the manufacturer and a passive tag that is affixed on the item by the retailer. When the customer buys the item, the item is scanned (either manually by a check-out person or automatically by the automated check-out system) at check-out and both the tags are read by the reader. The unclonable PUF-enabled tag is primarily used to provide evidence of tag-tampering or cloning while the retailer-affixed tag is primarily used to facilitate in-store processes such as inventory management and automated-checkout as well as reduce shrinkage due to theft, misplacement and processing errors. Together, the two tags help authenticate the tagged item and provide proof that the item is what the honest manufacturer claims it to be and that no one has tampered with its content from the time it was packaged.

3.2 Adversary Model

Based on its environment (i.e., a retail store), possible threats to the authenticity of the RFID-tagged item can come from manipulated manufacturer-placed tag or retailer-placed tag or both. Other forms of threats include any form of attack (e.g., replay attack) that would enable a dishonest 'customer' to pay less for the item than its retailer-intended price.

3.3 Assumptions

We assume honest manufacturer and retailer who are there for the long run. These manufacturers and retailers will not tamper with the tags nor switch tags, which is the subject of this study, since (1) they face penalties from regulatory agencies when the items they sell are not what they claim them to be and (2) there is no incentive for the retailer or the manufacturer to manipulate the tags.

We assume the adversary ($\mathcal{A}$) to follow the Dolev-Yao intruder model [7]. The adversary $\mathcal{A}$ has complete control over the communication between the RFID-tagged item and the retail store system whereby $\mathcal{A}$ can eavesdrop, block, modify, and inject messages anytime from/to any entity. However, appropriate keys are required to decrypt encrypted messages and the response from PUF for a given challenge cannot be exactly determined.

We are interested in ensuring that the customer pays exactly the retailer-set price and receives the exact item as promised in the transaction. Reduction in price due to discounts (e.g., coupons) is irrelevant for this study. We also do not consider the scenario where the retailer erroneously enters a wrong price for an item in the system.

3.4   Security Properties

The proposed protocol should guarantee the following security properties:

Correctness: The customer pays exactly the retailer-set price for an item.

Traceability: If a PUF-enabled tag is switched, its origin (i.e., the item in which it was embedded by its manufacturer) can be readily identified.

Accountability: When ticket-switching occurs, it is relatively easy to determine *when* and *where* a PUF-enabled tag or the other tag was switched (i.e., when separation of the tags from an item of interest occurred). This information can be used to immediately identify and catch the ticket-switcher in the act.

4   The Proposed Authentication Protocol

We want our authentication protocol to accomplish the following:

- Provide tamper-evidence
- Provide proof that the item is what it claims to be
- Allow for the retailer to place necessary information on the item - it's relatively easier with a retailer-placed tag
- Unclonable key

Tamper-resistance is provided by the unclonable (PUF) key, which is also *unclonable*. We allow for the manufacturer and retailer to place the information they deem necessary in separate tags. The manufacturer-placed tag is embedded in the item and inaccessible from the outside (i.e., it is not placed outside the item's packaging) and the retailer-placed tag is affixed on the item's packaging. While the retailer-placed tag can be switched with ease, the manufacturer-placed tag cannot be switched without damage to at least the packaging of the item.

As mentioned in Section 1, we assume the presence of two passive RFID tags for each item - a PUF-enabled tag that is embedded in the item by the manufacturer and another tag affixed on the item by the retailer. We use some of the guidelines from a recently proposed PUF-enabled mutual authentication protocol by van Herrewege et al. [26] in developing our authentication protocol. A PUF's response is different each time it's queried with the same challenge since it depends on both this challenge and any device- and ambient-condition- specific variations. However, a large number of PUF-based applications require reliability in its response and *fuzzy extractors* [6] are typically used along with PUFs for this purpose. *Secure sketch* in fuzzy extractor maps similar responses (i.e., based on the same *challenge*) to the same value while a *randomness extractor* extracts full-entropy bit-strings from a partially random source. Secure sketch first generates $(Gen())$ helper data (h) from the PUF's response $(h_{mi} = Gen(R'_{mi}))$ to a challenge (say, C_{mi}) and this helper data is used later to recover the PUF's noisy response (R'_{mi}) from its *true response* $(R'_{mi} = Rep(R_{mi}, h))$. We follow van Herrewege et al.'s recommendation to place the computationally intensive reproduction phase, Rep(), on the verifier and the efficient helper data generation phase, Gen(), on the PUF-enabled device. For a detailed and excellent description of $Gen()$, $Rep()$, fuzzy extractor, randomness extractor, and secure sketch, the reader is referred to [6].

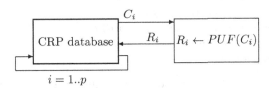

Fig. 2. PUF: Enrollment Phase

We borrow the essence of PUF-based model as presented in [26] to develop our authentication protocol. Specifically, we use the two stages from [26] as represented in Figures 2&3. Challenge-response pairs (CRPs) are generated during the enrollment stage, by repeatedly sending different challenges (C_i, where $i = 1..p$) to the tag's PUF and storing its response after 'error-correction' through helper data, and stored in the CRP database.

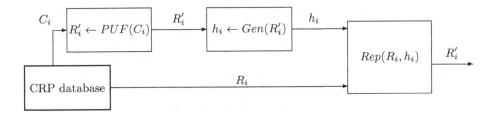

Fig. 3. PUF: Verification Phase

During the verification phase, a challenge (C_i) is chosen at random from the CRP database and sent to the tag. The tag's PUF takes this challenge as input and generates its response ($R'_i \leftarrow PUF(C_i)$). This response is then used by the tag to generate its corresponding helper ($h_i \leftarrow Gen(R'_i)$) data.

Along with the response (R_i) stored in the CRP database for this challenge, the helper data (h_i) can be used to generated the 'noisy' output from the tag's PUF $(R_i' \leftarrow Rep(R_i, h_i))$. We use the following notations:

- s_m, s_r, s_v, s_v': l-bit nonce
- k_m, k_r: manufacturer- and retailer- placed tag's shared secret keys
- ID_m, ID_r: (manufacturer- and retailer- placed) tag IDs
- C_{mi}: manufacturer tag's i^{th} PUF challenge, where $i = 1 \cdots p$
- R_{mi}: PUF's *true* (i.e., noise-corrected) response to C_{mi}
- R_{mi}': PUF's (noisy) response to C_{mi}
- t_{ms}, t_{me}: challenge-response start and end times for manufacturer tag
- t_{rs}, t_{re}: challenge-response start and end times for retailer tag
- Δ_m, Δ_r: 'round-trip' times to manufacturer- & retailer- placed tags
- f_k: keyed (with key k) encryption function
- $PUF(C_{mi})$: Physically Unclonable Function with C_{mi} as input
- h_{mi}: helper data[26] for the manufacturer-placed tag
- $Rep(R_{mi}, h_{mi})$: reproduction algorithm[26]
- $Gen(R_{mi})$: helper data generation algorithm[26]
- $auth$: authentication request
- $x \leftarrow y$: assign y's value to x

The proposed authentication protocol is presented in Figure 4. We assume that the verifier has access to the CRP database which contains previously recorded challenge-response pairs, represented by the set $\{C_{mi}, R_{mi}, ID_m\}$, for all PUFs. Since there are some similarities in what we intend to accomplish - i.e., *simultaneously* authenticate the two RFID tags as well as use information from a PUF-enabled RFID tag in a lightweight protocol to render ticket-switching difficult - and the purpose of protocols presented in [11] and [26], we borrowed ideas from both these papers as well as primitives from [6] (since several of these are used in [26]). Specifically, we use concepts from yoking-proof [11], reverse-fuzzy-extractors [26], and helper data [6].

The proposed protocol comprises two main timed 'components' that authenticate the manufacturer-applied and retailer-applied tags respectively. We ensure the simultaneous presence of these two tags in the item of interest through cryptography as well as by measuring the round-trip & processing time. The removal of either of these tags from the item would render the item inaccessible from the store's information system. We do not consider this possibility since this can be considered as a denial-of-service attack, which is outside the scope of this paper. We also note that the manufacturer-placed tag cannot be switched easily since switching it involves access to the inside of the sealed item that is inside its sealed package (e.g., a manufacturer-placed PUF-enabled RFID tag in a sealed package inside a sealed LEGO box). We try to accomplish this without revealing any secure information to a resourceful adversary.

We first authenticate the manufacturer-placed PUF-enabled RFID tag. To this end, the verifier first sends an authentication request along with a freshly-generated nonce (s_v). Upon receipt, the manufacturer-placed tag generates a fresh nonce (s_m) and encrypts this along with the verifier-generated nonce (s_v)

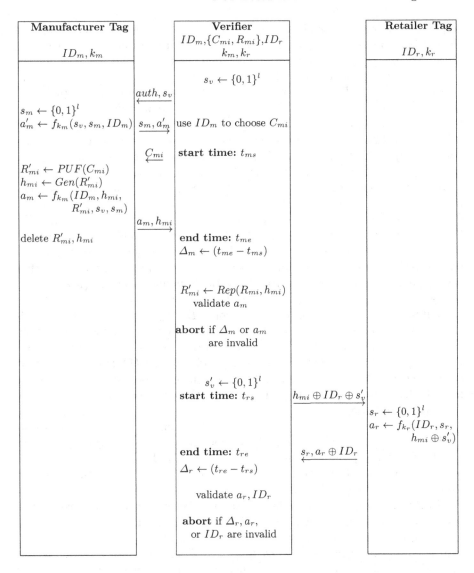

Fig. 4. The Proposed Protocol

and its ID (ID_m) and sends this encrypted value ($f_{k_m}(s_v, s_m, ID_m)$) to the verifier. The verifier decrypts the message and identifies the tag based on ID_m and randomly picks and sends a challenge (C_{mi}) for this tag from the CRP database to the manufacturer-placed tag. The verifier notes the time it takes for response from the manufacturer-placed tag. The measured response time is then compared with the required (known) time for round-trip plus the manufacturer tag's computation time. Here, the computation time dominates since it can be multiple orders of magnitude (vs. pure round-trip time) depending on the complexity of computation and the RFID tag's processing power. When the response time from the tag is longer than expected, it more than likely signifies the tag location to be farther than expected, and authentication is aborted.

In response, the manufacturer-placed tag generates its PUF-response for the challenge and associated helper data and then computes (a_m) - a keyed encryption (using k_m) of $(ID_m, h_{mi}, R'_{mi}, s_v, s_m)$. The manufacturer-placed tag sends (h_{mi}, a_m) to the verifier. R'_{mi}, h_{mi} are deleted from the manufacturer-placed tag to prevent *cold boot* attack [9]. The verifier ensures that the response was received in reasonable time and validates the received a_m. Here, validation essentially involves verifying that $a_m = f_{k_m}(ID_m, h_{mi}, R'_{mi}, s_v, s_m)$. If at least one of these (i.e., Δ_m or a_m) is invalid, the verifier aborts the authentication protocol.

When the manufacturer-placed tag is successfully authenticated, the verifier proceeds to authenticate the associated retailer-placed tag. This part of the protocol is also timed by the verifier. Since this tag is not assumed to be PUF-enabled, this part of the protocol is structurally different. To ensure a link between the two components and their authentication sequence, the verifier sends h_{mi} from the manufacturer-placed tag to the retailer along with a freshly-generated nonce (i.e., s'_v) and the tag's unique identifier (ID_r). Upon receipt of this message, the retailer-placed tag generates a fresh nonce and then computes a keyed encryption (using k_r) of $(ID_r, h_{mi} \oplus s'_v, s_r)$. It then sends this encrypted term (a_r) along with its ID and nonce to the verifier, which then validates the 'round-trip' time as well as a_r, ID_r. Validation by the verifier involves unpacking a_r and ID_r from $a_r \oplus ID_r$ and verifying ID_r and ensuring that $a_r = f_{k_r}(ID_r, s_r, h_{mi} \oplus s'_v)$. Again, if at least one of these (i.e., a_r, ID_r, Δ_r) is invalid, the verifier aborts the protocol. Note that neither of the tags validate the verifier's message.

There are two minor concerns in the proposed authentication protocol that are fortunately easily explained, and are therefore not of any major significance specifically to the proposed authentication protocol. These include the ability of an adversary to block or even modify messages between two entities and the measurement of round-trip times.

Clearly, an adversary can readily block any message between any two entities and prevent successful authentication. In the proposed authentication protocol, an active adversary can easily modify a message that will then be accepted as valid by its recipient: $h_{mi} \oplus ID_r \oplus s'_v$ sent from verifier to retailer tag can be modified to $h_{mi} \oplus ID_r \oplus s'_v \oplus \delta$, where δ is some random number, and the retailer tag would now use $h_{mi} \oplus s'_v \oplus \delta$ instead of $h_{mi} \oplus s'_v$ to generate a_r and the authentication would fail. Instead of going through all this, an adversary can just block the message from the retailer tag to the verifier and easily send a random number as response to the verifier, which then will abort the protocol. This type of attack can be successfully mounted on *any* existing RFID authentication protocol. However, since the proposed authentication protocol does not involve updates to any secret value during each protocol run that could potentially expose it to vulnerabilities associated with desynchronization or denial-of-service (DoS) attacks, we do not consider this eventuality.

While the round-trip times for messages between the verifier and each of the tags are individually bounded, the delay between querying these tags is not bounded. However, the verifier begins querying the retailer-placed tag if and as soon as the manufacturer-placed tag is verified and this minimal time delay to validate the response from the manufacturer-placed tag and to generate nonce s'_v would not allow for any type of attacks since (1) $(t_{rs} - t_{me})$ is negligible and therefore insufficient to, for example, detach and scan a tag separately and (2) the verifier has complete control over this in-between time period. One can question the very use of such time bounds since the separation possible (e.g., the entire length of a retail store) is relatively short for radio waves and therefore detecting location differences in such an environment necessitates extremely accurate (time-difference) measurements. However, we include this in our authentication protocol as an additional security measure. The use of round-trip times in RFID protocols is not new and it is commonly used, for example, in protocols that directly address relay attacks [10].

5   Security Properties and Analysis

Lemma 1. *The success probability of adversary $\mathcal{A}$ is bounded above by 2^{-2l}.*

Proof. For successful authentication, the adversary must be successful in submitting the exact information as expected by the verifier for simultaneous authentication of both the tags. Failure in either or both of these authentication stages would result in authentication failure for this item. There are two cases:
case a: The adversary can't successfully determine (h_{mi}, a_m) but knows $a_r \oplus ID_r$
case b: the adversary knows (h_{mi}, a_m) but not $a_r \oplus ID_r$.
In *case a*, the probability of success is bounded above by 2^{-2l} when $\mathcal{A}$ has no information and guesses each of the $2l$ bits. Similarly, for *case b*, when $\mathcal{A}$ needs to guess all l bits, the probability of its success is bounded above by 2^{-l}.   □

We first consider the security properties required of our protocol and the general setup and discuss its security properties.

Correctness: The retailer sets the price for each item that is for sale at the store and expects the customer to pay exactly that amount when an item is bought. Similarly, upon completion of the transaction, the customer expects to be charged the exact amount for which the item was offered for sale. Although the retail store may not be against the customer paying more, the customer certainly will not want to pay more. On the other hand, although the customer may not be against paying less, the retail store will not want to charge less. When a customer is charged less or more, the check-out system can be automated to raise a flag or trigger an alarm and appropriate action can then be taken.

Lemma 2. *The authentication protocol is correct if a pair of honest manufacturer and retailer tags are always successfully authenticated by a honest verifier.*

Proof. For tag authentication to succeed, both the manufacturer and the retailer tags simultaneously need to successfully authenticate themselves to the verifier.

For the manufacturer tag to successfully authenticate itself to the verifier [26], the following needs to be satisfied: $Rep(R_{mi}, Gen(R'_{mi})) = R'_{mi}$, $\forall (R_{mi}, R'_{mi})$. Note that a given challenge can detect up to d, the error correcting distance, and correct up to t ($t = \frac{(d-1)}{2}$) errors. The correctness property of *secure-sketch* [6] ensures that $Rep(R_{mi}, Gen(R'_{mi})) = R'_{mi}$ if distance$(R_{mi}, R'_{mi}) \leq t$. If the PUF generates responses of length l bits with a bit error rate of at most p, then probability(distance$(R_{mi}, R'_{mi}) \leq t) = binomial(t; l, p)$. The value of t is chosen such that this probability is very small and the *secure sketch* can recover R_{mi} from R'_{mi} with a very high probability.

For the retailer tag to successfully authenticate itself to the verifier, all it needs are h_{mi} and s'_v in addition to ID_r, s_r, k_r that it already knows. With this knowledge, it is guaranteed to successfully authenticate itself to the verifier.   □

Traceability: When a tag is switched with a tag from another item at the store, the 'original' item where this tag was taken from can be readily identified when necessary since the store information system has details on the identity of the tags as well as their associated items. However, a cloned tag does not have this property since the original tag from which the clone was made may no longer be on sale at this store or could have been from a different store altogether. However, since the embedded PUF tag cannot be cloned, only the retail store-affixed tag can be replaced with a cloned tag. Moreover, replacing just one of the two tags is useless since the item cannot be switched with one of lower price.

When a certain type (say, model) of item gets targeted frequently for ticket-switching, the retail store can initiate a process for better packaging for this type of item that is somewhat more tamper-resistant.

Accountability: Since the reader(s) on the retailer shelves continually communicate with the tags and monitor their presence, it is relatively easy to identify separation of one of the tags from the other. Therefore, it is difficult to displace an item from its intended display shelf, switch tags, and fail to return the item to its original shelf or initiate check-out without the system noticing this discrepancy. When this discrepancy is noticed by the system, it can instantiate necessary events that would result in identifying and capturing the ticket-switcher.

Attacks such as side-channel attack and hardware-tampering attack are rather difficult to mount given the difficulty with which secret information from a PUF-enabled tag can be obtained without compromising the tag. Modeling attack is also difficult in the proposed protocol since we do not directly use the response from the PUF-enabled tag. Tag impersonation attack cannot be mounted due to the difficulty with which response from PUF can be predicted.

6   Discussion

RFID tags are increasingly being used to prevent counterfeiting of expensive items as well as pharmaceutical items. The assumption here is that the RFID tags thus employed cannot be tampered with nor cloned. Unfortunately, a resourceful adversary can clone or tamper a low-cost passive RFID tag with reasonable effort. Recent initiatives to thwart such incidences have used watermarking, PUFs, among others. We considered watermarking and PUFs and settled on using PUFs, due to the appropriateness of their general characteristics and beneficial properties for the addressed problem, to develop our authentication protocol. Based on necessary requirements to address ticket-switching behavior, including the ability to deter as well as recognize when ticket-switching occurs, and the requirements of retailers in being able to place as much information as is necessary on the tags, we opted to use two tags per item. This paper is an attempt at exploring the the use of PUF and yoking concepts as potential candidates as solution to the ticket-switching problem. The solution presented in this paper can and should be refined for better characteristics (e.g., less complex in terms of communication and computation, stronger security).

The proposed protocol accomplishes authentication of the tags and consequently the RFID-tagged entity by the verifier. This one-way authentication is sufficient in most retail store settings. However, there may be scenarios (e.g., when the item is in transit in a supply chain) where two-way authentication is necessary. We are currently working on extending our protocol to accommodate two-way or mutual authentication of both tag(s) and verifier.

References

1. Armknecht, F., Maes, R., Sadeghi, A., Standaert, F., Wachsmann, C.: A Formal Foundation for the Security Features of Physical Functions. In: Proceedings of the IEEE Symposium on Security and Privacy, pp. 397–412 (2011)
2. Bassil, R., El-Beaino, W., Itani, W., Kayssi, A., Chehab, A.: PUMAP: A PUF-Based Ultra-Lightweight Mutual-Authentication RFID Protocol. International Journal of RFID Security and Cryptography 1(1/2), 58–66 (2012)
3. Bolotnyy, L., Robins, G.: Physically Unclonable Function-based Security and Privacy in RFID Systems. In: Proceedings of the Fifth IEEE International Conference on Pervasive Computing and Communications (PERCOM), pp. 211–220 (2007)
4. Curran, K., Lunney, T., Noman, A.N.M.: Tamper Detection for Low Cost RFID Tags; Using Watermarking with Chaotic Mapping. International Journal of Engineering and Technology 1(1), 27–32 (2011)
5. Devadas, S., Suh, E., Paral, S., Sowell, R., Ziola, T., Khandelwal, V.: Design and Implementation of PUF-Based "Unclonable" RFID ICs for Anti-Counterfeiting and Security Applications. In: Proceedings of the IEEE Int'l Conf. on RFID, pp. 58–64 (2008)
6. Dodis, Y., Ostrovsky, R., Reyzin, L., Smith, A.: Fuzzy Extractors: How to Generate Strong Keys from Biometrics and Other Noisy Data. SIAM Journal of Computing 38(1), 97–139 (2008)
7. Dolev, D., Yao, A.C.-C.: On the Security of Public Key Protocols. IEEE Transactions on Information Theory 29(2), 198–207 (1983)
8. Gandino, F., Montrucchio, B., Rebaudengo, M.: Tampering in RFID: A Survey on Risks and Defenses. Mobile Networks and Applications 15(4), 502–516 (2010)

9. Halderman, J.A., Schoen, S.D., Heninger, N., Clarkson, W., Paul, W., Calandrino, J.A., Feldman, A.J., Appelbaum, J., Felten, E.W.: Lest We Remember: Cold-boot Attacks on Encryption Keys. Communications of the ACM 52, 91–98 (2009)
10. Hancke, G.P., Kuhn, M.G.: An RFID Distance-bounding Protocol. In: Proceedings of IEEE/CreateNet SecureComm, pp. 67–73 (2005)
11. Juels, A.: "Yoking-Proofs" for RFID Tags. In: Proceedings of the International Workshop on Pervasive Computing and Communication Security, pp. 138–143 (2004)
12. Kardaş, S., Kiraz, M.S., Bingöl, M.A., Demirci, H.: A Novel RFID Distance Bounding Protocol Based on Physically Unclonable Functions. In: Juels, A., Paar, C. (eds.) RFIDSec 2011. LNCS, vol. 7055, pp. 78–93. Springer, Heidelberg (2012)
13. Maes, R., Verbauwhede, I.: Physically Unclonable Functions: a Study on the State of the Art and Future Research Directions. In: Naccache, D., Sadeghi, A. (eds.) Towards Hardware-Intrinsic Security and Cryptology, pp. 3–38. Springer (2010)
14. Noman, A.N.M., Curran, K., Lunney, T.: A Watermarking Based Tamper Detection Solution for RFID Tags. In: Proceedings of the International Conf. on Intelligent Information Hiding and Multimedia Signal Processing (IIH-MSP), pp. 98–101 (2010)
15. Pappu, S.R.: Physical One-Way Functions. PhD Thesis. MIT (2001)
16. Potdar, V., Chang, E.: Tamper Detection in RFID Tags using Fragile Watermarking. In: Proceedings of the IEEE International Conference on Industrial Technology (ICIT), pp. 2846–2852 (2006)
17. Reid, J., Gonzalez Nieto, J.M., Tang, T., Senadji, B.: Detecting Relay Attacks with Timing-based Protocols. In: Proceedings of ASIACCS, pp. 204–213 (2007)
18. Rührmair, U., Sehnke, F., Sölter, J., Dror, G., Devadas, S., Schmidhuber, J.: Modeling Attacks on Physical Unclonable Functions. In: Proceedings of the 17th ACM Conference on Computer and Communications Security (CCS), pp. 237–249 (2010)
19. Sadeghi, A.-R., Visconti, I., Wachsmann, C.: PUF-Enhanced RFID Security and Privacy. In: Secure Component and System Identification, SECSI (2010)
20. Schneier, B.: Schneier on Security - UPC Switching Scam (2008), http://www.schneier.com/blog/archives/2008/10/upc_switching_s.html
21. Schneier, B.: Schneier on Security - Bar Code Switching (2012), http://www.schneier.com/blog/archives/2012/05/bar_code_switch.html
22. Škorić, B., Tuyls, P., Ophey, W.: Robust Key Extraction from Physical Uncloneable Functions. In: Ioannidis, J., Keromytis, A.D., Yung, M. (eds.) ACNS 2005. LNCS, vol. 3531, pp. 407–422. Springer, Heidelberg (2005)
23. Agence France Press (2011), http://www.intothewine.fr/tags/trelissac-vin
24. Tuyls, P., Škorić, B., Stallinga, S., Akkermans, A.H.M., Ophey, W.: Information-Theoretic Security Analysis of Physical Uncloneable Functions. In: S. Patrick, A., Yung, M. (eds.) FC 2005. LNCS, vol. 3570, pp. 141–155. Springer, Heidelberg (2005)
25. Tuyls, P., Batina, L.: RFID-Tags for Anti-Counterfeiting. In: Pointcheval, D. (ed.) CT-RSA 2006. LNCS, vol. 3860, pp. 115–131. Springer, Heidelberg (2006)
26. Van Herrewege, A., Katzenbeisser, S., Maes, R., Peeters, R., Sadeghi, A.-R., Verbauwhede, I., Wachsmann, C.: Reverse Fuzzy Extractors: Enabling Lightweight Mutual Authentication for PUF-Enabled RFIDs. In: Keromytis, A.D. (ed.) FC 2012. LNCS, vol. 7397, pp. 374–389. Springer, Heidelberg (2012)
27. Yamamoto, A., Suzuki, S., Hada, H., Mitsugi, J., Teraoka, J.F., Nakamura, O.: A Tamper Detection Method for RFID Tag Data. In: IEEE International Conference on RFID, pp. 51–57 (2008)

Authenticating Email Search Results

Olga Ohrimenko, Hobart Reynolds, and Roberto Tamassia

Brown University, Providence RI 02912, USA
{olya,hcreynol,rt}@cs.brown.edu

Abstract. Alice uses a web mail service and searches through her emails by keywords and dates. How can Alice be sure that search results she gets contain all the relevant emails she received in the past? We consider this problem and provide a solution where Alice sends to the server authentication information for every new email. In response to a query, the server augments the results with a cryptographic proof computed using the authentication information. Alice uses the proof and a locally-stored cryptographic digest to verify the correctness of the result. Our method adds a small overhead to the usual interaction between the email client and server.

1 Introduction

Web-based email services are very popular for both individuals and corporations. Easy ways to manage mail along with generous free storage quotas (Gmail provides 10GB and HotMail offers "virtually unlimited" storage) are some of the appealing aspects of web mail. However, with increasingly large mailboxes, searching has become an essential feature of web email services. Consider the scenario where Alice recalls that several warning emails were sent in January about Eve's upcoming attacks. When she searches her mail she gets two emails as a result, however, she remembers that there were three. How does Alice know that the results she received are correct?

The trust between email account holders and their providers is most of the time unconditional. We store our private and work correspondence with mail servers in the clear. Although there is a question of privacy related to email content, in this paper we raise a different question. Given that mail services provide a large amount of free storage and maintain millions of accounts, how can we be sure that all of our emails are indeed stored, remain unmodified, and are returned to us when we need them? In 2011 a mail loss incident affecting $150,000$ Gmail users was reported.[1] In this case, the fact that emails were missing was easily noticeable since all of the mail was missing. However, it is much harder to detect an email loss when one does a search for emails from a specific time interval or containing given keywords. In this case, the user relies only on her memory. If some of the emails are indeed missing or have been modified, it is often impossible for a user to realize that such loss or corruption has occurred.

---

[1] http://www.bbc.com/news/technology-12600179

A. Jøsang, P. Samarati, and M. Petrocchi (Eds.): STM 2012, LNCS 7783, pp. 225–240, 2013.
© Springer-Verlag Berlin Heidelberg 2013

In this paper, we propose a protocol between an email user and the mail server that allows the server to prove that the emails returned to the user in response to a query are correct. Note that correctness implies *soundness* (only relevant messages are returned), *completeness* (all relevant messages are returned) and *integrity* (messages have not been modified). Proving the above properties for the search results allows a mail server to deny any accusations of lost or corrupt mail, thus increasing trust in web mail services.

Our solution is based on the usual interaction between the client and the mail server, where some of the protocols are augmented with additional information. While receiving or sending an email, the client computes a compact and unforgeable representation of the email with her secret key and sends it back to the server. The client keeps a single cryptographic digest (e.g., a SHA256 hash value) for the entire mailbox. This digest is updated each time an email is received, sent, or deleted. Whenever the client searches for emails (e.g., by a set of keywords and a time interval), the server computes the resulting list of relevant messages and assembles a proof that this list is sound and complete. The client then uses the digest it stores and the proof from the server to verify that the returned list of emails is indeed correct.

Besides providing cryptographically unforgeable security, our solution is efficient and scalable due to the small computational overhead it adds for the client and server. In particular, the size of the proof returned by the server and the verification time at the client are proportional to the number of emails returned in response to the query. Note that the proof size and verification time do not depend on the total number of email messages stored by the mail server. For example, when searching for emails with a popular word w from a particular date, the proof size is proportional to the set of emails from this date containing w, irrespectively of the total number of emails with word w. Thanks to their efficiency, the protocols executed by the client can be embedded as a plugin for a web browser.

1.1   Related Work

Authenticated data structures provide a cryptographic proof of their operations [25]. They have been developed for many fundamental problems, including membership queries [19], range queries [12], and select and join operations on databases in [5,19]. Goodrich *et al.* [11] study the authentication of keyword searches on the web using a three party model that relies on a trusted web crawler. Their work relies on an efficient method to verify result set intersection queries [21], which we deploy for our solution as well.

Regarding security issues for email, we note that there has been an extensive amount of work done on spam detection [2]. Also, the authentication of the sender's domain and the protection of the integrity of individual messages via cryptographic signatures has been deployed in the DomainKeys Identified Mail standard [13,18].

1.2   Contributions

The main contributions of our work can be summarized as follows:

- We have developed a method for the cryptographic verification of the soundness, completeness, and integrity of the list of emails returned by a mail server in response to a query consisting of a set of keywords and a time interval.
- We have shown that our method is highly scalable. In particular, the client stores only a private key and a single cryptographic digest. Also, the size of the proof returned by the server and the time taken by the client for verification is linear in the number of emails returned by the server in response to the query and logarithmic in the number of unique keywords in the corpus, irrespectively of the total number of messages stored by the server.
- We have implemented a system prototype for our method, which can be deployed as a browser plugin on the client side, and we have confirmed the practical efficiency of our method by conducting experiments on the Enron email corpus.

The specific problem we are considering has not been addressed before. Our solution builds on existing work on authenticated keyword searches and adds new techniques to fit the web email application, including an efficient method for supporting keyword searches restricted to a given *time interval*.

1.3   Structure of the Paper

The rest of this papers is organized as follows. Section 2 outlines our protocols and security properties. In Section 3, we describe our method for authenticating email search queries. Experimental results for a prototype implementation of our system are presented in Section 4. We discuss future research directions in Section 5.

2   System Overview

This section describes our email authentication protocols and overviews the architecture of our system.

2.1   Email Search Queries

An *email search query* consists of a set of keywords, K, and a timestamp interval, (t_{min}, t_{max}). In response to such a query, the mail server returns the list of emails that contain all the words in set K and whose timestamp is in interval (t_{min}, t_{max}). Note that a keyword may appear in the sender, recipient, subject or body of the message. This type of searches is common in the email setting since a user typically looks for emails using keywords she remembers and narrows down the result using the time interval during which she believes the email was received. Instead of returning all the relevant emails, which could be a very large list, the mail server typically returns the query results into pages, where the number of messages in a page is a parameter of the system. E.g., Gmail displays 20 messages at a time in decreasing chronological order.

Since searching over the sender, recipients, subject and body of the email can be done using the same search technique, we treat these components of the email as the *text part*. Using a day as the granularity of time for email search queries, we refer to the timestamp of the email as the *date part*.

2.2   Protocols

We consider two parties: the client and the mail server. The client has an account with the mail server and all the emails she receives first arrive at this server. Our system supports the traditional functions of the mail server: storing the client's emails, notifying the client of incoming emails, and returning emails or deleting emails as requested by the client. The client may retrieve a specific email message or issue an email search query. In addition, our system provides a layer of authentication on top of the traditional mail functionality: the mail server returns to the client a proof of the results of an email search query and the client verifies the query results using the proof and a single digest securely stored by the client.

The client stores a secret key and a single cryptographic digest associated with the entire mailbox stored at the server. This digest helps the client verify the results of an email search query. We use SHA256 so this digest is very compact. The mail server maintains an authenticated data structure of all the emails received but not deleted. This data structure allows the mail server to efficiently compute a proof for the results returned to the client in response to a query. The authentication process consists of two main protocols, update and query, which are described in detail in Section 3.

For every new email sent or received and for every email deleted, the client and the mail server execute the update protocol. This protocol yields a new value for the digest (reflecting the addition or deletion of an email) and some authentication information, which is used by the mail server to update the au-thenticated data structure. We illustrate this protocol in Figure 1(a). During the query phase (Figure 1(b)), the client issues an email search query. The mail server computes the result and a proof for it. The client then verifies the result using the proof and the digest.

2.3   Security Properties

Our system guarantees that once the update protocol has been executed for a new (or deleted) email, the mail server cannot hide this email from the query results (or include it into the query results) and create a proof that is verified by the client. Namely, if the verification succeeds, then the following properties hold for the email query results:

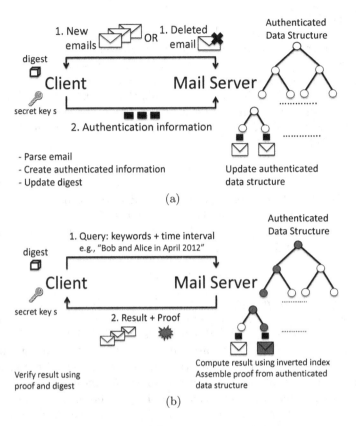

Fig. 1. Overview of our email authentication system. (a) Update protocol, which is executed each time the client receives, sends, or deletes an email. (b) Query protocol, which is executed each time the client issues an email search query.

- *Soundness:* each email in the result was received by the client and not deleted, contains all query keywords, and has a timestamp within the query interval;
- *Completeness:* the query results contain all the emails that were received by the client and not deleted, contain the query keywords, and have a timestamp within the query interval.

Also, for each email retrieved, if the verification succeeds, then the following property holds:

- *Integrity:* the email retrieved is identical to the one originally received.

In the next section, we show that our system supports the above security properties and has small communication and verification overhead. Namely, in the query protocol, the size of the proof and the time for the verification is linear in the size of the result and logarithmic in the number of unique keywords, but do not depend on the size of the email corpus stored at the mail server.

3 Solution

We first consider how the server computes an answer to an email search query and then describe the authentication layer. Let K be a set of keywords and $t_{\min}$ and $t_{\max}$ be timestamps such that $t_{\min} \leq t_{\max}$. The result R of the email search query $q = \{K, t_{\min}, t_{\max}\}$ is the set of emails that contains all keywords in K and have timestamp in the interval $[t_{\min}, t_{\max}]$. Let I_K be the set of emails that contain all keywords in K and let U_T be the set of emails with timestamp in $[t_{\min}, t_{\max}]$. We have

$$R = I_K \cap U_T. \tag{1}$$

Keyword Search. To support efficient keyword searches, an inverted index [26] maps every unique keyword, k, to the set, L_k, of ids of the emails containing this keyword, i.e., an inverted list. Thus, the set I_K of emails containing all keywords from a set K is given by

$$I_K = \cap_{k \in K} L_k. \tag{2}$$

Time Interval Search. We use a range tree [22] to efficiently answer time-interval queries. Let B be the number of distinct timestamps in an email corpus. We build a balanced binary tree with B leaves, where each leaf corresponds to a distinct timestamp and the leaves are ordered left to right by timestamp. A leaf v associated with timestamp t stores the set $T(v)$ of the ids of the emails with timestamp t. In our implementation, we assume that timestamps are days. Thus, set $T(v)$ has size typically greater than one. Each internal node, u, corresponds to the range of the timestamps of the leaves in its subtree. Also, node u stores the set $T(u)$ of the ids of emails with timestamp in this range. Thus, set $T(u)$ is recursively defined as $T(u) = T(left(u)) \cup T(right(u))$. The answer U_T to a time-interval query $(t_{\min}, t_{\max})$ can be computed as the union of the sets associated with the nodes of the range tree whose intervals cover the query interval. Note that any query interval can be covered by at most $2 \log B$ intervals associated with nodes of the range tree.

3.1 Set Intersection

Answering an email search query corresponds to computing the intersection of several sets of email ids: the sets of the inverted index associated with the query keywords and the sets of the range tree for the nodes whose intervals cover the query interval. See Equation 1 and Equation 2. Papamanthou et al. [21] describe a three-party protocol for authenticating set intersection. The technique is based on such cryptographic primitives as Merkle hash tree (for verifying the integrity of the sets used for intersection) and bilinear pairing (to verify the intersection itself). See [19] and [20] for details of these primitives. In this section we briefly describe how we adapt their protocol to our two-party model.

Let M be the number of unique keywords and B be the number of distinct timestamps in the email corpus. Note that there are $2B - 1$ nodes of the range tree. The server stores a list of sets of email ids $S = \{S[0], S[1], \ldots, S[n-1]\}$, where $n = M + 2B - 1$. A set $S[i]$ is either a set of the inverted index, i.e., L_k, or the set of emails received during the time interval associated with a node of the range tree. Let N be the number of emails in the collection. Since an email id is stored at $\log B$ nodes of the range tree and $B \leq N$, the space overhead at the server is $O(M + N \log B)$. The goal of the server is to prove that given an intersection query with set ids $V = \{v_1, v_2, \ldots, v_k\}$ the returned intersection I is indeed equal to $S[v_1] \cap S[v_2] \cap \ldots \cap S[v_k]$.

Setup. *Client:* The client keeps a secret key s and the root r of a Merkle hash tree (Algorithm 1). She sends to the server the sets in S, their accumulation values and exponentiations of a group generator. Here, an accumulation value of a set is a mapping from a set of email ids to an element of group $\mathbb{G}_1$ which is hard to compute without a secret key s.

Algorithm 1. Setup on the client side

Pick random secret key $s \in \mathbb{Z}_p^*$
Pick a cyclic multiplicative group of order p, $\mathbb{G}_1$
Let g be a generator of $\mathbb{G}_1$
Let G and setAccumulation be arrays of elements of $\mathbb{G}_1$ of size N and $|S|$, respectively
for $i \in \{0, 1, \ldots, |S| - 1\}$ **do**
  {compute polynomial $(S[i][0] + s)(S[i][1] + s) \ldots \}$
  setPolynomial = computePolynomial($S[i], s$)
  setAccumulation[i]=modExp(g, setPolynomial)
end for
r = buildMerkleHashTree(setAccumulation)
{compute exponentiations of g}
$G[0] = 1$
for $i \in \{1, \ldots, N\}$ **do**
  $G[i] = G[i-1] \times g$
end for

Server: The server builds a Merkle hash tree M on top of the values in setAccumulation. Note that he has to build a correct tree otherwise w.h.p. he will not be able to pass client's integrity check for values in setAccumulation. The following data structures are maintained by the server: **G**: set of exponentiations of a generator of group $\mathbb{G}_1$ received from the client; **S**: sets outsourced by the client to the server; **setAccumulation**: accumulation value for each set in S; **M**: Merkle hash tree over values in setAccumulation.

Update. The update protocol is executed when an email is added or deleted from the corpus. The client requests the accumulation values of the inverted lists that correspond to the unique keywords in the email. She also requests the accumulation values of the intervals that contain the timestamp of this email. If an email with id x is added to the collection she updates the accumulation values and sends them back: setAccumulation$[i]$ = modExp(setAccumulation$[i], s + x$). The technique for deletions is described in more detail in [11]. The corresponding Merkle tree paths have to be updated as well. The running time of the update protocol is $O(k \log B)$, where k is the number of unique keywords in the added or deleted message.

Intersection. This protocol is executed when the client asks the server to intersect a subset of sets from S, given by V, and return back the result of the intersection along with the proof. The client then uses the proof to verify that the answer is the correct intersection. *Server:* Given a set of ids V, the server computes the intersection I and its proof (Algorithm 2). The proof consists of the following components: an accumulation set representation of sets $S[v], \forall v \in V$; (2) a Merkle tree proof of every set in $S[v]$; subset witnesses showing that there is no element e such that $e \in I$ but $\exists v \in V, e \notin S[v]$; and completeness witnesses showing that there is no element e that appears in every set $S[v]$ but $e \notin I$. Note that proof elements are proportional to the size of the query with the exception of merkleProof which is logarithmic in the number of sets in S.

Client: The client verifies each part of the proof as shown in Algorithm 3 using her copy of the root of Merkle tree, r, and secret key s. She first verifies the integrity of the accumulation set representation that the server used to compute I using the Merkle tree part of the proof. To verify subset and completeness witnesses, the client uses a bilinearMap function, which takes two elements of group $\mathbb{G}_1$ and maps them to an element in a cyclic multiplicative group $\mathbb{G}_2$ of same order as $\mathbb{G}_1$ [20]. An important property of this function is that it is efficiently computable and result of bilinearMap(P^a, Q^b) is equal to bilinearMap$(P, Q)^{a \times b}$ where $P, Q \in \mathbb{G}_1$ and $a, b \in \mathbb{Z}_p$. Note that this functionality allows us to verify the subset and completeness conditions.

3.2   Email Search Queries

Recall that the parameters of an email search query are a set of keywords and a timestamp interval. If only keywords are given, the server can use the authenticated set intersection method described in Section 3.1. On the other hand, if only the time range is given the proof is simply a collection of Merkle tree proofs for the sets of nodes of the range tree whose intervals cover the query interval. If both search parameters are given, the server could execute separately a time range search and a keyword search, and let the client do the intersection. However, the two sets returned may be much larger than their intersection (e.g., a query for all emails from a particular day but containing a very popular term). In this section, we show how to efficiently authenticate email search queries.

Consider an email search query $q = \{K, t_{\min}, t_{\max}\}$. Let $K = \{k_1, k_2, \ldots, k_m\}$. The set of ids of the emails containing all keywords in K is

$$I_K = L_{k_1} \cap L_{k_2} \cap \ldots \cap L_{k_m}.$$

Algorithm 2. Computation of set intersection and the proof by the server

input V: vector of subscripts to intersect
output (1) I: intersection of sets in V; (2) accs: accumulators of the sets in V; (3)merkleProof: Merkle tree proof for every accumulation value; (4) subsetWitness; (5) completeWitness.
$I = \text{intersect}(S, V)$
$j = 0$
for $v \in V$
  $\text{accs}[j] = \text{setAccumulation}[v]$
  $\text{merkleProof}[j] = \text{computeMerkleProof}(M, v)$
  $j{+}{+}$
end for
$j = 0$
for $v \in V$
  $\text{subset} = \text{setDiff}(S[v], I);$
  {Compute coefficients of $\prod_{i \in \text{subset}}(i + s')$ since server does not know secret value s}
  $\text{subsetCoef} = \text{interpolatePolynomFFT}(\text{subset})$
  $\text{subsetWitness}[j] = 1$
  for $i \in \{0, 1, \ldots, |\text{subsetCoef}[j]| - 1\}$
    $\text{subsetWitness}[j] \times = \text{modExp}(G[i], \text{subsetCoef}[i])$
  $j{+}{+}$
  end for
end for
{If I is the correct intersection then accumulation values for subset witnesses have no common factors}
$\text{completeCoeff} = \text{extEuclidean}(\text{subsetCoef})$
for $j \in \{0, 1, \ldots, |V| - 1\}$
  $\text{completeWitness}[j] = \text{modExp}(G[j], \text{completeCoef}[j])$
end for
return I, accs, merkleProof, subsetWitness, completeWitness

Let $l_1, l_2, \ldots, l_t$ be nodes of the range tree whose time intervals cover the query range $(t_{\min}, t_{\max})$. The set of ids of the emails with timestamp in the query range is given by

$$U_T = T_{l_1} \cup T_{l_2} \cup \ldots \cup T_{l_t}.$$

The result of search query q is the set

$$R = I_K \cap U_T = (L_{k_1} \cap L_{k_2} \cap \ldots \cap L_{k_m}) \cap (T_{l_1} \cup T_{l_2} \cup \ldots \cup T_{l_t}).$$

We can rewrite the above equation as

$$R = (L_{k_1} \cap L_{k_2} \cap \ldots \cap L_{k_m} \cap T_{l_1}) \cup$$
$$(L_{k_1} \cap L_{k_2} \cap \ldots \cap L_{k_m} \cap T_{l_2}) \cup \ldots$$
$$(L_{k_1} \cap L_{k_2} \cap \ldots \cap L_{k_m} \cap T_{l_t}).$$

The server can authenticate each intersection using the method in Section 3.1. Also note that now the result can be at maximum of size $\log B$ where B is the

Algorithm 3. Verification of set intersection by the client

  input output of Algorithm 2.
  output accept/reject.
  querySize $= |V|$
  {Verify set accumulation values}
  for $i \in \{0, 1, \ldots, \text{querySize} - 1\}$
    {reject if one of the verification calls fails}
    verifyMerkleProof$(r, \text{accs}[i], \text{merkleProof}[i])$
  end for
  {compute polynomial $(I[0] + s)(I[1] + s) \ldots$}
  interPolyn $=$ computePolynomial(I, s)
  interAcc $=$ modExp$(g, \text{interPolyn})$
  {Verify subset witnesses}
  for $i \in \{0, 1, \ldots, \text{querySize} - 1\}$
    leftSideSubset $=$ bilinearMap(interAcc, subsetWitness$[i]$)
    rightSideSubset $=$ bilinearMap(accs$[i], g$)
    if leftSideSubset $\neq$ rightSideSubset **then**
      reject
    end if
  end for
  {Verify completeness witnesses}
  leftSideComplete $= 1$
  for $i \in \{0, 1, \ldots, \text{querySize} - 1\}$
    leftSideComplete $\times =$ bilinearMap(subsetWitness$[i]$, completeWitness$[i]$)
  end for
  rightSideComplete $=$ bilinearMap(g, g)
  if leftSideComplete $\neq$ rightSideComplete **then**
    reject
  end if
  accept

number of time ranges in the leaves of range tree. The authentication of each intersection

$$R_i = L_{k_1} \cap L_{k_2} \cap \ldots \cap L_{k_m} \cap T_{l_i}$$

involves computing subset and completeness witnesses for $m + 1$ sets. Since the computation time for both types of witnesses is linear in the size of sets that are intersected, it becomes expensive when query contains frequent keywords. Moreover, the server cannot reuse the computation of witnesses for multiple R_i's since these values depend on elements in T_{l_i}. We propose an important optimization on the server side: the server computes I_K and its proof, while using I_K to compute $R_i = I_K \cap T_{l_i}$ and a proof of only one intersection. This is a heuristic since the size of I_K may be much larger than the size of the final result R. However, as we show in the next section, the verification time on the client side is negligible even for large sizes of I_K.

The execution of an email search query by the server is shown in Algorithm 4. The client follows same verification steps as in Algorithm 3 to verify that I_K

Algorithm 4. Computation done by the server to construct the proof for email search query

---

input $\{K, t_{\min}, t_{\max}\}$: email search query

output (1) I_K: intersection of sets in K; (2) R: intersection of I_K and each time range in $(t_{\min}, t_{\max})$ of range tree; (3) accsI, accsT: accumulators of the sets in K and sets from range tree in interval $(t_{\min}, t_{\max})$; (4) merkleProofI, merkleProofR: Merkle proof for accumulation values above; (5) subsetWitnessI, subsetWitnessR; (6) completeWitnessI, completeWitnessR.

Call Algorithm 2 on input K

Let output of the above step be I_K, accsI, merkleProofI, subsetWitnessI, completeWitnessI

$T = \text{getIntervals}(\text{SegTree}, t_{\min}, t_{\max})$

$j = 0$

for $l \in T$

   accsT$[j]$ = setAccumulation$[l]$

   merkleProofR$[j]$ = computeMerkleProof(M, l)

   {Heuristic to avoid computing proof of I_K for every subset $R[j]$}

   $R[j]$ = intersectTwoSets$(S[l], I_K)$

   subsetWitnessR$[j]$ = computeSubsetWitness$(I_K, S[l], R[j])$

   completeWitnessR$[j]$ = computeCompleteWitness$(I_K, S[l], R[j])$

   $j{+}{+}$

end for

return I_K, R, accsI, accsT, merkleProofI, merkleProofR, subsetWitnessI, subsetWitnessR, completeWitnessI, completeWitnessR

---

is computed correctly. Then, she verifies each intersection in R also using Algorithm 3 but omitting the Merkle tree verification of set I_K, since verifying the correctness of I_K is sufficient.

The security of our method is based on the same assumptions as the method we adapt from [21] which relies on bilinear q-strong Diffie-Hellman assumption [3].

Further Optimizations and Extensions. We note that the time intervals that are higher in the range tree result in larger sets of email ids to be intersected. The server can replace a set $T(u)$ with smaller sets $T(left(u))$ and $T(right(u))$. The construction of the proof for these intersections is independent of each other and can be parallelized. One can split each of the children nodes further until a target set size is reached.

We can extend our solution to support the incremental verification of pages of query results. E.g., the server can provide a proof that the first page contains the 20 most recent results, the next page contains the next 20 and so on. The client can verify only the first page or any subsequence of result pages without having to scroll through all the pages. Our solution can be further extended to support labels assigned to emails (as in Gmail) and searches that include labels in addition to keywords and a time interval.

4   Performance

We extend the C++ implementation from [11] for authenticated set intersection to support email search queries. We run experiments on an 8-core Xeon 2.93 with 8GB RAM and 64-bit Debian Linux.

4.1   Data Set

We have conducted our experiments on the Enron Email Dataset [7]. This corpus contains 517,424 email messages with 612,091 unique terms, where the term/document distribution follows a power law with 75% of terms appearing in 6 or fewer emails. This corpus spans the time range of approximately 10 years, 1/1/1997-11/2/2007. The maximum number of emails from a single day is 3,309.

In our experiments, each leaf in the range tree corresponds to a single day. Note that the time span associated with a leaf can be configured to a smaller time interval, e.g., an hour, however, for this collection, a daily span was sufficient. For the query set we have generated 200 random keyword pairs from the corpus, where the lengths of the inverted lists vary from 50 to 7,986 emails. For date part of the query, we have picked intervals of 1 day, 7 days, 31 days, and 6 months, which contain 1,593, 9,114, 18,487 and 165,877 emails, respectively.

4.2   Query Phase

In Figure 2 we show the time for the sever to compute the proof of the result of a query with two keywords and various time ranges. The time is linear in the size of the inverted lists of the query keywords and the number of emails in the queried time range. The variation in times for lists of similar length is due to the difference in intersection sizes. The proof construction is highly parallelizable and could be optimized further on a machine with more cores.

In Figure 3 we show that the time for the client to verify the proof adds an insignificant overhead, which is linear in the size of the intersection of the keywords but is also affected by the size of the final set of results (spikes), i.e., after time range filter.

4.3   Update Phase

We now measure the overhead on the client side during the update phase. Recall that when a client receives an email she needs to update the accumulation values that correspond to the keywords in the email and time intervals of range tree that this email falls into. In Figure 4 we show the time it takes the client to execute the update protocol when 34 new emails of varying length are added. Each new email had a timestamp of the last day of the corpus affecting 7 time intervals in the range tree.

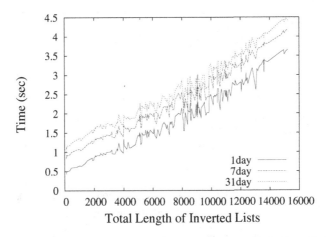

Fig. 2. Time for the server to compute a proof versus the lengths of inverted lists of query keywords. E.g., length of 4000 represents the total number of emails in the corpus where query keywords appear. Results are over 200 email search queries with two keywords of varying inverted list length over several time ranges.

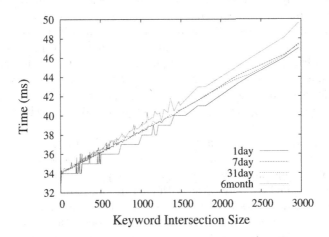

Fig. 3. Time for the client to verify the proof of an email search query as a function of the query answer, i.e., intersection size. Results are over the same query set as in Figure 2.

5 Future Research Directions

In this section, we outline directions for future research.

The approach proposed in this paper allows a user to verify that the list of messages returned in response to an email search query is correct with respect to the user's email corpus. However, it does not allow the user to verify that the emails she did not query for are still present at the mail server.

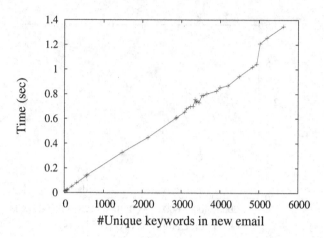

Fig. 4. Computational effort on the client side to add 34 new emails

For outsourced file systems, this goal can be achieved using protocols for provable data possession (see, e.g., [1,8]) and proofs of retrievability (see, e.g., [6,14]). These methods rely on the server storing authentication information that allows a user to verify probabilistically that her entire file system is stored by the server while downloading only a small amount of data. It would be interesting to investigate if one can combine the authentication information for proving possession of all emails with that for authenticating the search results to achieve both goals with small additional storage overhead. The idea of combining verification of search queries and proofs of possession has been also proposed in [16], where the resulting system can support verification of single keyword search over encrypted data.

User privacy is also a concern in web-based email servers. The user typically stores her emails unencrypted at the server to allow better service, e.g., keyword searches. Encrypting emails requires the server to perform searches on encrypted data (see, e.g., [4,17,15]). Also, even with encryption, information can be leaked from the pattern of access to the user's emails. For example, access to certain email messages could be correlated with publicly observable actions by the user. Several methods for protecting the access pattern to outsourced storage have been proposed, including data-oblivious computation (see, e.g., [9,10,23,24]). An ambitious research direction is to combine our authentication technique with the above methods for searching on encrypted data and for data-oblivious computation to perform searches on an encrypted email corpus while hiding the user's email search queries and the pattern of access to her emails.

Finally, it would be interesting to extend web mail clients to support the verification of query results and to provide visual feedback to the user on whether the verification succeeded or failed.

Acknowledgments. This research was supported in part by the National Science Foundation under grants CNS–1012060 and CNS–1228485, and by a NetApp Faculty Fellowship. We thank Michael Goodrich, James Lentini, Charalampos Papamanthou, Dan Rosenberg, and Nikos Triandopoulos for useful discussions. We are also grateful to Nathan Partlan, who developed components of an authentication system for Gmail.

References

1. Ateniese, G., Burns, R., Curtmola, R., Herring, J., Khan, O., Kissner, L., Peterson, Z., Song, D.: Remote data checking using provable data possession. ACM Trans. Inf. Syst. Secur. 14(1), 12:1–12:34 (2011)
2. Blanzieri, E., Bryl, A.: A survey of learning-based techniques of email spam filtering. Artif. Intell. Rev. 29(1), 63–92 (2008)
3. Boneh, D., Boyen, X.: Short signatures without random oracles and the SDH assumption in bilinear groups. J. Cryptology 21(2), 149–177 (2008)
4. Curtmola, R., Garay, J., Kamara, S., Ostrovsky, R.: Searchable symmetric encryption: improved definitions and efficient constructions. In: Proceedings of the 13th ACM Conference on Computer and Communications Security, CCS 2006, pp. 79–88. ACM, New York (2006)
5. Devanbu, P., Gertz, M., Martel, G., Stubblebine, S.G.: Authentic data publication over the internet. J. Comput. Secur. 11(3), 291–314 (2003)
6. Dodis, Y., Vadhan, S., Wichs, D.: Proofs of retrievability via hardness amplification. In: Reingold, O. (ed.) TCC 2009. LNCS, vol. 5444, pp. 109–127. Springer, Heidelberg (2009)
7. Enron Email Dataset, http://www.cs.cmu.edu/~enron/ (accessed on January 2012)
8. Erway, C., Küpçü, A., Papamanthou, C., Tamassia, R.: Dynamic provable data possession. In: Proceedings of the 16th ACM Conference on Computer and Communications Security, CCS 2009, pp. 213–222. ACM, New York (2009)
9. Goodrich, M.T., Mitzenmacher, M., Ohrimenko, O., Tamassia, R.: Oblivious RAM simulation with efficient worst-case access overhead. In: Proceedings of the 3rd ACM Workshop on Cloud Computing Security, CCSW 2011, pp. 95–100 (2011)
10. Goodrich, M.T., Mitzenmacher, M., Ohrimenko, O., Tamassia, R.: Privacy-preserving group data access via stateless oblivious RAM simulation. In: Proceedings of the 23rd Annual ACM-SIAM Symposium on Discrete Algorithms, SODA 2012, pp. 157–167. SIAM (2012)
11. Goodrich, M.T., Nguyen, D., Ohrimenko, O., Papamanthou, C., Tamassia, R., Triandopoulos, N., Lopes, C.V.: Efficient verification of web-content searching through authenticated web crawlers. PVLDB 5(10), 920–931 (2012)
12. Goodrich, M.T., Tamassia, R., Triandopoulos, N.: Efficient authenticated data structures for graph connectivity and geometric search problems. Algorithmica 60(3), 505–552 (2011)
13. Goodrich, M.T., Tamassia, R., Yao, D.: Accredited DomainKeys: a service architecture for improved email validation. In: Proceedings of the Conference on Email and Anti-Spam, CEAS 2005 (July 2005)
14. Juels, A., Kaliski Jr., B.S.: PORs: proofs of retrievability for large files. In: Proceedings of the 14th ACM Conference on Computer and Communications Security, CCS 2007, pp. 584–597. ACM, New York (2007)

15. Kamara, S., Papamanthou, C.: Parallel and dynamic searchable symmetric encryption. In: Financial Cryptography and Data Security, FC 2013 (to appear, 2013)
16. Kamara, S., Papamanthou, C., Roeder, T.: CS2: A searchable cryptographic cloud storage system. Technical report, Microsoft Research (2011), http://research.microsoft.com/pubs/148632/CS2.pdf
17. Kamara, S., Papamanthou, C., Roeder, T.: Dynamic searchable symmetric encryption. In: Proceedings of the 19th ACM Conference on Computer and Communications Security, CCS 2012, pp. 965–976. ACM, New York (2012)
18. Leiba, B., Fenton, J.: DomainKeys Identified Mail (DKIM): Using digital signatures for domain verification. In: Proceedings of the Conference on Email and Anti-Spam, CEAS 2007 (August 2007)
19. Merkle, R.C.: A certified digital signature. In: Brassard, G. (ed.) CRYPTO 1989. LNCS, vol. 435, pp. 218–238. Springer, Heidelberg (1990)
20. Nguyen, L.: Accumulators from bilinear pairings and applications. In: Menezes, A. (ed.) CT-RSA 2005. LNCS, vol. 3376, pp. 275–292. Springer, Heidelberg (2005)
21. Papamanthou, C., Tamassia, R., Triandopoulos, N.: Optimal verification of operations on dynamic sets. In: Rogaway, P. (ed.) CRYPTO 2011. LNCS, vol. 6841, pp. 91–110. Springer, Heidelberg (2011)
22. Preparata, F.P., Shamos, M.I.: Computational Geometry - An Introduction. Springer (1985)
23. Shi, E., Chan, T.H.H., Stefanov, E., Li, M.: Oblivious RAM with $o((\log n)^3)$ worst-case cost. In: Lee, D.H., Wang, X. (eds.) ASIACRYPT 2011. LNCS, vol. 7073, pp. 197–214. Springer, Heidelberg (2011)
24. Stefanov, E., Shi, E., Song, D.: Towards Practical Oblivious RAM. In: Proceedings of the 19th Network and Distributed System Security Symposium, NDSS 2012 (2012)
25. Tamassia, R.: Authenticated data structures. In: Di Battista, G., Zwick, U. (eds.) ESA 2003. LNCS, vol. 2832, pp. 2–5. Springer, Heidelberg (2003)
26. Zobel, J., Moffat, A.: Inverted files for text search engines. ACM Comput. Surv. 38(2) (2006)

Software Authentication to Enhance Trust in Body Sensor Networks

Joep de Groot[1], Vinh Bui[2], Jean-Paul Linnartz[1],
Johan Lukkien[2], and Richard Verhoeven[2]

[1] Signal Processing Systems Group, Electrical Engineering,
Eindhoven University of Technology, Eindhoven, The Netherlands
[2] System Architecture and Networking Group, Mathematics and Computer Science,
Eindhoven University of Technology, Eindhoven, The Netherlands

Abstract. This paper studies an approach to enhance the trust in the widespread use of Body Sensor Networks (BSN) in Healthcare. To address the wide variety in medical indications and differences between patients, we assume that such BSNs are programmable and highly flexible in their functionality. Yet this opens a vulnerability to malicious attacks and intrusion of the patient's privacy. We study the work flow in a typical medical scenario, we map the (implied or evidence-based) trust relations and we use this to propose a scheme for verifying the authenticity and trustworthiness without prohibitively interfering with common practices. Our proposed framework is currently being refined in the VITRUVIUS project, for instance to test the feasibility of its implementation.

1 Introduction

We witness a rapidly growing use of electronic systems that monitor our personal physiological and mental state by means of body related parameters. The user acceptance of Body Sensor Networks (BSN) will largely be determined by the confidence that human subjects have in the trustworthiness, security and privacy of such systems. The transparency of the underlying architecture can be an important factor, particularly if the software comes with clear certifications and its user interface clarifies which actors collect which kind of information. If used for medical applications, preferably the trust hierarchy of the system architecture lines up with the trust model that people have about the health care system of their country.

The requirements on privacy, trust and security are also very evident in lifestyle settings where monitoring is used for fitness, gaming, relaxation, ambient enhanced living, dietary advice, or infant and elderly monitoring. Various service providers may simultaneously offer different applications on a device that is owned by an end-user. Yet, also in a medical setting with devices under control of a care provider, there is a clear need to inform the patient about the various functions that his BSN executes simultaneously. A patient-centric approach allows the end-user to stay in control of the flow of his personal data.

A. Jøsang, P. Samarati, and M. Petrocchi (Eds.): STM 2012, LNCS 7783, pp. 241–256, 2013.

In most BSN deployments, the system consists of a central node or "body hub", supported by a few sensor nodes. The sensor nodes perform the actual measurements and communicate directly with the body hub, which acts as the central access point and handles all further communication with a back-end system via a secure Internet connection. Moreover, the sensor nodes will most likely become disposable products meant for one single use ("digital band aid"). This trend is accelerated by the 100,000 Lives Campaign from the Institute of Healthcare Improvement (IHI) [6] to promote large-scale continuous monitoring throughout for increasingly many patients, also in general wards.

To achieve a high flexibility of the functionality on BSNs, we foresee the use of downloadable software which has been customized to fulfill the end-user's or service provider's needs. Due to this downloadable software concept, the end-user is confronted with the risk of body spyware or malfunctioning software components, which affects his privacy and the trustworthiness of the system.

There is a high analogy with the current use of Apps on smart phones. A significant difference with the App scene is that when a private user downloads an application, he implicitly gives permission to access his private data. In the future, particularly in a medical setting, a doctor configures the package for a patient. This package can be highly individualized. Therefore it is not possible to give a one-time certification for this package. Moreover we foresee that there are a number of parties involved who collectively, but presumably not individually, can certify the trustworthiness of a software component.

This paper introduces an approach to solve key security and privacy issues related to downloadable software on a BSN. It protects the patients' privacy and trustworthiness of the system, i.e. it ensures that sensitivity and specificity are adequate and prevents leakage of privacy sensitive data. We also report some findings from our current implementation in the VITRUVIUS project [11].

The rest of this paper is organized as follows: Section 2 introduces preliminaries and some related work. Section 3 describes a BSN deployment scenario and the desired work flow as we foresee it. It clearly shows the need for a complete software security solution. After that, we discuss trust and security concerns, and our proposed solutions in Sections 4 and 5 respectively. Then, the system architecture is presented in Section 6. Section 7 describes a case study of the deployment protocol. The conclusion and future work are given in Section 8.

2 Preliminaries

Trust is a common and essential part of our human interaction. Although we deal with it on a daily basis it is difficult to unambiguously define it [3,14] or to capture it in an algebraic model [7,10,8,9], which can be evaluated by a computer. Based on these preceding studies we will analyze the trust in our patient scenario, as depicted in Figure 1 and in particular describe how trust is transferred from one actor to another. To do so we make use of the symbols ":" (transitivity) and "◇" (parallel paths) as defined in [10,8].

In a scenario, we map step by step the interactions with our patient Peter. We apply the models for trust relations as in [10,8]. The letters between parenthesis (A, B, properties) throughout the text indicate a trust relation from one actor to another. Only under certain preconditions [10] it can be concluded from (Alice trusts Bob) and (Bob trusts Charlie) that (Alice trusts Charlie). Importantly Alice must trust the referrals (sometimes called recommendations) by Bob. Therefore, we distinguish between functional trust (property f, solid arrow) and referral trust (property r, open arrow). Figure 1 summarizes the trust relations in our scenario.

While the above aspects are already modeled in previous publications, a new aspect, introduced in this paper is the evidence on which a trust relation is based. In many social settings, the evidence that a trustee provides to the trustor is not explicit, but can be implied by his environment. For instance, a doctor holding office in a hospital is trusted by patients as a qualified medical caregiver [15]. No patient will ask for his diploma during a consult. Yet, in our definition of a software architecture, it is important to recognize trust relations that are supported only as implied by circumstances (dashed line) and those in which evidence is given in the form of formal interaction, possibly including an authentication (solid line). In the latter case, the provision of a digital certificate can be introduced as a natural step in the work flow, while in the former case this may disrupt normal operations.

In some cases the trust is not direct (property d), but based on other functional and referral trusts. In such a case, we refer to indirect trust (property i) [10,8]. Since it is not possible to have evidence based indirect trust we extent the notation of implicit/evidence based trust with that of indirect trust by a fine dashed line. Some examples of these notations can be seen in Figure 1.

A final aspect is the purpose (or scope) of the trust. For simplicity we limit this to trustworthiness and security of the software implementation (P_S) and to trust in the adherence to medical regulations and procedures (P_M). In our security system, we do not explicitly model whether Peter trusts the diagnosis itself, but only whether Peter can trust the way of working.

In the paper we make use of a public key infrastructure (PKI) to strengthen some of the trust relations. We assume the PKI to be inherently secure, which implies the algorithms used cannot be compromised in a reasonable amount of time and we can appoint a certificate authority (CA) that can be trusted. These assumptions are common practice in the field of security. However, the role of our CA should not be confused with that of, for example a governmental medical authority, as they are independent organizations.

3 Deployment Scenario

This section follows a patient-centric perspective to describe a medical care cycle. Although we work out a specific scenario for a specific medical indication, in our opinion many interactions are representative for other treatments and our model represents a more generic work flow and its related security issues. The aim of this section is to gain insight in how we can establish an equivalent of human trust on a system that involves a BSN.

Our scenario starts with a visit of Peter to his general practitioner Gerard, after a few remarkable incidents. It is generally assumed that a patient trusts not only his GP personally $(P, G, df P_M)$ but also his referrals $(P, G, dr P_M)$ [15]. According to Gerard, Peter may suffer from epileptic seizures. Since Gerard is not an expert in the field of epilepsy, he refers Peter to epilepsy institute Indigo $(G, I, if P_M)$. In fact, Peter can maintain his trust in Gerard because he follows medical procedures, the trust is not affected by a limited knowledge of Gerard in certain medical disciplines.

Indigo is an institute specialized in epileptic disorders and is being recognized as such by the ministry of health $(M, I, df P_M)$. Indigo is allowed to provide health care under certain regulations. Indigo employs specialized doctors in the field of epilepsy, including neurologist Don, who is attending our patient Peter. At the time Don was employed by the institute he showed his medical qualifications to prove his competence $(I, D, df P_M)$.

Peter meets Don at Indigo $(P, D, if P_M)$ and describes to Don what has happened to him. Based on the symptoms, which are not life-threatening, Don decides Peter is allowed to go home while being monitored by a BSN. The BSN provides enough information for Don to come to a diagnosis.

Since Don is not experienced in placing the BSN nodes he delegates this to nurse practitioner Nancy. Nancy, a nurse employee at Indigo, is specialized in setting up BSNs. In Peter's presence, she unpacks sterile and shielded sensor nodes, and places them on Peter's body and explains how Peter can see their status and maintain the system. By opening the sterile package, she resets the functionality and configuration of the nodes. Moreover, she gives Peter the body hub and connects (pairs) the sensor nodes to the body hub. She tells Peter that the system does not have any functionality at the moment, but that will be provided by Don. *The prepackaged BSN nodes and body hub are labeled with a reference to their medical approval, e.g. in compliance with ISO 13485 (Requirement 3). This label is also available in electronic form in the institute's database.* Nancy is intentionally not included in the trust chain because there is no need to as we will show in Section 5.

In the meantime Don has chosen the algorithms $(D, H, df P_S)$ with some help of a domain expert software $(D, E, df P_S)$, which in his opinion are suitable to monitor Peter. Don configures the algorithms by setting their parameters, and by pressing a button he creates the software package for Peter. *We like to make sure the algorithms are medically approved, but can be customized for personalization. (Requirements 1 and 2)*

Upon creation of the software package a message appears on the screen of the body hub of Peter's BSN indicating that Don has created a package for him. The system inquires whether Peter approves the further download and installation of this package $(P, S, if P_S)$. *Here we want to be sure about two things: make sure the package is being sent to Peter's BSN (Requirements 3 and 4) and the system is able to verify the authenticity of the package (Requirement 5).*

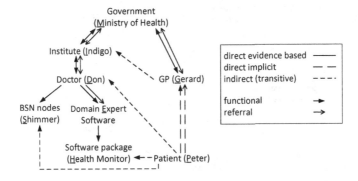

Fig. 1. Trust relations with a medical scope in our BSN deployment scenario

4   Trust

As the scenario showed, there are multiple trust relations. Some are direct functional trust relations, while others can be derived from these primary ones. Our goal is to reveal what proof is required to ensure that our patient Peter trusts the BSN and its underlying ICT or software implementation. In section 4.1, we analyze trust concerning medical regulations and protocols, i.e. trust with a medical scope (P_M), in 4.2 we will analyze the software equivalent (P_S). The resulting requirements are listed in section 4.3.

4.1   Medical

Under normal circumstances we may assume that our patient Peter implicitly trusts his general practitioner to be competent $((P, G, df P_M), (P, G, dr P_M))$ [15]. Gerard referred Peter to Indigo, this implies Gerard trusts Indigo to be able to treat Peter $(G, I, if P_M)$. Gerard trusts Indigo. This can be explained by the fact that they are both supervised by a higher entity like a government body, e.g. the ministry of health. This relation can be written down more formally, namely

$$(G, I, if P_M) = (G, M, dr P_M) : (M, I, df P_M) \tag{1}$$

Indigo employs Don, which also implies a mutual trust relationship $(I, D, df P_M)$. Due to this chain of trust relations we can state that Peter can trust Don $(P, D, if P_M)$ or more formally, namely

$$(P, D, if P_M) = (P, G, dr P_M) : (G, M, dr P_M) : (M, I, dr P_M) : (I, D, df P_M) \tag{2}$$

Finally, moving on to the BSN, there are two important trust relations we require, namely for Peter to trust the BSN hardware $(P, S, if P_M)$ and to trust the BSN software package $(P, H, if P_M)$. If we can make sure the directly involved person can either trust the BSN hardware or software, then all we have to do is

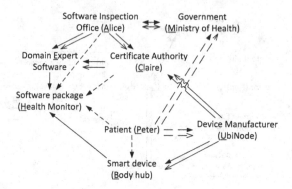

Fig. 2. Trust relations with a software scope

again refer this trust to Peter. For the BSN nodes this means we have to proof to Don that the BSN hardware has a medical approval $(D, S, df P_M)$, since he is the one recommending this system to Peter, so

$$(P, S, if P_M) = \ldots : (I, D, dr P_M) : (D, S, df P_M) \tag{3}$$

A similar relation $(P, H, if P_M)$ holds to the BSN software package. Don is using domain expert software, i.e. a Clinical Decision Support System (CDSS), to choose the BSN software. Therefore, this is not a direct trust relation. The domain expert software recommends and configures a software package for the BSN, therefore we assume the software to functionally trust the package it creates $(E, H, df P_M)$. This functional trust is subsequently required to ensure that Peter trusts the software on his BSN.

$$(P, H, if P_M) = \ldots : (I, D, dr P_M) : (D, E, df P_M) : (E, H, df P_M) \tag{4}$$

From above relation we can conclude that there are two primary relations to eventually provide a medically trustworthy BSN to Peter, namely the medical trust Don has in the BSN hardware $(D, S, df P_M)$ and software $(D, E, df P_M)$ he is using. Both relations cannot be considered self-evident and therefore we will propose a set of requirements to enhance them.

4.2   Software

A similar overview can be made for the ICT related trust (P_S). However, some of the actors in this diagram are not represented by a person, but for example by a software package or device with accompanying software. This implies that there is no interpersonal trust. For example an algorithm that verifies the authenticity of a download can be considered an evidence-based functional trust relation.

Similar to the medical trust, the ICT trust relations are based on an initial relation. This relation is, in our opinion, the trust that Peter has in the manu-facturer of the body hub hardware and the trust in a government body such as the Food and Drug Administration (FDA). Recently, the FDA indeed released regulations for certain equipment like cell phones that companies are planning to put at the center of connected health services [17]. Peter's trust in a device manufacturer can be based on the knowledge that Peter has about the brand's reputation, the medical approval or the trust neurologist Don expresses in it.

A commonly used assumption is that the device manufacturer pre-installs an operating system, and needs to include algorithms and root certificates to verify authenticity of downloaded packages, on the body hub. This implies that the manufacturer trusts one or more certificate authorities and their referrals. Moreover we assume the manufacturer trusts (functionally as well as in terms of referrals) his own product. This immediately leads to an indirect functional trust from Peter in the body hub.

$$(P, B, if P_S) = (P, U, dr P_S) : (U, B, df P_S) \tag{5}$$

Yet, as we will describe in the solutions section, this trust relation can be formalized by the implementation of a Physical Uncloneable Function.

As pointed out in the scenario, Don presumably uses the domain expert software, for example a Clinical Decision Support System (CDSS), which is able to help Don to follow procedures and which – in the future can be enabled to recommend and configure the personalized software for Peter. The expert tool has to be capable of certifying the generated package so the package's authenticity can be verified at the body hub. To guarantee integrity of the generated package, this software has to be trusted both in terms of functionality $(C, E, df P_S)$ and referrals $(C, E, dr P_S)$ by a CA. We have already seen an App, which provides support to physicians, getting certified for medical use [2]. Therefore, it is not surprising that clinical decision support, which recommends and configures the BSN software package in our scenario, might get a medical approval in the near future.

In our scenario, we foresee a specialized office, which is under government supervision $((M, A, df P_S), (M, A, dr P_S))$, taking care of medical software approval. Such an office can be part of for example the FDA (US) or MHRA (UK), but consist of software engineers. Once they are convinced of the correct functionality $(A, E, df P_S)$ and recommendations $(A, E, dr P_S)$ of our expert software, the CA can provide a public/private key-pair with accompanying certificate that is used by the domain expert software to certify its recommendations.

Finally, we can conclude that, based on above relations, Peter can trust the software that is being downloaded to his trusted device by two relations, hence

$$(P, H, if P_S) = ((P, U, dr P_S) : (U, B, dr P_S) : (B, H, df P_S)) \diamond \tag{6}$$
$$((P, M, dr P_S) : (M, A, dr P_S) : (A, E, dr P_S) : (E, H, df P_S))$$

4.3   Requirements

Our scenario revealed the need for building trust relations, and some security demands when deploying a BSN in a medical setting. In particular the trust relation $(D, S, df P_M)$ and $(D, H, df P_M)$ need to be strengthened by a technical measure, for which we use a digital signature, as for instance addressed in [10].

Moreover, the security demands, which are required to support the trust, can be formulated as

1. The BSN software will have to be functionally correct.
   To support: $(D, H, df P_M), (P, H, if P_M)$
2. The BSN software has to ensure the end-user's privacy by
   (a) only revealing those body parameters the algorithm is entitled to observe
   (b) not revealing what the package is monitoring if it is intercepted
   To support: $(P, H, if P_S)$
3. The BSN software should be executed at medically approved hardware.
   To support: $(D, S, df P_M), (P, S, if P_M)$
4. The BSN software package should end up at the intended user's BSN.
   To support: $(D, H, df P_M), (P, H, if P_M)$
5. The BSN system should be able to verify the authenticity of the received package.
   To support: $(P, H, if P_S)$

5   Proposed Solutions

The medical algorithms used in the library of the CDSS are being developed according to medically approved software development procedures. In our VITRU-VIUS project, this is an algorithm to detect epileptic seizures, but with tunable parameters and thresholds. We accomplish personalization of the algorithms by splitting the software package between signal processing algorithms (such as artifact filtering operations or parameter estimation) that translate sensor samples into a well-defined ontology, and a set of rules (say, 'if ... then ... else' statements) that can be executed in the rule engine of the CDSS. The former class can be seen as a Sensor Abstraction Layer that delivers a medical ontology as an appropriate interface to the executions of rules. We learned from our use case that a doctor searching for the right diagnoses for his patient may want to adjust the parameter settings to collect characteristics of any epileptic-like seizure for this particular patient. Nonetheless the CDSS should deliver a software package that also recognizes any seizure that formally falls within the definition of a (gold) standard and appropriately triggers the mandatory alarm procedures.

Such personalization makes it impractical to let an independent party approve the software composition for each patient individually. We propose that the Software Inspection Office (SIO) can release a type-approval for a generic algorithm. If the algorithms provide for configuration of specific parameters, the valid range of these parameters is also verified, approved and signed. Moreover, the SIO needs to validate the accompanying quality profile(s) [1], which describes the processing and memory demands and the behavior of the algorithm under certain configurations during execution.

The package is 'approved' if it satisfies two main requirements. Firstly a proper functionality of the algorithm needs to be guaranteed (Requirement 1),

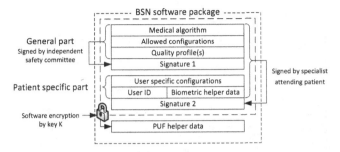

Fig. 3. Composition of the uploaded software packages including the two signatures

i.e. achieve a proper sensitivity and specificity. Secondly the algorithm should not leak any privacy sensitive information to parties who are not entitled to access that information (Requirement 2a). If both criteria are met, the SIO digitally signs the algorithm together with a specification of the allowed parameter range and quality profile, as depicted in Figure 3.

Bodyworn devices require a medical certification. Yet, in our system we also require that the patient trusts his device (Requirement 3) and its referrals and that such trust is evidence based. Hence, the device must be able to distinguish itself from a fake product, for instance, because only a genuine approved device would be able to unlock and execute protected software components.

It has been argued [5] that a Physically Uncloneable Function (PUF) can be used to bind the software to that particular device. This can be an appropriate solution for our scenario if the devices can be accompanied with a (digital) certificate which includes an encryption key and helper data based on the device's PUF [13]. This key is used to encrypt the final software package, while the helper data is sent along with the package to reproduce the key from the device's PUF. Figure 3 illustrates how this encryption is applied.

Moreover, the encryption can guarantee that if the package is intercepted it cannot be reverse engineered to reveal what kind of monitoring is deployed for that patient. This is needed to fulfill (Requirement 2b) on end-user privacy. Therefore, PUF can not only guarantee the use of correct and trustable hardware, it also enhances the end-users privacy.

Once a doctor personalizes a software package, our architecture needs to ensure that it will be executed at the BSN of the intended user (Requirement 4). A suitable solution studied in VITRUVIUS involves incorporating verifiable user identifier into the signed package.

Such a user-specific identifier may be derived from a protected biometric template in the future [12,4]. Besides the common modalities like fingerprints, face and iris's, it is also possible to extract biometrics from physiological signals [16], which are inherently being measured by the BSN sensor nodes. Moreover, since we foresee the use of a smart device, e.g. a smart phone, as the body hub a camera will most likely be available which enables face and iris scans. Yet in a medical setting, the False Rejection Rate of biometrics is still far from adequate to ensure sufficiently reliable operation in high acuity situations.

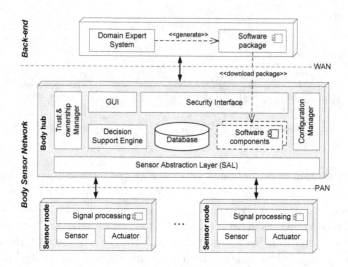

Fig. 4. The VITRUVIUS system architecture

Finally, the entire package, including the original signed package of medical algorithms, its configuration and user specific keys, will be signed by the (certified) CDSS under supervision of the attending doctor using his (certified) key, as depicted in Figure 3. Here we have to rely on a safe ICT infrastructure at the institute that protects the doctor's computer against attacks from both in- and outside the institute. In fact, hospitals are notoriously sloppy in restricting access which has led to broader security issues, but that is outside the scope of this paper. It can be subject to further study how a digital signature by a doctor can be guaranteed.

The doctor's signature allows the pre-installed verification software on the body hub to verify the authenticity of the package (Requirement 5). Here we opt for a doctor's signature instead of a signature by the institute, because of non-repudiation and trust reasons. Since the patient is more involved with the doctor than with the institute a signature by his doctor will strengthen his trust in the software and thus a more trustworthy BSN.

6   System Architecture

Our VITRUVIUS implementation of the proposed approach is shown in Figure 4. The BSN consists of sensor nodes together with the body hub, which is, among other things, capable of storing data and running application-specific, downloadable software components. The body hub controls the BSN and acts as the primary access point. The BSN connects to the back-end systems through the Internet, particularly between the domain expert system on the back-end and the *security interface* on the body hub. Through this connection, the back-end communicates with the BSN for the purposes of retrieving data and uploading the software packages.

As part of the back-end system, individualized software components (e.g. signal processing, database table, or decision-support rule) are configured and included into a software package together with their settings, quality profiles, and signatures by the domain expert system. The software package is downloaded, verified, installed, and activated on the body hub. With the help of our runtime BSN platform, the installed components are executed such that the BSN is configured towards a specific service, i.e., epileptic seizure monitoring.

At or near the body, a number of sensor nodes extract information from the body via dedicated sensors. Signal processing components, which pre-process the data (e.g. artefact rejection, signal validation and compression), are running either on these sensors or on the body hub. The body hub receives data from the sensors, stores it into the *database*, estimates key physiological parameters (e.g. heart rate, temperature) by means of signal processing components, and subsequently extracts key diagnostic information by means of the *decision-support engine*. This processing is according to the instructions and the settings from the software components. To satisfy the requirements mentioned in Section 4.3, the body hub has the following modules.

Security interface serves as a "body firewall" that shields the body hub from the outside world, verifies the package's signatures, blocks body spy-ware and only provides privacy-sensitive data to parties that can authenticate themselves as trustworthy. For example, the certification procedure can ensure that Peter or his care givers receive different information than doctor Don. Some parties, such as insurance companies, may only be informed about whether medically certified products are used according to professional protocols, doctors may be interested and allowed to use the raw physiological data, while care givers are best served with interpreted data (e.g. seizure events). For targeted applications the body hub can anonymize data and our architecture can ensure that the packages can be examined beforehand whether according to the latest insights it indeed does not leak any privacy.

Trust and ownership manager is capable of verifying the user identity (and possibly even extracts an unlock key from his biometrics). Moreover, the module constantly examines the current security and performance properties of the system at run-time; and verifies these properties at the system reconfiguration time, thereby authorizing configuration changes. The process of installing and executing a particular software component on the system might cause potential problems. For example, a new component may disable other components or processes running on the system by excessive use of system resources (e.g. CPU cycles, memory), unauthorized access or leakage of privacy information (e.g. a fitness application may access or leak epilepsy monitoring information). Regarding these aspects, we follow the design principles addressed in [1].

Configuration manager provides means for run-time download and installation of application-specific components. For instance, Peter wants to install a specific software package that is generated and advertised by doctor Don. In this case, Peter uses the User Interface to discover (e.g. via a QR-code) and install the advertised package on the body hub. In a sense it is similar to modern

Table 1. Notations used in the BSN deployment protocol

$c = \mathsf{Enc}(d, PK)$	Cypher text c from encryption on data d using public key PK
$d = \mathsf{Dec}(c, SK)$	Plain text d from encryption on data c using private key SK
$h = \mathsf{Hash}(d)$	Hash value h from data d
$s = \mathsf{Sign}(d, SK)$	Signature d on data d using private key SK
$c = \mathsf{Seal}(d, K)$	Cypher text c from symmetric encryption on data d using key K
$d = \mathsf{Unseal}(c, K)$	Plain text d from symmetric encryption on data c using key K
$k = \mathsf{Rep}(x, h)$	Recovery of key K from noisy signal x by using helper data h

smart phones that search and install Apps from an app-store, though with our security certification architecture in place. The configuration manager module together with the security interface module and the trust and ownership manager module inspects and verifies the downloaded package, verifies the future system integrity, and decrypts it and installs it on the system. After the installation, the components and the application are automatically configured according to their settings.

7   Deployment Protocol

The protocol can conceptually be split in three phases, namely a preparatory, a personalization and deployment phase. All three phases use cryptographic functions, of which an overview is given in Table 1. The preparatory phase consists of a phase of creating a set of algorithms and monitoring schemes that can be used by the originating institute or across multiple institutes, and a phase in which a particular institute prepares its facilities to roll out a particular monitoring solution.

1. Installation of a Software Inspection Office (SIO) by the government. Under supervision of the ministry of health, a group of experts are given the authority to certify the functionality and privacy of medical algorithms after appropriate inspection. This office has a similar role as existing healthcare approval agencies, but with a special expertise and mandate in medical software.
2. The ministry of health delegates to the CA the provision of certificates (and private keys) to qualified medical institutes and SIOs. Similar to many other governmental institutes, the SIO and institutes are authorized to respectively sign digitally the approved software and the individualized software
3. The certificate and the private key ($\mathsf{Cert}_{SIO}, SK_{SIO}$) are created and transferred to the SIO. We assume that the key distribution satisfies common security requirements.
4. Similarly, the certificate and the private key for the institute (Cert_I, SK_I) and qualified doctors (Cert_D, SK_D) are created and transferred to the institute and doctors, respectively.
5. An ICT specialist will install the domain expert software on the doctor's computer, which enables the individualization of pre-configured BSN software packages and its signing, together with the configuration and user identifier. This

requires the installation of the certificate and private key $(\mathsf{Cert_D}, \mathsf{SK_D})$ on the doctor's computer. We assume that the ICT infrastructure of the institute to be adequately protected against attacks.

6. An Algorithm Alg which can be used generically or for a class of medical purposes is developed at the institute or by a specialized company. It typically comprises of sensor node firmware, signal processing libraries, a set of clinical decision rules and an installation script. In our case, the algorithm will detect and report epileptic seizures. For each of the configurations for which approval is sought, which are described in the Allowed Configurations ACs, a quality profile QPs [1] will be created by assessing the behavior (CPU cycles, memory, etc.) of the software during runtime. Alongside with the package a document Doc is put up to describe its functionality, allowed configurations and detection accuracy.

7. The algorithm is submitted to the SIO, together with its allowed configurations, quality profiles and documentation $(\mathsf{Alg}, \mathsf{ACs}, \mathsf{QPs}, \mathsf{Doc}) \rightarrow \mathsf{SIO}$.

8. The algorithm (firmware, signal processing, decision rules, allowed settings, installation scripts, and quality profiles) is evaluated by the SIO. The SIO will assess whether the algorithm meets the claimed detection targets and whether it handles privacy sensitive data in a correct way.

9. Once the SIO accepts the algorithm, it will sign the entire package (algorithm, documentation, allowed configurations and quality profiles).

$$S_1 = \mathsf{Sign}((\mathsf{Alg} \,\|\, \mathsf{Doc} \,\|\, \mathsf{ACs} \,\|\, \mathsf{QPs}), \mathsf{SK_{SIO}}) \qquad (7)$$

10. The signed package $(\mathsf{Alg}, \mathsf{Doc}, \mathsf{ACs}, \mathsf{QPs}, S_1)$ is returned to the engineer at the institute or released for further distribution. Here, a societal trade off can be made whether the generic code is made public anyhow (to allow further scientific evaluation by independent researchers), or to keep the algorithm details confidential (e.g. to protect intellectual property or to avoid misuse).

11. The engineer adds the package to the library of the CDSS.

12. The engineer chooses and orders the suitable BSN hardware based on the institute's requirements, i.e., devices that meet specific requirements of the algorithms used at the institute. He also makes sure that these medically approved devices are accompanied with a digital certification $(\mathsf{Cert_{HW}})$.

13. The digital certificates are stored in the institutes database $(\mathsf{Cert_{HW}} \rightarrow \mathsf{DB_I})$ by means of the devices serial number until deployment of the devices.

Subsequently, we formulate the steps of the personalization phase.

1. The patient visits a specialist at the institute. If, in this interview the doctor concludes that monitoring with a BSN is possible, the patient is informed about the further procedure.

2. The patient is enrolled in the institute's database. Since the patient will carry a BSN the patient provides, besides the common personal details, a biometric identifier that can be reproduced by the BSN. This can be, for example, an ECG or ACM gait based feature or a face or iris biometric if the system is equipped with a camera. The identifier is stored as a protected biometric template [12,4] in the institute's database $(\mathsf{BioID_P} \rightarrow \mathsf{DB_I})$.

3. The doctor chooses from the available packages on his computer the one that is recommended to him by a CDSS for that particular patient and configures it for the patient by creating the user specific configuration USC, e.g. by filling in the patient's personal details or checking additional report options.

4. Once everything has been set, the doctor finalizes of the package. He selects the identity of his patient from the institute's database, which the software retrieves and includes as protected verification data (BioID, BioHD) for the biometric identity of the patient receiving the package.

5. The doctor signs the entire package by using his private key

$$S_2 = \mathsf{Sign}((\mathsf{Alg} \, \| \, \mathsf{Doc} \, \| \, \mathsf{ACs} \, \| \, \mathsf{QPs} \, \| \, S_1 \, \| \, \mathsf{USC} \, \| \, \mathsf{BioID} \, \| \, \mathsf{BioHD}), SK_D) \qquad (8)$$

6. Subsequently, he registers the hardware which will be used. For very specialized diagnostic cases (such as we encountered in VITRUVIUS), this involves the binding to a unique (e.g. PUF protected) identity of the body hub carried by the particular patient and a choice of the type of the sensor nodes. Once the receiving body hub is chosen, the software fetches the certificates of this hardware from the institute's database to read the encryption key K and PUF helper data PufHD from them. At the end, the package is encrypted by using the key

$$SP = \mathsf{Seal}((\mathsf{Alg}, \mathsf{Doc}, \mathsf{ACs}, \mathsf{QPs}, S_1, \mathsf{USC}, \mathsf{BioID}, \mathsf{BioHD}, S_2), K) \qquad (9)$$

The PUF helper data is sent along with the package to enable the body hub to reproduce the encryption key, i.e. $(SP, \mathsf{PufHD}) \to \mathsf{BSN}$. After the creation, the package will automatically become available for download to the BSN at a server of the institute for a limited time, e.g. a few days. For applications, in which less personalization occurs (e.g. general ward patient monitoring during routine treatments), the binding to a particular body hub can be automated as a standard procedure by the CDSS.

Finally, we formulate the deployment phase, which consists of the following steps and is depicted as a sequence diagram in Figure 5.

1. A trained nurse (practitioner) attaches the sensor nodes. By opening the sealed package, the nodes become active and their functionality is reset. She scans the QR-code printed on the sterile sensor package with the camera on the patient's body hub, so a pairing between nodes and the body hub is achieved.

2. The nurse instructs the patient how to obtain the software.

3. Search for package by patient. The pre-installed software contacts the (local) server offering BSN software. This can be a similar approach as Apps from an app-store for smart phones.

4. The package SP created in the development phase is found and downloaded.

5. The encryption key is reproduced by using the PUF helper data $K = \mathsf{Rep}(\mathsf{PUF}, \mathsf{PufHD})$ [13]. If the correct devices are used, this reproduced key will enable the device to decrypt the software package

$$(\mathsf{Alg}, \mathsf{Doc}, \mathsf{ACs}, \mathsf{QPs}, S_1, \mathsf{USC}, \mathsf{BioID}, \mathsf{BioHD}, S_2) = \mathsf{Unseal}(SP, K), \qquad (10)$$

otherwise the installation is aborted.

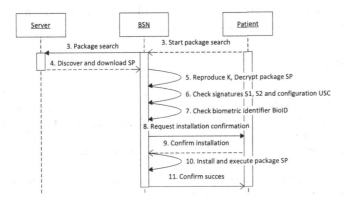

Fig. 5. Sequence diagram of the software package deployment

6. The package's signatures and configuration are inspected after decryption by using the keys from the Software Inspection Office's and the attending doctor's certificate. If decrypted signatures do not match the reconstructed values or the configuration is not within the allow ranges, the installation is aborted. In other words $\mathsf{Hash}(\mathsf{Alg} \,\|\, \mathsf{Doc} \,\|\, \mathsf{ACs} \,\|\, \mathsf{QPs})$ has to be equal to $\mathsf{Dec}(S_1, \mathsf{PK_{SIO}})$, $\mathsf{Hash}(\mathsf{Alg} \,\|\, \mathsf{Doc} \,\|\, \mathsf{ACs} \,\|\, \mathsf{QPs} \,\|\, S_1 \,\|\, \mathsf{USC} \,\|\, \mathsf{BioID} \,\|\, \mathsf{BioHD})$ has to be equal to $\mathsf{Dec}(S_2, \mathsf{PK_D})$ and USC has to be in ACs.

7. The biometric identifier is reconstructed by using the helper data [4]. The procedure continues if $\mathsf{Hash}(\mathsf{Rep}(\mathsf{Features}, \mathsf{BioHD}))$ matches BioID. Otherwise, an alternative identification of the patient is needed. We cannot simply abort the installation, because in false negative rates of existing biometric verification schemes are prohibitively high.

8. The installation software will inform the user that the package is approved and inquires whether he wishes to continue the installation.

9. The patient confirms the installation by pressing a button on the body hub.

10. The package is installed and executed.

11. Both the attending doctor and the patient receive a success confirmation.

8 Conclusion

In this work, we have analyzed the trust relations that occur in a representative BSN deployment scenario. Based on our findings we have identified the relations that required functional strengthening by means of certification and verification. These intermediate conclusions allowed us to formalize the security requirements. Based on these requirements we have subsequently proposed security solutions and studied the corresponding body hub software architecture. We described how this can be implemented in a protocol. We believe that via the formalization of trust relations, we contributed by proposing measures to strengthen the security of future systems. We took into account that certain medical trust relations are implicit and the hospital work flow would not allow the introduction of a digitally certified interaction during these phases of the treatment.

References

1. Bui, V.T., Lukkien, J.J., Verhoeven, R.: Toward a Trust Management Model for a Configurable Body Sensor Platform. In: Proceedings of the 6th ICST International Conference on Body Area Networks, Bodynets 2011, pp. 23–26 (November 2011)
2. Dolan, B.: First mobile medical app to get CE Mark in UK (January 2012), http://mobihealthnews.com/15707/first-mobile-medical-app-to-get-ce-mark-in-uk/
3. Gambetta, D.: Can We Trust Trust?. In: Trust: Making and Breaking Cooperative Relations, pp. 213–237. Basil Blackwell (1988)
4. de Groot, J., Linnartz, J.P.: Zero Leakage Quantization Scheme for Biometric Verification. In: 2011 IEEE International Conference on Acoustics, Speech and Signal Processing (ICASSP), pp. 1920–1923 (May 2011)
5. Holcomb, D., Burleson, W., Fu, K.: Power-Up SRAM State as an Identifying Fingerprint and Source of True Random Numbers. IEEE Transactions on Computers 58(9), 1198–1210 (2009)
6. Institute for Healthcare Improvement: Early Warning Systems: Scorecards That Save Lives, http://www.ihi.org/knowledge/Pages/ImprovementStories
7. Jøsang, A.: An Algebra for Assessing Trust in Certification Chains. In: Proceedings of the Network and Distributed Systems Security, NDSS (1999)
8. Jøsang, A., Hayward, R., Pope, S.: Trust Network Analysis with Subjective Logic. In: Proceedings of the 29th Australasian Computer Science Conference, ACSC 2006, vol. 48, pp. 85–94. Australian Computer Society, Inc., Darlinghurst (2006)
9. Jøsang, A., Ismail, R., Boyd, C.: A Survey of Trust and Reputation Systems for Online Service Provision. Decis. Support Syst. 43, 618–644 (2007)
10. Jøsang, A., Pope, S.: Semantic Constraints for Trust Transitivity. In: Proceedings of the 2nd Asia-Pacific conference on Conceptual modelling, APCCM 2005, vol. 43, pp. 59–68. Australian Computer Society, Inc., Darlinghurst (2005)
11. Linnartz, J.P., Lukkien, J., Benz, H., de Clercq, P., van Bussel, M.: VITRUVIUS Project Official Website (2008), http://vitruvius-project.com/
12. Linnartz, J.P., Tuyls, P.: New Shielding Functions to Enhance Privacy and Prevent Misuse of Biometric Templates. In: Kittler, J., Nixon, M.S. (eds.) AVBPA 2003. LNCS, vol. 2688, pp. 393–402. Springer, Heidelberg (2003)
13. Maes, R., Tuyls, P., Verbauwhede, I.: A soft decision helper data algorithm for SRAM PUFs. In: IEEE International Symposium on Information Theory, ISIT 2009, pp. 2101–2105, June 28 - July 3 (2009)
14. Mcknight, D.H., Chervany, N.L.: The Meanings of Trust. Technical Report MISRC Working Paper Series 4, University of Minnesota, Management Information Systems Research Center (1996)
15. Pearson, S.D., Raeke, L.H.: Patients' Trust in Physicians: Many theories, few measures, and little data. Journal of General Internal Medicine 15(7), 509–513 (2000)
16. Plataniotis, K., Hatzinakos, D., Lee, J.: ECG Biometric Recognition Without Fiducial Detection. In: 2006 Biometrics Symposium: Special Session on Research at the Biometric Consortium Conference, pp. 1–6, July19 - August 21 (2006)
17. Thompson, B.M.: FDA Regulation of Mobile Health. Tech. rep., MobiHealthNews (2010), http://mobihealthnews.com/research/fda-regulation-of-mobile-health/

YubiSecure? Formal Security Analysis Results for the Yubikey and YubiHSM

Robert Künnemann[1,2] and Graham Steel[2]

[1] LSV & INRIA Saclay – Île-de-France
[2] INRIA Project ProSecCo, Paris, France

Abstract. The Yubikey is a small hardware device designed to authenticate a user against network-based services. Despite its widespread adoption (over a million devices have been shipped by Yubico to more than 20 000 customers including Google and Microsoft), the Yubikey protocols have received relatively little security analysis in the academic literature. In the first part of this paper, we give a formal model for the operation of the Yubikey one-time password (OTP) protocol. We prove security properties of the protocol for an unbounded number of fresh OTPs using a protocol analysis tool, tamarin.

In the second part of the paper, we analyze the security of the protocol with respect to an adversary that has temporary access to the authentication server. To address this scenario, Yubico offers a small Hardware Security Module (HSM) called the YubiHSM, intended to protect keys even in the event of server compromise. We show if the same YubiHSM configuration is used both to set up Yubikeys and run the authentication protocol, then there is inevitably an attack that leaks all of the keys to the attacker. Our discovery of this attack lead to a Yubico security advisory in February 2012. For the case where separate servers are used for the two tasks, we give a configuration for which we can show using the same verification tool that if an adversary that can compromise the server running the Yubikey-protocol, but not the server used to set up new Yubikeys, then he cannot obtain the keys used to produce one-time passwords.

Keywords: Key management, Security APIs, Yubikey.

1   Introduction

The problem of user authentication is central to computer security and of increasing importance as the cloud computing paradigm becomes more prevalent. Many efforts have been made to replace or supplement user passwords with stronger authentication mechanisms [1]. The Yubikey is one such effort. Manufactured by the Swedish company Yubico, the Yubikey itself is a low cost ($25), thumb-sized USB device. In its typical configuration, it generates one-time passwords (OTPs) based on encryptions of a secret value, a running counter and some random values using a unique AES-128 key contained in the device. A Yubikey authentication server verifies an OTP only if it decrypts under the correct AES key to give a

A. Jøsang, P. Samarati, and M. Petrocchi (Eds.): STM 2012, LNCS 7783, pp. 257–272, 2013.

valid secret value with a counter larger than the last one accepted. The counter is therefore used as a means to prevent replay attacks. The system is used by a range of governments, universities and enterprises, e.g. Google, Microsoft, Agfa and Symantec [2].

Despite its widespread deployment, the Yubikey protocol has received little independent security analysis. Yubico themselves present some security arguments on their website [3]. A first independent analysis was given by blogger Fredrik Björck in 2009 [4], raising issues that Yubico responded to for a subsequent post [5]. The only formal analysis we are aware of was carried out by Vamanu [6], who succeeded in showing security for an abstract version of the Yubikey OTP protocol for a bounded number of fresh OTPs. In this paper, we use a new protocol analysis tool tamarin [7], not available at the time of Vamanu's analysis. We are able to prove the protocol secure in an abstract model for an unbounded number of fresh OTPs.

The aforementioned results assume that the authentication server remains secure. Unfortunately, such servers are sometimes breached, as in the case of the RSA SecurID system where attackers were able to compromise the secret seed values stored on the server and so fake logins for sensitive organisations such as Lockheed Martin [8]. RSA now use a Hardware Security Module (HSM) to protect seeds in the event of server compromise. Yubico also offer (and use themselves) an application specific HSM, the YubiHSM to protect the Yubikey AES keys in the event of an authentication server compromise by encrypting them under a master key stored inside the HSM. In the second part of our paper, we analyse the security of the YubiHSM API. First we show that due to an apparent oversight in the cryptographic design, an attacker with access to the server where Yubikey AES keys are generated is able to decrypt the encrypted keys and obtain them in clear. We informed Yubico of this problem in February 2012 and they issued a security advisory [9]. We then prove secrecy of keys in various configurations of YubiHSMs and servers, and suggest design changes that would allow a single server to be used securely.

All our analysis and proofs are in an abstract model of cryptography in the Dolev-Yao style, and make various assumptions (that we will make explicit) about the behaviour of the Yubikey and YubiHSM. At the end of the paper we will discuss how we could refine our models in future work.

The rest of the paper proceeds as follows. In section 2, we described the Yubikey and its OTP protocol. We model and analyse the security of this protocol in section 3. We then describe the YubiHSM in section 4, and the attacks we found in section 5. We model the HSM API and prove secrecy of the sensitive keys for various configurations in section 6. Finally we evaluate our results (7) and conclude (8).

2   The Yubikey Authentication Protocol

In the following, we will cover the authentication protocol as it pertains to version 2.0 of the Yubikey device [10].

The Yubikey is connected to the computer via the USB port. It identifies itself as a standard USB keyboard in order to be usable *out-of-the-box* in most environments using the operating system's native drivers. Since USB keyboards send "scan codes" rather than actual characters, a modified hexadecimal encoding, called *modhex* is employed, which uses characters that have the same position on many different keyboard layouts, including the German QUERTZ, the French AZERTY and the US QWERTY layout. Each keystroke carries 4 bits of information [10, Section 6.2].

The Yubikey can be configured to work in any of the following modes [10, Section 2.1]:

- *Yubikey OTP*, which is the method that is typically employed
- *OATH-HOTP*, where the OTP is generated according to the standard RFC 4226 HOTP algorithm,
- *Challenge-response mode*, where a client-side API is used to retrieve the OTP, instead of the keyboard emulation, and
- *Static mode*, where a (static) password is output instead of an OTP.

We will focus only on the Yubikey OTP mode, which we will explain in detail. Depending on the authentication module used on the server, there are four basic authentication modes [11, Section 3.4.1]:

- User Name + Password + YubiKey OTP
- User Name or YubiKey OTP + Password
- YubiKey OTP only
- User Name + Password

As the security provided by a user-chosen password is an orthogonal topic and the OTP is the main feature of the Yubikey, we will only focus on the third authentication mode.

The string emitted by the Yubikey is a 44-character string (i.e., 22 bytes of information in modhex encoding) and consists of the unique public ID (6 bytes) and the OTP (16 bytes) [12], encrypted its AES key. The length of the OTP is exactly the block-length of AES. It contains the following information in that order [10, Section 6.1].

- the unique secret ID (6 bytes)
- session counter (2 byte)
- timecode (3 byte)
- token counter (1 byte)
- a pseudo-random values (2 bytes)
- CRC-16 checksum (2 byte)

See Figure 1 for an example.

Yubico assigns an AES key and a public and secret ID to the Yubikey before shipment, but they can be overwritten. The Yubikey is *write-only* in this regard, thus it is not possible to retrieve secret ID nor the AES key. The session counter is incremented whenever the Yubikey is plugged in. Once it reaches its limit of

$2^{16} = 65536$, it cannot be used anymore. The timecode is incremented by an 8Hz internal clock. When it reaches its limit, the session is terminated, i.e., no more OTPs can be generated. This happens after approximately 24 days. The token counter is incremented whenever an OTP is generated. When it reaches its limit of 256, it restarts at 1 instead of terminating the session. The pseudo-random value of length two bytes is supposed to add entropy to the plain-text, while the CRC is supposed to detect transmission errors. It does not provide cryptographic integrity.

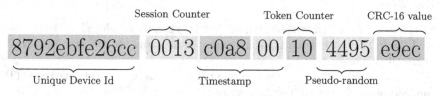

Fig. 1. Structure of the OTP (session: 19, token: 16)

A Yubikey stores public and secret ID *pid* and *sid*, and the AES key k, and is used in the following authentication protocol: The user provides a client C with the Yubikey's output *pid, otp* by filling it in a form. ("$\|$" denotes concatenation.)

$$C \rightarrow S : pid \parallel otp \parallel nonce \parallel$$
$$S \rightarrow C : otp \parallel nonce \parallel hmac \parallel status$$

where *nonce* is a randomly chosen value between 8 and 20 bytes, *hmac* is a MAC over the parameters using a key present on the server and the client. By *status*, we denote additional status information given in the response, containing an error code that indicates either success or where the verification of the OTP failed, the value of the internal timestamp, session counter and token counter when the key was pressed and more [13].

The server S accepts the token if and only if either the session counter is bigger than the last one received, or the session counter has the same value but the token counter is incremented. It is possible to verify if the timestamp is in a certain window with respect to the previous timestamp received, however, our model does not include the timing of messages, therefore we ignore this (optional) check.

3   Formal Analysis in the Case of an Uncompromised Server

We performed the analysis using the tamarin protocol prover [7], a new tool for the symbolic analysis of security protocols. It supports both falsification and verification of security goals which can be expressed as first-order formulas. The secrecy problem with unbounded nonces can be expressed in tamarin. Since this problem is undecidable [14], and due to the fact that the tool is sound and complete, it is not guaranteed to terminate. In order to achieve termination, some intervention is necessary: lemmas need to be used to cut branches in the proof attempt.

We are using tamarin for the analysis because it supports the modelling of explicit state, for example the last counter received for some Yubikey saved on the server. The popular protocol verification tool ProVerif [15], to take an example, represents protocol actions as Horn clauses, with the consequence that the set of predicates is monotonic: it is possible to derive new facts, but not to change or "forget" them. The Yubikey protocol, however, relies on the fact that once an OTP with a counter value has been accepted, the last counter value is updated. Certain OTP values that would have been accepted before will be rejected from this moment on. The resolution algorithm employed by ProVerif does not capture this (directly). There have been experiments with several abstractions that aim at incorporating state into Horn clauses [16,17], as well as the protocol analyser Scyther, but they have not been adequate for proving the absence of replay attacks for an unbounded number of sessions [6]. There is an extension that incorporates state synchronisation into the Strand Space Model [18], but as yet no tool support.

In tamarin, protocols are modelled as rewriting rules operating on a multiset of facts representing the protocol (Input/Output behaviour, long-term keys, short-term keys, session etc.). A *fact* $F(t_1, \ldots, t_k)$ consists of a fact symbol F or arity k and terms $t_1, \ldots, t_i$. We will denote the set of ground facts $\mathcal{G}$. The state of the system is a finite multiset of such facts, written $\mathcal{G}^{\#}$. There is a set of "special" fact symbols used to encode the adversary's knowledge (!K), freshness information (Fr) and messages on the network (In and Out). Other facts are used to represent the protocol state. The set of facts is partitioned into *linear* and *persistent* fact symbols. Linear facts can be consumed only once, persistent facts can be consumed arbitrarily often and are marked with an exclamation mark. Multiset rewriting rules are labelled by so-called *actions*. They consist of *premises* l, actions a and *conclusions* r, and are denoted $l - [a] \rightarrow r$. For example,

$$\mathsf{Out}(x) - [] \rightarrow\ !\mathsf{K}(x)$$

formalizes the adversary's capacity to eavesdrop all public communication,

$$!\mathsf{K}(x) - [\mathsf{K}(x)] \rightarrow \mathsf{In}(x)$$

his capacity to write on the network, i.e., the Dolev-Yao model. More formally, the labeled transition relation $\rightarrow_{\mathcal{M}} \subset \mathcal{G}^{\#} \times \mathcal{P}(\mathcal{G}) \times \mathcal{G}^{\#}$ and a set of ground instantiations of multiset rules $\mathcal{M}$ is defined by the following transition rule:

$$\frac{l - [a] \rightarrow r \in \mathcal{M} \quad lfacts(l) \subset^{\#} S \quad pfacts(l) \subset set(S)}{S \xrightarrow{set(a)}_{\mathcal{M}} ((S \setminus^{\#} lfacts(l)) \cup^{\#} mset(r))}$$

where *lfact* and *pfacts* denote the linear, respectively the permanent facts from a set, *set* and *mset* transform a multiset into a set and vice versa, and $\subset^{\#}, \setminus^{\#}, \cup^{\#}$ are the multiset equivalents of the subset relation, set difference and set union. The executions are then modelled by a set of traces defined as:

$$\{(A_1, \ldots, A_n) \ \mid \exists S_1, \ldots, S_n \in \mathcal{G}^{\#}. \ \emptyset \xrightarrow{A_1}_{\mathcal{M}} \ldots \xrightarrow{A_n}_{\mathcal{M}} S_n \wedge \forall i \neq j. \ \forall x.$$
$$(S_{i+1} \setminus^{\#} S_i) = \{\mathsf{Fr}(x)\} \Rightarrow S_{j+1} \setminus^{\#} S_j) \neq \{\mathsf{Fr}(x)\}\}$$

The second condition makes sure that each fresh name is indeed different in the trace.

An important part of the modelling of the Yubikey protocol's counter value was to determine whether one value is smaller than another. Our modelling employs a feature added to the development version of tamarin as of October 2012. Tamarin supports the union operator $\cup^{\#}$ for multisets of message terms. We model the counter as a multiset only consisting of the symbol "one". The cardinality of the multiset is the value of the counter. A counter value is considered smaller than another one, if the first multiset is included in the second. We enforce those semantics by adding an axiom that requires, for all instantiations of rules annotated with $\mathsf{Smaller}(a, b)$, that a is a subset of b:

$$\forall i, a, b. \ \mathsf{Smaller}(a, b)@i \Rightarrow \exists z. a + z = b$$

Note that i and j are timepoints and $\mathsf{Event}@i$ means that the trace contains a rule instantiation that produces the action Event at timepoint i. We had to simplify the modelling of the session and token counter: instead of having two counters, we just model a single counter. Since the Yubikey either increases the session counter and resets the token counter, or increases the token counter, it implements a complete lexicographical order on the pair (session counter, token counter).

The following rule models the initialisation of a Yubikey. A fresh public id, secret ID and Yubikey are drawn, and saved on the Server and the Yubikey.

$$\mathsf{Fr}(k), \mathsf{Fr}(pid), \mathsf{Fr}(sid) \ -\!\![\mathsf{Protocol}(), \mathsf{Init}(pid, k), \mathsf{ExtendedInit}(pid, sid, k)]\!\!\rightarrow$$
$$!\mathsf{Y}(pid, sid), \mathsf{Y\_counter}(pid, {}'1'), \mathsf{Server}(pid, sid, {}'\, 1'), !\mathsf{SharedKey}(pid, k),$$
$$\mathsf{Out}(pid)$$

The next rule models how the counter is increased when a Yubikey is plugged in. As mentioned before, we model both the session and the token counter as a single counter. We over-approximate in the case that the Yubikey increases the session token by allowing the adversary to instantiate the rule for any counter value that is higher than the previous one, using the $\mathsf{Smaller}$ action.

$$\mathsf{Y\_counter}(pid, otc), \mathsf{In}(tc) \ -\!\![\mathsf{Yubi}(pid, tc), \mathsf{Smaller}(otc, tc)]\!\!\rightarrow \mathsf{Y\_counter}(pid, tc)$$

Note that the adversary has to input tc. We can only express properties about the set of traces in tamarin, e. g., the terms the adversary constructs in a given trace, but not the terms he *could* construct in this trace. By requiring the adversary to produce all counter values, we can ensure that they are in !K, i. e., the adversary's knowledge.

When the button is pressed, an encryption is output in addition to increasing the counter:

$$!Y(pid, sid), Y\_counter(pid, tc), !SharedKey(pid, k), In(tc), Fr(npr), Fr(nonce)$$
$$-[YubiPress(pid, tc)]\rightarrow$$
$$Y\_counter(pid, tc +' 1'), Out(< pid, nonce, senc(< sid, tc, npr >, k) >)$$

The output can be used to authenticate with the server, in case that the counter inside the encryption is larger than the last counter stored on the server:

$$Server(pid, sid, otc), In(< pid, nonce, otp >), !SharedKey(pid, k), In(otc)$$
$$-[Login(pid, sid, tc, otp), LoginCounter(pid, otc, tc), Smaller(otc, tc)]\rightarrow$$
$$Server(pid, sid, tc)$$

for $otp = senc(< sid, tc, pr >, k)$. Tamarin is able to prove the following properties: First, the absence of replay attacks:

$$\neg(\exists i, j, pid, sid, x, otp_1, otp_2.$$
$$Login(pid, sid, x, otp_1)@i \wedge Login(pid, sid, x, otp_2)@j \wedge \neg(i = j))$$

Second, injective correspondence between pressing the button on a Yubikey and a successful login:

$$\forall pid, sid, x, otp, t_2.Login(pid, sid, x, otp)@t_2 \Rightarrow \exists t_1.YubiPress(pid, x)@t_1 \wedge$$
$$t_1 < t_2 \wedge \forall otp_2, t_3.Login(pid, sid, x, otp_2)@t_3 \Rightarrow t_3 = t_2$$

Third, the fact that the counter values associated to logins are monotonically increasing in time, which implies that a successful login invalidates previously collected OTPs.

$$\forall pid, otc_1, tc_1, otc_2, tc_2, t_1, t_2, t_3.Smaller(tc_1, tc_2)@t_3 \wedge$$
$$LoginCounter(pid, otc_1, tc_1)@t_1 \wedge LoginCounter(pid, otc_2, tc_2)@t_2 \Rightarrow t_1 < t_2$$

The source files and proofs are available at the following website: http://www.lsv.ens-cachan.fr/~kunneman/yubikey/analysis/yk.tar.gz.

The absence of replay attacks is proven by showing the following, stronger property to hold true:

$$\forall pid, otc_1, tc_1, otc_2, tc_2, t_1, t_2.$$
$$LoginCounter(pid, otc_1, tc_1)@t_1 \wedge LoginCounter(pid, otc_2, tc_2)@t_2 \wedge t_1 < t_2$$
$$\Rightarrow \exists z.tc_2 = z + tc_1$$

Intuitively, this means that counter values are increasing in time. Tamarin is able to prove the invariant, as well as the security properties completely automatically. Note that in this model, the adversary has no direct access to the server, he can only control the network. A stronger attack model is discussed in the next section.

4   The YubiHSM

The YubiHSM is also a USB device about 5 times thicker than a Yubikey. According to the Yubico literature it "provides a low-cost [\$500] way to move out sensitive information and cryptographic operations away from a vulnerable computer environment without having to invest in expensive dedicated Hardware Security Modules (HSMs)" [19]. The YubiHSM stores a very limited number of AES keys in a way that the server can use them to perform cryptographic operations without the key values ever appearing in the server's memory. These 'master keys' are generated during configuration time and can neither be modified nor read at runtime. The master keys are used to encrypt working keys which can then stored safely on the server's hard disk. The working keys are encrypted inside so-called AEADs (blocks produced by authenticated encryption with associated data). In order to produce or decrypt an AEAD, an AES key and a piece of associated data is required. The YubiHSM uses CCM mode to obtain an AEAD algorithm from the AES block cipher [20].

In the case of the Yubikey protocol, AEADs are used to store the keys the server shares with the Yubikeys, and the associated data is the public ID and the key-handle used to reference the AES key. The idea here is that since the master keys of the YubiHSM cannot be extracted, the attacker never learns the value of any Yubikey AES keys, even if he successfully attacks the server. While he is in control of the server, he is (of course) able to grant or deny authentication to any client at will. However, if the attack is detected and the attacker loses access to the server, it should not be necessary to replace or rewrite the Yubikeys that are in circulation in order to re-establish security.

5   Two Attacks on the Implementation of Authenticated Encryption

The YubiHSM provides access to about 22 commands that can be activated or de-activated globally, or per key, during configuration. We first examined the YubiHSM API in its default configuration, discovering the following two attacks which led to a security advisory given issued by Yubikey in February 2012 [9].

The attacks use the following two commands: AES_ECB_BLOCK_ENCRYPT takes a handle to an AES key and a plaintext of length of one AES block (16 Bytes) and applies the raw block cipher. YSM_AEAD_GENERATE takes a nonce, a handle to an AES key and some data and outputs an AEAD. More precisely, but still simplified for our purposes, it computes:

$$AEAD(nonce, kh, data) = \left(\left(\overset{\lceil \frac{|data|}{blocksize} \rceil}{\underset{i=0}{\|}} AES(k, counter_i) \right) \bigoplus data \right) \| mac$$

where k is the key referenced by the key-handle kh, $counter_i$ is a counter that is completely determined by $kh, nonce, i$ and the length of $data$ and $blocksize$ is 16 bytes. For the precise definition of mac and $counter$, we refer to RFC 3610 [20].

Figure 2 depicts the counter mode of operation, used to calculate the ciphertext body of the AEAD to which will be appended the MAC.

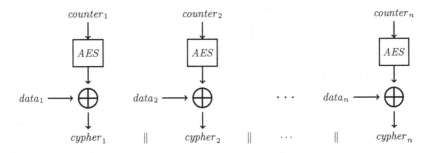

Fig. 2. AES in counter mode (simplified)

The AEADs used to store keys for decrypting OTPs in the Yubikey protocol are special cases: the plaintext is a concatenation of the respective Yubikey's AES key and secret device ID (22 bytes in total), and *nonce* consists of the Yubikey's public id.

An attacker with access to the command AES_ECB_BLOCK_ENCRYPT is able to decrypt an AEAD by recreating the blocks of the key-stream, i.e., $AES(k, counter_i)$. He xors the result with the AEAD truncated by 8 bytes (the length of *mac*) and yields *data*. When the attacker is able to compromise the server, he learns the AEAD and the key-handle used to produce it. Since the nonce is the public ID of the Yubikey, he can compute $counter_i$ and, using AES_-ECB_BLOCK_ENCRYPT the key-stream. It is in the nature of the counter-mode that encryption and decryption are the same operation. According to the reference manual[19, Section 4.3], "the YubiHSM intentionally does not provide any functions [sic] that decrypts an AEAD and returns it in clear text, either fully or partial [sic].". We therefore consider the protection of the AEAD's contents a security goal of the YubiHSM, which is violated by this attack. The attack can be prevented by disabling the AES_ECB_BLOCK_ENCRYPT command on the relevant key handles at configuration time.

The second attack uses only YSM_AEAD_GENERATE: if the attacker produces $AEAD(nonce, kh, 0^l)$ for the same handle kh and *nonce* a previously generated AEAD of length l was created with (he can discard *mac*). Again he directly recovers the key-stream. Once again, it is possible to decrypt AEADs. This attack is worse than the first one, because YSM_AEAD_GENERATE is necessary for the set-up of Yubikeys. Note that the attack applies also to the commands YSM_RANDOM_AEAD_GENERATE and YSM_BUFFER_-AEAD_GENERATE [19, p. 28-29].

This second attack is harder to prevent, since in order to set up Yubikeys with their AES keys, the YSM_AEAD_GENERATE command must at some point be enabled. The security advisory suggests that the threat can be "mitigated by observing that a YubiHSM used to generate AEADs is guarded closely to not permit maliciously crafted input." In the next section, we try to interpret this advice into a concrete configuration for which we can prove security of the sensitive keys. Then, in section 7, we describe practical ways in which this configuration could be used.

6 Analysis in the Case of Server Compromise

In the following, we will assume the following corruption scenario: in addition to the capacities described in Section 3, the attacker can read the AEADs stored on the server and he can access the HSM. Every AEAD is created using the same key on the HSM, the handle to this key is made public. The public ID is given to the adversary when the Yubikey is set up. Counter values are guessable, so there is no need to give the adversary explicit access to this data. The adversary is still not able to directly read the data stored on the Yubikey or YubiHSM. Note that in this situation, the attacker can trivially approve or deny authorisation requests to the server, hence we cannot expect to show absence of replay attacks. We are rather interested in whether the attacker can recover the secret keys used to create OTPs, which would allow him to continue to obtain authorisation even once he is denied access to the server.

We model the xor operator in a very simplified manner. The equational theory we employ allows to recover the two attacks described in Section 5, but it does not capture all attacks that the xor-operator might permit in this context. For this reason, the positive security results in this section have to be taken with caution. We model xor using the function symbols xor, $dexor1$ and $dexor2$ and the equations $dexor1(xor(a, b), a) = b$ and $dexor2(xor(a, b), b) = a$. Using this equational theory, we are able to rediscover the attacks described in the previous section. The current version of tamarin (0.8.2.1) does not have built-in support yet, but it is planned for future releases.

The counter values are modelled as before. We initialise the YubiHSM with exactly one key-handle:

$$\mathsf{Fr}(k), \mathsf{Fr}(kh) \,\text{--}[\mathsf{MasterKey}(k), \mathsf{OneTime}()]\!\!\rightarrow\! !\mathsf{HSM}(kh, k), \mathsf{Out}(kh),$$
$$\mathsf{!YSM\_AEAD\_YUBIKEY\_OTP\_DECODE}(kh)$$

We make sure that this rule is only instantiated once by adding a corresponding axiom $\forall i, j.\ \mathsf{OneTime}@i \wedge \mathsf{OneTime}@j \Rightarrow i = j$.

The following rules model the fact that the adversary can communicate with the YubiHSM and read the list of AEADs stored on the authentication server.

$$\mathsf{OutHSM}(x) \,\text{--}[\mathsf{HSMRead}(x)]\!\!\rightarrow \qquad\qquad [\mathsf{Out}(x)]$$
$$\mathsf{In}(x) \,\text{--}[\mathsf{HSMWrite}(x)]\!\!\rightarrow \qquad\qquad [\mathsf{InHSM}(x)]$$
$$!\mathsf{S\_AEAD}(pid, aead) \,\text{--}[\mathsf{AEADRead}(aead), \mathsf{HSMRead}(aead)]\!\!\rightarrow \quad [\mathsf{Out}(aead)]$$

The next rules aim at modelling the HSM. We modelled a set of 4 rules in total, but only YSM_AEAD_YUBIKEY_OTP_DECODE is used. (YSM_AEAD_-GENERATE is directly incorporated into the rule BuyANewYubikey, see below.)

InHSM($< did, kh, aead, otp >$), !HSM(kh, k),
    !YSM_AEAD_YUBIKEY_OTP_DECODE(kh)
$-$[OtpDecode($k2, k, < did, sc, rand >, sc, xor(senc(ks, k), < k2, did >), mac$)
    OtpDecodeMaster($k2, k$)]$\mapsto$ OutHSM(sc)

where $ks =$ keystream(kh, N), $mac =$ mac($< k2, did >, k$), $aead =< $xor($senc(ks, k), < k2, did >), mac >$ and $otp =$ senc($< did, sc, rand >, k2$).

The rules for emitting the OTP and the login are modelled in a way very similar to Section 3, but of course we model the encryption used inside the AEAD in more detail. Here, the server-side rule for the login.

In($< pid, nonce, senc(< sid, tc, pr >, k2) >$), !HSM($kh, k$), !S_sid($pid, sid$),
    !S_AEAD($pid, aead$),   S_Counter(pid, otc)
$-$[Login($pid, tc, senc(< sid, tc, pr >, k2)$)), Smaller($otc, tc$)]$\mapsto$
    S_Counter(pid, tc)

where ks, mac and $aead$ are defined as before.

Tamarin is able to prove that, within our limited model of xor, the adversary never learns a Yubikey AES key or a YubiHSM master key - in other words, AEADs, as well as the key used to produce them, stay confidential. The proof does not need human intervention, however, some additional typing invariants are needed in order to reach termination. For instance, the following invariant is used to proof that a key k_2 shared between the authentication server and the Yubikey can only be learned when the key used to encrypt the AEADs is leaked.

$$\forall t_1, t_2, pid, k2.\text{Init}(pid, k2)@t_1 \wedge \text{K}(k2)@t_2$$
$$\Rightarrow \exists t_3, t_4, k.\text{K}(k)@t_3 \wedge \text{MasterKey}(k)@t_4 \wedge t_3 < t_2$$

7   Evaluation

The positive and negative results in this paper provide formal criteria to evaluate the security of the Yubikey protocol in different scenarios.

Positive Results: Under the assumption that the adversary can control the network, but is not able to compromise the client or the authentication server, we have shown he cannot mount replay attack. Furthermore, if a YubiHSM is used configured such that YSM_AEAD_YUBIKEY_OTP_DECODE is the only available command, then even in case the adversary is able to compromise the server, the Yubikey AES keys remain secure. All these results are subject to our abstract modelling of cryptography and the algebraic properties of XOR of course.

Since the Yubikeys need to be provisioned with their AES keys and secret identities must be stored in the AEADs, we propose two set-ups that can be used to obtain the configuration used in the analysis:

1. *One Server, One YubiHSM:* There is a set-up phase which serves the purpose of producing AEADs (using any of the YSM_AEAD_GENERATE commands) and writing the key and secret/public identity on the Yubikey. This phase should take place in a secure environment. Afterwards, the YubiHSM is returned to configuration mode and all commands disabled except YSM_-AEAD_YUBIKEY_OTP_DECODE. In this set-up, only one YubiHSM is needed, but it is not possible to add new Yubikeys once the second phase has begun without taking the server off-line and returning the YubiHSM to configuration mode. Note that switching the YubiHSM into configuration mode requires physical access to the device, hence would not be possible for an attacker who has remotely compromised the server.

2. *Two Servers, Two YubiHSMs:* There is one server that handles the authentication protocol, and one that handles the set-up of the Yubikeys. The latter is isolated from the network and only used for this very purpose, so we consider it a secure environment. We configure two YubiHSMs such that they store the same master-key (the key used to produce AEADs). The first is used for the authentication server and has only YSM_AEAD_YUBIKEY_-OTP_DECODE set to true, the second is used in the set-up server and has only YSM_AEAD_GENERATE set to true. The set-up server produces the list of public ids and corresponding AEADs, which is transferred to the authentication server in a secure way, for example in fixed intervals (every night) using fresh USB keys. The transfer does not necessarily have to provide integrity or secrecy (as the adversary can block the authentication via the network, anyway), but it should only be allowed in one direction.

Reading between the lines (since no YubiHSM configuration details are given) it seems that Yubico themselves use this set-up to provision Yubikeys [21].

Negative Results: In case either of the permissions AES_ECB_BLOCK_EN-CRYPT or YSM_AEAD_GENERATE are activated on a master key handle (which by default they both are), the YubiHSM does protect the keys used to produce one-time passwords encrypted under that master key. Since YSM_-AEAD_GENERATE (or YSM_BUFFER_AEAD_GENERATE) are needed in order to set a Yubikey up, this means that separate setup and authorisation configurations have to be used in order to benefit from the use of the YubiHSM, i.e., have a higher level of security than in the case where the keys are stored unencrypted on the hard disk. Unfortunately, open source code available on the web in e.g. the yhsmpam project [22], designed to use the YubiHSM to protect passwords from server compromise, uses the insecure configuration, i.e. one YubiHSM with both YSM_AEAD_GENERATE and (in this case) YSM_-AEAD_DECRYPT_CMP enabled, and hence would not provide the security intended.

Possible changes to the YubiHSM: We will now discuss two possible counter-measures against this kind of attack that could be incorporated into future versions of the YubiHSM to allow a single device to be used securely, the first which may be seen as a kind of stop-gap measure, the second which is a more satisfactory solution using more suitable crypto:

1. *AEAD_GENERATE with a randomly drawn nonce:* All three YubiHSM commands to generate AEADs (YSM_AEAD_GENERATE, YSM_BUF-FER_AEAD_GENERATE and YSM_RANDOM_AEAD_GENERATE) allow the user to supply the nonce that is used. This would not be possible if they were replaced by a command similar to YSM_AEAD_GENERATE that chooses the nonce randomly and outputs it at the end, so it is possible to use the nonce as the public ID of the Yubikey. However, even in this case there is an online guessing attack on the HSM: an AEAD can be decrypted if the right nonce is guessed. We can assume that the adversary has gathered a set of honestly generated OTPs, so he is able to recognize the correct nonce. Since the nonce space is rather small (2^{48}) in comparison to the key-space of AES-128, the adversary could perform a brute-force search. We measured the amount of time it takes to perform 10 000 YSM_AEAD_GENERATE operations on the YubiHSM. The average value is 0.2178 ms, so it would take approximately 1900 years to traverse the nonce space. Even so this is not completely reassuring.

2. *SIV-mode:* The SIV mode of operation [23] is designed to be resistant to repeated IVs. It is an authenticated encryption mode that works by deriving the IV from the MAC that will be used for authentication. As such it is deterministic - two identical plaintexts will have an identical ciphertext - but the encryption function cannot be inverted in the same way as CCM mode by giving the same IV (the encryption function does not take an IV as input, the only way to force the same IV to be used is to give the same plaintext). This would seem to suit the requirements of the YubiHSM very well, since it is only keys that will be encrypted hence the chances of repeating a plaintext are negligible. Even if the same key is put on two different Yubikeys, they will have different private IDs yielding different AEADs. In our view this is the most satisfactory solution.

Methodology: Since the tamarin prover could not derive the results in this paper without auxiliary lemmas, we think it is valuable to give some information about the way we derived those results.

We first modelled the protocol using multiset rewriting rules, which was a straight-forward task. Then, we stated a sanity lemma saying "There does not exist a trace that corresponds to a successful protocol run" to verify that our model is sane. Tamarin should be able to derive a counter-example, which is a proof that a correct protocol run is possible.

We stated the security property we wanted to prove, e.g., the absence of replay-attacks. Since tamarin did not produce a proof on its own, we investigated the proof derivation in interactive mode. We deduced lemmas that seemed necessary to cut branches in the proof that are looping, so-called typing invariants. An example is YSM_AEAD_YUBIKEY_OTP_DECODE: it outputs a subterm of its input, namely the counter value. Whenever tamarin tries to derive a term t, it uses backward induction to find combination of AEAD and OTP that allows to conclude that the result of this operation is t. Meier, Cremers and Basin propose a technique they call *decryption-chain reasoning* in [24, Section 3b] that we used to formulate our typing invariant. Once the invariant is stated, it needs to be proven. Sometimes the invariant depends on another invariant, that needs to be found manually. We used trial and error to find a set of invariants that lead to a successful verification of the security property, and then minimised this set of lemmas by experimentally deleting them to find out which ones were strictly necessary.

All in all, it took about 1 month to do the analysis presented in this work. The modelling of the protocol took no more than half a day. Finding a first modelling of the natural numbers and the "Is smaller than" relation took a week, since at this time, the multiset union operator was not available in tamarin. We employed a modelling that build the "Is smaller than" as a set of permanent facts from an "Is Successor" of relation:

$$\mathsf{In}(0), \mathsf{In}(S(0)) \ -\![\mathsf{IsSucc}(0, S(0)), \mathsf{IsZero}(0)]\!\rightarrow \quad !\mathsf{Succ}(0, S(0))$$
$$\mathsf{In}(y), \mathsf{In}(S(y)), !\mathsf{Succ}(x, y) \ -\![\mathsf{IsSucc}(y, S(y))]\!\rightarrow \quad !\mathsf{Succ}(y, S(y))$$
$$!\mathsf{Succ}(x, y) \ -\![\mathsf{IsSmaller}(x, y)]\!\rightarrow \quad !\mathsf{Smaller}(x, y)$$
$$!\mathsf{Smaller}(x, y), !\mathsf{Succ}(y, z) \ -\![\mathsf{IsSmaller}(x, z)]\!\rightarrow \quad !\mathsf{Smaller}(x, z)$$

An additional axiom is needed to enforce transitivity. Using this modelling, it was also possible to derive all results covered in this paper. We consider the modelling using the multiset data type more natural, whereas this modelling does not rely on the support of associativity, commutativity and a neutral element in equational theories, as is needed to model multisets with the empty multiset and multiset union. It might be interesting for similar use cases with other tools that may not support such equational theories. The sample files available for download include this second modelling as well.

The lion's share of the time was spent in searching the right invariants for termination. The running time of tamarin is acceptable: proving the absence of replay-attacks in case of an uncompromised server takes around 35 seconds, proving confidentiality of keys in the case of a compromised server takes around 50 seconds, both on a 2.4GHz Intel Core 2 Duo with 4GB RAM.

8   Conclusions

We were able to show the absence of replay-attacks of the Yubikey protocol in the formal model. This has been attempted before, using a variety of protocol analysis tools, but it was previously only possible for a fixed number of nonces. This shows, that verification based on multiset-rewriting rules is a promising approach for realistic protocols, as long as the right invariants can be found.

Perhaps surprisingly, the modelling of a monotonically increasing counter proves to be a surmountable problem.

To evaluate the YubiHSM, a small device that can potentially perform cryptographic operations without revealing the key to the computer it is connected to, we considered a more challenging scenario. Here, the attacker can access the server and communicate with this device. Two attacks show that in the default configuration, the encryption operations are implemented in a way such that they do not provide confidentiality of plaintexts. The user must either set up the authentication server and the YubiHSM such that provisioning and authorisation commands are never available at the same time on the same server. We proposed a change to the cryptographic design that would relax this restriction.

We learned that it is possible to obtain formal results on the YubiKey and YubiHSM for an unbounded model using tamarin, which gives us hope for the unbounded formal analysis of other Security APIs, for example PKCS#11 and the TPM. However, there are plenty of improvements to be made: we currently treat the session and token counter on the Yubikey as a single value, and simplify the algebraic theory of xor considerably. The treatment of xor is expected to be included in future versions of the tamarin tool. Our own work will concentrate on developing a methodology for deriving the lemmas tamarin needs to obtain a proof automatically, thus permitting more automation and more expressive models.

References

1. Bonneau, J., Herley, C., van Oorschot, P.C., Stajano, F.: The quest to replace passwords: a framework for comparative evaluation of Web authentication schemes. Technical Report UCAM-CL-TR-817, University of Cambridge, Computer Laboratory (March 2012); Shorter version appears in Proceedings of IEEE Symposium on Security and Privacy (2012)
2. Yubico AB: Yubico customer list, http://www.yubico.com/references
3. Yubico AB: Yubikey security evaluation: Discussion of security properties and best practices v2.0. (September 2009), http://static.yubico.com/var/uploads/pdfs/Security_Evaluation_2009-09-09.pdf
4. Björck, F.: Yubikey security weaknesses. On Security DJ Blog (February 2009), http://web.archive.org/web/20100203110742/http://security.dj/?p=4
5. Björck, F.: Increased security for yubikey. On Security DJ Blog (August 2009), http://web.archive.org/web/20100725005817/http://security.dj/?p=154
6. Vamanu, L.: Formal analysis of Yubikey. Master's thesis, École normale supérieure de Cachan (August 2011), http://n.ethz.ch/~lvamanu/download/YubiKeyAnalysis.pdf
7. Schmidt, B., Meier, S., Cremers, C.J.F., Basin, D.A.: Automated analysis of diffie-hellman protocols and advanced security properties. In: Proceedings of the 25th IEEE Computer Security Foundations Symposium, CSF 2012, pp. 78–94 (2012)
8. Kaminsky, D.: On the RSA SecurID compromise (June 2011), http://dankaminsky.com/2011/06/09/securid/
9. Yubico Inc.: Yubihsm 1.0 security advisory 2012-01 (February 2012) (published online), http://static.yubico.com/var/uploads/pdfs/SecurityAdvisory%202012-02-13.pdf

10. Yubico AB Kungsgatan 37, 111 56 Stockholm Sweden: The YubiKey Manual - Usage, configuration and introduction of basic concepts (Version 2.2) (June 2010), http://www.yubico.com/documentation
11. Yubico AB Kungsgatan 37, 111 56 Stockholm Sweden: YubiKey Authentication Module Design Guide and Best Practices (Version 1.0), http://www.yubico.com/documentation
12. Kamikaze28, et al.: Specification of the Yubikey operation in the Yubico wiki (June 2012), http://wiki.yubico.com/wiki/index.php/Yubikey
13. The yubikey-val-server-php project: Validation protocol version 2.0. (October 2011), http://code.google.com/p/yubikey-val-server-php/wiki/ValidationProtocolV20
14. Durgin, N., Lincoln, P., Mitchell, J., Scedrov, A.: Undecidability of bounded security protocols. In: Heintze, N., Clarke, E. (eds.) Proceedings of the Workshop on Formal Methods and Security Protocols — FMSP, Trento, Italy (1999), Electronic proceedings, http://www.cs.bell-labs.com/who/nch/fmsp99/program.html
15. Blanchet, B.: Automatic verification of correspondences for security protocols. Journal of Computer Security 17(4), 363–434 (2009)
16. Arapinis, M., Ritter, E., Ryan, M.D.: Statverif: Verification of stateful processes. In: CSF, pp. 33–47. IEEE Computer Society (2011)
17. Mödersheim, S.: Abstraction by set-membership: verifying security protocols and web services with databases. In: [25], pp. 351–360
18. Guttman, J.D.: State and progress in strand spaces: Proving fair exchange. J. Autom. Reasoning 48(2), 159–195 (2012)
19. Yubico AB Kungsgatan 37, 111 56 Stockholm Sweden: Yubico YubiHSM - Cryptographic Hardware Security Module (Version 1.0) (September 2011), http://www.yubico.com/documentation
20. Whiting, D., Housley, R., Ferguson, N.: Counter with CBC-MAC (CCM). RFC 3610 (Informational) (September 2003)
21. Yubico AB Kungsgatan 37, 111 56 Stockholm Sweden: Yubicloud Validation Service - (Version 1.1) (May 2012), http://www.yubico.com/documentation
22. Habets, T.: Yubihsm login helper program, http://code.google.com/p/yhsmpam/
23. Rogaway, P., Shrimpton, T.: Deterministic authenticated encryption: A provable-security treatment of the keywrap problem (2006)
24. Meier, S., Cremers, C.J.F., Basin, D.A.: Strong invariants for the efficient construction of machine-checked protocol security proofs. In: [25], pp. 231–245
25. Al-Shaer, E., Keromytis, A.D., Shmatikov, V. (eds.) Proceedings of the 17th ACM Conference on Computer and Communications Security, CCS 2010, Chicago, Illinois, USA, October 4-8. ACM (2010)

Boosting Model Checking
to Analyse Large ARBAC Policies

Silvio Ranise[1], Anh Truong[1], and Alessandro Armando[1,2]

[1] Security and Trust Unit, FBK-Irst, Trento, Italia
[2] DIST, Università degli Studi di Genova, Italia

Abstract. The administration of access control policies is a task of paramount importance for distributed systems. A crucial analysis problem is to foresee if a set of administrators can give a user an access permission. We consider this analysis problem in the context of the Administrative Role-Based Access Control (ARBAC), one of the most widespread administrative models. Given the difficulty of taking into account the effect of all possible administrative actions, automated analysis techniques are needed. In this paper, we describe how a model checker can scale up to handle very large ARBAC policies while ensuring completeness. An extensive experimentation shows that an implementation of our techniques performs significantly better than MOHAWK, a recently proposed tool that has become the reference for finding errors in ARBAC policies.

1 Introduction

The administration of access control policies is a task of paramount importance for the flexibility and security of many distributed systems. For flexibility, administrative actions are carried out by several security officers. For security, the capabilities of performing such operations must be limited to selected parts of the access control policies since officers can only be partially trusted. Indeed, flexibility and security are opposing forces and avoiding under- or over-constrained specifications of administrative actions is of paramount importance. In this respect, it is crucial to foresee if a user can get a certain permission by a sequence of administrative actions executed by a set of administrators. Since it is difficult to take into account the effect of all possible administrative actions, push-button analysis techniques are needed.

Role-Based Access Control (RBAC) [12] is one of the most widespread authorization model and Administrative RBAC (ARBAC) [5] is the corresponding widely used administrative model. In RBAC, access control policies are specified by assigning users to roles that in turn are assigned to permissions. ARBAC allows for the specification of rules that permit to modify selected parts of a RBAC policy. The analysis problem consists of establishing if a certain user can be assigned to a certain role (or permission) by a sequence of administrative actions. Several automated analysis techniques (see, e.g., [11,10,14]) have been developed for solving this problem in the ARBAC model. Recently, a tool called ASASP [2] has been shown (in [4]) to perform better than the state-of-the-art tool

A. Jøsang, P. Samarati, and M. Petrocchi (Eds.): STM 2012, LNCS 7783, pp. 273–288, 2013.

RBACPAT [8] on the set of benchmark problems in [14] and (in [3]) to be able to tackle more expressive ARBAC policies that RBACPAT cannot handle. More recently, another tool called MOHAWK has been shown (in [9]) to scale much better than RBAC-PAT on the problems in [14] and more complex ones.

In this paper, we investigate how the model checking techniques underlying ASASP can scale up to solve the largest problem instances in [9]. In fact, preliminary experiments showed that ASASP can only handle instances of moderate size in [9]. This has lead us to develop a new version of ASASP, called ASASPXL, with the goal of boosting the model checking techniques underlying ASASP and guaranteeing to find errors in ARBAC policies if they exist. This is in contrast with the approach of MOHAWK, which—as said in [9]— is incomplete, i.e. it may miss errors in a buggy policy. An extensive experimental comparison on the benchmark problems in [9] shows that ASASPXL performs significantly better than MOHAWK.

Plan of the paper. Section 2 introduces the ARBAC model and the related analysis problem. Section 3 briefly reviews the model checking technique underlying ASASP. Section 4 describes the techniques that we have designed for scalability. Section 5 summarizes the findings of our experiments. Section 6 concludes.

2   Administrative Role-Based Access Control

In *Role-Based Access Control (RBAC)* [12], access decisions are based on the roles that individual users have as part of an organization. Permissions are grouped by role name and correspond to various uses of a resource. Roles can have overlapping responsibilities and privileges, i.e. users belonging to different roles may have common permissions. To allow for compact specifications of RBAC policies, role hierarchies are used to reflect the natural structure of an enterprise and make the specification of policies more compact by requiring that one role may implicitly include the permissions that are associated with others.

RBAC policies need to be maintained according to the evolving needs of the organization. For flexibility and scalability, large systems usually require several administrators, and thus there is a need not only to have a consistent RBAC policy but also to ensure that the policy is modified by administrators who are allowed to do so. Several administrative frameworks have been proposed. One of the most popular administrative frameworks is Administrative RBAC (AR-BAC) [5] that controls how RBAC policies may evolve through administrative actions that assign or revoke user memberships into roles. Since administrators can be only partially trusted, administration privileges must be limited to selected parts of the RBAC policies, called *administrative domains*. The ARBAC model defines administrative domains by using RBAC itself to control how security officers can delegate (part of) their administrative permissions to trusted users. Despite such restrictions, it is very difficult to foresee if a subset of the security officers can maliciously (or inadvertently) assign a role to an untrusted user that enable him/her to get access to security-sensitive resources.

Formalization. Let U be a set of users, R a set of roles, and P a set of permissions. Users are associated to roles by a binary relation $UA \subseteq U \times R$ and roles are associated to permissions by another binary relation $PA \subseteq R \times P$. A role hierarchy is a partial order $\succeq$ on R, where $r_1 \succeq r_2$ means that r_1 is *more senior than* r_2 for $r_1, r_2 \in R$. A user u is a *member* of role r when $(u, r) \in UA$. A user u *has permission* p if there exists a role $r \in R$ such that $(p, r) \in PA$ and u is a member of r. A *RBAC policy* is a tuple $(U, R, P, UA, PA, \succeq)$.

Usually (see, e.g., [14]), administrators may only update the relation UA while PA and $\succeq$ are assumed constant. An administrative domain is specified by a *pre-condition*, i.e. a finite set of expressions of the forms r or $\bar{r}$ (for $r \in R$). A user $u \in U$ *satisfies* a pre-condition C if, for each $\ell \in C$, u is a member of r when ℓ is r or u is not a member of r when ℓ is $\bar{r}$ for $r \in R$. Permission to assign users to roles is specified by a ternary relation *can_assign* containing tuples of the form (C_a, C, r) where C_a and C are pre-conditions, and r a role. Permission to revoke users from roles is specified by a binary relation *can_revoke* containing tuples of the form (C_a, r) where C_a is a pre-condition and r a role. In both cases, we say that C_a is the *administrative pre-condition*, C is a *(simple) pre-condition*, r is the *target role*, and a user u_a satisfying C_a is the *administrator*. When there exist users satisfying the administrative and the simple (if the case) pre-conditions of an administrative action, the action is *enabled*. The relation *can_revoke* is only binary because simple pre-conditions are useless when revoking roles (see, e.g., [14]). The semantics of the administrative actions in $\psi := (can\_assign, can\_revoke)$ is given by the binary relation $\rightarrow_\psi$ defined as follows: $UA \rightarrow_\psi UA'$ iff there exist users u_a and u in U such that either (i) there exists $(C_a, C, r) \in can\_assign$, u_a satisfies C_a, u satisfies C (i.e. (C_a, C, r) is enabled), and $UA' = UA \cup \{(u, r)\}$ or (ii) there exists $(C_a, r) \in can\_revoke$, u_a satisfies C_a (i.e. (C_a, r) is enabled), and $UA' = UA \setminus \{(u, r)\}$. A *run* of the administrative actions in $\psi := (can\_assign, can\_revoke)$ is a possibly infinite sequence $UA_0, UA_1, ..., UA_n, ...$ such that $UA_i \rightarrow_\psi UA_{i+1}$ for $i \geq 0$.

A pair (u_g, R_g) is called a *(RBAC) goal* for $u_g \in U$ and R_g a finite set of roles. The cardinality $|R_g|$ of R_g is the *size* of the goal. Given an initial RBAC policy UA_0, a goal (u_g, R_g), and administrative actions $\psi = (can\_assign, can\_revoke)$; (an instance of) the *user-role reachability problem*, identified by the tuple $\langle UA, \psi, (u_g, R_g)\rangle$, consists of checking if there exists a finite sequence $UA_0, UA_1, ..., UA_n$ (for $n \geq 0$) where (i) $UA_i \rightarrow_\psi UA_{i+1}$ for each $i = 0, ..., n - 1$ and (ii) u_g is a member of each role of R_g in UA_n.

The user-role reachability problem defined here is the same of that in [14,9]. In the rest of the paper, we focus on problem instances where U and R are finite, P plays no role, and $\succeq$ can be ignored (see, e.g., [13]). Thus, a RBAC policy is a tuple (U, R, UA) or simply UA when U and R are clear from the context.

3   Model Checking Modulo Theories and ARBAC Policies

Prologue. Model Checking Modulo Theories (MCMT) [7] is a framework to solve reachability problems for infinite state systems that can be represented by transition systems whose set of states and transitions are encoded as constraints in first-order logic. Such symbolic transition systems have been used as abstractions of parametrised protocols, sequential programs manipulating arrays, timed system, etc (see again [7] for an overview).

The main idea underlying the MCMT framework is to use a backward reachability procedure that repeatedly computes pre-images of the set of *goal* states, that is usually obtained by complementing a certain safety property that the system should satisfy. The set of backward reachable states of the system is obtained by taking the union of the pre-images. At each iteration of the procedure, it is checked whether the intersection with the initial set of states is non-empty (*safety* test) and the *unsafety* of the system (i.e. there exists a (finite) sequence of transitions that leads the system from an initial state to one satisfying the goal) is returned. Otherwise, when the intersection is empty, it is checked if the set of backward reachable states is contained in the set computed at the previous iteration (*fix-point* test) and the *safety* of the system (i.e. no (finite) sequence of transitions leads the system from an initial state to one satisfying the goal) is returned. Since sets of states and transitions are represented by first-order constraints, the computation of pre-images reduces to simple symbolic manipulations and testing safety and fix-point to solving a particular class of constraint satisfiability problems, called Satisfiability Modulo Theories (SMT) problems, for which scalable and efficient SMT solvers are currently available (e.g., Z3 [1]).

Enter ASASP. In [4,3], it is studied how the MCMT approach can be used to solve (variants of) the user-role reachability problem. On the theoretical side, it is shown that the backward reachability procedure described above decides (variants of) the user-role reachability problem. On the practical side, extensive experiments have shown that an automated tool, called ASASP [2] implementing (a refinement of) the backward reachability procedure, has a good *trade-off* between *scalability* and *expressiveness*. The success of ASASP in terms of scalability is discussed in [4]: it performs significantly better than the state-of-the-art tool RBAC-PAT [8] on a set of synthetic instances of the user-role reachability problem proposed in [14]. There are two main reasons for the efficiency of ASASP: (1) the use of the Z3 SMT solver for quickly discharging the proof obligations encoding safety and fix-point tests and (2) the use of a *divide et impera* heuristics to decompose the goal of a user-role reachability problems into sub-goals (see [2] for more on this issue). The success of ASASP in terms of expressiveness is reported in [3]: it successfully solves instances of the user-role reachability problems in which role hierarchies and attributes (ranging over infinite sets of values) are used to define administrative domains that RBAC-PAT is not capable of tackling because of the following two reasons. First, the separate administration restriction (see, e.g., [14]) does not hold for the variants of the user-role reachability problem considered in [3]. Such a restriction—that distinguishes administrators from simple users—allows to solve instances of user-role reachability problems by considering only one user at a time. Second, the assumption that the cardinality of the set U of users is bounded is also not satisfied. Despite this, designers of administrative rules can still know, by using ASASP, whether security properties are satisfied or not, regardless of the number of users.

Enter MOHAWK. Immediately after ASASP, a new tool, called MOHAWK [9], has been proposed for the analysis of ARBAC policies especially tuned to error-finding rather than verification (as it is the case of both RBAC-PAT and ASASP). In [9], it is shown that MOHAWK outperforms RBAC-PAT on the problems in [14] and on a new set of much larger instances of the user-role reachability problem. It was natural to run ASASP on these new benchmark problems: rather disappointingly, it could tackle problem instances containing up to 200 roles and 1,000 administrative operations but it was unable to scale up and handle the largest instances containing 80,000 roles and 400,000 administrative operations. This is in line with the following observation of [9]: "model checking does not scale adequately for verifying policies of very large sizes." The reason of the bad scalability of ASASP can be traced back to the fact that it was designed to handle instances of the user-role reachability problems with a relatively compact but complex specification (e.g., involving attributes ranging over infinite domains). In contrast, the problem instances in [9] are quite large with very simple specifications in which there is a bounded but large number of roles, the role hierarchy is not used, and the separate administration restriction holds. (Notice that the absence of a role hierarchy is without loss of generality; see, e.g., [13].)

Exit ASASP **Enter** MCMT. What were we supposed to do to make a tool based on the MCMT approach capable of efficiently solving the user-role reachability problem instances in [9]? One possibility was to extend ASASP with new heuristics to obtain the desired scalability. The other option was to re-use (possibly off-the-shelf) a well-engineered model checker in which to encode the user-role reachability problem for ARBAC policies. Our choice was to build a new analysis tool on top of MCMT [2], the first implementation of the MCMT approach. The advantage of this choice are twofold. First, we do not have to undergo a major re-implementation of ASASP that takes time and may insert bugs, but we only need to write a translator from instances of the user-role reachability problem to reachability problems in MCMT input language, a routine programming task. Second, we can re-use a better engineered incarnation of the MCMT approach that supports some features (e.g., the reuse of previous computations) that may be exploited to significantly improve performances, as we will see in Section 4.

MCMT **at Work.** In [2], the development of ASASP is justified with the fact that it was not possible to encode user-role reachability problems in the input language of MCMT because (a) it supports only unary relations and (b) it does not allow transitions to have more than two parameters. Limitation (a) prevents the representation of the relation $UA \subseteq U \times R$ and limitation (b) does not allow to handle role hierarchies and to overcome the separate administration restriction (see [4] for a discussion about these issues). In this respect, the limited expressiveness required to specify the ARBAC policies in [9] makes the two limitations above unproblematic. Concerning (a), it is not necessary to use the binary relation UA to record user-role assignments, since the set R of roles is finite. It is sufficient to replace UA with a finite collection of sets, one per role. Formally, let $R = \{r_1, ..., r_n\}$ for $n \geq 1$, define $U_{r_i} = \{u | (u, r_i) \in UA\}$ for $i = 1, ..., n$. Straightforward modifications to the definition of $\rightarrow_\psi$ (for ψ a pair of relations *can_assign* and *can_revoke*)—given in Section 2—allows one to replace UA with the U_{r_i}'s. Concerning (b), since the role-hierarchy has been eliminated and the separate administration restriction is enforced, the definition of $\rightarrow_\psi$, for a given tuple in *can_assign* or *can_revoke*, is parametric with respect to just two users, namely the administrator and the user to which the administrative action is going to be applied. These observations enable us to use MCMT for the automated analysis of the instances of the user-role reachability problem in [9]. To this end, we have written a translator of instances of the user-role reachability problems to reachability problems expressed in MCMT input language. To keep technicalities to a minimum, we illustrate the translation on a problem from [14].

Example 1. According to [14], we consider just one user and omit administrative users and roles so that the tuples in *can_assign* are pairs composed of a simple pre-condition and a target role and the pairs in *can_revoke* reduce to target roles only. Let $U = \{u_1\}$, $R = \{r_1, ..., r_8\}$, initially $UA := \{(u_1, r_1), (u_1, r_4), (u_1, r_7)\}$, the tuples $(\{r_1\}, r_2)$, $(\{r_2\}, r_3)$, $(\{r_3, \overline{r_4}\}, r_5)$, $(\{r_5\}, r_6)$, $(\{\overline{r_2}\}, r_7)$, and $(\{r_7\}, r_8)$ are in *can_assign* whereas the elements (r_1), (r_2), (r_3), (r_5), (r_6), and (r_7) are in *can_revoke*. The goal of the problem is $(u_1, \{r_6\})$.

To formalize this problem instance in MCMT, we introduce a unary relation u_r per role $r \in R$. The initial relation UA can thus be expressed as

$$\forall x. \left[\begin{array}{l} u_{r_1}(x) \leftrightarrow x = u_1 \wedge u_{r_4}(x) \leftrightarrow x = u_1 \wedge u_{r_7}(x) \leftrightarrow x = u_1 \wedge u_{r_a}(x) \leftrightarrow x = u_2 \wedge \\ \neg u_{r_2}(x) \wedge \neg u_{r_3}(x) \wedge \neg u_{r_5}(x) \wedge \neg u_{r_6}(x) \end{array} \right].$$

For instance, $(\{r_5\}, r_6)$ in *can_assign* is formalized as

$$\exists x. \left[u_{r_5}(x) \wedge \forall y.(u'_{r_6}(y) \leftrightarrow (y = x \vee u_{r_6}(y))) \right]$$

and (r_1) in *can_revoke* as $\exists x. \left[u_{r_1}(x) \wedge \forall y.(u'_{r_1}(y) \leftrightarrow (y \neq x \wedge u_{r_1}(y))) \right]$, where u_r and u'_r indicate the value of U_r immediately before and after, respectively, of the execution of the administrative action (we also have omitted—for the sake of compactness—identical updates, i.e. a conjunct $\forall y.(u'_r(y) \leftrightarrow u_r(y))$ for each role r distinct from the target goal in the tuple of *can_assign* or *can_revoke*). The other administrative actions are translated in a similar way. The goal can be represented as $\exists x.u_{r_6}(x) \wedge x = u_1$. The pre-image of the goal with respect to $(\{r_5\}, r_6)$ is the set of states from which it is possible to reach the goal by using the administrative action $(\{r_5\}, r_6)$. This is formalized as the formula

$$\exists u'_{r_1}, ..., u'_{r_8}.(\exists x.(u'_{r_6}(x) \wedge x = u_1) \wedge \exists x. \left[u_{r_5}(x) \wedge \forall y.(u'_{r_6}(y) \leftrightarrow (y = x \vee u_{r_6}(y))) \right]),$$

that can be shown equivalent to $\exists x.u_{r_5}(x) \wedge x = u_1$ (see [4] for details). On this problem, MCMT returns **unreachable** and we conclude that $(u_1, \{r_6\})$ is unreachable, confirming the result of [14]. □

4   MCMT's New Clothes for Analysing ARBAC Policies

The design of the techniques used to enable MCMT to scale up to handle the largest instances of the user-role reachability problem in [9] have been guided by the following two simple observations:

(O1) The main source of complexity is the huge number of administrative operations; thus, for scalability, the original problem must be split into smaller sub-problems by using a heuristics that tries to maximize the probability of MCMT to return **reachable**.

(O2) The invocations of MCMT are computationally very expensive; thus, heuristics to minimize their numbers and reuse the findings of state space explorations of previous sub-problems to speed up the solution of newer ones are of paramount importance for scalability.

The main idea is to generate a sequence $P_0, ..., P_{n-1}, P_n$ of problem instances with a fixed goal and an increasingly larger sub-set of the administrative operations. Key to speed up the solution of problem P_{k+1} (for $0 \leq k < n$) is the capability of MCMT to reuse the information gathered when exploring the search spaces of problems $P_0, ..., P_k$. Figure 1 shows the architecture of the tool, called ASASPXL, in which we have implemented these ideas.

It takes as input an instance of the user-role reachability problem (in the format of MOHAWK) and returns **reachable**, when there exists a finite sequence of administrative operations that lead from the initial RBAC policy to one satisfying the goal, and **unreachable** otherwise. We now describe the internal workings of the various modules of ASASPXL except for the **Translator** and MCMT that have already been discussed in Section 3.

4.1   Useful Administrative Operations

After observation **(O1)**, the idea is to extract increasingly larger sub-sets of the tuples in ψ so as to generate a sequence of increasingly more precise

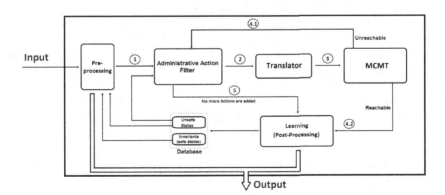

Fig. 1. ASASPXL architecture

approximations of the original instance of the user-role reachability problem. The heuristics to do this is based on the following notion of an administrative action being useful.

Definition 1. Let ψ be administrative actions and R_g a set of roles. A tuple in ψ is 0-*useful* iff its target role is in R_g. A tuple in ψ is k-*useful* (for $k > 0$) iff it is $(k-1)$-useful or its target role occurs (possibly negated) in the simple pre-condition of a $(k-1)$-useful transition. A tuple t in ψ is *useful* iff there exists $k \geq 0$ such that t is k-useful.

The set of all k-useful tuples in $\psi = (can\_assign, can\_revoke)$ is denoted with $\psi^{\leq k} = (can\_assign^{\leq k}, can\_revoke^{\leq k})$. It is easy to see that $can\_assign^{\leq k} \subseteq can\_assign^{\leq k+1}$ and $can\_revoke^{\leq k} \subseteq can\_revoke^{\leq k+1}$ (abbreviated by $\psi^{\leq k} \subseteq \psi^{\leq k+1}$) for $k \geq 0$. Since the sets can_assign and can_revoke in ψ are bounded, there must exists a value $\tilde{k} \geq 0$ such that $\psi^{\leq \tilde{k}} = \psi^{\leq \tilde{k}+1}$ (that abbreviates $\psi^{\leq \tilde{k}} \subseteq \psi^{\leq \tilde{k}+1}$ and $\psi^{\leq \tilde{k}+1} \subseteq \psi^{\leq \tilde{k}}$) or, equivalently, $\psi^{\leq \tilde{k}}$ is the (least) fix-point, also denoted with $lfp(\psi)$, of useful tuples in ψ. Indeed, a tuple in ψ is useful iff it is in $lfp(\psi)$.

Example 2. Let ψ be the administrative actions in Example 1 and $R_g := \{r_6\}$. The sets of k-useful tuples for $k \geq 0$ are the following:

$$\psi^{\leq 0} := (\{(\{r_5\}, r_6)\}, \{r_6\}) \qquad \psi^{\leq 1} := \psi^{\leq 0} \cup (\{(\{r_3, \overline{r_4}\}, r_5)\}, \{r_5\})$$
$$\psi^{\leq 2} := \psi^{\leq 1} \cup (\{(\{r_2\}, r_3)\}, \{r_3\}) \qquad \psi^{\leq 3} := \psi^{\leq 2} \cup (\{(\{r_1\}, r_2)\}, \{r_2\})$$
$$\psi^{\leq 4} := \psi^{\leq 3} \cup (\emptyset, \{r_1\}) \qquad \psi^{\leq k} := \psi^{\leq 4} \text{ for } k > 4,$$

where $(can\_assign_1, can\_revoke_1) \cup (can\_assign_2, can\_revoke_2)$ abbreviates $(can\_assign_1 \cup can\_assign_2, can\_revoke_1 \cup can\_revoke_2)$. Notice that $\psi^{\leq 4} = lfp(\psi)$.

Now, consider the following instance of the user-role reachability problem: $\langle UA, \psi^{\leq 4}, (u_1, \{r_6\}) \rangle$ where UA the initial user-role assignment relation in Example 1. After translation, MCMT returns **unreachable** on this problem instance. We obtain the same result if we run the tool on the translation of the following problem instance: $\langle UA, \psi^{\leq 4}, (u_1, \{r_6\}) \rangle$. Interestingly, if we ask MCMT to return also the sets of user-role assignment relations that have been explored during backward reachability for the two instances (this feature of MCMT will be discussed in Section 4.3 below), we immediately realize that they are identical. This is not by accident as the following proposition shows.   □

Proposition 1. A goal (u_g, R_g) is unreachable from an initial user-role assignment relation UA by using the administrative operations in ψ iff (u_g, R_g) is unreachable from UA by using the administrative operations in $lfp(\psi)$.

The proof of this fact consists of showing that the pre-image of the fix-point set of backward reachable states with respect to any of the administrative operations in ψ but not in $lfp(\psi)$ (denoted with $\psi \setminus lfp(\psi)$) is redundant and can thus be safely discarded. We illustrate this with an example.

Example 3. Consider again the problem instance in Example 1. The set of backward reachable states that MCMT visits during backward reachability is

$$\exists x. \left[\begin{array}{l} (u_{r_6}(x) \wedge x = u_1) \vee (u_{r_5}(x) \wedge x = u_1) \vee (u_{r_3}(x) \wedge \neg u_{r_4}(x) \wedge x = u_1) \vee \\ (u_{r_2}(x) \wedge \neg u_{r_4}(x) \wedge x = u_1) \vee (u_{r_1}(x) \wedge \neg u_{r_4}(x) \wedge x = u_1) \end{array} \right], \quad (1)$$

obtained by considering the tuples in $\psi^{\leq 4}$ only, as observed in Example 2. (It is possible to tell MCMT to save to a file the symbolic representation—such as (1)— of the set of backward reachable states visited during backward reachability.) Now, the pre-image of (1) with respect to $(\{r_7\}, r_8) \in \psi \setminus \psi^{\leq 4}$ is the formula $(1) \wedge \exists x.u_{r_7}(x)$ as r_8 does not occur in (1). Indeed, such a formula trivially implies (1) (or, equivalently, the conjunction of (1) with the negation of (1) $\wedge \exists x.u_{r_7}(x)$ is unsatisfiable) and the fix-point test is successful, confirming that (1) is also a fix-point with respect to the administrative operations in $\psi^{\leq 4} \cup \{(\{r_7\}, r_8)\}$. Similar observations hold for the other tuples in $\psi \setminus \psi^{\leq 4}$ allowing us to conclude that (1) is also a fix-point with respect to ψ. □

A formal proof of the proposition can be obtained by adapting the framework in [4] to the slightly different symbolic representation for ARBAC policies adopted in this paper.

The module **Administrative action filter** in Figure 1 uses the notion of k-useful tuple to build a sequence of increasingly precise instances of user-role reachability problem. Such a sequence is terminated either when the goal is found to be reachable or when the fix-point of useful administrative operations is detected (by Proposition 1, this is enough to conclude that a goal is unreachable with respect to the whole set of administrative operations). Given an instance $\langle UA, \psi, (u_g, R_g) \rangle$ of the user-role reachability problem, the **Administrative action filter** works as follows:

1. Let $k := 0$ and UT be the set of k-useful tuples in ψ
2. Repeat
   (a) **Translate** the instance $\langle UA, UT, (u_g, R_g) \rangle$ of the user-role reachability problem to MCMT input language
   (b) If MCMT returns **reachable**, then return **reachable**
   (c) Let $k := k + 1$, $PUT := UT$, and UT be the set of k-useful tuples in ψ
3. Until $PUT = UT$
4. Return **unreachable**

Initially, UT contains $\psi^{\leq 0}$. At iteration $k \geq 1$, UT stores $\psi^{\leq k}$ and PUT contains $\psi^{\leq (k-1)}$. For $k \geq 0$, the instance $\langle UA, \psi^{\leq k}, (u_g, R_g) \rangle$ of the user-role reachability problem is translated to MCMT input language (step 2(a)). In case MCMT discovers that the goal (u_g, R_g) is reachable with the sub-set $\psi^{\leq k}$ of the administrative operations, *a fortiori* (u_g, R_g) is reachable with respect to the whole set ψ, and the module returns (step 2(b)). Otherwise, a new instance of the user-role reachability problem is considered at the next iteration if the condition at step 3 does not hold, i.e. PUT does not yet store $lfp(\psi)$. If the condition at step 3 holds, by Proposition 1, we can exit the loop and return the unreachability of the goal with respect to the whole set ψ of administrative operations. The termination of the loop is guaranteed by the existence of $lfp(\psi)$. Notice how two instances of the user-role reachability problem at iterations k and $k+1$ only differ for the administrative actions in $\psi^{\leq(k+1)} \setminus \psi^{\leq k}$ while they share those in $\psi^{\leq k}$ since $\psi^{\leq k} \subseteq \psi^{\leq(k+1)}$.

4.2   Reducing the Number of Invocations to the Model Checker

Recall the first part of observation (**O2**) that suggests to find ways to reduce the number of invocations to MCMT. Our idea is to exploit two interesting capabilities of MCMT: (a) saving (to a file) the symbolic representation of the state space explored when the goal is unreachable and (b) returning a sequence of transitions that lead from the initial state to a state satisfying the goal.

The crucial observation to exploit capability (a) is that the negation of the formula representing the (fix-point) set F of backward reachable states (e.g., formula (1) in Example 3 above) is the (strongest) invariant whose intersection with the set G of states satisfying the goal is empty (see [7] for more on this point). The negation of the formula representing F (together with the other components of the instance of the user-role reachability problem that has generated it) is stored by the **Learning (Post-Processing)** module to the database labelled **Invariants** in Figure 1 and it is used in the module **Pre-processing** (see Figure 1) as follows. Assume that a new instance of the user-role reachability problem shares the same initial user-role assignment relation and the same set of administrative operations associated to a formula φ stored in the database **Invariants**. If the formula representing the new goal is such that in conjunction with φ is unsatisfiable, then we can immediately conclude that also the new goal is unreachable. We illustrate this with an example.

Example 4. Consider again the instance of the user-role reachability problem in Example 1 and formula (1) representing the the symbolic representation of the set of backward reachable states that have been visited during backward reachability. The conjunction of (1) with that representing the initial relation UA (reported in Example 1) is unsatisfiable (safety check) and MCMT returns **unreachable** (as anticipated in Example 1). At this point, the negation of (1), i.e.

$$\forall x. \begin{bmatrix} (x = u_1 \rightarrow \neg u_{r_6}(x)) \wedge (x = u_1 \rightarrow \neg u_{r_5}(x)) \wedge (x = u_1 \wedge u_{r_3}(x) \rightarrow u_{r_4}(x)) \wedge \\ (x = u_1 \wedge u_{r_2}(x) \rightarrow u_{r_4}(x)) \wedge (x = u_1 \wedge u_{r_1}(x) \rightarrow u_{r_4}(x)) \end{bmatrix} \quad (2)$$

is stored in the database **Invariants** together with the initial user-role assignment relation and administrative operations of Example 1.

Now, consider that the next instance of the user-role reachability problem to solve is composed of the same initial user-role assignment relation and administrative operations and the goal is $(u_1, \{r_5\})$. Since the conjunction of the symbolic representation of the goal, $\exists x.(x = u_1 \wedge u_{r_5}(x))$, with (2) is obviously unsatisfiable (this can be quickly established by an available SMT solver), our system immediately returns **unreachable** also for this instance without invoking MCMT.   □

Now, we turn to the problem of exploiting capability (b) of MCMT, i.e. returning a sequence σ of transitions leading from the initial state to a state satisfying the goal. For this, notice that each state generated by applying a transition in σ is indeed also reachable. The symbolic representation G of the sets of user-role assignment relations generated by the application of the administrative operations in σ (together with the initial user-role assignment relation and the sequence σ) are stored by the **Learning (Post-Processing)** module to the database labelled **Unsafe States** in Figure 1 and are used by the module **Pre-processing** (see again Figure 1) as follows. Assume that a new instance of the user-role reachability problem shares the same initial user-role assignment relation and contains at least the administrative operations in σ associated to the sequence γ of user-role assignment relations generated by the applications of the operations in σ. If the goal g of a new problem instance is in γ, then we can immediately conclude that g is reachable. We illustrate this with an example.

Example 5. Consider the following instance of the user-role reachability problem: $\langle UA, \psi, (u_1, \{r_2, r_8\}) \rangle$, where UA and ψ are those of Example 1. On the translated reachability problem, MCMT returns `reachable` with the following sequence $\sigma = (\{r_7\}, r_8); (\{r_1\}, r_2)$ of administrative operations. The sequence γ of states obtained by computing the pre-image of the goal with respect to the administrative operations in σ contains the goal itself $g_0 := \exists x.(x = u_1 \wedge u_{r_2}(x) \wedge u_{r_8}(x))$, the pre-image of g_0 with respect to $(\{r_1\}, r_2)$, i.e. $g_1 := \exists x.(x = u_1 \wedge u_{r_1}(x) \wedge u_{r_8}(x))$, and the pre-image of g_1 with respect to $(\{r_7\}, r_8)$, i.e. $\exists x.(x = u_1 \wedge u_{r_1}(x) \wedge u_{r_7}(x))$. This information is stored in the database **Unsafe States**.

If we now consider the following instance of the user-role reachability problem: $\langle UA, \psi, (u_1, \{r_1, r_8\}) \rangle$, where UA and ψ are again as in Example 1, ASASPXL immediately returns `reachable` without invoking MCMT because the symbolic representation of this goal is equal to g_1 in the database **Unsafe States**.   □

This concludes the description of the internal workings of the **Pre-processing** module in Figure 1 that tries to minimize the number of invocations of MCMT (first part of observation (**O2**)). The description of the **Learning (Post-processing)** module will be finished in the following (sub-)section.

4.3 Reusing Previously Visited States

Recall the second part of observation (**O2**) that suggests to re-use as much as possible the results of previous invocations of the model checker. Our idea is to save the sets of user-role assignment relations visited when solving the instance $P_k = \langle UA, \psi^{\le k}, (u_g, R_g) \rangle$ of the user-role reachability problem generated by the **Administrative action filter** module (see Section 4.1) so as to avoid to visit them again when solving the next instance $P_{k+1} = \langle UA, \psi^{\le (k+1)}, (u_g, R_g) \rangle$. As observed above (see the last sentence of Section 4.1), two successive instances P_k and P_{k+1} of the user-role reachability problem generated by the **Administrative action filter** module only differ for the administrative actions in $\psi^{\le (k+1)} \setminus \psi^{\le k}$ and share those in $\psi^{\le k}$. When solving P_{k+1}, it would thus be desirable to visit only the states generated by the actions in $\psi^{\le (k+1)} \setminus \psi^{\le k}$ and avoid to recompute those generated by the actions in $\psi^{\le k}$, that have already been visited when solving P_k.

The description of the missing part of the internal workings of the **Learning** (**Post-processing**) module can be completed as follows. Consider sub-problem $P_k = \langle UA, \psi^{\leq k}, (u_g, R_g) \rangle$ for $k \geq 0$. There are two cases to consider depending on the fact that (u_g, R_g) is reachable or not.

First, assume that MCMT has found (u_g, R_g) to be unreachable and that φ is the formula representing the complement of the set of backward reachable states. Before solving sub-problem P_{k+1}, the **Learning** module deletes from $\psi^{\leq (k+1)}$ the administrative actions whose symbolic representation of the (simple) pre-condition implies φ. The correctness of doing this is stated in the following proposition.

Proposition 2. Let $\langle UA, \psi, (u_g, R_g) \rangle$ be an instance of the user-role reachability problem such that (u_g, R_g) is unreachable and F is the set of backward reachable states. If $t \notin \psi$ is an administrative operation whose simple pre-condition is contained in F, then (u_g, R_g) is also unreachable when considering the instance $\langle UA, \psi \cup \{t\}, (u_g, R_g) \rangle$ of the user-role reachability problem.

The proof of this fact is based on the following two observations. First, if t is not useful then we can safely ignore it by Proposition 1. Second, if t is useful then the pre-image of F with respect to t is contained in F because, by assumption, its simple pre-condition is contained in F. We illustrate this with an example.

Example 6. Consider the instance of the user-role reachability problem in Example 1. The goal is unreachable and the set of backward reachable states F is symbolically represented as (1). Consider $t_1 = (\{r_2, \overline{r_4}\}, r_8)$: this is not useful, the pre-image of F with respect to t_1 is redundant by Proposition 1, F is a fix-point also with respect to $\psi \cup \{t_1\}$, and the goal is still unreachable. Consider now $t_2 = (\{r_2, \overline{r_4}\}, r_3)$: the pre-image of F with respect to t_2 is symbolically represented by the formula $\exists x.(u_{r_2}(x) \wedge \neg u_{r_4}(x) \wedge x = u_1)$. An available SMT solver easily shows that this formula implies (1), F is a fix-point also with respect to $\psi \cup \{t_2\}$, and the goal is still unreachable. ☐

The second case of operation for the **Learning** module is when MCMT finds (u_g, R_g) to be reachable by a sequence $\sigma = t_1; \cdots; t_n$ of administrative operations. Let $g_1; \cdots; g_n$ be the sequence of user-role assignment relations obtained by applying t_j to g_{j-1} for $j = 1, ..., n$ with $g_0 = UA$. Before solving a new instance of the user-role reachability problem with the same initial user-role assignment relation UA and whose administrative actions contain those in σ, the **Learning** module adds to $\psi^{\leq (k+1)}$ the transition having as (simple) "pre-condition" UA and as "update" g_j, for $j = 2, ...n$. (Notice that the additional transitions do not enlarge the set of reachable states.) We illustrate this with an example.

Example 7. Consider again the first instance of the user-role reachability problem of Example 5: $\langle UA, \psi, (u_1, \{r_2, r_8\}) \rangle$ where UA and ψ are those in Example 1. As already said, the goal is reachable with the sequence $\sigma = (\{r_7\}, r_8); (\{r_1\}, r_2)$. Thus, the **Learning** module would add the following (redundant) transition:

$$\exists x. \left(\begin{array}{l} u_{r_1}(x) \wedge u_{r_4}(x) \wedge u_{r_7}(x) \wedge \\ \forall y.(u'_{r_2}(y) \leftrightarrow (y = x \vee u_{r_2}(y))) \wedge \forall y.(u'_{r_8}(y) \leftrightarrow (y = x \vee u_{r_8}(y))) \end{array} \right),$$

where identical updates have been omitted for the sake of simplicity.

Consider now the following new instance of the user-role reachability problem: $\langle UA, \psi, (u_1, \{r_3\})\rangle$. It is immediate to see that the goal is reachable by the sequence $\sigma' = \sigma; (\{r_2\}, r_3)$ of administrative operations. Because of the availability of the additional transition above—whose execution has the same effect of the (atomic) sequential execution of the administrative actions in σ—the reachability of the goal can be detected in two steps instead of three.   □

As illustrated in the example, the hope is that establishing the reachability (if the case) of the goal of a new instance of the user-role reachability problem could be done by using one of the additional transitions whose effects is equivalent to the execution of several transitions, thereby speeding up the search procedure.

This concludes the description of the internal workings of the **Learning (Post-processing)** module in Figure 1.

4.4   Putting Things Together

We now describe the flow of execution among the various modules in ASASPXL (see Figure 1). The input instance $P = \langle UA, \psi, (u_g, R_g)\rangle$ of the user-role reachability problem is given to the **Pre-processing** module that searches the databases **Unsafe states** and **Invariants (Safe states)** to see whether the goal can be declared `reachable` or `unreachable` because of the cached results of previous invocations to the model checker (Section 4.2). If no previous information allows us to conclude, the instance is passed (arrow labelled with 1) to the **Administrative Action Filter** that computes a sequence $P_1, ..., P_k$ of increasingly precise approximations of P by using the notion of useful administrative operations (Section 4.1). Each P_k is sent (arrow labelled with 2) to the **Translator** that converts the problem instance to a reachability problem in MCMT input language. At this point, the model checker is invoked (arrow labelled with 3) on the resulting problem and two outcomes are possible. If the goal is unreachable, then control is given back to the **Administrative Action Filter** (arrow labelled 4.1) that considers a more precise approximation of the problem (if any) that is translated and solved again by MCMT. If this is not possible, control is passed to the **Learning** module (arrow labelled 5) that declares the instance of the user-role reachability problem to be `unreachable` and updates the database **Invariants** (Section 4.2). Instead, if the goal is found reachable by MCMT, then control is passed directly to the **Learning** module (arrow labelled 4.2) that declares the instance of the user-role reachability problem to be `reachable` and updates the database **Unsafe states** (Section 4.2).

The completeness of ASASPXL derives from the properties discussed in Sections 4.1, 4.2, and 4.3 as well as the correctness of the encoding in the module **Translation** (see end of Section 3).

5   Experiments

We have implemented ASASPXL in Python and have conducted an exhaustive experimental evaluation to compare it with MOHAWK on the set of "Complex Policies" in [9], composed of three synthetic test suites: **Test suite 1**—whose problem instances can be solved in polynomial time, **Test suite 2**—that are NP-complete, and **Test suite 3**—that are PSPACE-complete. We do not consider the "Simple Policies" in [9] as their solving time is very low and are not suited to evaluate the scalability of the tools. We do not consider other tools (e.g., RBAC-PAT [8]) as the experiments in [9] clearly shows that MOHAWK is superior. For example, RBAC-PAT when performing backward reachability is reported to seg-fault on problem instances containing at least 20 roles and 100 rules in all test suites while it is significantly slower than MOHAWK when run in forward reachability mode; e.g.,

Table 1. Experimental results on the "complex" benchmarks in [9]

Test suite	# Roles, # Rules	MOHAWK (Slicing time + Verification time)		ASASPXL	Variance	
					MOHAWK	ASASPXL
Test suite 1	3, 15	**0.42**	(0.17 + 0.25)	0.12	0.00034	0.00126
	5, 25	**0.50**	(0.20 + 0.30)	0.22	0.00104	0.02188
	20, 100	**0.60**	(0.28 + 0.32)	0.11	0.00048	0.00314
	40, 200	**0.94**	(0.39 + 0.55)	0.10	0.19242	0.00294
	200, 1000	**2.65**	(1.25 + 1.40)	0.18	0.7027	0.02758
	500, 2500	**4.87**	(2.27 + 2.60)	0.43	7.0337	0.29594
	4000, 20000	**16.90**	(11.41 + 5.49)	1.64	1.26694	0.11166
	20000, 80000	**71.56**	(44.70 + 26.86)	24.17	7.56264	0.27724
	30000, 120000	**195.54**	(119.39 + 76.15)	59.08	66.4833	0.38058
	40000, 200000	**455.14**	(263.82 + 191.32)	109.07	32.35406	2.42496
	80000, 400000	**2786.33**	(1600.22 + 1186.11)	398.63	1251.832	0.51542
Test suite 2	3, 15	**0.40**	(0.16 + 0.24)	0.12	0.00046	0.00204
	5, 25	**0.50**	(0.19 + 0.31)	0.21	0.0019	0.02012
	20, 100	**0.54**	(0.25 + 0.29)	0.10	0.00036	0.00242
	40, 200	**1.21**	(0.37 + 0.84)	0.10	1.07136	0.00108
	200, 1000	**2.54**	(1.24 + 1.30)	0.14	0.6452	0.01008
	500, 2500	**5.02**	(2.29 + 2.73)	0.43	5.91882	0.32836
	4000, 20000	**14.33**	(9.65 + 4.68)	1.48	0.53058	0.06206
	20000, 80000	**74.32**	(45.35 + 28.97)	24.99	13.9347	0.0716
	30000, 120000	**194.85**	(115.58 + 79.27)	57.09	42.39056	0.18292
	40000, 200000	**470.89**	(262.39 + 208.50)	98.49	585.6608	0.26196
	80000, 400000	**2753.12**	(1589.97 + 1163.15)	360.96	1493.596	3.19596
Test suite 3	3, 15	**0.41**	(0.17 + 0.24)	0.09	0.00012	0.00078
	5, 25	**0.47**	(0.19 + 0.28)	0.08	0.00164	0.0001
	20, 100	**0.77**	(0.29 + 0.48)	0.54	0.0771	0.08822
	40, 200	**0.77**	(0.38 + 0.39)	0.37	0.0012	0.00468
	200, 1000	**5.93**	(1.53 + 4.4)	1.51	47.2814	0.20348
	500, 2500	**3.78**	(2.05 + 1.73)	1.12	0.05662	0.00298
	4000, 20000	**14.05**	(9.96 + 4.09)	11.13	0.09255	0.317425
	20000, 80000	**80.61**	(48.64 + 31.97)	27.25	23.98093	2.974775
	30000, 120000	**259.15**	(148.35 + 110.80)	97.55	325.5216	6343.912
	40000, 200000	**604.17**	(346.10 + 258.07)	110.65	1247.141	110.9948
	80000, 400000	**3477.19**	(1951.41 + 1525.78)	402.22	2776.703	0.50856

according to [9], the instances with 20,000 roles and 80,000 rules in the three test suites are solved in around a minute by MOHAWK while RBAC-PAT goes in time out after 60 minutes.

For each set of ARBAC policies in the test suites, we have generated an instance of the user-role reachability problem by considering an empty initial user-role assignment relation and 5 distinct (randomly generated) goals that are selected to be reachable (this kind of instances of the user-role reachability problem are said to be instances of the error-finding problem in [9]).

Table 1 reports the results of running ASASPXL and MOHAWK on these instances. Column 1 reports the name of the test suite, column 2 contains the number of roles and administrative operations in the policy, column 3 and 4 the average times (in seconds) taken by MOHAWK and ASASPXL, respectively, to solve the five instances of the user-role reachability problem associated to an ARBAC policy, and column 5 the variance in solving times for MOHAWK and ASASPXL, respectively. For MOHAWK, in column 3 we report also the time spent in the slicing phase (a technique for eliminating irrelevant users, roles, and administrative operations that are non relevant to solve a certain instance of the user-role reachability problem, see [9,14] for more details) and the verification phase (i.e. the abstract-check-refine model checking technique described in [9]). All experiments were performed on an Intel Core 2 Duo T6600 (2.2 GHz) CPU with 2 GB Ram running Ubuntu 11.10.[1]

The results clearly show that ASASPXL performs significantly better than MOHAWK. In many cases, ASASPXL overall time is less than MOHAWK Verification time (see column 3), i.e. even disregarding the Slicing time. Furthermore, the behaviour of ASASPXL is more predictable than MOHAWK since the variance of the latter is much larger (see the last column of the table). The results also demonstrate the effectiveness of our approach and nicely complement the theoretical properties discussed in Section 4 that aim to guarantee that ASASPXL will not miss errors (if any). This is in contrast with MOHAWK, that, as said in [9], is incomplete and thus may not find all errors.

6 Conclusions

We have presented techniques to enable a model checker to solve large instances of the user-role reachability problem for ARBAC policies. The model checker is assumed to provide some basic functionalities such as the capability of storing the already visited sets of states for later reuse and that of returning the sequence of transitions that lead from an initial state to a state satisfying the goal (if the case). In our implementation, we have used MCMT but any model checker with these features can be plugged in. (This is so because we work under the separate administration restriction and the capability of MCMT to handle infinite state systems is not used since—as observed in, e.g., [14]—it is possible to consider just

---

[1] We thank the authors of MOHAWK for making available to us the latest version of their tool. We also thank the support team of NuSMV for their help with the installation of the tool, a necessary pre-requisite for using MOHAWK.

one administrator without loss of generality.) We have shown that the proposed techniques do not miss errors in buggy policies; this is in contrast with MOHAWK that is incomplete. We have also provided evidence that an implementation of the proposed techniques, called ASASPXL, performs significantly better than MOHAWK on the larger problem instances in [9].

As future work, we plan to design and implement ASASP 2.0, a tool that combines the flexibility of ASASP [2] with the scalability of ASASPXL. To this end, we are currently collecting a database of heterogeneous problem instances that will help us to understand the right level of expressiveness. In this respect, the benchmark problems recently proposed in [6] (together with those in [3]) will be of particular interest since the analysis must be done with respect to a finite but unknown number of users. For such problems, the capability of MCMT to handle infinite state systems will be key.

Acknowledgements. This work was partially supported by the "Automated Security Analysis of Identity and Access Management Systems (SIAM)" project funded by Provincia Autonoma di Trento in the context of the "team 2009 - Incoming" COFUND action of the European Commission (FP7).

References

1. http://research.microsoft.com/en-us/um/redmond/projects/z3
2. Alberti, F., Armando, A., Ranise, S.: ASASP: Automated Symbolic Analysis of Security Policies. In: Bjørner, N., Sofronie-Stokkermans, V. (eds.) CADE 2011. LNCS, vol. 6803, pp. 26–33. Springer, Heidelberg (2011)
3. Alberti, F., Armando, A., Ranise, S.: Efficient Symbolic Automated Analysis of Administrative Role Based Access Control Policies. In: ASIACCS, ACM Pr. (2011)
4. Armando, A., Ranise, S.: Automated Symbolic Analysis of ARBAC-Policies. In: Cuellar, J., Lopez, J., Barthe, G., Pretschner, A. (eds.) STM 2010. LNCS, vol. 6710, pp. 17–34. Springer, Heidelberg (2011)
5. Crampton, J.: Understanding and developing role-based administrative models. In: Proc. 12th CCS, pp. 158–167. ACM Press (2005)
6. Ferrara, A.L., Madhusudan, P., Parlato, G.: Security Analysis of Access Control Policies through Program Verification. In: CSF (2012)
7. Ghilardi, S., Ranise, S.: Backward Reachability of Array-based Systems by SMT solving: Termination and Invariant Synthesis. In: LMCS, vol. 6(4) (2010)
8. Gofman, M.I., Luo, R., Solomon, A.C., Zhang, Y., Yang, P., Stoller, S.D.: Rbac-Pat: A policy analysis tool for role based access control. In: Kowalewski, S., Philippou, A. (eds.) TACAS 2009. LNCS, vol. 5505, pp. 46–49. Springer, Heidelberg (2009)
9. Jayaraman, K., Ganesh, V., Tripunitara, M., Rinard, M., Chapin, S.: Automatic Error Finding for Access-Control Policies. In: CCS, ACM (2011)
10. Jha, S., Li, N., Tripunitara, M.V., Wang, Q., Winsborough, H.: Towards formal verification of role-based access control policies. IEEE TDSC 5(4), 242–255 (2008)
11. Li, N., Tripunitara, M.V.: Security analysis in role-based access control. ACM TISSEC 9(4), 391–420 (2006)
12. Sandhu, R., Coyne, E., Feinstein, H., Youmann, C.: Role-Based Access Control Models. IEEE Computer 2(29), 38–47 (1996)
13. Sasturkar, A., Yang, P., Stoller, S.D., Ramakrishnan, C.R.: Policy analysis for administrative role based access control. In: CSF. IEEE Press (July 2006)
14. Stoller, S.D., Yang, P., Ramakrishnan, C.R., Gofman, M.I.: Efficient policy analysis for administrative role based access control. In: CCS. ACM Press (2007)

Constrained Role Mining

Carlo Blundo[1] and Stelvio Cimato[2]

[1] DI, Università degli studi di Salerno – 84011 Fisciano, Italy
[2] DI, Università degli studi di Milano – 26013 Crema, Italy

Abstract. Role Based Access Control (RBAC) is a very popular access control model, for a long time investigated and widely deployed in the security architecture of different enterprises. To implement RBAC, roles have to be firstly identified within the considered organization. Usually the process of (automatically) defining the roles in a bottom up way, starting from the permissions assigned to each user, is called *role mining*. In literature, the role mining problem has been formally analyzed and several techniques have been proposed in order to obtain a set of valid roles.

Recently, the problem of defining different kind of constraints on the number and the size of the roles included in the resulting role set has been addressed. In this paper we provide a formal definition of the role mining problem under the cardinality constraint, i.e. restricting the maximum number of permissions that can be included in a role. We discuss formally the computational complexity of the problem and propose a novel heuristic. Furthermore we present experimental results obtained after the application of the proposed heuristic on both real and synthetic datasets, and compare the resulting performance to previous proposals.

1 Introduction

Role Based Access Control (RBAC) is a very popular access control model, for a long time investigated and widely deployed in the security architecture of different enterprises, since the early 1990s [4,7]. The goal of RBAC is to provide and manage access to restricted resources in an efficient way. To implement RBAC, roles have to be firstly identified within the considered organization, collecting sets of permissions in roles and then assigning roles according to the responsibilities and qualifications of each employee. The advantage coming from the adoption of the RBAC model is that access control can be centralized and decoupled from users and the costs and the overhead of the security management can be reduced.

The correct definition of the set of roles which satisfies the needs of the organization is the most difficult and costly task to be performed during the implementation of a RBAC system. Such an activity is often referred to as *role engineering* and includes the correct identification of roles from the current structural organization of the enterprise. Mainly this task, i.e. the extraction of a complete and efficient set of roles, can be performed using two approaches: *top-down* or

A. Jøsang, P. Samarati, and M. Petrocchi (Eds.): STM 2012, LNCS 7783, pp. 289–304, 2013.

bottom-up role engineering. In the first case, roles are defined after that the functionalities of the organization have been well analyzed, and elicitation activities have been performed. The top down approach usually is labor intensive and involves a large amount of work and time done by humans especially in large enterprises with a large number of business processes, as reported in some case study are available in the literature [19]. On the other hand, the bottom-up process, often denoted also as *role mining*, starts from the analysis of the current set of permissions assigned to users, and tries to aggregate them in order to extract and define roles. Obviously, hybrid approaches can exist in which both directions, top-down and bottom-up, can be used in subsequent steps of the analysis in order to refine the returned set of roles.

Bottom-up approach to role mining has been more investigated, since many techniques borrowed from data mining can be applied in an automatic way to the existing configuration of user-permission assignments. A RBAC system can be easily constructed in this way and a starting set of roles can be fastly generated. The problem with such an approach, is that the quality and the number of returned roles often are not so good, since no semantics is taken into consideration when the role mining process is started. In many situations the returned set of roles might not match any functional organization within the analyzed enterprise and the existing business processes might not be adequately represented. An accurate analysis of the returned results is needed to better tune the retrieved representation of roles to the current organizational requirements of the enterprise. A formal definition of the Role Mining Problem (RMP) and some of its variants has been given and deeply analyzed in [24]. There, the NP-completeness of the (decisional) RMP problem has been proved, and the formulation of RMP as a graph covering problem has been done in [6,27].

The problem of imposing constraints on the set of roles resulting after the role mining process has been considered in the past. Statically or dynamically mutually exclusive roles constraints have been included in RBAC models [20] and in the NASI/NIST standards [7]. According to these constraints, for examples, no user can be assigned contemporary a given set of mutually exclusive roles, or no user can activate simultaneously a set of roles in the same session. Such constraints are often used as mechanisms to achieve Separation Of Duty principles (SOD), preventing one user from having a large number of roles to complete a task, or imposing restrictions on the minimum number of users needed to perform a critical activity [15].

Constraints are then important since they simply allow the role engineer to express some restrictions directly impacting the security of the returned organizational structure. And this is even more valuable when an automatic process, such as role mining, is used to generate the roles and implement the required security policy.

Recently, a simple classification of the constraints on the cardinality of the number of roles, users and permissions for a given RBAC system has been proposed [16]. The first heuristic taking into account a cardinality constraint on the number of permissions contained in a role has been proposed by [14]. In this work, however, the proposed results have been compared only w.r. to other heuristics which were not able to consider constraints on roles. Role-usage cardinality constraints have been considered in [11], where two approaches, one based on role priority, the other on permission coverage, have been presented.

In this work we propose a novel heuristic for mining RBAC roles under cardinality constraint. The algorithm is based on a previous proposal [1], where an initial candidate role set was constructed by considering one role for each user on the basis of the current assignment of permissions. The role set is then refined and updated by eliminating the roles obtained as union of other roles already included in the set and ensuring that the cardinality constraint is respected. The resulting procedure is very efficient in terms of computation time and quality of returned role set. To this aim we present the results obtained by running our heuristics on different datasets, some available over the network, some artificially created. The results are compared with our implementation of the algorithm presented in [14] and analyzed in terms of the metrics presented in [18].

The remainder of this paper is organized as follows. In the next section we discuss related works. Section 2 contains the preliminary concepts needed to define the constrained role mining problem and the discussion on its complexity. In section 4 we introduce our heuristics and compare the solution with related work in section 5. Finally Section 7 presents our conclusions and ongoing work.

2   Constrained RMP

In this section we introduce the CONSTRAINED ROLE MINING PROBLEM and analyze its computational complexity showing that it is NP-complete while its optimization version is NP-hard.

The notation we use is borrowed from the NIST standard for *Core Role-Based Access Control* (Core RBAC) [7] and it is adapted to our needs. We denote with $\mathcal{U} = \{u_1, \ldots, u_n\}$ the set of users, with $\mathcal{P} = \{p_1, \ldots, p_m\}$ the set of permissions, and with $\mathcal{R} = \{r_1, \ldots, r_s\}$ the set of roles, where, for any $r \in \mathcal{R}$, we have $r \subseteq \mathcal{P}$. We also define the following relations. $\mathcal{URA} \subseteq \mathcal{U} \times \mathcal{R}$ is a many-to-many mapping *user-to-role* assignment relation. $\mathcal{RPA} \subseteq \mathcal{R} \times \mathcal{P}$ is a many-to-many mapping *role-to-permission* assignment relation. $\mathcal{UPA} \subseteq \mathcal{U} \times \mathcal{P}$ is a many-to-many mapping *user-to-permission* assignment relation. $\mathcal{RH} \subseteq \mathcal{R} \times \mathcal{R}$ is a partial order over $\mathcal{R}$, which is called a *role hierarchy*. When $(r_1, r_2) \in \mathcal{RH}$, we say that the role r_1 is senior to r_2.

When needed, we will represent the assignment relations by binary matrices. For instance, by UPA we denote the $\mathcal{UPA}$'s matrix representation. The binary matrix UPA satisfies $\text{UPA}[i][j] = 1$ if and only if $(u_i, p_j) \in \mathcal{UPA}$. This means that user u_i possesses permission p_j. In a similar way, we define the matrices URA, RPA, and RH.

Given the $n \times m$ users-to-permissions assignment matrix UPA, the *role mining problem* (see [24], [6], and [8]) consists in finding an $n \times k$ binary matrix URA and a $k \times m$ binary matrix RPA such that, $\text{UPA} = \text{URA} \otimes \text{RPA}$, where, the operator $\otimes$ is such that, for $1 \leq i \leq n$ and $1 \leq j \leq m$, $\mathsf{UPA}[i][j] = \bigvee_{h=1}^{k}(\mathsf{URA}[i][h] \wedge \mathsf{RPA}[h][j])$. Therefore, in solving a role mining problem, we are looking for a factorization of the matrix UPA. The smallest value k for which UPA can be factorized as $\mathsf{URA} \otimes \mathsf{RPA}$ is referred to as the *binary rank* of UPA. A *candidate* role consists of a set of permissions along with a user-to-role assignment. The union of the candidate roles is referred to as *candidate role-set*. A candidate role-set is called *complete* if the permissions described by any UPA's row can be exactly *covered* by the union of some candidate roles. In other words, a candidate role-set is complete if and only if it is a *solution* of the *equation* $\mathsf{URA} \otimes \mathsf{RPA}$. In this paper we consider only complete candidate role-set.

By adding a constraint t on the number of permissions that can be assigned to any role, the *t-constrained role mining problem* can be defined, as follows. Given an $n \times m$ users-to-permissions assignment matrix UPA and a positive integer $t > 1$, find an $n \times k$ binary matrix URA and a $k \times m$ binary matrix RPA such that $\mathsf{UPA} = \mathsf{URA} \otimes \mathsf{RPA}$ and, for any $1 \leq i \leq k$, one has $|\{j : \mathsf{RPA}[i][j] = 1\}| \leq t$. The computational complexity of the above define problem will be discussed in the next section.

2.1 NP-Completeness

The computational complexity of the ROLE MINING PROBLEM (and of some of its variants) was considered in several papers (see, for instance, [24], [3], [6], and [25]). where it was shown its NP-completeness (by reducing it to the SET BASIS DECISION PROBLEM). The decisional version of the t-CONSTRAINED ROLE MINING PROBLEM can be defined, as follows:

Problem 1. (*t*-CONSTRAINED ROLE MINING DECISION PROBLEM) Given a set of users $\mathcal{U}$, a set of permissions $\mathcal{P}$, a user-permission assignment $\mathcal{UPA}$, and two positive integers t and k, with $t > 1$ and $k < \min\{|\mathcal{U}|, |\mathcal{P}|\}$, are there a set of roles $\mathcal{R}$, a user-to-role assignment $\mathcal{URA}$, and a role-to-permission assignment $\mathcal{RPA}$ such that $|\mathcal{R}| \leq k$, $\mathsf{UPA} = \mathsf{URA} \otimes \mathsf{RPA}$, and, for any $r \in \mathcal{R}$, $|r| \leq t$?

Theorem 1. *The t*-CONSTRAINED ROLE MINING DECISION PROBLEM *is NP-complete.*

To prove that the above defined problem is NP-complete it is necessary to show that it is in NP, and that another NP-complete problem can be reduced to it in polynomial time. It is very easy to show that the ROLE MINING DECISION PROBLEM can be used in the proof of the above theorem, proving then the NP-completeness of the t-CONSTRAINED ROLE MINING DECISION PROBLEM. Similarly, the optimization version of the t-CONSTRAINED ROLE MINING PROBLEM can be defined and its NP-hardness proved.

In [23], Stockmeyer proved that the SET BASIS DECISION PROBLEM is NP-complete by reducing to it the VERTEX COVER DECISION PROBLEM (one of Karp's 21 NP-complete problems [12], see also problem GT1 in [9]). The VERTEX COVER OPTIMIZATION PROBLEM is APX-complete [5], that is, it cannot be approximated within any constant factor in polynomial time unless P=NP. Therefore, we have the following simple non-approximability result:

Theorem 2. *The t-*CONSTRAINED ROLE MINING OPTIMIZATION PROBLEM *cannot be approximated within any constant factor in polynomial time unless P=NP.*

3   Related Works

Role engineering has been firstly introduced by Coyne et al in [4] where the definition of a top down process for the definition of roles has been discussed. Along the same research line, several other works have been presented [19], but recently, the focus of role engineering has turned to consider more automated techniques, based on the bottom up approach, where data mining techniques are applied for the definition of roles [13]. Role mining algorithms have been presented based on set covering [3], graph theory [6,27], subset enumeration [26], database tiling [24]. The theoretical aspects of the RMP have been considered in [25,24,3], where the complexity of the problem has been analyzed and its equivalence to other known optimization problem showed. Another interrelated problem, i.e. dealing with the semantic meaning of roles, has been addressed in [17].

Cardinality constraints on the number of permissions included in a role have been firstly considered in [14], and a heuristic algorithm called Constrained Role Miner (CRM) has been proposed. The CRM algorithm takes in input the UPA matrix and returns a set of roles, each one satisfying the given cardinality constraint. CRM is based on the idea of clustering users having the same set of permissions and selecting, as candidate roles, the roles composed of the set of permissions satisfying the constraint and having the highest number of associated users. In [14], the performances of the algorithm are evaluated on real world datasets considering different metrics (such as the number of returned roles, the sum of the size of the user assignment and permission assignment matrices and so on), with respect to other previously proposed algorithms. However the comparison is performed without considering constraints, since the other algorithms return a complete set of roles but have not the capability of managing constraints. In section 5 we evaluate our proposal against the result obtained after our implementation of the CRM algorithm, considering both real world and synthetic datasets. A different kind of cardinality constraints, considering the number of user-role assignments, have been considered in [10]. Such constraints can be useful when the number of persons that can be assigned to a given role (e.g. the number of directors, managers, etc) in a given organization is known or can be fixed. In the paper, three algorithms have been proposed based on a graph approach, where the role mining problem is mapped to the problem of finding minimum biclique cover of the edges of a bipartite graph. The three heuristics are obtained by modifying the basic greedy algorithm proposed in [6], and experimental results on real world datasets are reported considering some constraints on the number of users that can be assigned to any role. Finally cardinality constraints have also been considered in [16] where a representation of the constraints in terms of association rules is proposed: permissions are regarded as attributes, and each user-permission assignment as a transaction. To generate mutually exclusive permissions constraints, i.e. set of permissions that cannot be assigned to the same role, an algorithm is proposed, based on known techniques for mining association rules in databases, and its performance evaluated on synthetically generated datasets.

4   Heuristics

In this section we present a family of heuristics. Each heuristic takes as input the matrix UPA and returns a complete role set satisfying the cardinality constraint (i.e., at most t permissions are associated to each role). We borrow the ideas from the heuristics presented in [1] and we adapt them to handle the cardinality constraint.

The basic idea is to select from UPA all rows having less than t permissions in an order that will be defined below. Such rows will correspond to candidate roles that will be added to the candidate role-set. If there is no row having at most t permissions, then a row is selected and, t of the permissions included in the row are chosen (the way we select such row and permissions gives rise to different heuristics). The selected permissions produce a role that is added to the candidate role-set. Then, all rows *covered* by the candidate role-set are removed from UPA and the procedure is iterated until the UPA matrix contains some rows.

The above sketched procedure is more formally described by Algorithm 1 where we use the following notation. Given an $a \times b$ binary matrix M, for $1 \leq i \leq a$, with M[i] we denote the M's i-th row; while, with |M[i]| we denote the number of ones appearing in M[i]. The procedures NUMCOLS(M) and NUMROWS(M), return the number of columns and rows, respectively, of the matrix M. For a set S and an integer h, the procedure FIRST(S, h) returns the first h elements listed in the set S. Given a user-permission assignment matrix UPA, a new candidate role is generated by selecting a UPA's row having the least number of permissions with ties broken at random (Lines 6-8 of Algorithm 1). If the number of permissions associated to the selected row (i.e., the number of 1s in UPA[$selectedRow$]) is at most t, then a new role is created (Line 9 of Algorithm 1) and is added to the candidate role-set (Line 21 of Algorithm 1). In this algorithm, the matrix *uncoveredP* represents the users' permissions that are not covered by the roles in *candidateRoles*. Once a role (i.e, *newRole*) to be added to the *candidateRoles* set is discovered, the procedure SETTOZERO updates the matrix *uncoveredP* according to *newRole*. All rows whose permissions are covered by the candidate roles are removed from both matrices *uncoveredP* and UPA (Lines 22-23 of Algorithm 1), running the procedure REMOVECOVEREDUSERS [1]. Algorithm 1 halts when all UPA's rows have been removed (Line 5 of Algorithm 1).

---

[1] Actually, in our implementation SETTOZERO updates both *uncoveredP* and UPA, but in Algorithm 1, for the sake of clarity, we prefer to keep separate the updating of such matrices.

Algorithm 1. t-SMA$_R$(UPA, t, *selection*)

1: *candidateRoles* $\leftarrow \emptyset$
2: *uncoveredP* $\leftarrow$ UPA
3: $np \leftarrow$ NUMCOLS(UPA) /* np is equal to the number of permissions */
4: $nr \leftarrow$ NUMROWS(UPA) /* nr is equal to the number of users */
5: **while** NUMROWS(UPA) > 0 **do**
6:     $m \leftarrow \min\{|\text{UPA}[i]| : 1 \leq i \leq nr\}$
7:     *candidateRows* $\leftarrow \{i : 1 \leq i \leq nr$ and $|\text{UPA}[i]| = m\}$
8:     *selectedRow* $\leftarrow_R$ *candidateRows*
9:     *newRole* $\leftarrow \{p_j : 1 \leq j \leq np$ and $\text{UPA}[selectedRow][j] = 1\}$
10:     **if** $|newRole| > t$ and *selection* $== 0$ **then**
11:         *newRole* $\leftarrow$ FIRST(*newRole*, t)
12:     **else if** $|newRole| > t$ and *selection* $== 1$ **then**
13:         $m \leftarrow \min\{|uncoveredP[i]| : 1 \leq i \leq nr\}$
14:         *candidateRows* $\leftarrow \{i : 1 \leq i \leq nr$ and $|uncoveredP[i]| = m\}$
15:         *selectedRow* $\leftarrow_R$ *candidateRows*
16:         *newRole* $\leftarrow \{p_j : 1 \leq j \leq np$ and $uncoveredP[selectedRow][j] = 1\}$
17:         **if** $|newRole| > t$ **then**
18:             *newRole* $\leftarrow$ FIRST(*newRole*, t)
19:         **end if**
20:     **end if**
21:     *candidateRoles* $\leftarrow$ *candidateRoles* $\cup \{newRole\}$
22:     *uncoveredP* $\leftarrow$ setToZero(UPA, *uncoveredP*, *newRole*)
23:     UPA $\leftarrow$ REMOVECOVEREDUSERS(UPA, *candidateRoles*)
24: **end while**
25: **return** *candidateRoles*

If the number of permissions exceeds the cardinality constraint, then two possible ways of selecting the role to be added to the candidate role-set have been considered. These two possibilities gave rise to two heuristics referred to as *t*-SMA$_R$-0 and *t*-SMA$_R$-1, respectively. In *t*-SMA$_R$-0 (i.e., when *selection* is set to 0 in Algorithm 1), the new role will simply contain the first t permissions associated to the selected row (Lines 10-11 of Algorithm 1). While, in *t*-SMA$_R$-1 (i.e., when *selection* is set to 1 in Algorithm 1) one of the rows (Lines 13-16 of Algorithm 1) of the matrix *uncoveredP* having the least number of permissions is selected, ties broken at random. If the selected row is associated to more than t permissions, then the new role will include only its first t permissions (Lines 17-19 of Algorithm 1).

Algorithm 1 returns a set of roles (i.e., rows and subsets of rows) exactly covering the UPA matrix. As described in [1], it is possible to consider the covering of the matrix UPA by using its its columns (instead of the rows). We refer to such a *new* heuristic based on columns as *t*-SMA$_C$. The only difference between heuristics *t*-SMA$_R$ and *t*-SMA$_C$ is the way a role is computed. Heuristic *t*-SMA$_C$ selects a permission p (i.e., a UPA column) associated to the least number of users.

Setting $\mathcal{U}(p) = \{u \in \mathcal{U} : (u, p) \in \mathcal{URA}\}$ (i.e, all users having permission p), the role r_p induced by permission p is defined as $r_p = \{p' : \mathcal{U}(p) \subseteq \mathcal{U}(p')\} \cup \{p\}$. If $|r_p| \leq t$, then the role is added to the candidate role-set; otherwise, we a role including the "first" t permissions in r_p is added to the candidate role-set. As for heuristics t-SMA$_R$, rows covered by roles in the candidate role-set are removed. The process is iterated until the UPA matrix contains some rows (t-SMA$_C$'s pseudo-code is quite similar to the one for t-SMA$_R$, hence it is omitted).

5   Experimental Results

In this section we evaluate the proposed heuristic by presenting some experimental results obtained executing our heuristics on several input test cases and report some comparisons of their performance to previous proposals. We compare our heuristics with the one described in [14] (from now on denoted CRM). As far as we know, [14] is the only paper to have considered the problem of constructing a role set under cardinality constraints on the roles. In this sense, that is the first comparison between two heuristics dealing with cardinality constraints, since in [14] much of the discussion of the experimental results focused on the comparisons with other heuristics having no limitations on the size of the roles.

Dataset	#Users	#Perms	|UPA|	min#Perms	max#Perms	Density
Healtcare	46	46	1,486	7	46	70.23%
Domino	79	231	730	1	209	4.00%
Emea	35	3,046	7,220	9	554	6.77%
Firewall1	365	709	31,951	1	617	12.35%
Firewall2	325	590	36,428	6	590	19.00%
Apj	2,044	1,164	6,841	1	58	0.29%
Americas large	3,485	10,127	185,294	1	733	0.53%
Americas small	3,477	1,587	105,205	1	310	1.91%
Customer	10,021	277	45,427	0	25	1.64%

Fig. 1. Real-world datasets

The comparison takes into account the metrics introduced in [18]. The goal is to validate our proposal, by showing that its performance, regarding both the execution speed and the *quality* of the returned role set, is equivalent or better than the one returned by CRM. We would like to point out that, using our implementation of CRM, in some cases we obtained different values from the ones presented in [14]. This could be due to different choices in the two implementations (for instance, in our implementation, ties broken at random while it is not clear how they are handled in [14]). Moreover, we had to resolve some ambiguities we found in the description of Algorithm 2 in [14].

All heuristics have been implemented by using Scilab [22] Version 5.3.0 on a MacBook Pro running Mac OS X 10.6.7 (2.66 Ghz Intel Core i7, 4GB 1067Mhz

Dataset	Heuristic	Parameters						
		NR	|RH|	|URA|	|UPA|	S1	S2	CPU time
Healtcare	t-SMA$_R$	16	25	352	429	806	822	0.0107
	t-SMA$_C$	14	23	317	354	694	708	0.0263
	CRM	14	0	317	53	370	384	0.0940
Domino	t-SMA$_R$	20	30	142	627	799	819	0.0176
	t-SMA$_C$	22	42	186	628	856	878	0.0720
	CRM	20	0	177	564	741	761	0.1604
Emea	t-SMA$_R$	34	0	35	7211	7246	7280	0.1425
	t-SMA$_C$	40	20	63	7514	7597	7637	0.0787
	CRM	34	0	35	7211	7246	7280	1.8257
Firewall 1	t-SMA$_R$	71	90	2048	4398	6536	6607	0.8944
	t-SMA$_C$	74	102	3130	2800	6032	6106	0.1266
	CRM	68	10	2465	840	3315	3383	2.6367
Firewall 2	t-SMA$_R$	10	13	836	1119	1968	1978	0.0601
	t-SMA$_C$	10	10	963	998	1971	1981	0.0385
	CRM	10	0	963	591	1554	1564	0.1246
Apj	t-SMA$_R$	475	304	3152	2764	6220	6695	39.0043
	t-SMA$_C$	465	320	3578	2455	6353	6818	4.5203
	CRM	455	3	3488	1391	4882	5337	184.9613
Americas small	t-SMA$_R$	225	276	5045	17680	23001	23226	21.7423
	t-SMA$_C$	204	383	11936	8580	20899	21103	2.5487
	CRM	209	70	15580	3249	18899	19108	54.4594
Americas large	t-SMA$_R$	430	115	3653	103541	107309	107739	157.7549
	t-SMA$_C$	612	1647	10579	84559	96785	97397	24.4408
	CRM	415	32	4333	87118	91483	91898	796.2600
Customer	t-SMA$_R$	1154	4559	46511	7519	58589	59743	255.4128
	t-SMA$_C$	276	218	45425	531	46174	46450	9.3343
	CRM	277	2	45443	279	45724	46001	425.8314

Fig. 2. Results of the three heuristics over the real-world datasets

DDR3 SDRAM). In the next section, we compare our heuristics with respect to CRM over available real-world datasets; while, in Section 5.2, we present the results obtained running the implementation of the heuristics over synthetically generated datasets.

5.1 Real-World Datasets

In this section we evaluate the performance of the CRM heuristic and of our t-SMA$_R$ and t-SMA$_C$ heuristics, by comparing the results obtained using as input the real-world datasets listed in Table 1, Such real-world datasets are available online at HP Labs [21] and have been used for evaluation of several other role mining heuristics [6,18,14]. The datasets *Americas small* and *Americas large* have been obtained from Cisco firewalls granting access to the HP network to authenticated users (users' access depends on their profiles). Similar datasets are *Apj* and *Emea*. The *Healthcare* dataset was obtained from the US Veteran's Administration; the *Domino* dataset was obtained from a Lotus Domino server; *Customer* is based on the access control graph obtained from the IT department of an HP customer. Finally, the *Firewall1* and *Firewall2* datasets are obtained as result of executing an analysis algorithm on Checkpoint firewalls. The main characteristics of the nine datasets are reported in Table 1, where the number of users and permissions (second and third columns, respectively), the overall number of permissions (i.e., |UPA|), the minimum and maximum number of permissions assigned to a user (sixth and seventh column, respectively), and the UPA's density (i.e., the ratio between |UPA| and the UPA size – #Users × #Perms) are listed.

The considered metrics are obtained by selecting different values for the weights as suggested in [18], when the general *weighted structural complexity* as a criterion to measure the quality of the returned RBAC configuration is adopted. In our case, we focused on the number of roles (NR), the size of the role hierarchy (|RH|), the size of the user-to-role assignment matrix (|URA|), the size of the role-to-permission assignment matrix (|RPA|), the sum |URA| + |RPA| + |RH| denoted by $S1$, the size of NR + |URA| + |UPA| + |RH| denoted by $S2$, and the execution time expressed in seconds. This is not at all equivalent to real-world time, but we used those data to compare CPU usage among different heuristics as it is irrespective of background processes that might slow down the execution.

Firstly the heuristics have been tested when there is no constraint on the role size (i.e., we set t equal to the max number of permissions). In this case, in Algorithm 1, setting the parameter *selection* either to 0 or to 1 has no effect on the returned candidate role-set. The results obtained by running the three heuristics are listed in Figure 2, where both heuristics t-SMA$_R$-0 and t-SMA$_R$-1 are denoted by t-SMA$_R$. Both our heuristics behave pretty well on the nine datasets. Considering the size of the candidate role-set generated by the heuristics, in four cases out of nine (i.e., *Healtcare, Domino, Emea*, and *Firewall2*) our heuristics provide the same results as CRM. In four cases out of nine (i.e., *Firewall1, Apj, Americas small*, and *Americas large*) CRM returns a (not so much) smaller role-set. Finally, for the *Customer* dataset t-SMA$_C$ returns the smallest role-set. Considering the CPU time, our heuristics outperform CRM with improvements ranging from 50% to 90%. Considering also the $S1$ and $S2$ parameters, it is possible to observe that CRM has a better performance, except for the *Emea* dataset.

The proposed heuristics have also been evaluated considering different values for the threshold constraint. Tests have been performed on all the nine datasets, but due to space limitation, here only the results for the *America small* dataset with $t \in \{22 + 12 \cdot i \mid 0 \leq i \leq 24\}$ (see Figure 3) are reported. In general, there are few differences between the behavior of t-SMA$_R$-0 and t-SMA$_R$-1. Indeed, the graphics associated to them almost overlap. As expected, the number of roles increases when the constraint value decreases, i.e. when few permissions can be assigned to each role. Our heuristics always return a smaller role-set than the one computed by CRM. It is possible to observe that the value of the constraint

t does not affect much the computation time of our heuristics (the same happens to CRM unless $t < 46$). Anyway, CRM's computation time is 2.5 times larger than t-SMA$_C$'s time and about 20 times larger than t-SMA$_R$-0's (t-SMA$_R$-1) computation time.

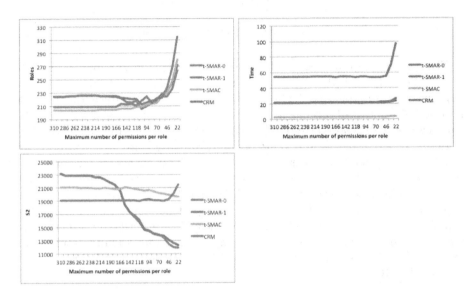

Fig. 3. Comparison of the four heuristics run on the America small dataset

Finally, considering the $S2$ parameter, according to Figure 3, in our heuristics as the value of t decreases, the $S2$ parameter decreases as well, while for heuristic CRM, the value of the $S2$ parameter does not change much unless $t < 46$. For $310 \leq t \leq 166$, CRM generates solutions with smaller values for $S2$ with respect to our heuristics, while, for $166 < t \leq 22$, our heuristics have better performance.

5.2 Synthetic Datasets

In this section, we report the performance evaluation of our heuristics on synthetic datasets. We followed the approach suggested in [26] generating the datasets by a synthetic data generator. Such a generator takes as input five parameters: the number of roles NR, the number of users NU, the number of permissions NP, the maximal number of roles MRU that can be assigned to each user, and the maximal number of permissions MPR each role can have. To generate the role-to-permission assignment, for each role r, the generator chooses a random number $N_r \in [1, MPR]$, then it randomly chooses N_r permissions from $\mathcal{P}$ and assigns them to r. In this way, the RPA matrix is constructed. To obtain the URA matrix, the generator, for each user u, chooses a random number $M_r \in [1, MRU]$, then it randomly chooses M_r roles from the generated ones and assigns them to u. Then, the UPA matrix is implicitly defined.

NR	NU	NP	MRU	MPR
100	2000	100	3	10
100	2000	500	3	50
100	2000	1000	3	100
100	2000	2000	3	200

Fig. 4. Test parameters with fixed NP/MPR ratio

The datasets have been generated using the parameters summarized in Figure 4. As the synthetic data generator is randomized, for each set of parameters, ten runs have been considered. On each randomly generated dataset (i.e. for each returned UPA matrix) both our heuristics and CRM were run and for a specific parameter set, all reported results have been averaged over the ten runs.

In all the experiments, the value of the cardinality constraint has been set equal to the maximum number of permissions that can be assigned to each role (i.e., $t = MPR$). The heuristics have been tested on several different datasets obtained by keeping constant some of the parameters while others ranged over different values. For the sake of brevity, we report here only the results of the experiments on the test parameters reported in Figure 4, where the maximum number of permission per roles ranges from 10 to 200 (and then the same holds for the value of constraint parameter t), while the ratio NP/MRP is constant and equal to 10.

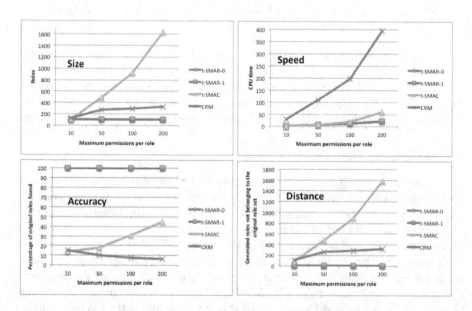

Fig. 5. Comparison of the four heuristics run on the synthetic dataset for fixed NP/MPR ratio: Role-set size, CPU time, Accuracy, and distance

MPR	Heuristic	Parameters						
		NR	$|RH|$	$|URA|$	$|UPA|$	S1	S2	CPU time
10	t-SMA$_R$-0	99.8	59.9	5548.6	503.4	6111.9	6211.7	1.245
	t-SMA$_R$-1	99.8	59.9	5548.6	503.4	6111.9	6211.7	1.261
	t-SMA$_C$	99.6	15.3	16611.3	115.5	16742.1	16841.7	0.299
	CRM	126.1	70.6	18274.9	171.3	18516.8	18642.9	28.223
50	t-SMA$_R$-0	101.9	17.5	3673.5	2550.4	6111.9	6343.3	5.735
	t-SMA$_R$-1	102.2	21.3	3677	2550.4	6111.9	6350.9	5.735
	t-SMA$_C$	490.5	502	82506.2	1035.9	84044.1	84534.6	5.845
	CRM	269.4	383	30337.3	2292.6	18516.8	33012.9	110.091
100	t-SMA$_R$-0	101.4	12.3	3622.6	4820.7	8455.6	8557.0	11.809
	t-SMA$_R$-1	101.5	13.8	3622.9	4820.7	8457.4	8558.9	11.807
	t-SMA$_C$	924.6	1674.4	152401.2	2978.7	157054.3	157978.9	19.383
	CRM	289.9	393.0	31625.3	4564.0	36582.3	36872.2	195.959
200	t-SMA$_R$-0	100.0	3.1	3451.1	9914.5	13368.7	13468.7	21.838
	t-SMA$_R$-1	100.0	3.1	3451.1	9914.5	13368.7	13468.7	21.806
	t-SMA$_C$	1634.0	4301.4	270813.9	7924.0	283039.3	284673.3	59.069
	CRM	329.5	476.1	34188.6	9741.2	44405.9	44735.4	393.904

Fig. 6. Results of the four heuristics over synthetic datasets

For each set of parameters the size of the complete role-set generated running the heuristics, as well as the CPU time needed to compute the complete role-set (see Figure 5) are reported. The heuristics are also evaluated considering also *Accuracy* and *Distance*. *Accuracy* is defined as the ratio between the number of generated roles exactly matching the *original* roles and the size of role sets generated by the synthetic data generator (i.e., we measure the percentage of original roles found by the heuristics). Given a complete role-set generated by any of the heuristics, the *Distance* parameter measures how *different* is the role-set generated by the heuristic from the original one (i.e., if R_G is the role-set generated by the synthetic data generator and R_F is the role-set computed by the heuristic, then $Distance = |R_F \backslash R_G|$). According to data summarized in Figure 5, results returned by t-SMA$_R$-0 and t-SMA$_R$-1 are identical and the graphics associated to them overlap. Both heuristics are much better than CRM. Indeed, they compute in few seconds a role-set having 100% *Accuracy* and null *Distance* meaning that the role-set generate by the synthetic data generator is completely reconstructed for all the considered test cases. Notice that CRM's *Accuracy* is less than 20% and *Distance* and CPU time increases as the maximum number of permissions per role does. Both t-SMA$_R$-0 and t-SMA$_R$-1 heuristics, always return a role-set containing about 100 roles, while CRM returns a much larger role-set (i.e., 4 to 15 times larger). We also evaluated all heuristics using the metrics considered in Section 5.1. Results are summarized in Figure 6 where it is possible to observe that, although in some case CRM returns good values for $|UPA|$, in general its performances are not very good.

6   Extensions

In this section we briefly discuss some possible extensions to the heuristics we presented.

Preprocessing. The presented heuristics start building the role-set from scratch, i.e. by selecting rows of the UPA matirix as candidate roles. It would be possible as well to consider already generated candidate role sets as input to the proposed algorithm (considering, for example, set intersection as in [24].

Postprocessing. Improved results can be obtained by reducing the size of the role hierarchy RH, running the *lattice-based* postprocessing procedure defined in [6]. According to this procedure, each role $r \in \mathcal{R}$ containing some other roles is substituted with the role r', where $r' = r \setminus \bigcup_{r_c \, : \, r_c \subset r} r_c$. For lack of space, we do not show here the complete results, but when our heuristics are executed on the examined real datasets, in six cases out than nine they return better results compared to CRM [2]. Notice, however, that in this case the role hierarchy is flattened, and this can limit the application in practice (since RBAC3 is not satisfied).

Other Constraints. Other categories of the constraints can be considered, and our heuristics can be simply adapted to compute a compliant role set. Considering, for example, the constraint k on the number of roles that can be assigned to each user, the users-role matrix URA returned by $t\text{-SMA}_R$ can be used as input to a procedure that filters out the users violating the constraint, and applies a greedy strategy to cover all the permissions for those users. The simple strategy consists in selecting the first $k - 1$ roles from the ones assigned to the users, each time picking the role covering the greatest number of uncovered permissions, and then collecting the remaining permissions in the last k-th role (the greedy strategy is the same used in the *classical* approximation algorithm for set covering). Other simple constraints, listed in RBAC2 (such as mutual exclusion of roles, users, etc), can also be considered, by changing the condition at step 10 of Algorithm 1.

7   Conclusions

The role mining process, usually, returns a role infrastructure on the basis of the relationships among users and permissions contained in the UPA matrix. However, the definition of a role-set really reflecting the internal functionalities of the examined organization remains a challenging task. The need for managing different kind of constraints in role engineering has recently been the focus of many works in literature [14,10,16,11]. The definition and the management of constraints in role mining are very important aspects in role mining, since they allow the role engineer to control the automatic process and introduce some rules that can have impact on the retrieved structure. In this paper, we have proposed a heuristic capable of returning a complete role-set satisfying constraints on the maximum number of permissions included in each role. The comparisons made show how the results in terms of accuracy, distance, size, and computation time improve on a previously presented algorithm [14]. Our simple algorithm is easily extensible to consider other kinds of cardinality constraints, such as maximum number of users assigned to a role or mutually exclusive permissions or roles [16]. Furthermore, it is possible to investigate on the definition of other kinds of constraints regarding the role hierarchy and the semantic associated to each role [17], and try to adapt the proposed algorithm in order to return a role set satisfying the newly defined constraints.

References

1. Blundo, C., Cimato, S.: A simple role mining algorithm. In: Proceedings of the 2010 ACM Symposium on Applied Computing, SAC 2010, pp. 1958–1962. ACM, New York (2010), http://doi.acm.org/10.1145/1774088.1774503
2. Blundo, C., Cimato, S.: Constrained role mining. arXiv:1203.3744v1 [cs.CR] (2012)
3. Chen, L., Crampton, J.: Set covering problems in role-based access control. In: Backes, M., Ning, P. (eds.) ESORICS 2009. LNCS, vol. 5789, pp. 689–704. Springer, Heidelberg (2009)
4. Coyne, E.J.: Role engineering. In: ACM Workshop on Role-Based Access Control (1995)
5. Dinur, I., Safra, S.: On the hardness of approximating minimum vertex cover. Annals of Mathematics 162 (2004, 2005)
6. Ene, A., Horne, W., Milosavljevic, N., Rao, P., Schreiber, R., Tarjan, R.E.: Fast exact and heuristic methods for role minimization problems. In: Proc. of the 13th ACM Symposium on Access Control Models and Technologies, pp. 1–10. ACM (2008)
7. Ferraiolo, D.F., Sandhu, R.S., Gavrila, S.I., Kuhn, D.R., Chandramouli, R.: Proposed NIST standard for role-based access control. ACM Transaction on Information System Security 4(3), 224–274 (2001)
8. Frank, M., Basin, D.A., Buhmann, J.M.: A class of probabilistic models for role engineering. In: ACM Conference on Computer and Communications Security, pp. 299–310. ACM (2008)
9. Garey, M.R., Johnson, D.S.: Computers and Intractability, A Guide to the Theory of NP- Completeness. W.H. Freeman and Company (1979)
10. Hingankar, M., Sural, S.: Towards role mining with restricted user-role assignment. In: 2nd International Conference on Wireless Communication, Vehicular Technology, Information Theory and Aerospace Electronic Systems Technology (Wireless VITAE), pp. 1–5 (February 28, 2011- March 3, 2011)
11. John, J., Sural, S., Atluri, V., Vaidya, J.: Role mining under role-usage cardinality constraint. In: Proc. of the 12th IFIP Conference on Security, pp. 705–716 (2012)
12. Karp, R.M.: Reducibility Among Combinatorial Problems. In: Miller, R.E., Thatcher, J.W. (eds.) Complexity of Computer Computations, pp. 85–103. Plenum Press (1972)
13. Kuhlmann, M., Shohat, D., Schimpf, G.: Role mining - revealing business roles for security administration using data mining technology. In: Proc. of the 8th ACM Symposium on Access Control Models and Technologies, pp. 179–186. ACM, New York (2003), http://doi.acm.org/10.1145/775412.775435

14. Kumar, R., Sural, S., Gupta, A.: Mining rbac roles under cardinality constraint. In: Jha, S., Mathuria, A. (eds.) ICISS 2010. LNCS, vol. 6503, pp. 171–185. Springer, Heidelberg (2010), http://portal.acm.org/citation.cfm?id=1940366.1940383

15. Li, N., Tripunitara, M.V., Bizri, Z.: On mutually exclusive roles and separation-of-duty. ACM Trans. Inf. Syst. Secur. 10 (May 2007), http://doi.acm.org/10.1145/1237500.1237501

16. Ma, X., Li, R., Lu, Z., Wang, W.: Mining constraints in role-based access control. Mathematical and Computer Modelling (2011), http://linkinghub.elsevier.com/retrieve/pii/S0895717711000719

17. Molloy, I., Chen, H., Li, T., Wang, Q., Li, N., Bertino, E., Calo, S., Lobo, J.: Mining roles with semantic meanings. In: Proc. of the 13th ACM Symposium on Access Control Models and Technologies, pp. 21–30. ACM (2008)

18. Molloy, I., Li, N., Li, T., Mao, Z., Wang, Q., Lobo, J.: Evaluating role mining algorithms. In: SACMAT 2009, pp. 95–104 (2009)

19. Roeckle, H., Schimpf, G., Weidinger, R.: Process-oriented approach for role-finding to implement role-based security administration in a large industrial organization. In: Proceedings of the Fifth ACM Workshop on Role-Based Access Control, RBAC 2000, pp. 103–110. ACM (2000), http://doi.acm.org/10.1145/344287.344308

20. Sandhu, R.S., Coyne, E.J., Feinstein, H.L., Youman, C.E.: Role-based access control models. Computer 29, 38–47 (1996)

21. Schreiber, R.: Datasets used for role mining experiments, http://www.hpl.hp.com/personal/Robert_Schreiber/

22. Scilab Consortium. Scilab: The Free Software for Numerical Computation (Ver 530 (for Mac OS X 1067)), http://www.scilab.org/

23. Stockmeyer, L.J.: The minimal set basis problem is NP-complete. Tech. Rep. RC 5431, IBM Research (May 1975)

24. Vaidya, J., Atluri, V., Guo, Q.: The role mining problem: finding a minimal descriptive set of roles. In: Proc. of the 12th ACM Symposium on Access Control Models and Technologies, pp. 175–184. ACM (2007)

25. Vaidya, J., Atluri, V., Guo, Q.: The role mining problem: A formal perspective. ACM Trans. Inf. Syst. Secur. 13(3) (2010)

26. Vaidya, J., Atluri, V., Warner, J.: Roleminer: mining roles using subset enumeration. In: CCS 2006, pp. 144–153. ACM (2006)

27. Zhang, D., Ramamohanarao, K., Ebringer, T.: Role engineering using graph optimisation. In: Proc. of the 12th ACM Symposium on Access Control Models and Technologies, pp. 139–144. ACM (2007)

A Datalog Semantics for Paralocks

Bart van Delft, Niklas Broberg, and David Sands

Chalmers University of Technology, Sweden

Abstract. Broberg and Sands (POPL'10) introduced a logic-based policy language, *Paralocks*, suitable for static information-flow control in programs. Although Paralocks comes with a precise information-flow semantics for programs, the logic-based semantics of policies, describing how policies are combined and compared, is less well developed. This makes the algorithms for policy comparison and computation ad-hoc, and their security guarantees less intuitive. In this paper we provide a new semantics for Paralocks policies based on Datalog. By doing so we are able to show that the ad-hoc semantics from earlier work coincides with the natural Datalog interpretation. Furthermore we show that by having a Datalog-inspired semantics, we can borrow language extensions and algorithms from Datalog for the benefit of Paralocks. We explore how these extensions and algorithms interact with the design and implementation of *Paragon*, a language combining Paralocks with Java.

1 Introduction

Information flow is at the heart of many security policies. One way to build secure software is to ensure that all information flows conform to an intended policy – for example that trusted data is only influenced by trusted sources, or that confidential data never flows to public channels. Paralocks is a policy language for specifying flexible and dynamic information flow policies [4]. The language allows for the formulation of simple but expressive policies that are dynamic in the sense that they vary over time, but are still statically known at compile time. The *Paragon* [3] programming language is an integration of Paralocks policies with the Java programming language. The *Paragon* compiler's main job is to check that information will only flow according to the specified policies.

It is noted in [3,4] that certain parts of Paralocks show great similarities with Datalog, a well-known query language for deductive databases. Datalog is a popular language for formalising access control and authorisation policies [10,11,15], but as far as we know no other work has used Datalog for information flow policies. A key difference is that we are mainly interested in comparing and combining policies, rather than in simply answering queries. In this work we reify the correspondence with Datalog and replace the original semantics[1] of Paralocks with one that is directly inspired by Datalog. In this paper we show

---

[1] The term "semantics" can be interpreted to mean two different things: either the dynamic semantics of information flow, or the semantics of operations on policies. What we deal with in this paper is the latter: the semantics of the Paralocks lattice and its operations. While the information-flow dimension of the semantics builds on the policy lattice, it is largely orthogonal to the issues studied in this paper.

A. Jøsang, P. Samarati, and M. Petrocchi (Eds.): STM 2012, LNCS 7783, pp. 305–320, 2013.

1. how this new Datalog semantics for Paralocks can be related to the original semantics from [4],
2. how Paralocks can benefit from its new semantics by incorporating results from the extensive Datalog literature, and
3. what impact extensions imported from Datalog would have in a practical enforcement of Paralocks (i.e. Paragon).

The Paralocks semantics from [4] is mainly of an algorithmic nature, making its security guarantees less intuitive. A relation between Horn clauses and policy evaluation is made, but this relation was rather informal, and led to an unclear and inaccurate connection between the logical connectives (conjunction, disjunction and implication) and the policy operations (meet, join and comparison). We demonstrate that the Datalog semantics provides a more natural specification from which we are able to show the soundness and completeness of the original implementation-oriented definitions of the policy operations (Section 3).

For point 2, we identify two ways in which results from Datalog research can positively be adopted in information flow analysis: *language extensions* (Section 4) and *algorithms* (Section 5).

The Datalog language has been extended in several directions and for some of these extensions it seems natural to include these in a policy specification language as well. In this work we investigate two extensions, known as Datalog with negation [19] (Section 4.1) and Datalog with constraints [14] (Section 4.3), and discuss what effect these extensions have on the Paralocks language.

On a different tack, several algorithms have been proposed in Datalog literature that operate on Datalog programs. One operation that is of particular interest is the containment operation, since it resembles the problem of policy comparison in Paralocks. This operation checks if one policy is less restrictive than another, and is thus at the core of the whole information flow analysis. We identify two subclasses of containment problems for Datalog programs that relate to Paralocks policies, and show (Section 5) that in general problems of one of these classes, uniform containment, can also be solved by algorithms from the other, conjunctive query containment. We also show how the discussed language extensions require the adoption of other Datalog results in the algorithms for policy comparison.

Finally, with point 3 we consider each of the extensions and algorithms in the practical context of Paragon. Since they affect what expectations are placed on the information flow analysis, not all of them are as easily deployable in practice as they are in theory.

These developments are preceded by a more detailed summary of the Paragon policy language, which follows in the next section.

2   Paralocks

Paralocks is a language for specifying dynamic information flow policies for data in a program. The intended usage is to annotate data sinks and sources in a program with policies that specify how data may flow between them. The flows in the program can then be validated using a static analysis, to ensure that they adhere to the policies as specified. Paralocks itself is inherently agnostic to the underlying programming language in which it is deployed. An integration of Paralocks with Java is currently being developed under the name Paragon, and we will use Java as our example throughout this section. We begin by presenting Paralocks, both intuitively and formally. We then continue by pointing out some of the practical issues that arise when integrating Paralocks with Java.

2.1 Information Flow Basics

Denning and Denning [9] pioneered a static (compile-time) approach to specifying and verifying the information flows occurring in a program. The core idea is that program variables (inputs, outputs, etc) are each labelled with a policy, where the set of all policies forms a complete lattice. A simple and standard example would be a trivial lattice consisting of two security levels, *Public* and *Secret*, and the policy comparison ordering *Public* $\sqsubseteq$ *Secret*. Information flows in a program must follow the policy. Consider a simple assignment x = y. Here the data contained in variable y flows to x, a so called *direct flow*. For this assignment to be secure we require the policy on y to be *no more restrictive than* the policy on x. The intuition is that the data in y should not be allowed to flow anywhere via x that it would not already be allowed to flow to without going via x. To validate this flow, we need to determine that $policy(y) \sqsubseteq policy(x)$.

If data is computed from several different sources, and is then assigned to a variable, e.g. x = y+z, then none of the policies on y and z respectively may be more restrictive than that on x. To simplify such comparisons we take the effective policy of an expression to be the *least upper bound* of all the policies on the various sources it is computed from. To validate this flow, we thus need to determine that $policy(y) \sqcup policy(z) \sqsubseteq policy(x)$.

The same operations are needed to track *indirect flows*, such as in the program if (x) { y=0; }. Here the value of y is indirectly affected by the value of x, causing a flow that must be validated by checking that $policy(x) \sqsubseteq policy(y)$.

Finally, if data is written to several different sinks within a conditional branch, e.g. if (x) { y=0; z=0; }, then none of the policies on y and z respectively may be *less* restrictive than the one on x. To simplify such comparisons we compute the *greatest lower bound* of all the policies on the various sinks. To validate the flows in the above program, we thus need to determine that $policy(x) \sqsubseteq policy(y) \sqcap policy(z)$.

The use of the Paralocks policy language follows this general approach. What sets Paralocks apart is the specific lattice used – a much richer language for specifying policies than the simple Denning-style lattice – together with a component that allows for a much-needed dynamic interpretation of policies.

2.2 Paralocks

Labelling a data source with a Paralocks policy specifies to whom the data may flow, *and under what conditions*. The two basic building blocks of policies are thus *actors* to whom the data may flow, and *locks*, which represent conditions (typically security-relevant properties of the system). A lock is said to be *open* when the condition it represents is fulfilled, and *closed* when it is not. As an example, the policy $\{A, B \Rightarrow x\}$ specifies that data with this policy may flow to actor x, assuming locks A and B are open. Locks thus provide the possibility for a dependence between the dynamic system state and the policy to be enforced.

At any given point in a program we can conservatively approximate the set of locks that are known to be open (via a static analysis such as a type system). We denote this set the *current lock state*. All policy comparisons are then done in the context of this lock state. Thus, as an example, if the lock A is known to be open, then the policies $\{A \Rightarrow x\}$ and $\{x\}$ (short for $\{\Rightarrow x\}$) are equivalent.

Locks may be parameterised over actors, forming lock *families* (hence the name *Para*(-meterised) *locks*). Clauses in a policy may quantify over actor parameters; for example, the policy $\{\forall x.A(x) \Rightarrow x\}$ specifies that the data may flow to any actor a for whom the corresponding lock $A(a)$ is open.

With these intuitions in hand, we can now go on and define Paralocks policies and operations formally.

Definition 1. *Paralocks policies.*

- *Policies are built from* actor identifiers a, b, *etc. referring to concrete actors, and* parametrised locks, *ranged over by* σ, σ' *etc. Each parameterised lock has a fixed arity,* $arity(\sigma) \geq 0$.
- *A lock is a term* $\sigma(a_1, \ldots, a_n)$ *where* $arity(\sigma) = n$. *The symbols* Σ, Σ' *range over sets of locks, and a lock state LS is a set of locks without free variables.*
- *A clause c is a term of the form* $\forall a_1, \ldots, a_n.\Sigma \Rightarrow a$, *in which a and zero or more actor identifiers in Σ may have been replaced with the quantified variables $a_1, \ldots, a_n$. We call a the* head *of the clause, and Σ its* body.
- *A* policy *is a set of clauses, written* $\{c_1; \ldots; c_n\}$.

Each Paralocks policy can be read as a conjunction of definite first-order Horn clauses. That is, each policy clause $\forall a_1, \ldots a_n.\{\sigma_1(\vec{b_1}); \ldots; \sigma_m(\vec{b_m})\} \Rightarrow a$ can be read as the Horn clause $\forall a_1, \ldots a_n.(\sigma_1(\vec{b_1}) \wedge \cdots \wedge \sigma_m(\vec{b_m})) \Rightarrow Flow(a)$, where $Flow$ is a special reserved lock that does not occur anywhere else[2].

A policy p allows information to flow to actor a in lock state LS if the Horn clause representation implies the validity of $Flow(a)$, denoted $p \cup LS \vDash Flow(a)$. The set of all allowed information flows according to a policy under a given lock state is $p(LS) = \{Flow(a) \mid p \cup LS \vDash Flow(a)\}$. The restrictions on the $Flow$ parametrised lock ensure that it cannot be opened directly, and no recursive clauses are possible.

In the original Paralocks work, the meet and join operations were viewed intuitively from a logical perspective as relating to conjunction and disjunction respectively. With that perspective the join operation is viewed as an approximation of logical disjunction of Horn clauses, since (conjunctions of) Horn clauses

---

[2] $\vec{b_i}$ are vectors of actor identifiers and variables, their lengths depending on the arity of the locks in which they appear.

are not closed under disjunction. This mismatch of semantic domains led to an algorithmic, ad-hoc definition of the join and meet operations. In section 3 we will show, using Datalog to provide the desired semantics for policies, that these definitions of meet and join are in fact the desired ones, not just approximations.

Paralocks can be extended by generalising the lock state to allow recursive rules. A recursive rule is very similar to a policy clause as defined above, but where the head can be an arbitrary lock predicate. This allows for convenient definitions of *properties* of lock families; one useful example is transitivity, e.g. $\{L(a,b), L(b,c) \Rightarrow L(a,c)\}$. An ordinary open lock is then equivalent to a rule with that lock as the head and an empty body. Policies are interpreted as before, only now interpreted in the context of a generalised, possibly recursive lock state. For the rest of this paper we will assume the existence of recursive rules.

Paragon Paragon [3] is an extension of Java that integrates Paralocks policies. In Paragon, fields and variables are annotated with Paralocks policies to specify how they may be used in a program.

Paragon allows recursive rules but with the restriction that a recursive rule may only be introduced when a lock is declared, and then only with that lock as the head of the rule. This allows the use of *global* lock properties, guaranteed to hold throughout the program, but will not allow e.g. transitivity to be turned on and off during program execution.

For convenience we define a specialised notation for policy semantics for this scenario, where the global recursive rules are separated from the lock state: $p(G, LS) = \{Flow(a) \mid p \cup G \cup LS \models Flow(a)\}$. In a given program, all policies will be interpreted in the context of the same G.

3 A Datalog Semantics for Paralocks

In this section we introduce Datalog, a well-established deductive database query language, based on logic programming [6,8,19]. We demonstrate how its semantics can be used as an alternative semantics for Paralocks.

3.1 Datalog

We start with some definitions and terminology of a basic variant of Datalog found in literature, see e.g. [6,12,19]. In this paper $a, b, c, \ldots$ are *constants*, $X, Y, Z, \ldots$ are *variables* and $p, q, r, \ldots$ are *predicates*. Each predicate has a fixed arity ≥ 0. A *term* t is either a constant or a variable and $A = p(t_1, \ldots, t_n)$ is an *atom* provided that p is an n-ary predicate. A ground atom, i.e. one containing no variables, is called a *fact*. A *rule* r is of the form $A_0 :- A_1, \ldots, A_m$ with $m \geq 0$ and each A an atom. A_0 is called the *head* of the rule, $A_1, \ldots, A_m$ the *body* of the rule. A rule is called *safe* if all variables occurring in A_0 occur at least once in the body of that rule. A set of rules is called a *database schema*.

Predicates that appear in the head of a rule are called *intensional* predicates, whereas those appearing only in the body of rules are called *extensional* predicates. A set of ground atoms (facts) on extensional predicates is called an *extensional database* or EDB.

A *query Q* is a set of rules that together define a predicate q, i.e. all rules have the predicate q as their head and q does not occur anywhere else than within Q.

Definition 2 (Answer sets). *The* answer set *to a query Q on an EDB with database schema D, written $Q(D, \text{EDB})$, is the set of all facts on q that can be derived using the deductive rules in both Q and D.*

We omit a formal definition of "the facts that can be derived". The standard operational version of the definition is obtained by iterating an *immediate consequence operator*, starting with the set EDB. The immediate consequence operator, given a set of facts DB, computes DB plus all facts which are an instance of the head of a rule in $Q \cup D$, and for which the corresponding instance of the body is contained in DB. Provided that the rules in Q and D are all safe, a fixed point can be reached in a finite number of iterations of the immediate consequence operator, and this is the set of derivable facts.

Assume two queries Q_1 and Q_2 defining the same predicate q. The query Q_1 is *contained* in Q_2 in the presence of a database schema D if for all EDBs each fact on q that can be derived by Q_1 can also be derived by Q_2. Similar, Q_1 is *uniformly contained* in Q_2 in the presence of a database schema D if for all DB (i.e. facts on both extensional and intensional atoms) each fact on q that can be derived by Q_1 can also be derived by Q_2 [16].

Definition 3 (Datalog Containment)
Regular containment
$Q_1 \preceq Q_2$ *in database schema DS iff* $\forall \text{EDB}.Q_1(DS, \text{EDB}) \subseteq Q_2(DS, \text{EDB})$.
Uniform containment
$Q_1 \preceq^u Q_2$ *in database schema DS iff* $\forall DB.Q_1(DS, DB) \subseteq Q_2(DS, DB)$.

3.2   Paralocks and Datalog

It is fairly straightforward to see how the different elements of Paralocks can be related to Datalog. Lock families correspond to predicates, the lock state to an EDB, clauses are just a different syntax for rules, and the global policy is equivalent to a database schema. The information flow policies themselves correspond to Datalog queries, and therefore the policy evaluation $p(G, LS)$ can be translated into the query evaluation $Q(D, \text{EDB})$ where each policy p can be seen as a query defining the distinguished predicate $Flow$.

The policy ordering is slightly tricky. As is common in information flow lattices, Paralocks defines the top element to be the most restrictive policy. In Datalog ordering, the query with the largest answer set is considered to be the top element. Thus the policy ordering corresponds to the *inverse* of Datalog query containment.

Two complications need to be addressed in this translation. To ensure termination of query evaluation or containment, all rules have to be safe. This does not hold for Paralocks, but by adding the distinguished atom $IsActor(X)$ to the body of a rule if the head is $Flow(X)$ we can make the each clause safe. We then add the guarantee that $IsActor(a)$ is opened at the point that actor a is created.

A second issue arises from the explicit difference in Datalog between extensional and intensional predicates. By direct translation, the Paralocks lock state is a set of both extensional and intensional predicates, whereas the algorithms for query evaluation and containment are defined explicitly only on EDBs.

Somewhat surprisingly, it turns out there is no absolute need for our translation to completely resemble Datalog in this respect. Instead of considering regular containment, we identify our policy ordering as being an instance of uniform containment (Definition 3). In general, uniform containment is considered to be just an approximation to real containment, but for our purpose it closely matches policy ordering. A similar situation is found by Dougherty *et al.* [11] who use Datalog and uniform containment for formalising dynamic access policies.

3.3   A Datalog Semantics

We show how the three policy operations of Paralocks – meet, join and policy ordering – can be semantically defined. The original definitions of meet and join, being of a more algorithmic nature, are shown to be correct computations of these operations. The original ordering check is replaced with an algorithm for uniform containment originating from Datalog, discussed further in Section 5.

Definition 4 (Policy operations). *Suppose that $\sqcup$ and $\sqcap$ are total binary operations of type Policy $\times$ Policy $\rightarrow$ Policy. Then we say that $\sqcap$ is the* meet *operation if for any policies p_1, p_2 and global policy G it holds that $\forall LS.(p_1 \sqcap p_2)(G, LS) = p_1(G, LS) \cup p_2(G, LS)$. Similarly, $\sqcup$ is the* join *operation if $\forall LS.(p_1 \sqcup p_2)(G, LS) = p_1(G, LS) \cap p_2(G, LS)$.*

In the context of global policy G, the binary ordering relation $\sqsubseteq$ on policies is defined as follows: p_1 at most as restrictive as p_2, written $p_1 \sqsubseteq p_2 \iff \forall LS.p_2(G, LS) \subseteq p_1(G, LS)$.

Note that the meet and join operations are *specifications* of the desired operations, but *a priori* we do not know whether they exist. There are two things to note in the definition of policy ordering. First, as mentioned in Section 3.2, the direction of the relation is inversed compared to the original Datalog one from Definition 3. Second, it quantifies over *all* possible lock states. However when policies are compared in programs we must be able to take advantage of our knowledge about what locks are known to be open at a given program point, and the standard Datalog ordering is too static for our needs. We therefore adapt this last definition so that it uses the additional knowledge that at least locks L will be open at the point of comparison; $p_1 \sqsubseteq_L p_2$ means that p_1 is no more restrictive than p_2 when at least locks L are open:

Definition 5 (Lock state aware ordering). *In the context of a global policy G, and for any lock state L, let $\sqsubseteq_L$ be the partial ordering on policies defined as: $p_1 \sqsubseteq_L p_2 \iff \forall LS.L \subseteq LS \Rightarrow p_2(G, LS) \subseteq p_1(G, LS)$.*

An algorithm for computation of the meet is straightforward since Datalog queries are effectively closed under conjunction.

Theorem 1. *The meet of two policies,* $p_1 \sqcap p_2$, *can be computed as* $p_1 \cup p_2$.

Proof. Both p_1 and p_2 only define rules on the predicate *Flow*, therefore the immediate consequence operator derives the same set of facts F for all other predicates in both $p_1(G, LS)$ and $p_2(G, LS)$, for any lock state LS. Since *Flow* does not appear in the body of any rule, the union of the facts on *Flow* that p_1 and p_2 derive individually from F, is the same that the policy $p_1 \cup p_2$ would derive on F, hence $p_1(G, LS) \cup p_2(G, LS) = (p_1 \cup p_2)(G, LS)$.

For the crucial join operation it is not as obvious that there exists a computation exactly matching the semantics. In the original work an ad-hoc definition was argued to be sound but not complete [4]. By working with Datalog rather than arbitrary Horn clauses we can now show it to be both sound and complete:

Theorem 2. *The join of two policies,* $p_1 \sqcup p_2$, *can be computed as*

$$
\begin{aligned}
p_1 \sqcup p_2 = {} & \{\Sigma_1 \cup \Sigma_2 \Rightarrow x \mid \Sigma_1 \Rightarrow x \in p_1; \Sigma_2 \Rightarrow x \in p_2\} \\
& \cup \{\Sigma_1 \cup \Sigma_2 \Rightarrow a \mid \Sigma_1 \Rightarrow a \in p_1; \Sigma_2 \Rightarrow a \in p_2\} \\
& \cup \{\Sigma_1 \cup \Sigma_2[x \mapsto a] \Rightarrow a \mid \Sigma_1 \Rightarrow a \in p_1; \Sigma_2 \Rightarrow x \in p_2\} \\
& \cup \{\Sigma_1[x \mapsto a] \cup \Sigma_2 \Rightarrow a \mid \Sigma_1 \Rightarrow x \in p_1; \Sigma_2 \Rightarrow a \in p_2\}
\end{aligned}
$$

Proof. We have to show that for any lock state LS, actor a:

$$
\begin{aligned}
Flow(a) \in p_1(G, LS) \\
Flow(a) \in p_2(G, LS)
\end{aligned}
\iff Flow(a) \in (p_1 \sqcup p_2)(G, LS)
$$

$\Longrightarrow$: In order for $Flow(a) \in p_1(G, LS)$ and $Flow(a) \in p_2(G, LS)$ to hold there must be a clause in p_1 and a clause in p_2 that allow for the derivation of $Flow(a)$. It is clear from the definition of $\sqcup$ that for each combination of two clauses in p_1 and p_2 that agree on their heads (after possible substitution), there exists a single clause in $p_1 \sqcup p_2$ that derives the same fact.

$\Longleftarrow$: Similarly, each clause in $p_1 \sqcup p_2$ can be split into two clauses with one in p_1 and one in p_2, possibly with a variable in the head instead of a constant.

That the policy ordering can be given a complete algorithm as well is however not directly obvious. Since recursion is possible in general, Datalog literature tells us that the question of containment is undecidable [17]. The relatively mild restriction that Paralocks places on the query predicate, i.e. *Flow*, as shown in Section 2, to appear only as the head of policy clauses and nowhere else, gives us both a decidable problem and an algorithm to compute the ordering.

Theorem 3. *The ordering check whether a policy* p_1 *is at most as restrictive as a policy* p_2, $p_1 \sqsubseteq p_2$, *can be computed using the uniform containment check from Sagiv [16] as* $p_2 \preceq^u p_1$.

Proof. The correctness of the algorithm has been demonstrated by Sagiv [16].

A sound and complete computation for the policy ordering in the presence of a lock state can be obtained via a small modification to Sagiv's algorithm, which we demonstrate in Section 5.2.

This gives us a natural Datalog semantics for Paralocks, and at the same time demonstrates that we can use the same algorithmic implementations for meet and join operations as before. For policy ordering we actually find a better-suited method from Datalog containment which we discuss in detail in Section 5, incorporating the extensions made to the policy language in Section 4.

4   Adopting Datalog Extensions into Paralocks

With a Datalog semantics for Paralocks in place, a whole area of research becomes available to enrich the information flow framework. In this section we consider two popular extensions to regular Datalog: Datalog with negation, and Datalog with constraints. We describe how they could be incorporated into Paralocks, and what consequences they would have on the Paragon compiler.

4.1   Datalog with Negation

One common extension to regular Datalog is the inclusion of negation in the body of rules. For example, consider a Chinese-wall information policy [2] in which consultants may work for company A or company B, but not both at the same time. To model this company A's data would be given the policy $\{\forall x.\, ConsultsForA\,(x),\, \neg\, ConsultsForB\,(x) \Rightarrow x\}$ (symmetrically for company B).

To ensure termination and decidability of Datalog queries it is well-known that negation cannot be added arbitrarily. Rules need to be *safe* with respect to negation, meaning that each variable occurring in a negated atom should appear in at least one positive atom in the same body. In the same way we ensured safety of rules in Section 3.2, we can add a positive $IsActor(X)$ atom for each variable in the body of a rule to make it safe. In addition, the set of rules defining a predicate needs to be stratified. That is, if a recursive path occurs in the definition of a predicate, negation should not be included in that path. For example, consider the database schema (or: global policy):

$$\{\quad A(X) :- B(X), \neg D(X) \qquad D(X) :- B(X), \neg A(X) \quad\}$$

and an EDB $\{B(a)\}$. Under the query $Q = \{F(X) :- A(X)\}$ there are two possible answer sets depending on whether the first or second rule in the database schema gets evaluated first. Stratification of rules is required to prevent this non-determinism[3]. These concepts could be translated directly into Paralocks. Inclusion of negation is however only straightforward if we ignore the practical issues stemming from the information-flow analysis itself.

---

[3] Technically, this still does not suffice and some additional restriction on the evaluation algorithm applies [19].

The main complication arises from the particular property we have on policy ordering with respect to the lock state. Before introducing negation, this property was easily formulated: the policy ordering has to hold in each lock state at least containing the current one (Definition 5). In the presence of negation we loose monotonicity; the absence of a lock can now make a policy more liberal as well as more restrictive, making the notion of a 'more permissive lock state' complicated.

4.2 Datalog with Negation and Paragon

The effects of negation on the Paragon compiler would be numerous. To understand why we must understand a bit more about methods-handling in Paragon. Methods are annotated in several ways, including annotations that specify the policies of the method's arguments, returned value and side-effects. Of particular relevance here, is that methods must specify how they interact with the lock state, to allow the analysis to conservatively approximate the current lock state across method calls. Each method should thus detail what locks it *may* close, what locks it *will definitely* open.

To provide enough information for the ordering check, the analysis would need to track both an upper and a lower bound on the set of opened locks. Method signatures then also need to specify which locks are definitely closed and which might be opened. This would result in an additional burden to the programmer and error messages from the compiler would presumably become so complicated that they would only confuse the user. Finally, although we do not have any concrete evidence to support this, the conservative approximation of the lower and upper bound on opened locks is likely to result in the compiler becoming very conservative as well. This means that writing programs involving negation that actually type-check would become a tedious assignment.

These practical considerations make us reject the idea of adopting negation from Datalog directly into Paragon, despite the two languages being so similar. Instead we consider a different tack and attempt to simulate negation with a *dual lock*. During type-checking we replace each occurrence of a negated lock $\neg L$ with a (fresh) lock nL. Any statement that opens or closes L is extended with a statement that performs the inverse operation on nL. Starting the analysis with a lock state in which all nL locks are open, the type system matches the expectations from the programmer.

To give the formal guarantee that both locks will never be open at the same time we can adopt the "Datalog with integrity constraints" extension [19]. This extension allows for the specification of rules without heads; if a database satisfies its body that integrity constraint is violated. For each lock L used in negated form we add the integrity constraint $\leftarrow L, nL$.

What we cannot guarantee is that at least (and in combination with the paragraph above: exactly) one of the two locks is open. If we could, this would imply that we are able to express negation without having the stratification requirement. That is why the analysis starts with the nL locks being open at the start of the analysis. There is clearly a practical issue associated with this. Suppose we have a lock L of arity k, When we create a new actor we must open all of the negative locks that can involve that actor. For nL alone this means that we must open $k(m + 1)^{(k-1)}$ locks where m is the number of other actors. In examples of Paralocks policies encountered so far k is at most 2 but this still seems too costly. One reasonable compromise would be to limit negation to unary locks (as used in the Chinese wall policy sketched previously). This would mean that creation of a new actor would entail opening n (negative) locks, where n is the number of unary locks.

In this way we can extend our policy language with some negation possibilities, without obtaining the complications that would arise from adopting the natural negation from Datalog.

4.3 Datalog with Constraints

Another interesting extension to Datalog is called *Datalog with Constraints*, or Datalog^c [14]. This extension allows the bodies of rules to be extended with constraints on the domain elements. For example, for natural numbers one could have the rule $A(X) :- B(X), X > 11$. Li and Mitchell [14] present several examples of constraint domains. In our scenario we are considering a constraint domain that is only indirectly included by Li and Mitchell; the only two constraints applicable on actors are that they are either equal or unequal. Having constraints on the inequality of actors (the equality constraint is already implicitly present in standard Datalog) allows for separation-of-interest policies:

$$\{\forall x, y, z. WorksFor(y, x), WorksFor(z, x), y \neq x, z \neq x, y \neq z \Rightarrow IsBoss(x)\}$$

i.e. an actor is a boss if at least two different actors are working for her. This notion of difference is not expressible in the current definition of Paralocks.

Concretely, we can include the notion of a *constraint rule*, which is of the Datalog / Paragon form:

$$A_0 :- A_1, \ldots, A_m, \phi \qquad\qquad A_1, \ldots, A_m, \phi \Rightarrow A_0$$

where ϕ is a conjunction of what is called *primitive constraints*, i.e. of the forms $x = y$ and $x \neq y$. A rule is *safe* if all variables occurring in ϕ occur also in $A_0, \ldots, A_m$. This implies that facts are no longer ground atoms, but can contain constrained variables, e.g. $IsBoss(X) :- X \neq Alice$. These are called *constraint facts*. The evaluation of a query thus no longer returns an answer set consisting of facts, but one of constraint facts. p_1 is now at most as restrictive as p_2 if any constraint fact derivable by p_2 is logically entailed by at least one fact in p_1. The definition for the ordering check needs to be updated accordingly:

Definition 6 (Lock state aware ordering with constraints). *In the context of global policy G, and for any lock state L, $\sqsubseteq_L^c$ is the constraints and lock state aware ordering relation defined by $p_1 \sqsubseteq_L^c p_2 \iff \forall LS. L \subseteq LS \Rightarrow \forall f_2 \in p_2(G, LS). \exists f_1 \in p_1(G, LS). f_1 \vDash f_2$.*

As for Datalog with negation, the area of Datalog with constraints is well studied and can easily be incorporated into Paralocks. The algorithm for checking the policy ordering is easily modified to work with constraints using results from Datalog literature, as we will show in Section 5.

4.4 Datalog with Constraints and Paragon

As with negation the story becomes more involved when considering the practical application of constraints in Paragon. In Paragon, actors can be referred to by variables and may therefore be aliased. For example, whether the opening of lock $L(a)$ followed by the closing of lock $L(b)$ results in lock $L(a)$ being open depends on whether or not the program variables a and b are aliases for the same concrete actor. In the current implementation without constraints Paragon takes the conservative approach and assumes that a close statement on $L(b)$ closes lock L for all potential aliases of b. The current analysis only needs to track whether two program variables may alias or not. When constraints on actors can be added in policies we need to have an aliasing analysis that also tracks whether program variables are must-aliases.

5 Algorithms for Policy Ordering

In the previous section we explored how the Datalog semantics provided us with extension possibilities to the Paralocks policy language. In this section we consider the use of algorithms developed for Datalog. In one direction this can give us policy evaluation algorithms with a lower average complexity than the standard operational semantics (see e.g. [1]). More importantly, though, is that an algorithm for policy ordering can be found in Datalog query containment algorithms.

5.1 Uniform and Conjunctive Query Containment

We consider two Datalog containment relations that correspond to policy ordering: uniform containment and conjunctive query containment. We already mentioned uniform containment as a candidate in Section 3.2. In this section we introduce conjunctive query containment as a second option.

A *conjunctive query* (CQ) is a query that only has extensional predicates in the bodies of its rules. The decision whether a conjunctive query is (regularly, Definition 3) contained in another, possibly non conjunctive query, is known as the CQ containment problem.

Sagiv already noted in his introduction of uniform containment [16] that any CQ containment problem can be solved with a uniform containment algorithm. We show that the opposite direction holds as well. That is, each uniform containment problem, such as the policy ordering for Paralocks, can be addressed with a CQ containment algorithm. Since there is a much larger body of work on algorithms for CQ containment [5,7,12] than there is for uniform containment, this increases the collection of containment algorithms for any uniform containment problem. We can transform a uniform containment problem into a CQ containment problem as follows:

Definition 7 (Uniform containment problem transformation)
Suppose that we have a uniform containment problem $Q_1 \preceq^u Q_2$ with database schema DS such that the predicate defined by Q_1 does not occur in the body of any rule. The CQ transformed version $\tau(Q_1, Q_2, DS) = (R_1, R_2, DS', \theta, \theta^{-1})$ where

- *$\vec{p}$ is the set of all intensional predicates in DS,*
- *θ is a substitution mapping each predicate $p \in \vec{p}$ to a fresh predicate p^E,*
- *θ^{-1} is the inverse of θ,*
- *$R_1 = Q_1 \theta$,*
- *$R_2 = Q_2$, and*
- *$DS' = DS \cup \{p(\vec{X}) :- p^E(\vec{X}) \mid p \mapsto p^E \in \theta\}$.*

Note that the resulting R_1 only has atoms on p^E predicates, i.e. extensional atoms in its body. We show that the transformed problem holds in a regular containment check iff the original problem holds in a uniform containment check:

Theorem 4. *Given a transformation $\tau(Q_1, Q_2, DS) = (R_1, R_2, DS', \theta, \theta^{-1})$*

$$Q_1 \preceq^u Q_2 \iff R_1 \preceq R_2$$

Proof. $\Longrightarrow$: We have $\forall DB.Q_1(DS, DB) \subseteq Q_2(DS, DB)$. For any EDB, we need to show that $R_1(DS', \text{EDB}) \subseteq R_2(DS', \text{EDB})$. Let $\delta = \text{EDB} \cup \text{EDB}\theta^{-1}$. Since R_1 is only defined on extensional predicates, all facts are derived directly from the EDB; DS' is not used. $Q_1 = R_1\theta^{-1}$, so $R_1(DS', \text{EDB}) \subseteq Q_1(DS, \delta)$. By assumption, $R_1(DS', \text{EDB}) \subseteq Q_2(DS, \delta)$. And also $R_1(DS', \text{EDB}) \subseteq Q_2(DS', \text{EDB})$ since the $p(\vec{X}) :- p^E(\vec{X})$ rules in DS' can derive the set $\text{EDB}\theta^{-1}$. Since $Q_2 = R_2$, we obtain $R_1(DS', \text{EDB}) \subseteq R_2(DS', \text{EDB})$.

$\Longleftarrow$: We have $\forall \text{EDB}.R_1(DS', \text{EDB}) \subseteq R_2(DS', \text{EDB})$. Let q be the predicate defined by both Q_1 and Q_2. For any DB, we need to show that for any fact $q(\vec{y})$ such that $q(\vec{y}) \in Q_1(DS, DB)$, it also holds that $q(\vec{y}) \in Q_2(DS, DB)$. $q(\vec{y})$ is derived using a rule $r \in Q_1$. Consider $s =$ the set of (intensional) $p(\vec{x})$ facts used in r to derive $q(\vec{y})$. Safely ignoring the filtering of q predicate on the definition of an answer set, this means that $s \subseteq Q_1(DS, DB)$, and since Q_1 cannot contribute to this also $s \subseteq Q_2(DS, DB)$ (*). Let $\delta = s\theta$, i.e. δ is an EDB. It follows that $q(\vec{y}) \in R_1(\emptyset, \delta)$, since $R_1 = Q_1\theta$; therefore also $q(\vec{y}) \in R_1(DS', \delta)$. By assumption follows $q(\vec{y}) \in R_2(DS', \delta)$ and $R_2 = Q_2$ thus $q(\vec{y}) \in Q_2(DS', \delta)$. Combining this with (*) gives us $q(\vec{y}) \in Q_2(DS, DB)$.

5.2   Checking Policy Ordering

Since uniform containment appears as the most natural Datalog interpretation for policy ordering we adopt the algorithm from Sagiv [16] as our basic implementation. The connection with CQ containment allows us to switch to a different algorithm in the future if that becomes favourable for reasons of flexibility or complexity, and already we incorporate some ideas borrowed from CQ algorithms (Section 5.3). The algorithm from Sagiv works by testing all canonical databases[4] and can be summarised as follows:

To check if $p_1 \preceq^u p_2$ (i.e. $p_2 \sqsubseteq p_1$), consider each rule $r = head :- body$ in p_1 individually. Let θ be a substitution such that all distinct variables in $body$ are mapped to distinct fresh constants, i.e. constants not yet present in p_1, p_2 or the global policy G. Uniform containment holds iff for each rule the iterated check $head\theta \in p_2(G, body\theta)$ holds. That this algorithm tests all relevant (canonical) databases and therefore should only succeed if the containment holds over all databases should be quite intuitive. For a proof we refer to [16].

This algorithm checks for ordering as per Definition 4. Converting it into an ordering check as per Definition 5 that takes the current lock state into account requires not that much alteration; given the current lock state L we simply replace the iterated check by $head\theta \in p_2(G, L \cup body\theta)$.

The complexity of the algorithm is directly influenced by the number of rules in p_1 and the complexity of deciding whether $head\theta \in p_2(G, L \cup body\theta)$. That is, the complexity of the ordering algorithm is in the same order of complexity as query evaluation, which has worst case complexity EXPTIME-complete [8]. This complexity is dictated by the (maximum) sum of all arities of the predicates in the bodies of all clauses. In our use of Paralocks to model information flow policies and idioms so far we have not come across any predicates with an arity greater than two or clauses with more than three atoms in the body, which gives the indication that the impact of this complexity is still low. Further practical studies are required to confirm this suspicion.

5.3   Policy Ordering with Extensions

In this section we consider how the ordering operation based on uniform containment as described above needs to be adapted to include the extensions discussed in Section 4.

Negation. For the inclusion of negation we do not use the natural Datalog negation but instead simulate negation by giving each lock L a counterpart nL (Section 4.1), therefore no changes to the ordering operation are required.

Constraints. Extending the work by Sagiv, Ullman briefly considers constraint domains [18] using results on CQ containment from Klug [13]. Here we instead choose to translate the method deployed by Farré *et al.* [12]. The essence of both methods [12,13] is however the same. To quantify over all databases the algorithms enumerate, as in Section 5.2, all relevant canonical databases. The Constructive Query Containment (CQC) method introduced by Farré *et al.* [12]

---

[4] A canonical database is a representative of the family of databases that can be obtained by all possible one-to-one replacements of constants.

incorporates so-called Variable Instantiation Patterns (VIPs) for this purpose[5]. Since in our domain actors are only equal or unequal we adopt the *negation VIP* into our ordering check. The resulting algorithm is as follows:

Given K the set of all constant actors appearing in p_1, p_2 and G, for each rule $r = head :- body$ in p_1 let $\vec{x}$ be the set of all variables. Let $\Theta = s(\vec{x}, K)$ be a *set* of substitutions, where:

$$s(\{x\} \cup \vec{x}, K) = \bigcup_{k \in K} \{\{x \mapsto k\} \cup \theta \mid \theta \in s(\vec{x}, K)\}$$
$$\cup \ \{\{x \mapsto k_n\} \cup \theta \mid \theta \in s(\vec{x}, K \cup \{k_n\})\} \quad k_n \notin K$$
$$s(\emptyset, K) = \emptyset$$

p_2 is at most as restrictive as p_1 iff for each rule, each $\theta \in \Theta$, the iterative check $head\theta \in p_2(G, L \cup body\theta)$ holds.

Textually, Θ is a list of substitution-combinations in which each variable in *body* is mapped to one of the existing constants or a fresh constant. This ensures that the algorithm tests all canonical databases. The number of iterative checks that needs to be performed increases with a factor V^K where V is the number of variables in a rule, and K the total number of constants. In general we expect this cost increase to be modest, since the (small) cases we encountered so far almost never had more than one concrete actor in a policy or global rule.

6 Conclusions

By changing the semantics for Paralocks policies from its original ad-hoc version to one based on Datalog, we have provided a more natural and intuitive understanding of the language. Still, the original semantics coincides with the Datalog version, and due to its algorithmic nature provides a good guidance for implementation. Another advantage is that we can transfer language extensions and algorithms from Datalog into Paralocks, although practical considerations arising from the use of Paralocks in a type checker must be taken into account.

The algorithms and extensions discussed in this work are to be added to the next generation of Paragon, an information-flow aware compiler for Java. We also aim to improve the feedback from the compiler by incorporating the discussed algorithm for policy ordering, since it allows us not only to say where in the program an illegal information flow occurs, but also to provide more feedback as to why this flow is illegal.

Acknowledgments. This work has been partly funded by the Swedish research agencies VR and SSF, and the European Commission EC FP7-ICT-STREP WebSand project. Thanks to the ProSec group at Chalmers, in particular to Wolfgang Ahrendt and Pablo Buiras for discussions and feedback.

---

[5] The entire CQC method seems a tempting candidate to be used instead of uniform containment, but unfortunately does not perform well in the presence of recursive rules.

References

1. Bancilhon, F., Maier, D., Sagiv, Y., Ullman, J.D.: Magic sets and other strange ways to implement logic programs (extended abstract). In: Proceedings of the Fifth ACM SIGACT-SIGMOD Symposium on Principles of Database Systems, PODS 1986, pp. 1–15. ACM, New York (1986)
2. Brewer, D.F.C., Nash, M.J.: The Chinese Wall Security Policy. In: Proceedings of the 1989 IEEE Symposium on Security and Privacy, pp. 206–214 (1989)
3. Broberg, N.: Practical, Flexible Programming with Information Flow Control. Ph.D. thesis, Chalmers, Göteborg University, Göteborg, Sweden (2011)
4. Broberg, N., Sands, D.: Paralocks – Role-Based Information Flow Control and Beyond. In: Proceedings of the 37th Annual ACM SIGACT-SIGPLAN Symposium on Principles of Programming Languages, POPL (2010)
5. Calvanese, D., De Giacomo, G., Lenzerini, M.: On the decidability of query containment under constraints. In: Proceedings of the Seventeenth ACM SIGACT-SIGMOD-SIGART Symposium on Principles of Database Systems, PODS 1998, pp. 149–158. ACM, New York (1998)
6. Ceri, S., Gottlob, G., Tanca, L.: What You Always Wanted to Know About Datalog (And Never Dared to Ask). IEEE Trans. on Knowl. and Data Eng. 1(1), 146–166 (1989)
7. Chekuri, C., Rajaraman, A.: Conjunctive query containment revisited. Theoretical Computer Science 239(2), 211–229 (2000)
8. Dantsin, E., Eiter, T., Gottlob, G., Voronkov, A.: Complexity and expressive power of logic programming. ACM Computing Surveys 33, 374–425 (2001)
9. Denning, D.E., Denning, P.J.: Certification of programs for secure information flow. Comm. of the ACM 20(7), 504–513 (1977)
10. DeTreville, J.: Binder, a logic-based security language. In: IEEE Symposium on Security and Privacy, pp. 105–113 (2002)
11. Dougherty, D.J., Fisler, K., Krishnamurthi, S.: Specifying and Reasoning About Dynamic Access-Control Policies. In: Furbach, U., Shankar, N. (eds.) IJCAR 2006. LNCS (LNAI), vol. 4130, pp. 632–646. Springer, Heidelberg (2006)
12. Farré, C., Teniente, E., Urpì, T.: Checking query containment with the CQC method. Data & Knowledge Engineering 53(2), 163–223 (2005)
13. Klug, A.: On Conjunctive Queries Containing Inequalities. J. ACM 35(1), 146–160 (1988)
14. Li, N., Mitchell, J.C.: Datalog with Constraints: A Foundation for Trust Management Languages. In: Dahl, V. (ed.) PADL 2003. LNCS, vol. 2562, pp. 58–73. Springer, Heidelberg (2002)
15. Li, N., Mitchell, J.C., Winsborough, W.H.: Design of a role-based trust-management framework. In: IEEE Symposium on Security and Privacy, pp. 114–130 (2002)
16. Sagiv, Y.: Optimizing Datalog Programs. In: Foundations of Deductive Databases and Logic Programming, pp. 659–698. Morgan Kaufmann (1988)
17. Shmueli, O.: Decidability and expressiveness aspects of logic queries. In: Proceedings of the Sixth ACM SIGACT-SIGMOD-SIGART Symposium on Principles of Database Systems, PODS 1987, pp. 237–249 (1987)
18. Ullman, J.: Information integration using logical views. In: Afrati, F.N., Kolaitis, P.G. (eds.) ICDT 1997. LNCS, vol. 1186, pp. 19–40. Springer, Heidelberg (1997)
19. Ullman, J.D.: Principles of Database and Knowledge-Base Systems, Volume I. Computer Science Press (1988)

Author Index